STRIPPED TO THE BONE

The Wave or Adventures with Cassiopaea by Laura Knight-Jadczyk

Riding the Wave (vol. 1)
Soul Hackers (vol. 2)
Stripped to the Bone (vol. 3)
Through a Glass Darkly (vol. 4)
Petty Tyrants & Facing the Unknown (vols. 5 & 6)
Almost Human (vol. 7)
Debugging the Universe (vol. 8)

Other books by Laura Knight-Jadczyk

The Secret History of the World and How to Get Out Alive
9/11: The Ultimate Truth (with Joe Quinn)
*High Strangeness: Hyperdimensions and the Process of
    Alien Abduction*

volume 3 of
LAURA KNIGHT-JADCZYK'S
THE WAVE
OR ADVENTURES WITH CASSIOPAEA

STRIPPED TO THE BONE

THE PATH TO FREEDOM
IN THE PRISON OF LIFE

Red Pill Press

Copyright © 2000, 2010 Laura Knight-Jadczyk
Cassiopaean materials Copyright © 1994–2010
Arkadiusz Jadczyk and Laura Knight-Jadczyk

http://www.cassiopaea.org/

ISBN-10: 1-897244-52-5
ISBN-13: 978-1-897244-52-4

3RD EDITION
Second printing September 2011.

All Rights Reserved. No part of this publication may be reproduced, stored in a retrieval system, or transmitted in any form or by any means, electronic, mechanical, or otherwise, other than for "fair use", without the written consent of the author.

Red Pill Press
10020-100 Ave.
Grande Prairie, AB
T8V 0V3, Canada
http://www.redpillpress.com/

Printed in Canada

TABLE OF CONTENTS

Introduction 7

Chapter 20
Black Lightning Strikes 11

Chapter 21
Roswell Revisited 76

Chapter 22
The Nexus Seven Meet the Cassiopaeans 129

Chapter 23
Lucifer and the Pot of Gold 185

Chapter 24
The Bacchantes Meet Apollo at Stonehenge 228

Chapter 25
A Walk in Nature among the Names of God 267

Chapter 26
The Tree of Life 305

Chapter 27
Stripped to the Bone 342

Appendix
Cult-ivating Terror 395

Bibliography 415

INTRODUCTION

Stripped to the Bone follows *Soul Hackers* in the Wave series. However, as a bit of a refresher for new and old readers, I will begin this volume with a summary of the main topics covered so far. This will also serve as an introduction to my work in superluminal communication, which forms the 10% inspiration behind the 90% perspiration of the research of our organization, Quantum Future Group, Inc.

First, however, I will insert some comments about the central inspiration for this book written by my husband, theoretical/mathematical physicist, Arkadiusz Jadczyk. Even though this introduction may help to orient you, please remember that the Wave series was written for online reading and the volumes should be read in order for total comprehension. It was written in a dynamic process as an interaction between the author and the readers. It was broken up into individual books because, were we to attempt to published it all together in one volume, it would be enormous and prohibitively expensive.

> The term "Cassiopaeans" appears in several places in this book and requires some explanation. After a two-year-long experiment in what we have come to call "superluminal communication" using a spirit board, a source identifying itself as the Cassiopaeans told us, "we are you in the future." Modern physics does not provide us with practical means for this type of communication and theories on this subject are not yet well developed; they are, in fact, inconclusive and controversial. While communication into the past cannot be dismissed in current theories as impossible, it is perhaps improbable. However, the more improbably is a given phenomenon, the more information is carried by its occurrence, and for this reason we did not dismiss the possibility of the truth of the source. Instead, we decided to continue the communications as a form of a controlled experiment in "superluminal thought transfer", even if it was clear that the

term should be considered as a tentative indication of only one out of several possible interpretations.[1]

The information received from this experiment is presented in the context of broad ranging historical, scientific and other metaphysical material and offers the clues that have led to the worldview and inferences presented by us in our numerous publications on the Web and in print. Perhaps it is only our own subconscious mind that presents itself as a source, but even if it is so, does that tell us more? Do we really know what "unconscious" or "subconscious" mind is and of what it is capable?

We sometimes ask ourselves if the Cs are who they say they are, because we do not take anything as unquestionable truth. We take everything with a grain of salt, even if we consider that there is a good chance that it is truth. We are constantly analyzing this material as well as a great quantity of other material that comes to our attention from numerous fields of science and mysticism.

We invite the reader to share in our seeking of Truth by reading with an open, but skeptical mind. We do not encourage devotee-ism or true belief. We *do* encourage the seeking of knowledge and awareness in all fields of endeavor as the best way to discern lies from truth. The one thing we can tell the reader is this: we work very hard, many hours a day, and have done so for many years, to discover the bottom line of our existence on Earth. It is our vocation, our quest, and our job. We constantly seek to validate and/or refine what we understand to be either possible or probable or both. We do this in the sincere hope that all of mankind will benefit, if not now, then at some point in one of our probable futures.

In volume one, *Riding the Wave,* we introduced the Wave, a subject of some scope and complexity. As the Cs describe it, the Wave is a term used to describe a Macro-Cosmic Quantum Wave Collapse. This is presumably a naturally occurring cosmic phenomenon that produces both physical and metaphysical changes to the Earth's cosmic environment, theorized to be statistically probable sometime in the early 21st century. It is variously described by other sources as the planetary shift to fourth density, the "shift of the ages", "ascension", "the harvest", etc., and is most often slated to take place at the end of 2012 (as per the Mayan calendar). However, contrary to what the New Agers are saying about this event, it doesn't look like it's as simple as Earth and all its inhabitants spontaneously entering a new era of spiritual awakening and rebirth. There's no free lunch!

---

[1] I tell the story of the beginnings of our experiment in the introductory installment of our *Knowledge and Being* video series, which can be viewed for free at these addresses:
http://www.youtube.com/user/cassiopaeaorg/
http://www.cassiopaea.org/knowledge_and_being/

While *Riding the Wave* provided some of the theoretical underpinnings of the concept of the Wave, in volume two, *Soul Hackers,* I began sharing practical, real-life applications of the concepts by telling my own story. The things I learned relate to what the Cs have called simple "karmic understandings." I related my personal experiences with channeling and its many pitfalls, as well as my experiences with New Age religions and beliefs, including my experience with my own Éiriú Eolas meditation program (although I didn't have a name for it at the time). Those experiences provided me with lessons – confirmed by research – that showed me the beginnings of a new way of life, as well as the hidden hands at work behind both mainstream and New Age belief systems. And it led into some pretty dark territory!

I ended *Soul Hackers* with Dr. D. Corydon Hammond's infamous Greenbaum lecture and its implications for the New Age community. The whole idea of Greenbauming put the New Age movement in a completely different light for me, and it is with this frightening concept that we begin.

CHAPTER 20
BLACK LIGHTNING STRIKES ...
OR MARJOE GORTNER
MEETS TED PATRICK

After reading about Greenbaum programming, we more or less have some idea of the kinds of things that might be going on in the so-called real world, i.e., human engineered mind programming; and we have a lot to think about. We have also talked about people who may have enormous creative potential and who may be special targets for mind-programming activities, whether human originated or from another density, and we have talked about what seems to be, more or less, an ongoing experiment in social and philosophical control whereby masses of people can be influenced to think in certain "loops" that may have no basis in reality.

When speaking of these mind-programming activities, we have to ask, are we talking about just a small group? Certainly, the logistics of such activity make us think that it must be a somewhat limited activity. Of course, many readers of this material will think that whatever ideas they espouse on the subject, based upon their religious or cultural upbringing, are exempt from questioning – *they* are the right ones. Or, they have attached themselves to this or that teaching, whether it be channeled or scientific or ethnic or whatever, and because it feels right, or because their "guide" or inner guidance system of whatever nature, has confirmed it for them, it is *not* subject to being a program. In fact, this is one of the very control mechanisms we'll be talking about in this chapter.

On the subject of the logistics of mind programming, I want to remind the reader of the following:

January 21, 1995
Q: (L) How "long", and I put long in quotes, because we know, as you say, there is no time, but how long, as we measure it, have the Grays been interacting with our race? The Grays, not the Lizards; the Grays, the cybergenetic probes?
A: *Time travelers, therefore, "Time is ongoing".*

Q: (L) Okay, recently I read a couple of books J gave me, *Knight in Shining Armor* [by Jude Deveraux] and *Replay* [by Ken Grimwood]. Both of these books described time travel.[2]

A: No, not finished with answer. Do you understand the gravity of last response?

Q: (L) They are time travelers, they can move forward and backward in time, they can play games with our heads ... (T) They can set up the past to create a future they want. (D) They can organize things so that they can create the energy that they need ... (L) They can also make things look good, make them feel good, make them seem good, they can make you have an idea one minute, and then the next minute, create some sort of situation that confirms that idea ...

A: *When you asked how long, of course it is totally unlimited, is it not?*

Q: (L) That's not good. If they were to move back through space-time and alter an event in our past, would that alteration in the past instantaneously alter our present as well?

A: *Has over and over and over.*

Q: (D) So they do it over and over and over, constantly? (L) So, at each ...

A: You just are not yet aware, and have no idea of the ramifications!!!

Q: (L) We're getting a little glimmer! (T) The ramifications of being able to move in and out of time and manipulate it the way you want ... (J) And the ramifications of what they're doing to us and what they will do to us, over and over. (L) So, in other words, our only real prayer in this whole damn situation is to get out of this density level. That's what they're saying, that's what it sounds like to me.

A: Close.

Q: (L) Because, otherwise, we're just literally, as in that book, stuck in the replay over and over and over, and the Holocaust could happen over and over, and we could just, you know ... Genghis Khan, Attila the Hun ... over and over and over again. (T) We're stuck in a time loop; they're putting us in a time loop. (J) Are we in a time loop?

A: Yes.

I once had what I thought was a rather silly idea. I was reading alien abduction cases, and the descriptions were so similar that I wondered if it was the same few guys who constantly traveled back and forth in time over and over again abducting first one person, then another and then another and so on. If they could keep going back to the same moment in time, but to a different person, the same little

---

[2] The reader might like to look these books up on amazon.com and read them for an entertaining presentation of how time loops might work for the human being. The issue of how we might be controlled thereby is an altogether more grim and serious subject. The book *Replay* comes closest to describing what it might be like to be trapped in an endlessly repeating loop.

group could abduct millions of people, seemingly *simultaneously*. It may not have been such a silly idea. Some of you may remember what Ark wrote about channeling in *High Strangeness*:

> We need now to return to our question: if communications from the future are possible, why don't we receive these broadcasts on a daily basis? If our minds can serve as receivers, then why aren't we all aware of the transmissions?
>
> I think that the answer has to do with multiple realities and branching universes, and perhaps any civilization, which would receive messages from the future on a daily basis, has ceased to exist because communication through time is a very dangerous game. You produce paradoxes and these paradoxes remove the paradoxical universes from the repository of possible universes; if you create a universe with paradoxes, it destroys itself either completely or partially. Perhaps just intelligence is removed from this universe because it is intelligence that creates paradox. Perhaps we are very fortunate that even if we can receive some of these messages from the future, we still continue to exist.
>
> Suppose our civilization were to advance to the point where everyone can communicate with themselves in the past; they have a computer with a special program and peripheral device that does this. It becomes the latest fad: everyone is communicating with themselves in the past to warn of dangers or upcoming calamities or bad choices, or to give lottery numbers or winning horses. But, what is seen as a 'bad choice' or 'calamity' for one could be seen to be a 'good event' or 'benefit' to someone else!
>
> So, the next step would be that 'hackers' would begin to break into the systems and send false communications into the past to deliberately create bad choices and calamities for some in order to produce benefits for themselves or others.
>
> Then, the first individual would see that false information has been sent and would go into their system and go back even earlier to warn themselves that false information was going to be sent back by an 'imposter' and how to tell that it was false.
>
> Then the hacker would see this, and go back in time to an even earlier moment and give false information that someone was going to send false information (that was really true) that false information (that was really false) was going to be sent, thereby confusing the issue.
>
> This process could go on endlessly with constant and repeated communications into the past, one contradicting the other, one signal canceling out the other, with the result that it would be exactly the same as if there were no communication into the past!
>
> There is, also, the very interesting possibility that the above scenario is exactly what is taking place in our world.

Then, we have that most interesting remark (also quoted in *High Strangeness*) made by our demon-possessed subject, Ann Haywood, who said:

> "She puts the robe around me and then my mind separates from my body. I can look back and see it lying there. Then we go up through the ceiling, pop out the roof, and fly into space. One night the Lady *took me back in time*. We were in a foreign country and the people wore old-fashioned clothes. *The Lady took on the appearance of a beautiful woman in a blue robe. She performed miracles for them* ..." Suddenly Ann's face turned ashen and she asked to be excused. Her scream of pain was heard from the bathroom where she had taken refuge. When Ann came out, she was sniffling and holding her abdomen. The Lady had savagely attacked her for revealing that *down through history, creatures like the Lady have taken the form of saints. They then use the gullibility of humankind to misguide and misinform people so that they believe they are seeing miracles performed.* Ann begged the newsman to delete that portion of the interview. (Osborn 1983; emphasis added)

If these ideas are anywhere close to what we must deal with, then I can only quote from Laurel and Hardy: It's a fine pickle we've gotten ourselves into, isn't it Ollie?

A correspondent recently wrote to me:

> The last parts of [volume two, *Soul Hackers*] were a lot about mind programming. Well, something happened in "real life" that in a way REALLY scared me. I only have started to realize very recently that this might/could be just another example of how STS 4D tries "to get to us", "us" being especially the more "active" ones in the field, meaning those that work "in the field", so to speak. (I am a magazine publisher, specializing in metaphysical subjects.)
>
> Logically, that's not so much to these STS guys' liking and the "bag of tricks" they may have available is phenomenal. I would like to ask you to give your opinion about what happened to me. Was it an incredible scheme of manipulation, defying all credibility, just set up to deceive me, or what?
>
> A first remark: 4D STS can somehow "monitor" our "weakest" spots. For some it is money, others power, others wealth, still others fame, etc. I guess mine would be "in the emotional area", and do they know how to "move in" ...
>
> It starts in the fall of 1996; I was in LA attending a "Mind, Body, Spirit" event, to see if there was anything there worthwhile that I wanted to cover. There happened to be one, just one, metaphysical teaching that really got my attention ... It just felt good, peaceful, mystical ...
>
> I talked with two guys; they were extremely polite and gave me a book. I read it later on and, well, I sort of liked it. It was a sort of story, bordering reality and SF [Science Fiction] (At least, so I thought). It was

clearly an introduction book. Easy to read, to get people's attention – just introducing the subject.

Now, we jump to the spring of 1997. I saw a specific web site (about walk-ins) and just "registered" it. Nothing to do with the aforementioned "New Age Teaching". End of June 1997: I attend a New Age trade show in Birmingham; guess what, there they (the aforementioned New Age group, NOT the "walk-in" group) were again! I had lunch with the two people in the booth. Nice meeting. And I offered to help them.

Then, second week of September 1997 ... I am driving on the M25 around London, and "out of nowhere" a sort of telepathic communication gets started. Not frightening, it was actually "funny" in a strange way. It never had happened to me like that (at that time I was guessing that "my guidance" was really moving up a notch! Well, I didn't know the Cs web site yet). It was about a conference I should attend somewhere nearby Glastonbury, UK. The conference was about walk-ins. I found out the dates. (Coincidence! It was just the weekend I had decided to "keep free for me"!) So, I went.

Very nice conference it was. And there I meet "someone". Yup, an American girl. Stunning redhead! All kinds of the strangest things start to happen ... Synchronicities all over the place, people actually started saying things about me when looking at her – talking about a magic (or should I say "magick"??) weekend! It didn't stop there ... "Romance" followed – oh so swiftly ... TOO swiftly I'd say now. A real "love bite"!

Well, hey, I was experiencing a living fairytale here! So, she decides to stay after the weekend. But guess what? She just "happened" to be deeply involved in this very same New Age teaching I had recently become aware of and had decided to become involved in!! And, as it just "happened", I was just going to a show to "introduce" the material there. Well, she could come along and help, right??? Give a little talk, meet the people. What a coincidence!

But now, she starts "bombarding" me with the principles of this "teaching". At times, I even had to get a bit aggressive to avoid this continual effort to "brainwash" me. At this point, the group sent me a second book, and somehow, this changed my views entirely regarding this teaching. (Divine STO intervention?) After reading this second book, I could see that this teaching was a THREAT of the worst kind!

But, because of this woman, and the emotional ties, I kept this to myself because there were plans to visit the group's European HQ. I thought that, at least, I would be able to examine things further and make a more thorough assessment. While there, I experienced, (no kidding), what I think was a direct attack of psychic black magic. It freaked me out!! It was me – psychically – against eight or so tough people! It actually made me sick.

And of course, there were the ongoing big confrontations with the girl about this, so she went home. One month later I was in the US to try to figure out what the meaning of all this was. I don't think I ever lived through a more confusing month than the month of November 1997.

To make a long story short: Because I was not willing to be brainwashed by this group, I went back home a "heartbroken man".

> Couldn't figure out what the heck had happened. This was nothing like me, still it happened TO me. There followed 15 months of silence. Oh yes, I DID get regular mailings from that group – a continuous barrage of material.
>
> The story had another chapter in a "less dense" way just this past year. A last meeting in the states with the redhead where she made a last "attempt" (pretty forced...) to "turn me on" to that teaching, right? Well, it didn't work. After a last e-mail conversation with her, the mailings also stopped from the main HQ.
>
> Conclusion: can it be that this whole "play" was just staged to get me "hooked up" in that bl**dy teaching??? They probably considered me "useful" for their organization? I never could figure out where they got their funds from – and they were WELL funded!
>
> The scary part is, how could all these – at first sight – totally non-related events be set up and coordinated??? The whole thing played out in 3-4 countries, on several continents, involved different, non-related (I guess...) organizations; a concerted attack on me where I am "weakest", the most incredible "miracles" happened to make it seem that "the hand of God" was upon me, in contradiction to what I KNEW to be true about this teaching – that it was a real THREAT to mankind! Just a big cosmic drama.
>
> The thing is, I believe it to be possible that not one of them (maybe 1 or 2 of the "heads" in the UK excepted, they gave me a very "strange" feeling) *is consciously aware of what's going on!*
>
> "They" (whoever or whatever was behind this) made one HUGE mistake: the timing was just too perfect ... The same day that this manipulation was finally stopped by me, a new one was started – or at least it was tried!! I am getting VERRRRY careful now.
>
> OK, I know, Knowledge Protects ... I learned that part at least. But how many others are led into similar things in similar ways and don't have the knowledge about New Age teachings that I did so that, with the second book I was able to discern and make a decision, against all the synchronicities and "confirmations" and so forth that have become "bread and butter" for the New Age set?

This correspondent was really on the fast track, I would say, but this is not the only story of this kind I have heard, not to mention what I have lived personally. My correspondent makes some crucial points about our subject here when he asks, "The scary part is, how could all these – at first sight – totally non-related events be set up and coordinated?" And he adds, "The thing is, I believe it to be possible that not one of them (maybe one or two of the heads in the UK excepted, they gave me a very strange feeling) is *consciously aware of what's going on!*"

Oh, so true! The most useful tools of fourth-density STS are those who simply do not believe in a control system, and do not think that they, themselves, can be used. The instant you think this, is the instant you are vulnerable.

In answer to the question of how such a cosmic drama could be orchestrated, just keep in mind the time travel factor, and the following:

> November 19, 1994
>
> A: Disinformation comes from seemingly reliable sources. It is extremely important for you to not gather false knowledge, as it is more damaging than no knowledge at all. Remember knowledge protects, ignorance endangers. The information you speak of, T, was given to you deliberately because you and J and others have been targeted due to your intense interest in level of density 4 through 7 subject matter. You have already been documented as a "threat". [...] Remember, disinformation is very effective when delivered by highly trained sources because *hypnotic and transdimensional techniques are used* thereby causing electronic anomalies to follow suggestion *causing perceived confirmation to occur.*
>
> Q: (T) What I want to know is who has the power and ability to set up these kinds of confirmations or synchronicities?
>
> A: Same forces spreading disinformation: Brotherhood / Consortium / Illuminati / New World Order / "Antichrist" / Lizards.
>
> Q: (T) But I'm just a nobody. Why would they go to all trouble ...
>
> A: Several answers follow: number one, *Nobody is a "nobody"*. Number two, *it is no trouble at all for aforementioned forces to give seemingly individualized attention to anybody*. Number three, T has been targeted and so has J and others because you are on the right track. Number four, this area is currently a "hot bed" of activity and extremely rapidly expanding awareness.

When I was first reading the Greenbaum material, I kept thinking that this was more or less a shadow of what hyperdimensional beings must be capable of doing. The fact that we are even aware of the Greenbaum program is due to errors or glitches in the programs of some of the people. What about the people who have no glitches? What about the people who are perfectly programmed via truly alien technology? How could we ever tell? At one point, we questioned the Cassiopaeans a bit more closely about fourth-density programming:

> July 19, 1995
>
> Q: (L) Our first question is: In a previous session we were given a small dissertation on the process of abduction. It was described for us in some detail. [This is included in *High Strangeness*.] Now, what we would like to know is, if our souls are abducted from our bodies and then used as a pattern for remolecularization in fourth density, is there ever, at any time, a remolecularized clone that is retained in fourth density even after the soul has been returned to its original body?
>
> A: No, it's not possible.

Q: (L) So, they don't keep a pattern or clone of any of us after they have abducted us, "they" being a general term?
A: No.
Q: (L) Do any of the STS beings have the ability to cause us physical problems, or mental or emotional problems when not in direct contact with us?
A: Certainly.
Q: (L) How is this done?
A: A number of different methods used.
Q: (L) Could you give us one or two examples of how this is done?
A: There are many: sound wave manipulation of the ultra-high frequency range would be one.
Q: (L) What do these sound waves in the ultra-high frequencies do?
A: *They can alter chemical balances within the body of the subject, thereby also the brain, using the physical path to cause distress by altering these chemical imbalances into place.*
Q: (L) Do these ultra-high frequency sound waves ever carry messages in terms of pre-coded suggestions that are triggered by these waves?
A: Messages are not carried in ultra-high frequency sound waves. Now, you are talking about an entirely different method. *Sound wave focusing is designed to alter body and brain chemistry in order to alter such things as physical sensations, emotions, and so forth, which then may lead to the altering of mental thought patterns.* But messages are not sent by ultra-high frequency sound waves. *Messages are sent by something called Free Formal Imaging.*
Q: (L) And what does that describe?
A: That describes the transference of thought.
Q: (L) And how is that done? At what frequency is it done?
A: Not correct concept. There is no "frequency" as such involved. There is methodology that, again, unfortunately, you do not understand. However, since you seek answers to all questions, the only possible way to explain is to simply say a thought is formed in one realm and sent to a second realm, which is yours.
Q: (L) Okay. Can it be sent to a directed target?
A: Absolutely.
Q: (L) Now, the question has arisen that, since other-dimensional beings have the ability to kidnap or abduct or forcibly extract souls, do they also have the capability of manipulating our soul essences after they have left our bodies during the transition to fifth density?
A: Not correct. You see when your physical body expires, and you enter fifth density, this is done one way and one way only: by passing through a conduit which opens specifically for the purpose of transference from third density to fifth density. Now, something often referred to in your terminology as a silver thread, is like a closed

line, which opens when this conduit is needed. That's rather awkward, but it's the only way to describe it. So that when the physical body terminates, this line is opened forming a conduit through which the soul passes naturally. However, part of the existence of this conduit is that it is absolutely impenetrable by any force from any density level. Therefore, souls in the process of transferring from third density to fifth density cannot in any way be molested or tampered with. And it should be mentioned here also that the soul imprint of the physical body always has a connection to fifth density and that is through the so-called "silver thread" that always exists as the third density soul's doorway to fifth density. It can be opened at a moment's notice whenever needed. When it is opened it becomes a conduit. Through that conduit the soul passes. And it is not subject to interference by anything. This is not a deliberate construction; it is merely the natural process. Once it is passing through the conduit produced by the opening of the silver thread, then, of course, it cannot be tampered with. Do you understand?

Q: (L) Yes, but why do so many souls, when they leave the body, not traverse this conduit, and why do they stay earthbound, and why do they attach to other bodies? Why does this condition exist?

A: That is a complicated question, however the best answer is choice is involved there for those souls who wish not to leave the plane of third density. The only possibility to do this is to be detached from the now expired physical body but still be within the third density plane, which, of course, is not natural, but nonetheless can occur. In situations such as this, though it has been incorrectly reported, the silver thread is still attached and still remains a thread rather than a conduit. The soul is still attached to the silver thread but detached from the host body, which has now expired. So the effect is very similar to being consciously aware of third density surroundings without a third density unit to accompany. Do you understand?

Q: (L) Yes. Okay ...

A: Also, please be aware of the fact that once the soul leaves the confines of the physical body, the illusion of time passage is no longer apparent even when the soul remains on the third density plane. Therefore, it appears to that soul that no time whatsoever has passed. And, we mention this merely for you to contemplate all of the various meanings behind this.

Free Formal Imaging. A most interesting concept. I wonder how many people think they have guides or guardian angels and they are really just being manipulated by such messages? And, the above exchange makes it clear that the problem is even more difficult since the Cassiopaeans are suggesting that body chemicals can be manipulated by sound waves, and that these chemicals – including hormones one would guess – affect one's thinking. As noted earlier, any woman who has ever suffered PMS knows how true that is!

But, excluding normal cyclical fluctuations, it seems that the same PMS-type state, and even others more precisely formulated, can be artificially stimulated in the individual by this sound wave technology. What about stimulation of pleasure chemicals? How easy would it be for them to implant an idea, send a voice message via an idea construct, and then simultaneously stimulate the pleasure centers of the brain so that the individual is washed through and through with warmth and love, thereby being convinced that the idea that is being contemplated is very positive and life affirming when it is, in fact, actually the opposite.

At the same time, we understand one of the means by which an individual can be blocked from retrieving memories by having a pain block installed, and later stimulated.

The point is: it becomes almost impossible to trust one's emotions when considering this factor. So, again, we see the necessity for knowledge about the environment and thoughtful examination of our internal state at all times in order to avoid such traps.

Just how powerful this type of manipulation can be in human hands, is exemplified in a couple of brief remarks about the Branch Davidians at Waco:

> October 5, 1994
>
> Q: (L) Did the United States government deliberately murder the Branch Davidians at Waco?
>
> A: Close. Led them to destroy themselves.
>
> Q: (L) How?
>
> A: Psychological warfare tactics.
>
> Q: (L) Did the US government set their compound on fire?
>
> A: No.
>
> Q: (L) Who set the compound on fire?
>
> A: Branch Davidians. ELF and subliminals, as well as other means drove them crazy.

The fact that the use of ELF and other sound frequencies is ubiquitous was mentioned by the Cassiopaeans one night to a researcher who had recently been through what she described as a "severe psychic attack".

> February 25, 1995
> Q: (CD) The thing the other night ... was I being bombarded by ELF frequencies?
> A: All are.

Q: (L) All in the room?
A: All are.
Q: (CD) Am I in physical danger?
A: That is not the point. You can be harassed.
Q: (BP) Cannot unconditional love and faith overcome all of this?
A: More is needed. Knowledge protects.

Please note that another guest who was well and truly inured in the New Age teachings suggested "love and faith" as the solution to the problem. This is exactly the kind of teachings that are being promulgated to make seekers weak and vulnerable to manipulation. Just as Don Elkins could have very well survived the assaults on him if he had been able to pursue the questions about attack from negative forces, so might many seekers be able to avoid similar traps, and many other kinds of traps as well.

In addition to sound, it seems that there are other technologies to keep the human population deaf and blind. The next excerpt is interesting because it followed a suggestion for a series of questions made by the Cassiopaeans themselves in response to an unspoken question:

November 18, 1995
A: Strobe lights are used for 3rd density mind control.
Q: (L) Strobe lights located where? What brought that up?
A: We have picked up your thought waves, which are progress oriented, and are trying to assist you in your increased learning and progress frequency wave. You see, this increases the energy level!!
Q: (L) Okay. You mentioned the strobe lights. Are these strobe lights that are used to control minds, are these something that we would or might come in contact with on a daily basis?
A: Do you not already know? We didn't say: some strobe lights, we said: strobe lights, i.e., all-inclusive!
Q: (T) Strobe lights come in many forms and types. TV is a strobe light. Computer screens are a strobe light. Light bulbs strobe, fluorescent strobe, streetlights strobe.
A: Police cars, ambulances, fire trucks ... How long has this been true? Have you noticed any changes lately??!!??
Q: (F) Twenty years ago there were no strobe lights on any of those vehicles mentioned. They had the old flasher-type lights. Now, more and more and more there are strobe lights appearing in all kinds of places. (L) And now, they even have them on school buses! (T) And the regular city buses have them too, now. (L) Okay, is the strobe of a strobe light set at a certain frequency in order to do certain things?
A: Hypnotic opener.

Q: (L) What is the purpose of the hypnotic opener being used in this way?

A: You don't notice the craft. Opener. Is precursor to suggestion, which is auditory in nature?

Q: (T) What suggestion?

A: Put on your thinking caps. Networking is not making assumptions. Bold unilateral statement of "fact" is.

Q: (T) Oh. Phrase your statements in the form of a question! Cosmic Jeopardy! I'd like "Hypnotic Openers" for $200, Alex! (L) Okay, you said the "suggestion is auditory in nature". If this is the case, where is the suggestion coming from in auditory format?

A: Where do you normally receive auditory suggestions from?

Q: (L) Radio, television ... (T) Telephone ... (L) Is that what we are talking about?

A: Yes.

Q: (L) If you encounter a strobe while driving, or you are sitting in front of your television, then the suggestions can be put into you better because of this hypnotically opened state? Is that it?

A: Yes.

Q: (L) What are these suggestions designed to do, to suggest? In a general sense, to not see the craft?

A: Yes.

Q: (T) Do we get these signals from the radio in the car even if it is turned off?

A: Depends upon whether or not there is another source.

Q: (T) Another source such as?

A: ELP, for example. Extremely Low Pulse.

Q: (T) ELF, Extremely Low Frequency, and ELP, Extremely Low Pulse – is this the same thing?

A: Sometimes.

Q: (T) This would be an external pulse or frequency?

A: Yes.

Q: (T) Would it be originating from the source of the strobe?

A: No. They act in unison.

Q: (L) And this process prevents us from seeing something, such as craft flying in our skies at any given time?

A: Or maybe see them as something else.

Q: (L) Now, we have to stop for a minute because I want to tell you something. In the past few months, I have really been watching the sky carefully every opportunity I get. On three or four separate occasions I have seen what I thought was an ordinary airplane, and I would watch it carefully and then scan to the left or right, and when I looked back at the place where this plane should be, based on observable speed and direction, there would be nothing there. I have stood there and searched and searched and found nothing. These things just vanished. I knew I had seen it, I knew I wasn't crazy, I knew it couldn't have gone away that completely – and having it happen several times has just really unsettled me. What are the implications of this, other than the fact that we could be completely overflown at all times for any number of purposes and we could be, as a mass of people, completely unaware of it?

A: Yes, monoatomic gold!

Q: (L) And what does the reference to monoatomic gold mean? We have wondered about obtaining and taking some of this monoatomic gold.

A: Are you serious? How about some small helpings of arsenic, anyone?

Q: (L) Okay, my feeling is that there is some negative energy behind that, even though David Hudson is trying to be a positive person and do positive things, and that ... It may be that he is being manipulated.

A: This is often true!

Q: (L) I think that taking something like that to transform your consciousness without doing the work or having it occur naturally is a violation of the free will of the Higher Self. That's what I think. (F) Well, did Jesus or other great masters take this gold powder?

A: No.

Q: (L) Did Adolph Hitler take this kind of powder, or something similar?

A: Yes.

Q: (F) That paints a rather bleak picture, doesn't it? (L) Could this powder be utilized to transform a person to a very positive entity doing great good?

A: Or could it be utilized to transform an entire race of beings into hypnotic submission!!!!!!!!!!!

Q: (F) Wow! (L) Put it in the water. (F) Or even just advertise it as the "Manna from Heaven" and get the biggest corporations in the world to ... I mean, you know that if this guy were not meant to spread this stuff all around, by now he'd be running into roadblocks, you wouldn't be allowed to get tapes like that out there. That was one thing I was suspicious of, like why he hasn't even been stopped, if it's really as wonderful as he claims ... I mean it just doesn't fit. Anything that's really, really good, and it's going to go against the control system. [...] Are they just going to sit back and say, "Oh, yeah, we'll just let this gold powder get spread round everywhere, and everybody will take it and develop super psychic powers and wake up", just like that? I don't think so! The fact that it is being promulgated from the "other side" tells us that there is a plan here.

A: Total entrapment of the being, mind, body and soul. Strobes use minute gold filament.

Q: (L) How can that compare with taking monoatomic gold internally?
A: What composes minute filament, do you suppose? Hint, it ain't from Fort Knox!
Q: (T) Monoatomic gold.
A: Bingo. You see, this has extraordinary properties.
Q: (T) I'm sure it does! The thing is, if it does what Hudson says it does, the power structure would have shut him down – he wouldn't have gotten this far with it. So, if they are letting him do it, it's because it doesn't do what he says it does, it does the opposite. When you take the stuff for so many days, you complete the program; it restructures your genes. Isn't that what happened to us before? Do we want to do it again? (L) And, wasn't it said that light was used to cancel certain DNA factors? (J) Exactly! (L) Okay, how do we block this kind of control?
A: You don't. Knowledge protects.

Regarding the ELF control factor, we had a personal experience at one point that could give some clues to others who are searching. In 1997, Ark had several research obligations in Europe and one of them was in Göttingen. When he arrived at the institute, he was assigned an office and would walk from the hotel to the office at the University every day. But there was a strange problem. As soon as he would get settled in to work, he became so sleepy that he could simply not stay awake. He tried everything from getting up and moving around to drinking coffee or tea, and nothing worked. He tried going to sleep earlier to make sure he was well rested, but he simply could not sleep in a way so as to get good rest. Even if he felt relatively rested in the hotel, the instant he would enter the office and begin working, the drugged sensation would wash over him and he would become almost incoherent. We were in constant contact by email and phone, and I was becoming very worried about him.

Well, he finally noticed that when he was down in the basement library of the University, he was not sleepy, so he took his notebook computer down there to work and spent as little time in the office as possible. I decided to ask a few questions about this situation:

May 31, 1997

Q: (L) Ark has been having a problem sleeping at night and staying awake in the office. The building is a number 9, but there is also the Max Planck Institute across the street. Is it the number 9, or the Max Planck Institute across the street?
A: Well, we vote for Max!
Q: (L) So, what are they doing over there in that building that is affecting him?

A: Better question: What are "they" doing on 4th density that is affecting him?

Q: (L) Since that is a better question, what *are* they doing on fourth density that is affecting Ark? Is he being abducted from this building?

A: No.

Q: (L) Are they STS or STO?

A: STS.

Q: (L) Are they zapping him with some kind of frequency modulation?

A: Close.

Q: (L) Why is it more effective in that building than in the basement or at his hotel?

A: Because of Max.

Q: (L) Okay, they are using whatever is going on in that building to zap Ark. Anything else they are doing there?

A: Yes.

Q: (L) Could you tell me what?

A: No. It would not be in your best interests to know.

Q: (L) Is there anything else they are doing to Ark?

A: Yes.

Q: (L) Can you tell me?

A: Body chemistry alteration.

Q: (L) In what sense is there body chemistry alteration going on?

A: Brain wave factors.

Q: (L) Is there something he can do for protection?

A: He soon will leave the area.

Q: (L) Well, during the time he is there, how much damage can they do?

A: Probably not much.

Q: (L) Anything else?

A: One shot of whiskey per day will help.

Q: (L) Well, that is a bizarre thing to say! A shot of whiskey?! That will help his brain chemistry?

A: Some.

Q: (L) What is this altering of his brain chemistry designed to do?

A: Befuddle.

Q: (L) Well, I think it is working. Any other suggestion besides staying in the hotel, or the basement, and drinking a shot of whiskey a day?

A: No need.

Q: (L) And you are not going to tell us what they are doing over there in the Max Planck Institute?

A: As Carlos Allende would say: "If you knew, you would die of shock."

Well, many of the things going on here on the Big Blue Marble certainly aren't friendly for sure! But, as the Cassiopaeans noted, Ark was soon to leave Göttingen for Dijon for a couple of weeks, after which he traveled to Florence. The time in Dijon was as bad, if not worse, than the time in Göttingen. At the point of the next transcript, he was already in Florence.

July 5, 1997

Q: (L) This past couple of weeks that Ark spent in Dijon were miserable. What was the fundamental reason for these conditions and this misery?

A: Near ELF transmitter. Also the water supply is loaded with fluoride.

Q: (L) He is gone from Dijon now. Whatever it was in Göttingen, you said he would be gone soon and not to worry. So ... he is no longer near the ELF transmitter ... he is no longer drinking the water ...

A: Fluoride is toxic, and deposits in fatty tissues, and lymph system. Aside from the obvious possible negative consequences, it can make one more susceptible to electromagnetic wave frequencies that are designed to make one open to mind alteration!

Q: (L) Okay. You have my undivided attention. How does he get the fluoride out of his system?

A: Recommend daily ingestion of Goldenseal root, as well as vinegar and garlic in moderation, along with up to an hour per every two days of light aerobic exercise.

Q: (L) Well, this sounds serious. Anything else that will help?

A: This is a good start. Arkadiusz, or as we like to call him, Arkady, is the primary target of your trio, for now. Great potential dangers lurk ...

Q: (L) So this really is like the Grail Quest? He has to go through a magic forest, chop heads off dragons, keep his eyes open and not be led astray by deceptive images and tricks ... the whole thing!

A: Where to get the influence for the inspiration behind that story? Imagine how much your cause would be damaged without him? Where would your ambition for the quest go? You must be extremely vigilant when it comes to him and his safety. He still does not completely fathom the depths of the situation. Until he is here, thus more protected, and it will not be easy to get him here, danger awaits the greeting of each new day. Vigilance! Vigilance! Vigilance!!!!!

Q: (L) That is completely depressing. Help me out here!

A: Now ... Calm down! No need for depression. Would you rather be left with a lack of knowledge, and in an ever-increasing state of false security-oriented oblivion, only to be struck by lightning?!? Of course not!!! So remember ... Knowledge protects, ignorance endangers!!

Q: (L) Well, you said that it was going to be difficult for him to get home. The travel arrangements have already been made. Are you saying difficult in a general sense, or is there going to be some major move made, some plan going on at other levels, or behind the scenes, to prevent him? [And there was, as it turned out, but that is another story, best saved for later!]

A: There always is that. Have you not seen the evidence already? Must be aware. Think of it as a war. Expect every possible move/or occurrence. Victory comes from being forewarned, and therefore, forearmed.

Q: (L) Is that, as Frank said, the key? To turn up the vigilance volume to maximum?

A: Always. Don't be like the sentry who fell into a peaceful, pleasure filled, dreamy sleep while on watch! He did not even feel the blade as it pierced his heart!

Q: (L) Well, that is not friendly. Now I really am depressed! Tell me: is what we are doing so important that this kind of energy has to be concentrated on us?

A: Yes.

Q: (L) Can we quit?

A: Look at it this way: make it your goal to succeed, and then you have not to fear. Arkadiusz must be made aware that dangers lurk everywhere, potentially. He has spent a lifetime building a strong sense of security, based upon his own natural self-assured state of being. But now is the "time" to learn that this is not enough.

Q: (L) Is there any specific danger in Florence that you can point out, or back in Wroclaw?

A: No specific dangers. Just remember: there are forces "out there" that wish to see your project, and you, fail. You two have both previously felt the sting of these forces acutely. He has not so much, until now.

Q: (L) Anything further on this?

A: We could go on and on. The point is: warn Arkadiusz! Knowledge protects ...

Q: (L) Well, I certainly will. Could this WM who has just come into the picture be part of the attack forces?

A: Anyone and everyone could be. Remember, *they work through persons; they are not normally the persons themselves.*

The notion that the process of graduating from third density is exemplified in the stories of the Grail Quest brings up the point that many of the tests and trials of the Grail hero involved great deception. He was not just challenged by obviously dangerous or threatening things in his reality, though that did happen. The greatest dangers came from those ploys and traps that were designed to seduce him through kindness, sympathy, love and beauty. It was only after he had made the right choice that the true form of the illusion was revealed to him. He was not granted any proof beforehand, nor was he given any insight other than the fact that following the illusion was a distraction from the ultimate goal.

That brings us back to the idea that the so-called aliens, or hyperdimensional beings, work *through* humans, via mind programming, emotional manipulation, and other methods. How is one to tell if they are interacting with a disseminator of disinformation posing as a teacher or guru or great saint or channel or even personal guides or guardian angels?

One individual suggested that we should be able to separate the reliable sources from disinformation because the latter would be given out by people who had apparent ego issues, or that they were clearly out for money.

I would like to suggest just the opposite would be true in the most hard-core cases. Yes, we have a lot of folks out there who are stuck in their egos, whose egos are being manipulated to send them out to proclaim this or that teaching involving a hierarchy in which they, naturally, have a very high position. Those people who are in it for the money and the glory are easy enough to spot if you look close enough. Even Sai Baba, a South Indian guru who claimed to be the reincarnation of the Maharashtrian saint, Sai Baba of Shirdi, has fallen from grace because many people have become aware of the clever shell game of manipulations he has been playing all these years.

But it is the others – the perfectly programmed individuals that will be discerned with only great difficulty. And, the problem we face is the following: they really believe in what they are saying or doing. They are dedicated and driven to preach, convert, suffer, and sacrifice for the sake of their message!

Consider the Unification Church and its adherents often known colloquially as Moonies as an example. Consider the sacrifice and suffering of these people, begging on street corners, witnessing in airports and parks, accosting strangers with their message. Think of the many recent inside stories about the ways and means of their conversions. Think of the fact that they have all more or less given up a normal life, they have given all they own to their church. They have suffered hunger, cold, sleep deprivation, and so on for the sake of this belief system. They are truly sincere and dedicated. They have no ego at all. Could that be another clue?

Are they programmed in the same way we have been talking about? Are techniques such as the Greenbaum method being used here? The fact is it isn't even necessary. One good Master Programmer can do a lot with an ignorant person. The question is, what kind of people are susceptible to these Master Programmers? In 1931, Aldous Huxley wrote *Brave New World*, in which he stated:

> "The older dictators fell because they never could supply their subjects with enough bread, enough circuses, enough miracles and mysteries. Nor did they possess a really effective system of mind-manipulation.
>
> "Under a scientific dictator, education will really work – with the result that most men and women will grow up to love their servitude and will never dream of revolution. There seems to be no good reason why a thoroughly scientific dictatorship should ever be overthrown."

Aldous Huxley also made an early connection between the effects experienced by those partaking of psychedelic drugs and the experiences of Eastern Mysticism and this set the consciousness-raising bomb off with a bang. Along came Timothy Leary, and Richard Alpert AKA Baba Ram Dass, with their LSD and other modes of mind marvels, leading the parade of those who were "turned on, tuned in".

Abraham Maslow became a father figure to the new wave of those desiring to fill the gaping hole of their reality with peak experiences. Maslow cited psychedelic drugs as one of the means in which even ordinary people could have a little of what the Eastern Mystics worked many years to develop. Now, it could be had for a weekend seminar at Big Sur, or a study by mail course at only $29.95 per lesson. What a deal!

Peak Experiences – experience, experience, and experience – became the pot of gold at the end of the rainbow of the 1960s. No one needed to live in existential despair any longer. Everyone could become a spiritual voyager and achieve extended periods in realms of consciousness they had only heard about in veiled, mysterious allusions passed down through the ages. Encounter groups, radical therapies, old and new combinations of theories and practice came rolling off the conveyor belt of techno-spirituality. The intangibles of spirit had been harnessed. Anyone could evoke some desirable experience by manipulating awareness at the basic physical and psychological levels. Never mind that all of this bypassed the vital processes of reason and conscious decision making.

By its very nature, the whole techno-spiritual machine operated completely without critical thinking; it tapped the bottomless pit of feeling and emotion – primal being. Never mind that much of this emotion was negative, confusing, anxious and fearful. Let's just get it all out here in the open and have a party with it!

Each of the many techniques developed during this time were completely capable of producing an emotional high of one sort or another. There were endless peak experiences, and dramatic personal breakthroughs. The mixtures of Zen, yoga, meditation, and drugs along with strict mechanical technology, were a veritable adventure in awareness. The only problem was: in the midst of all this peaking, mind-blowing, turning on and tuning in, ecstasy and encountering, many people encountered things that perhaps ought not have been awakened. Boundaries were breached into invisible and terrifying realms of consciousness. William Chittick translator of the works of the great Sufi Shaykh, Ibn al-'Arabi, wrote:

> Nowadays most people interested in the spirituality of the East desire the 'experience', though they may call what they are after intimate communion with God. Those familiar with the standards and norms of spiritual experience set down by disciplined paths like Sufism are usually appalled at the way Westerners seize upon any apparition from the domain outside of normal consciousness as a manifestation of the 'spiritual'. In fact, there are innumerable realms in the unseen world, some of them far more dangerous than the worst jungles of the visible world.
>
> "So preserve yourselves, my brothers, from the calamities of this place, for distinguishing it is extremely difficult! *Souls find it sweet, and then within it they are duped*, since they become completely enamored of it." (*Futuhat* III 38.23, in Chittick 1989, 263)

By the end of the decade of the '60s, the human potential movement had become a veritable potpourri of religion, science, mysticism, magick and the occult. The drug use got out of hand, the techniques began to show serious flaws with a number of tragedies resulting in crime or madness, and the whole idea of human beings becoming "psychic supermen" hit the skids.

The promise of the '60s decayed into an aimless lethargy – old hippies living in communes, braiding their gray locks and lusting after the sweet young teeny boppers while they fired up another bong and reminisced about the good old days at Esalen.

But wait! Something else happened here. Remember, this is America, the home of the free ... market, that is. Many people suggest that the subsequent proliferation of the New Age consciousness raising movement was the result of big business seeing a pile of money to be made in the development of slick, newly packaged psychoanalysis and psychodrama. There was, indeed, mass distribution and Madison Avenue marketing of things like Mind Dynamics, Arica, Silva Mind Control, Transcendental Meditation, and on and on. Individual entrepreneurs knew a good thing when they saw it. However, there is more to this than meets the eye. This is important to our subject, so bear with me.

What happened was that many of the mind-wounded ran straight back into the arms of their childhood faith; but many more became victims of the many up and coming cults that were happy to take them in and patch the holes in their psyches, or fix them up for a few weekends of witnessing on the street corner and some door-to-door proselytizing. The odd thing is that most of these new cults were simply variations of the old cults. Instead of Jesus coming to save us, the aliens were going to do it!

Many of the cults, and even the old religions, took advantage of the new marketing strategies and polished up their images, sent their people to advertising classes and then out into the world in massive fundraising and recruitment drives. The Hare Krishna group, among others, even hired their own ad men.

So, the race was on again. Only now, it was like buying Coca-Cola. The "pause that refreshes" right here in this very tape set, consciousness raising course, or cult practice! It had become a form of spiritual masturbation where everyone met their own needs in private. You could put on your strobe glasses, listen to your astral travel tape, channel your very own guides, and get high without ever leaving the farm. You could change your beliefs, create your own reality, and indulge your inner child by mail, by golly!

What nobody seems to be talking about, however, is the concomitant changes in our world that very well may be the direct result of this so-called shift in consciousness. Nobody wants to talk about the hard reality of what is really going on out there. One correspondent described it so well that I will reproduce his comments:

> I think I am noticing a vast world of things going on that, just a few short years ago, would never have happened. Almost everywhere I look, when I see circumstances and reactions and goings-on, the thought explodes into my head, 'What in the world is going on here?' Let me list what I see:
>
> The modern-day Roman circus spectaculars of Elians, O.J.s and Monicas.
>
> The appeal of today's *non-music*, music that appeals to the most base of human emotion and response.
>
> The opiate of the mindless drone and flicker of constant television.
>
> The dangled carrot of a manipulated and contrived economy.
>
> The apathy toward the government and their meaningless platitudes.

> The increase in violence and attacks from close and least expected sources, which appear to be designed by outside forces to provide an energy feeding frenzy as well as divert those seeking awareness and understanding from a path of discovery.
>
> The dark side of Tesla genius.
>
> The easy access of Internet porn and the proliferation of cyber-sex as an option to replace 'real life'.

And to the above I would add:

> One out of every 100 Americans living in a prison, a figure unprecedented in our history.
>
> The numbers of people on prescription, mind altering drugs is even higher than the number of people in physical prisons.
>
> We are now diagnosing and drugging our children for behavior that was once considered to be normal for a child.
>
> Gang proliferation throughout all levels of society, where once such things existed only among the very poor and disadvantaged.
>
> Children becoming violent at a young age more frequently than ever before.
>
> Mass killings so common they aren't even reported on the front page anymore.

And, while I have your ear: what's up with the way kids dress nowadays? Well, it's not even just kids, it's ubiquitous. It seems that human beings, under the influence of Madison Avenue and the motivation masters of greed and degradation, get up early in the morning to figure out how to dress themselves, arrange their hair, and decorate their bodies in as repulsive a way as possible.

I am continuously revolted by clerks in stores with multiple body piercings, tattoos that look more like dirt smudges or bruises than art, hair that looks like it was arranged by Attila the Hun, make-up that looks like it was applied by Vlad the Impaler. Young people wear clothing that make them look like rejects from the Oklahoma dust bowl days. Chains and chunks of metal clank from every part of their person as they display their ornaments to their peers, resembling a combination of ancient Mongol warriors and concentration camp survivors.

And it's clearly not the proclaimed "personal expression", because it is more of a uniform than anything else. They demand to have the same look, the same brand of clothing, the same body parts pierced, or to think of new and more bizarre ways to do it, is overwhelming every parent I know. I have had to draw the line in my own house, telling my kids that they won't eat at my table if the way they look makes my stomach churn.

Who or what is inspiring these manifestations of purely barbaric, mechanistic behavior? Who is turning humanity into beings who accept what used to be the trappings of slavery as if it were the latest style? And what's more, to convince them that it is expressive or attractive? What is going on when physical self-mutilation and self-defacement, mind numbing and body jarring music, and things that are just plain ugly are considered normal? And, not just normal, but *attractive*.

While the above might appear as a rant, look more closely and try to discern what this tendency says about our society. What is it telling us? *Those who have bought into the New Age bonanza seem to have shut off their minds and the effect on their offspring is frightening*. We have become part of a reality that is ripe for being taken over by the first "strong man" who comes along with signs and wonders. When we think back over all of this "awakening of America", we find that the origins of the movement are traceable to the arts. So, let's take another look at something the Cassiopaeans said:

September 21, 1996

Q: (T) Is there any significance to the ID4 [Independence Day] movie?

A: Sure.

Q: (L) What was the primary intention of the makers of this movie? The primary message that they attempted to convey?

A: Infuse thinking patterns with [planchette swirled a few times here] concept of aliens. Part of a larger project called "Project Awaken".

Q: (L) And who is behind, or in charge of, this project?

A: Thor's Pantheum. Sub-select trainees for transfer of enlightenment frequency graduation.

Q: (L) Well, is this group STS or STO?

A: *Both*.

Q: (T) They're working together? Bipartisan?

A: No.

Q: (J) Are they aware of each other? Working on this?

A: Yes. There is more to all of this than you could dream. An army of Aryan psychic projectors.

Q: (L) And what do they project?

A: Themselves ... Right in to one's head.

Q: (L) And, when they project themselves right into someone's head, what does that someone perceive?

A: Inspiration.

Q: (L) Inspiration to do something?

A: And ...

Q: (L) To do something, and to understand or perceive something?

A: Yes.

Q: (L) So, how many are in this army?

A: 1.6 million.

Q: (L) When they're doing this projecting into someone's head, where are they projecting from?

A: Mostly subterranean.

Q: (L) Are they third or fourth-density beings?

A: Both.

Q: (T) Let me back up to a question here. If they can do all this projecting on their own, what was the point of the movie?

A: No, you misunderstand ... This is *an intense activity, directed towards influencing the high level creative forces.*

Q: (L) Was there something subliminal in the movie? That opened something?

A: Sure. Not for you, but for others.

Q: (L) What made us immune?

A: You already have the knowledge.

Q: (L) What are these high-level creative forces that need to be influenced, or desirable of being influenced?

A: *Those in the creative arts.*

Q: (L) So in other words this group is using their projecting ability to influence those in the creative arts to produce things that will therefore influence the people on the planet. Is that it?

A: Yes.

Q: (L) Can we say that they are stimulating people in a positive way?

A: Maybe.

Q: (J) Can we say that they are stimulating people in a negative way?

A: Maybe.

Q: (L) So, there's probably a little of both. And you say that we are immune to it because we already have knowledge. Now, when you say we have knowledge, do you mean just knowledge in particular about aliens and alien realities and alien potentials and so forth?

A: Yes.

Well, that certainly is interesting. But, indeed, we have both STS and STO in operation here. And when you consider the time travel element, well, the game becomes infinitely more interesting.

In terms of mind programming, this question about what is done via the media always arises. There are many conspiracy theorists who are certain we're being viciously manipulated in this way. But, the simple fact is: it isn't even necessary to go to such lengths!

November 16, 1994

Q: (L) We are aware that we are being manipulated by the media. We would like to know what types of methods do they use and what is their objective? What kind of technical means do they use to project mental manipulation by way of TV or movies?
A: Simple bombardment visual and verbal most of the time.
Q: (L) Do they use subliminal implantation of ideas in TV and movies?
A: Yes, but not needed most often.
Q: (L) The music that kids listen to, is there any effort to program them in this media?
A: Yes.
Q: (L) Do they use subliminals there?
A: Yes.
Q: (L) Do they use electronic signals?
A: Yes.
Q: (L) Do they use electronic signals on television programming?
A: Have but not that often.
Q: (L) Is there any signal being sent over the test of the emergency broadcast signal?
A: No.

At this point, I am going to quote several longer passages from a book by Richard Dolan, *UFOs and the National Security State*. This material came out after *The Wave* series was first published, and not only confirms my working hypothesis at the time, it also adds important details to the understanding of the problems we face.

> From the 1940s to the 1970s, military personnel from the United States and many other nations encountered unidentified flying objects, visually and on radar, sometimes at close range. These instances happened not scores of times, but hundreds of times, perhaps even thousands. Sometimes the encounter was nothing more than a solid radar return of an object moving at an incomprehensible speed, performing impossible maneuvers. Sometimes it included the violation of sensitive airspace. Often it involved the dispatch of one or more jets to intercept the object. At times, crew members claimed to see a metallic, disc-like object, sometimes with portholes, sometimes with lights, frequently engaged in what appeared to be intelligent, evasive maneuvers. In a very few cases, it involved the crash and military retrieval of a UFO. In a few others, it involved injury and even death to military personnel. In the large majority of instances recorded in *UFOs and the National Security State*, military personnel who encountered UFOs were adamant that they did not see a natural phenomenon.

This is clearly a serious development, and it was treated as such by those groups we may call the national security state. The CIA, NSA, and all branches of military intelligence received UFO reports and discussed the matter as something of serious concern. There is also evidence, provided by former Blue Book chief Edward Ruppelt, of an 'Above Top Secret' group with access to all UFO data, a group that straddled the worlds of government, military, and industry.

At the same time, the military created the fiction, for public consumption only, that the UFO problem was nothing to be concerned about – certainly not the result of little green men. Aided by a heavy-handed official media and culture, it tried to convince the public that the Air Force's Project Blue Book was the appropriate tool for looking into this purely academic concern. Blue Book was fundamentally a public relations tool, not an investigative body. Throughout its existence, it was under orders to debunk ...

Some intelligence agency, most likely CIA, appears to have surveilled civilian UFO groups ... In 1952, the Aerial Phenomena Research Organization (APRO) was founded in Sturgeon Bay, Wisconsin, by Coral Lorenzen. It soon became one of America's most influential and respected UFO organizations. Months before the first appearance of the organization's periodical, the APRO Bulletin, *a man claiming an intelligence background became an active supporter and attempted to lead the organization into 'metaphysical areas of research'*. Coral Lorenzen said she 'gently parried' these attempts. She later discovered light embossing on a letter she received from him, and used a soft pencil to discern what looked like an intelligence report about her. During the summer of 1952, two suspicious men posing as painting contractors called on her and engaged her in conversation. The men did not seem interested in selling any services. After they left, they parked their car where they had a clear view of the back of her home. These two men also visited APRO's treasurer and secretary the same day, but apparently not any other homes in the neighborhood.

It is worth mentioning that, by 1952, 74 percent of the CIA's money (and 60 percent of personnel) went toward covert operations ... Contrary to the 1947 National Security Act, which stipulated that the CIA's activities be confined outside the United States, *the agency had already infiltrated and financed many U.S. labor, business, church, university, student, and cultural groups, usually channeling the money through various foundations.* In 1952, it began opening the mail through a new program known as HT Lingual, which targeted correspondence between U.S. citizens and communist nations. For twenty-one years, with FBI help, the program photographed two million envelopes and opened 215,000 letters. No one, not even the president was exempt. By 1952, also, the CIA was using unwitting subjects to test the effects of LSD ...

In March 1965 ... FBI offices were asked to compile lists of reliable reporters who could be called on for COINTELPRO work. Hoover was meanwhile busy gathering data on antiwar groups as well as members of Congress. That summer, US Army intelligence agents began to infiltrate and spy on a wide range of political groups involving about one thousand investigators and three hundred officers collecting questionable political utterances ...

The CIA also controlled an army of thirty-six thousand men ... which cost perhaps $300 million annually. Although Congress never authorized this activity, there was little to fear, considering the agency's classified budget and its many private sources of income.

The HT Lingual program remained aggressive. By the early 1970s, the New York City component examined over 2 million mail items per year, photographed over thirty thousand envelopes, and opened eight thousand to nine thousand letters. In 1971, CIA Director Richard Helms gave a rare public address, in which he insisted that the CIA did not surveil domestic targets. 'The nation must to a degree take it on faith,' he said, 'that we who lead the CIA are honorable men, devoted to the nation's service.'

Meanwhile, CIA mind-control guru Sid Gottlieb had developed a strong interest in electronic stimulation of the brain, which he persuaded Helms to support. The idea was to program a human being to attack and kill upon command, to be done through the CIA's Operation Often.

The NSA was examining over 150,000 telegrams per month, as part of Operation Shamrock ...

Hoover, increasingly paranoid about exposure of the enormity of FBI activities, severed all relations with the CIA in the spring of 1970, and soon thereafter with all other intelligence agencies ...

One of Nixon's most persistent goals was the reorganization of the intelligence community, an immense undertaking. The most famous result of his efforts was the Huston Plan, named after Tom Huston, his point man on the project. At the June 1970 meeting in the Oval Office, all the main players attended: Haldeman, Ehrlichmann, Huston, and intelligence chiefs Hoover (FBI), Helms (CIA), Adm. Noel Gaylor (NSA), and Lt. Gen. Donald Bennet (DIA). Nixon made it clear he wanted a major effort against domestic dissidents. The group was chaired by Hoover and named the Inter Agency Committee on Intelligence (ICI). Even the formidable presence of the now cautious Hoover, however, could not prevent its far-reaching recommendations: expanded mail openings, resumption of illegal entries and 'black bag' jobs, electronic surveillance of Americans and foreigners within the U.S., an increase in the number of 'campus sources', and expansion of the army's counterintelligence mission.

Nixon endorsed the plan in mid-July but would not sign it, nor would Haldeman and Ehrlichmann. Who, then, at the White House, put his name to this dramatic authorization? Why, Nixon's young staffer, Tom Huston. Hoover easily torpedoed the plan on July 23, when he announced that he would certainly go along, just as soon as he received written authorization from the president for all these break-ins and wiretaps. Thus, the plan to 'institutionalize burglary as presidential policy' failed. In practice, it made little difference, as these agencies were already engaging in many of the practices for which they sought approval. They did not cease simply because official sanction was not forthcoming. In some cases, they even expanded their activities.

The first cracks in the facade appeared in 1971. With intelligence community break-ins widespread, Hoover ended the COINTELPRO program in April, not due to any recognition of impropriety but to fear of exposure. The bureau continued to be aggressive against its COINTELPRO targets, but was less systematic. Hoover's fears proved well justified, for in May 1971, burglars broke into the FBI Field Office at Media, Pennsylvania, escaping with about a thousand documents and exposing the FBI's massive surveillance of blacks, students, radicals, and other mischievous groups. The word 'COINTELPRO' escaped into society.

Then, on June 13, 1971, the New York Times began publishing a series of highly sensitive documents known as the Pentagon Papers. These were a classified history of the Vietnam War, leaked by Daniel Ellsberg, whom the White House immediately sought to smear and discredit. In September, a group of Cuban-Americans connected with the CIA, along with G. Gordon Liddy and E. Howard Hunt, broke into the office of Ellsberg's psychiatrist. These people were Richard Nixon's personal covert action squad, nicknamed the 'plumbers group'. In April 1972, it was almost certainly Nixon people who broke into the home of CBS White House correspondent Dan Rather.

Also in April 1972, the residence of J. Edgar Hoover was broken into twice. According to Hoover biographer Anthony Summers, the second break in allowed for the placement of a poison (thiophosphate) into Hoover's personal toilet articles. The chemical is a compound used in insecticides, highly toxic if taken orally, inhaled, or absorbed through the skin. It causes fatal heart seizure and is detectable only if an autopsy is performed within hours of death. J. Edgar Hoover died between 2 a.m. and 3 a.m. on May 2, 1972. He received no autopsy, and the cause was ascribed to cardiac arrest, although Hoover's doctor claimed he had been in good health. That morning, about twenty government agents methodically ransacked Hoover's residence, but Hoover's secretary destroyed countless files before anyone reached them. The official establishment lionized and glorified Hoover, and twenty-five thousand people flocked to the Capitol to pay homage to him. Nixon called him 'a great force for good in our national life.' Privately, Nixon feared Hoover even in death. A year later, he spoke of the old Director as though he were still alive: 'He's got files on everybody, goddamn it!'

Shortly after Hoover's death, Nixon's plumbers group burglarized the Chilean embassy in Washington. Then, on June 17, 1972, they were caught while breaking into the Democratic National Committee in Washington's Watergate Office Building. Many believe Watergate was just the tip of the iceberg, since there had been at least a hundred similar types of break-ins, all apparently politically motivated, all unsolved, an unknown number of which were connected to Nixon. ... It took some time before the FBI realized the break-in was not a CIA operation ...

Nixon's several failed attempts to reorganize the intelligence community showed that he was no better than his predecessors at controlling this sprawling octopus. Dissatisfied with and mistrustful of Helms, Nixon fired him following his reelection to the presidency in November 1972. Helms now began two months of vigorous cleanup at the CIA, closing down such vulnerable programs as Operation Often. During his last days as CDI in January 1973, Helms ordered Gottlieb, also on his way out to destroy all files relating to MK-Ultra, MK-Search, and related endeavors in mind control. Among other things, Helms was worried that the lawsuits of Ewen Cameron's former patients could blaze a trail straight to Langley. Inexplicably, Gottlieb failed to destroy about 130 incriminating boxes in the archives. Had he destroyed these, MK-Ultra might have remained unknown to this day. Meanwhile, the CIA was also working to prevent the publication of an expose by former agent Victor Marchetti. HT Lingual and the NSA's Minaret programs also ended in 1973, the latter in order to prevent exposure during the Weathermen Trial ...

James Schlesinger, a CIA outsider, replaced Helms, then named William Colby as head of clandestine services. At Colby's urging, Schlesinger soon ordered CIA employees to report all suspected violations of the law, or of the CIA's charter, to the CIA's Inspector General. The result was a 693 page report called 'Potential Flap Activities', known more commonly as The Family Jewels. It discussed Operation Chaos, bits of MK-Ultra (although nothing significant), illegal domestic wiretaps and bugging, and so on. As amazing as these revelations were, there is little doubt that much, much more never surfaced. Schlesinger fired about one thousand CIA officers, then left the agency in July 1973 to take over at the Pentagon ...

Classified information spilled out throughout 1973. People learned that the FBI actually wiretapped reporters and White House officials ... The National Security apparatus suddenly looked vulnerable ... and the president most of all ... [Shortly thereafter, Nixon fell from power.]

In 1969, and into the early 1970s, the American National Security state was at its most expansive. This belied a losing effort in Southeast Asia. But while the Vietnam front was being lost and domestic dissent remained widespread, the UFO front appeared to be won. Flying saucers were relegated to a remote corner of cold war history as a curiosity in cultural paranoia and mass hysteria.

The UFO phenomenon, however, did not go away after the Condon Report debunked it. Odd, unexplained, and even fantastic events continued to be reported by sober, reliable people. Although the intense media fixation of 1940s or 1960s was no longer the rule in the 1970s, evidence for the reality of UFOs as something extraordinary, and even alien, did not escape the public.

Nor, it appears, the classified world. JANAP-146 and CIRVIS remained in effect, for example, indicating that UFO reports were still being routed through those channels. Moreover, journalist Howard Blum noted that since 1972, the NSA had been 'secretly monitoring and often assessing worldwide allegations of UFO activity.' It was mandatory, Blum wrote, to 'Flash-report' Fort Meade on all intercepted flying objects; 'and these installations are required to track and Flash-report on any signals or electronic intelligence that might have an extraterrestrial origin.' In February 1974, the French Defense Minister, Robert Galley, confirmed in a radio interview that his department was very interested in UFO reports and 'that it had been interested since the great wave of 1954 ...' His department's records contained 'some baffling radar/visual incidents.' The UFO phenomenon was global, Galley said, and he expressed his conviction that 'we must regard these phenomena with an attitude of completely open mind ... It is undeniable that there are facts that are unexplained or badly explained.'

The great advantage to UFO secrecy henceforth was the official deniability that the military now possessed. Previously, those who disbelieved Air Force denials about UFOs always replied with the unanswerable question: then why investigate UFO reports through Project Blue Book? Now, however, the Air Force no longer officially investigated UFOs. With Blue Book gone, the last link to official sanction was removed from the UFO problem, and it was taken in toto to where the national security elite had always wanted it to be: deep within the classified world. (Dolan, 2002; emphasis added)

As I quoted in *High Strangeness*, Dolan also mentions Dr. Jose Delgado's experiments in ESB (Electrical Stimulation of the Brain), which could not only evoke fear and pleasure, but hallucinations.

In 1968, George Estabrooks, another spook scientist, spoke indiscreetly to a reporter for the *Providence Evening Bulletin*. "The key to creating an effective spy or assassin, rests in creating a multiple personality with the aid of hypnosis," a procedure which he described as "child's play." By early 1969, teams within the CIA were running a number of bizarre experiments in mind control under the name Operation Often. In addition to the normal assortment of chemists, biologists, and conventional scientists, *the operation employed psychics and experts in demonology.*

The compiled evidence – which includes government documents – suggests that a group of specialists working in the shadows of numerous national security organizations, set up and executed the largest cover-up in the history of government; *and that the Human Potential movement and the subsequent New Age movements, were key elements of this cover-up.* In other words, they not only have used the colorful community of alternative ideas as an unwitting tool of disinformation, it is highly probable that most of it was literally created by them as COINTELPRO. Though the name stands for Counterintelligence Program, the targets were not enemy spies. The FBI set out to eliminate "radical" political opposition inside the U.S. What a lot of people do not realize is that this was a high level psychological operation specifically set up to vector ideological trends – beliefs, memes, etc.

> [T]he cover up of UFO information is nothing unique. A state capable of conducting terminal mind-control experiments, biological spraying of American cities, illegal mail and cable interceptions, nationwide domestic surveillance by its military, human plutonium and syphilis injections, sundry coups and assassinations, ongoing media manipulations and flat-out public lying on a continual basis, would surely be capable of lying about UFOs, too. Indeed, it was the very institutions involved in such unsavory and subterranean activities that were most interested in maintaining UFO secrecy.
>
> What could they have been so concerned about? As everyone likes to ask, why the secrecy? Surely, if the military truly believed what it said for years about UFOs – that they are usually misidentifications of natural phenomena – it would hardly be interested in the problems. But that is not the case ...
>
> [I]t is within the national security apparatus, and not among civilians, where most of the pieces to this puzzle exist. UFOs have national security implications, if for no other reason than that they have involved the military personnel of many nations. The subject is therefore subject to secrecy protocols, a situation that has existed for over fifty years, and is unlikely to end any time soon. ... The military dimension to the UFO problem remains locked away within the classified world.
>
> Some believe this is as it ought to be. Can the public really handle the truth about aliens? If the presence of others constitutes a threat to humanity, for example, what could the average person even do about it? There are those who believe that secrecy about UFOs is in the public's best interest. Whatever the value of this sentiment – which I do not share – the 'public interest' has never been the main

concern of those making the decisions. Ultimately, a national security apparatus exists not to protect the public but itself. The attachment of Americans to the fiction of a representative government, or – God forbid – a democracy, has clouded their ability to see their society for what it is: an oligarchy that uses the forms of democracy to appease and distract the public. [It is] folly to imagine that an oligarchy is not concerned with maintaining its position, to the exclusion of all else.

If we accept the reality of an alien presence, as the UFO evidence suggests, we must be willing to consider that presence as a threat. The record of military encounters with UFOs suggests that this is the case. Since the public is completely unprepared to meet this threat, one can only hope that those groups which have been dealing with it will act in the public interest. During the period of review [covered by Dolan's book], those groups did not always work in the public interest when it came to other matters. There is little reason to believe it was, or is, any different regarding an alien presence.

Since the 1970s, the subject of UFOs has become more complex. Encounters are as widespread as ever, and even more plentiful than in the early years. At the same time, UFOs have received a thoroughly schizophrenic cultural treatment. Within popular culture, UFOs and aliens possess a cachet they never had during the cold war. Yet, the bastions of 'official culture' – academia, mainstream media, government, and the elements of national security – continue to ignore the subject or else treat it as a joke. One can plainly see that neither ABC Nightly News nor the American Historical Review deems the subject worthy of analysis …

Throughout most of the [last] century's last three decades, very little effort was expended by the larger organizations either to end government UFO secrecy or, it appears, to reach the public with a coherent message. Instead, they have spent their efforts squirreling away huge amounts of data for … who knows what end?

In addition to these, there now exist organizations that serve in a kind of professional debunking capacity. The military and intelligence community continue to show myriad connections with UFO organizations, and several instances of UFO disinformation planted by intelligence personnel are known. The result has been three decades of fragmentation and perennial wheel-spinning …

UFOs have continued to intersect with the militaries of the world. Unauthorized airspace violations by unknown vehicles continue to occur; attempted interceptions continue to take place; secrecy orders are as severe as ever. For all of our sophisticated, secret, technology, these objects do not appear to be under our control. Through the cultural static, that signal is clear. (Dolan, 2002)

But all the while, the UFOs kept coming, and people kept seeing them, and some have seen through the easy answers provided by the New Age and are still asking questions.

There are, of course, many who are skeptical regarding the idea of alien manipulation, the control system, and even the mind programming experiments of the various human agencies, some of which have been exposed in government documents. That is understandable, when considering the factors discussed in *High Strangeness*. However, I think that a modification of Pascal's Wager can most appropriately be applied to this situation: better to accept the possibility in case it is true, than to disregard it and be wrong. Certainly, if it is not true, considering it as a possibility and factoring it into analyses of reality won't hurt. By the same token, if it is true, and that possibility is disregarded, the consequences could be fatal.

Even with the evidence that points in the direction of *something* going on behind the scenes, and this evidence indicating that what is known is only the tip of the iceberg, there are still die-hard skeptics out there doing things that could be not only dangerous to one's health, but actually part of the programming experimentation itself.

> December 3, 1994
>
> Q: (L) I received an article from P about experiments by a fellow named Persinger who has been trying to duplicate the "abduction" experience by subjecting people to EM fields in a sensory deprivation chamber. I would like comments on that, and second ...
>
> A: Nonsense, some have closed mind inspired by fear.
>
> Q: (L) My concern is that if he is doing this to people, and we have talked about electromagnetic energy blowing holes in the dimensional boundaries, my concern is that this experimentation could be detrimental to the persons being experimented on; is this a possibility?
>
> A: Yes.
>
> Q: (L) What could be the results of subjecting someone to these electromagnetic fields?
>
> A: Cessation of body.
>
> Q: (L) In other words, it could kill them?
>
> A: Yes.
>
> Q: (L) Could it also open doors between dimensions and allow other things to enter in?
>
> A: Yes.
>
> Q: (L) Could they be subjected to spirit or demonic possession by this method?
>
> A: Yes.

Q: (L) Could they also be being subjected to further programming by aliens through this method?

A: Yes.

Q: (L) Anything else you wish to say on this?

A: Always keep open mind.

Referring back to our little historical discussion above, can we possibly think that all of the human potential movement activity was deliberately designed to prepare the meat for roasting, so to speak?

Just exactly how this is done in a more or less ordinary way, by which I exclude any idea of aliens or Secret Government projects being involved, follows the same general line as religious programming that takes place in churches and evangelists' tents across the country. An interesting series of remarks were made about it by Marjoe Gortner, former Evangelist, in an interview with Flo Conway and Jim Siegelman in their book *Snapping* (1978):

> "As the preacher, I'm working with the crowd, watching the crowd, trying to bring them to that high point at a certain time in the evening. I let everything build up to that moment when they're all in ecstasy. The crowd builds up and you have to watch that you don't stop it. You start off saying you've heard that tonight's going to be a great night; then you begin the whole pitch and keep it rolling."

For Marjoe, who had seen it a million times, the divine moment of religious ecstasy had no mystical quality at all. It was a simple matter of group frenzy that had its counterpart in every crowd.

> "It's the same as a rock-and-roll concert. You have an opening number with a strong entrance; then you go through a lot of the old standards, building up to your hit song at the end."

The hit song, however, was spiritual rebirth, the product of a time-tested recipe for evangelical religion to which the preacher and every member of the audience contribute some small but active ingredient. Afterwards, according to Marjoe, the only fitting encore to the overwhelming moment of being saved is a personal demonstration of the power of that newfound faith. This is the motivating factor that prompts speaking in tongues, also known as the "receiving of the Holy Ghost". As Marjoe explained it, this well-known evangelical tradition required even greater participation on the part of the tongues recipient and the entire audience.

> "After you've been saved," Marjoe continued, "the next step is what they call 'the infilling of the Holy Spirit.' They say to the new convert, 'Well, now you're saved, but you've got to get the Holy Ghost.' So you come back to get the tongues experience. Some people will get it the same night; others will go for weeks or years before they can speak in tongues. You hear it, you hear everyone at night talking in it in the church, and they're all saying, 'We love you

and we hope you're going to get it by tonight.' Then one night you go down there and they all try to get you to get it, and you go into very much of a trance – not quite a frenzy, but it is an incredible experience.

"During that moment the person forgets all about his problems. He is surrounded by people whom he trusts and they're all saying, 'We love you. It's okay. You're accepted in Christ. We're with you, let it go, relax.' And sooner or later, he starts to speak it out and go *dut-dut-dut.* Then everyone goes, 'That's it! You've got it!' and the button is pushed and he will in fact start to speak in tongues and just take off: *dhandayelomosatayleesaso* ... and on and on."

Marjoe paused. We were dumbfounded by his demonstration, although he hadn't gone into the jerking, trance-like ecstasy that is commonly associated with the tongues moment. ... Yet even in this restrained demonstration, he seemed almost uncannily to be triggering some innate releasing or babbling mechanism. We asked him how he brought it about.

"You'll never get it with that attitude," he joked. Then he went on to explain the true nature of the experience.

"Tongues is something you learn," he emphasized. "It is a releasing that you teach yourself. You are told by your peers, the church and the Bible – if you accept it literally – that the Holy Ghost spake in another tongue; and you become convinced that it is the ultimate expression of the spirit flowing through you. The first time maybe you'll just go *dut-dut-dut-dut* and that's about all that will get out. Then you'll hear other people and the next night you may go *dut-dut-dut-UM-dut-DEET-dut-dut* and it gets a little better. The next thing you know, it's *elahandosatelayeekcondelemosandreyaseya* ... and it's a new language you've got down."

Except that, according to Marjoe, it's not a real language at all. Contrary to most religious understanding, speaking in tongues is by no means passive spiritual possession. It must be actively acquired and practiced. Although the "gift" of tongues is a product of human and not supernatural origin, Marjoe displayed tremendous respect for the experience as an expression of spirituality and fellowship.

"I really don't put it down," he said. "I never have. It's just that I analyze it and look at it from a very rational point of view. I don't see it as coming from God and say that at a certain point the Holy Spirit zaps you with a super whammy on the head and you've 'gone for tongues' and there it is. Tongues is a process that people build up to. Then, as you start to do something, just as when you practice the scales on the piano, you get better at it."

During his years on the Bible belt circuit, Marjoe came to see the evangelical experience as a form of popular entertainment, a kind of participatory divine theater that *provided its audiences with profound emotional rewards.*

"The people out there don't see it as entertainment," he confessed, "although that is in fact the way it is. Those people don't go to movies, they don't go to bars and drink, they don't go to rock-and-roll concerts – but everyone has to have an emotional release. So they go to revivals and they dance around and talk in tongues. It's socially approved and that is their escape.

"It was my duty to give them the best show possible," he said. "Say you've got a timid little preacher in North Carolina or somewhere. He'll bring in visiting evangelists to keep his church going. We'd come in and hit the crowd up and we were superstars. It's the charisma of the evangelist that the audience believes in and comes to see.

"When I was traveling, I'd see someone who wanted to get saved in one of my meetings, and he was so open and bubbly in his desire to get the Holy Ghost. It was wonderful and very fresh. But four years later I'd return and that person might be a hard-nosed intolerant Christian because he was better than anyone who drinks and better than the world because he had Christ. That's when the danger comes in. People want an experience. They want to feel good and their lives can be helped by it. But then as you start moving into the operation of the thing, you get into controlling people and power and money.

"Moon's [Unification Church] is doing the same thing I do, only he's taken it one step further. He's suggesting to people that he *is* the Messiah. In my religion, the old-time religion, it's total blasphemy to suggest that. Moon has gone too far, but that's a very heavy number on people, because everyone wants to meet a Messiah."

Marjoe was quick to point out that Moon's preaching powers, like his own, were by no means divine or even innate. Marjoe acknowledged that his power over an audience derived primarily from the skills he perfected as a child, techniques of rhetoric and public speaking that have passed down from the Greeks.

"It's the same whether you're a preacher, a lawyer or a salesman," he told us. "You start off with a person's thought processes and then gradually sway him around to another way of thinking in a very short time."

Many of the techniques he commanded were simple and age-old, but *so effective that they proved equally powerful even when an audience had been explicitly forewarned of their use.* Toward the end of our conversation, Marjoe told us a story that revealed the finesse of his skills. In contrast to the massive physical experiences, intense group rituals and intimate personal crises that [are popular in the New Age crowd], Marjoe demonstrated how *words alone, artfully manipulated, may be used to influence groups and individuals*, even to the point of evoking the overwhelming emotional response of being "saved".

"I lecture in about twenty colleges a year," he began, "and I do a faith-healing demonstration – but I always make them ask for it. I tell them that I don't believe in it, that I use a lot of tricks; and the title of the lecture is Rhetoric and Charisma, so I've already told them how large masses are manipulated by a charismatic figure. I've given them the whole rap explaining how it's done, but they still want to see it. So I throw it all right back at them. I say, 'No, you don't really want to see it.' And they say, 'Oh, yes. We do. We do!' And I say, 'But you don't believe in it anyway, so I can't do it.' And they say, 'We believe. We believe!' So after about twenty minutes of this I ask for a volunteer, and I have a girl come up and I say, 'So you want to feel better?' You're just up here for a good time and you want to impress all these people and you want to make an ass out of me and an ass out of this whole thing, so why don't you go back and sit down?' I really get hard on her, and she says, 'No, no, I believe!' And I keep going back and forth until she's almost in tears. And then, even though this is in a college crowd and I'm only doing it as a joke, I just say my same old line, *In the name of Jesus!*

And touch her on the head, and WHAM! They fall down flat every time!" (Conway and Siegelman 1978; emphasis added)

So the programming begins. During the early contacts, a potential convert can be manipulated with absolute precision by the rhetorical ploys described by Marjoe. Conversations using similar Neuro Linguistic Programming techniques also build rapport, as does the use of confrontation and direct emotional assault.

Once the individual has been drawn into the teaching, they are bombarded with ideas and doctrines that they cannot fit together while at the same time being led through ceremonies or rituals that induce intense emotional highs and peak experiences.

They are then subjected to more personal encounters in which these experiences are given the prescribed interpretation that is being inculcated. During this period, they are usually involved in intensive repetitive things, which can be as simple as the order of worship in an ordinary church. There can be orders to "stand up, sit down, kneel, pray, sing, stand up, sit down, sing, pray" and so on. More intense formats include chanting and meditation that can induce physical and psychic highs. The end result is, of course, that all of this *stops the mind*. And when that happens, the individual is completely open to suggestion and command.

The convert is instructed at this time to "refrain from doubt", and "do not question the wisdom of the teaching". The oldest version of this mind program is, of course, what we consider to be the standard religious teachings. But we can certainly see from all of the above that they are as much mind control as any New Age teaching or so-called cult. As a matter of fact, the key to being a Christian is "the surrender of the intellect, the emotions, and the will". To whom? Well, it's said that it is to the "One, True God". But would the "One, True God" really forbid doubt and questioning if there was no doubt or question that he *was* the "One, True God"?

In the end, however, the result of all of these programs is the same: under the cumulative pressures of whatever specific mode of programming is employed, the individual's will gives way and they slide into a state of mind in which they literally are no longer capable of thinking for themselves.

This type of comprehensive assault strikes at the very heart of consciousness by undermining the processes of thinking and reflection that are crucial to individual awareness and free will.

Yet, the converts and adherents of religions and cults or many New Age teachings have a different name for what is happening to them: happiness. They have found peace. In the labor for the cult, they are in a daily state of spiritual high, an emotional peak experience that never ends! And, if it does falter for just a moment or two, the leaders and associates work quickly to bolster the high – to get them back down to the church for another infusion. And they go because they can then return to the state of bliss that is their reward or unquestioning devotion.

Successful self-help therapy, religious, or New Age philosophy graduates often achieve a sustained state of euphoria. Their problems are solved because – well, because they *have* no problems. They have stopped worrying about the things that were bothering them. They no longer strive to change and grow and learn and do and accomplish. They are content in their condition of a shutoff mind, their state of not thinking. Conway and Siegelman ask:

> What kind of cultural environment breeds this widespread need to shut off the mind? It could be argued that the need is universal, that everyone – from Athenians to Sufis to voodoo tribesmen to modern Americans – must have some periodic release from the ordeal of being human. In that sense, the rituals and techniques which throughout history have been used to create peak experiences and moments of enlightenment may be looked on as vital sources of rest and relaxation for the mind, momentary breathing spells that hold great powers of insight, healing and renewal.
>
> But what value can there be in engineering these experiences to shut down the workings of the mind altogether, to persistently stunt the processes of thought and leave people numb to their own feelings and the world around them? *Throughout history, this systematic stilling of human awareness has proved an efficient method of con-*

> *trolling members of tribes, societies and whole nations in which little value is placed upon individuality.* The state of mind it produces has a tradition that dates back to the dawn of civilization.
>
> In the remote bush country of Australia, aboriginal tribes still engage in rituals perfected more than 16,000 years ago to induce a state of mind in their adolescents that is surprisingly similar to the plight of many of society's brightest youth today and people of all ages.
>
> In recent years, aboriginal Dream Time has been hailed as a state of profound sophistication in human awareness. Anthropologists point to the aborigine's physical endurance, spiritual satisfaction and telepathic powers as marks of advanced evolution in a tribe that may represent humankind's longest unbroken line of cultural development. However, they make the error of implying that this efficient and admittedly remarkable form of social control in a *primitive, unchanging environment* holds some promise for the future of our vastly more complex and fast-changing technological society. (Conway and Siegelman 1978; emphasis added)

We need to make careful note that this mode of consciousness exists for the very purpose of keeping the aborigine primitive and unchanging. It's no surprise that they still live as they did many thousands of years ago. That should give us pause.

> In all the world, there is nothing quite so impenetrable as a human mind snapped shut with bliss. No call to reason, no emotional appeal can get through its armor of self-proclaimed joy. (Conway and Siegelman 1978)

It doesn't matter who it is, whether it is a graduate of some group therapy, a born-again Christian, a meditator, or the follower of this week's channel o'choice. If you ask a question, the individual will spin around and around in circles of nonsensical beliefs and dogma. If you interrupt and repeat your question, they simply start right where they left off, or go back to the beginning of the loop and start over again.

Such people are not just simply incapable of carrying on a conversation. They are completely programmed. And they don't have to be hauled in by aliens or Dr. Greenbaum to get that way.

Even though they were not talking about the kinds of programming we have been discussing, some of the work of Flo Conway and Jim Siegelman in their book *Snapping* is applicable to the present problem. They ask:

> How do you reach such people? Can they be made to think and feel again? Is there any way to reunite them with their former personalities and the world around them? (Conway and Siegelman 1978)

The answer that seems to be obvious to Siegelman and Conway is interesting because it falls into the same trap as the cults they're talking about. It effectively makes a cult out of thinking in a specific way – the correct way – as defined by another arbitrary "expert" or authority, in this case Ted Patrick.

> A man named Ted Patrick developed the first remedy. A controversial figure dubbed by the cult world [as] Black Lightning, Patrick was the first to point out publicly what the cults were doing to America's youth. He investigated the ploys by which many converts were ensnared and delved into the methods many cults used to manipulate the mind.
>
> ... In unsuccessful attempts to free cult members from their invisible prisons, Patrick was repeatedly thrown into real ones. ... In July 1976, ... Patrick was sentenced to serve a year in prison for a cult kidnapping he did not in fact perform. ... Early in 1977, we first visited Ted Patrick in the Theo Lacy Facility of the Orange County Jail to learn about deprogramming from the man who coined the term.
>
> "The cults completely destroy the mind," he said without qualification. *"They destroy your ability to question things, and in destroying your ability to think,* they also destroy your ability to feel. ... They have the ability to come up to you and talk about anything they feel you're interested in. Their technique is to get your attention, then your trust. The minute they get your trust, just like that they can put you in the cult."
>
> It was the classic sales pitch, carried off so smoothly that it amounted to what Patrick called "on-the-spot hypnosis".
>
> It was in 1971 that Patrick infiltrated the Children of God ... In his brief encounter with the Children of God, though he was alert to the cult's tactics, Patrick found that he was not immune to their effects.
>
> "You can feel it coming on," he explained ... "Thinking, to a cult member is like being stabbed in the heart with a dagger. ... It's very painful because they've been told that the mind is Satan and thinking is the machinery of the Devil. ... *When you deprogram people, you force them to think.* The only thing I do is shoot them challenging questions. I hit them with things that they haven't been programmed to respond to. I know what the cults do and how they do it, so I shoot them the right questions; and they get frustrated when they can't answer. They think they have the answer; they've been given answers to everything. But I keep them off balance and this forces them to begin questioning, to open their minds. When the mind gets to a certain point, they can see through all the lies that they've been programmed to believe. They realize that they've been duped and they come out of it. Their minds start working again."
>
> That, according to Patrick, was all there was to deprogramming. Yet since Patrick began deprogramming cult members, both the man and his procedure had taken on monstrous proportions in the public

eye. ... Cult members had been warned that Black Lightning was an agent of Satan who would subject them to unimaginable tortures to get them to renounce their beliefs. ... No ex-cult member, parent or other reliable witness we talked to ever substantiated any of those charges. In truth, Patrick told us, and others later confirmed, many of the distortions that had been disseminated about the deprogramming were part of a coordinated campaign by several cults to discredit his methods. In the end, he said, the propaganda only worked to his advantage.

"The cults tell them that I rape the women and beat them. They say I lock them in closets and stuff bones down their throats." Patrick laughed. "What they don't know is that they're making my job easier. They come in here frightened to death of me, and then, because of all the stuff they've been told, I can just sit there and look at them and I'll deprogram them just like that. They'll be thinking, 'What the hell is he going to do now?' They're waiting for me to slap them or beat them and already their minds are working."

In the beginning, Patrick admitted, he developed his method by trial and error, attempting to reason with cult members and learning each cult's rituals and beliefs until he cracked the code. Refining his procedure with each case, he came to understand exactly what was needed to pierce the cult's mental shield. Like a diamond cutter he probed with his questions the rough surface of speech and behavior until he found the key point of contention at the center of each cult member's encapsulated beliefs. Once he found that point, Patrick hit it head on, until the entire programmed state of mind gave way, revealing the cult member's original identity and true personality that had become trapped inside.

"The first time I lay eyes on a person," he said, "I can tell if his mind is working or not. Then, as I begin to question him, I can determine exactly how he has been programmed. From then on, it's all a matter of language. It's talking and knowing what to talk about. I start challenging every statement the person makes. I start moving his mind, slowly, pushing it with questions, and I watch every move that mind makes. I know everything it is going to do, and when I hit on that one certain point that strikes home, I push it. I stay with that question – whether it's about God, the Devil or that person's having rejected his parents. I keep pushing and pushing. I don't let him get around it with the lies he's been told. Then there'll be a minute, a second, when the mind snaps, when the person realizes he's been lied to by the cult and he just snaps out of it. It's like turning on the light in a dark room. They're in an almost unconscious state of mind, and then I switch the mind from unconsciousness to consciousness, and it snaps, just like that." (Conway and Siegelman 1978; emphasis added)

The question is, why is what Patrick doing any different from what the cults he claims to consider so dangerous doing?

> It was Patrick's term for what happens in deprogramming. And in almost every case, according to Patrick, it came about just that suddenly. When deprogramming has been accomplished, the cult member's appearance undergoes a sharp, drastic change. He comes out of his trance-like state and his ability to think for himself is restored. "It's like seeing a person change from a werewolf into a man. It's a beautiful thing." (Conway and Siegelman 1978)

That is certainly a loaded statement. Patrick assumes, *a priori*, that the so-called cult member is doing something that harms others or deprives them of their rights or freedoms, and yet he forcefully deprograms them against their will. Notice that he uses the pejorative description "werewolf". That seems to be verbal manipulation. Don't misunderstand me. I think that those individuals who are trapped in silly cults are definitely victims; but they are victims of themselves, not of something out there.

> Snapping is a phenomenon that appears to have extreme moments at both ends. A moment of sudden, intense change may occur when a person enters a cult, during lectures, rituals and physical ordeals. Another change may take place with equal, or ever greater, abruptness when the subject is deprogrammed and made to think again. Once this breakthrough is achieved, however, the person is not just "snapped out" and home free. Deprogramming always requires a period of rehabilitation to counteract an interim condition Patrick called "floating".
>
> "Deprogramming is like taking a car out of the garage that hasn't been driven for a year," he said. "The battery has gone down, and in order to start it up you've got to put jumper cables on it. It will start up then, but if you turn the key off right away it will go dead again. So you keep the motor running until it builds up its own power. This is what rehabilitation is. Once we get the mind working, we keep it working long enough so that the person gets in the habit of thinking and making decisions again." (Conway and Siegelman 1978)

Siegelman and Conway now come to the crucial question:

> The grave questions Patrick first flamboyantly brought to public attention are not ones we can choose to like or dislike – nor will they simply go away if we ignore them. *Is an individual free to give up his freedom of thought?* May a religion, popular therapy, political movement, or any other enterprise systematically attack human thought and feeling in the name of God, the pursuit of happiness, personal growths or spiritual fulfilment? These are questions that Americans, perhaps more than others, are not prepared to deal with,

because they challenge long-standing constitutional principles and cultural assumptions about the nature of the mind, personality and human freedom itself. ... In a statement more prescient at the time than either of us knew, Patrick became somber, concerned over what he saw as the public's growing apathy in the face of the cult world's increasing wealth, power and social legitimacy.

The cult movement is the greatest threat and danger to this country that we have ever had. But the people won't wake up, the government, Congress, the Justice Department won't wake up until something bad happens. (Conway and Siegelman 1978)

When I originally wrote *The Wave*, I saw the idea of cult deprogramming as similar to what we do and similar to what the Cassiopaeans did for me. The big difference was, of course, that I *asked* for the information that was received; no one kidnapped me and beat me over the head to wake me up. However, given the nature of the world, where knowledge *is* power, and the nature of the research we do – helping people to think, to acquire knowledge, which includes knowledge of religion and religious states – it is hardly surprising that we would be targeted with the kind of libel and defamation for which COINTELPRO is famous: they started calling *us* a cult.

That said, considering the work we do, the slander directed towards us was an astonishing blow to me, and of course, to our body of work. It was only much later I realized that the accusations were being made for the very purpose of diverting people from reading my work and therefore diverting them from engaging in the very deprogramming process we discussed. After all, if so many people were being freed from the cultic hold of mainstream religion by reading it and realizing that science and religious feeling are not mutually exclusive, it's clear that the Powers That Be knew that something had to be done.

In fact, in articles posted on our website and every day as part of our Signs of the Times (http://sott.net) news website, we report on the many inconsistencies and hypocrisies that are evident in the major organized religions and their New Age offshoots and the controlling influences they obviously exert upon many millions of people. At the same time, we are attempting to discern true religion – a marriage of science and mysticism. After all, religion means "to bring back together", to become whole (re- = back + ligare = bind together. I.E. bas: *leg = to collect).

One of the most remarkable things about this however, is that anyone is free to look objectively at our work and stated intentions and quickly and clearly see that we fail miserably in terms of cult qualifications as they are presented in the world today, which are essentially fascist in nature. As a slight diversion, I want to suggest that the reader consider this issue of "cults" more closely, by reading an article on the website by Joe Quinn called "Cult-ivating Terror", which is included here as an appendix. As Joe shows quite well, the definition of cult has changed greatly in the years since Jim Jones, David Koresh, Heaven's Gate, etc. Mainstream religions are no longer referred to as cults, which are seen to have a strong element of coercion.

Every definition of cult requires that the group in question have some form of religious aspect or worship as a fundamental basis or their raison d'être. Of course, this could be said of any religious group, but it really becomes a problem when it takes the form of the glorification of a single individual as godlike rather than focusing on an idea or ideal as the object of cultic value. At the same time, we have to consider that there are some – probably very few – human beings whose accomplishments or work do make them worthy of being held in high esteem (take Gurdjieff, for example). There is certainly something to be said for achieving higher levels of consciousness and conscience, and such individuals who have done so could be examples and role models and helpers. In short, they should be ready to wash other people's feet.

But there's a difference between high esteem and believing that someone is going to save you. No one can save anyone, they can only teach, show a way, set an example, and perhaps support others with advice, material support, emotional support, etc. In fact, those who claim to offer such salvation are often psychopaths. Such leaders never admit to being wrong or even normal humans. They worship themselves and expect worship from their followers. The unfortunate thing is that there is any number of whacko snake-oil types out there who are waiting to snag people – most of whom are abysmally ignorant – who seek out religions (cults) because they are trying to get relief.

In his book *The Corruption of Reality*, John Schumaker points out that human beings seem to come hardwired with a need to dissociate. I think that this is actually a need to make contact with the higher self. Nevertheless, this hardwiring is present in all brains whether that individual could be considered potentially souled or not. In some people the brain's ability to dissociate can simply be a normal way of coping, or can result in Dissociative Identity Disorder (DID), or other mental disorders. In the potentially souled individual, the brain's capacity to dissociate could be utilized as it may have originally been intended: a means of shutting down the physical and connecting with the spiritual.

In any event, it seems clear from the evidence Schumaker presents that it is a hardwired function just waiting to be taken advantage of by any snake-oil salesman that comes along. It is also abundantly evident that those who do not utilize this ability of the brain – those who suppress it – suffer from other disorders.

There is an epidemic in the world today that doesn't get near enough attention – the epidemic of stress. According to the latest statistics, human beings are 100 times more likely to have significant emotional and mental problems than people born a hundred years ago. Adult rates of depression and anxiety have tripled just since 1990. Over 80% of people who go to a doctor with physical problems also complain of excessive stress. These problems are increasing so fast that, within the next ten years or so, the primary causes of early death and disability will be stress, outranking most diseases, accidents and violence.

But we keep coming back to that little problem that people need to know how to 1) deal with their stress in a healthy way, i.e. using dissociative techniques positively; 2) use dissociative techniques to fuse the many aspects of the conscious mind while, at the same time, making direct contact with the higher self. Those true and workable techniques (which work because of the hard-wiring of the brain) have been taken and utilized by the snake-oilers to line their own pockets, to inculcate into people ideas and beliefs that are patently false and have no relationship to reality. They have been used to turn large groups of people against other large groups of people for the personal agendas of the snake-oil types and their cronies (the marriage between religion and politics is ancient), to foment wars, pogroms, persecutions, and so on.

In the end, the problem is not so much the issue of "cult" or "religion" per se, but who or what is creating it, promulgating it, and for what reason. It may very well be that there is only one true Christianity and only one true religion – the common understanding held between all individuals with developed conscience and consciousness – but that doesn't mean that anybody really knows what it is. We think we are getting close to it by means of both inspiration followed by hard research and experimentation, but it's still only an approximation. Now, we see through a glass darkly ... a work in progress.

In light of the above analysis of the status of cults in our society and just what qualifies any group for cult status, it is clear from our perspective – and surely from anyone who has taken even a cursory glance at our work and research – that our detractors and those that would seek to slander and defame us, must find another pigeon-hole in which to stuff us, or another allegation to level at us, for we simply do not qualify for the cult label in the modern definition with all its accompanying negative connotations.

We do not practice any forms of coercion or manipulation; they are anathema to the common morals we share as human beings. We simply attempt to offer an opportunity to those who feel they may understand the application of the theories we have developed, and to provide a safe environment for them to do so. Above all we value free will and the right for each person to decide and choose for themselves. At the same time we are not so naive to fail as to realize that to some this concept is detestable. So detestable, in fact, that they want very much to shut us down, drive us off the Internet, and if possible, destroy us completely.

Alternatively, for those that prefer to ignore reason and objective evidence, they may continue to label us a cult as they wish. However in such a case, in the interest of logical consistency, they should also assign the cult moniker to every other research body and organization that honestly pursues its goals, openly seeks to network with other researchers with the necessary skills, and freely offers the results of its work in a public forum for the scrutiny of all – *for that is what we do.*

Our broad research goals are clearly defined, nothing other than an honest desire to pursue these goals as part of a network of like-minded individuals is asked or required of any potential group members. Our online school is still free to any applicant who is qualified by virtue of being as free as possible of cultic thinking and beliefs. No one is required to pay anything at all, and we ask only for donations that are commensurate with the perceived value of our work by the participant. No one has ever been excluded for financial reasons from full participation in every aspect of our work. As an innate function of the research we do and the networking principles that guide it, any benefits are shared equally by all.

It is indeed a lamentable state of affairs that we feel obliged to address the question of cults at all. However, the explosion in recent years of groups of all shapes and forms has given rise to many charlatans and disinformation artists. From the evidence available, it appears that many of them have less than honorable intentions towards their prospective audience and potential members. In fact, we have investigated many of these disinformation groups and artists in our research and the results are published on our website. In this respect we are happy to be able to contribute to the efforts of all those that seek objective and verifiable truth in the face of lies and deceit, whatever their origin.

We hope that, as a result of this brief analysis, we may have provided the reader with a slightly deeper understanding of the "cult" label and phenomena. As with all our research, our goal was to provide as balanced and objective analysis as possible and as a result help to shed further light on this rather complicated subject. In particular, we hope we have drawn attention to the various factors that have lead to the current climate in which the "cult" label can so easily be used to unfairly discredit and malign a group or organization, which may nevertheless possess genuinely honest intentions and information.

What is interesting is the fact that the issue of cults was brought to the attention of the world in the context of variations on Christianity. It was only later applied to other types of groups such as UFO cults, including the various instances of mass suicides like the Solar Temple cult in Switzerland and Heaven's Gate. The progression of this process has continued so that now, it is the very type of Christianity that was originally labeled cult has taken over the world via the Christian Right Dominionists.

These are, admittedly, extremes, but the fact is that deprogramming was not initially looked on favorably in this country, and rightly so. Many deprogrammers who followed Ted Patrick have spent years in the courts fighting lawsuits, or years in prisons serving sentences for violating a person's right to give up their free will to any cult they choose. What is strangely contradictory about this, however, is the fact that now, the cult deprogrammer in the service of the mainstream religions has become an "expert". We should have seen the handwriting on the wall when the government called in self-proclaimed "expert" Rick Ross to advise them on how to handle the Branch Davidians, resulting in their murder and immolation at Waco. And most of all, we notice that the biggest cults – the mainstream religions – are allowed to continue to deceive people exactly as small groups are accused of doing.

The important thing about the above described deprogramming process is that it is a down-to-earth example of what the Cassiopaeans talk about when they say over and over again, "knowledge protects, ignorance endangers", with the huge exception that a person has the right to choose whether or not they will be deprogrammed. It also exemplifies in a very dramatic way, the process by which the Cassiopaeans communicate. They are deprogramming us because we *asked*.

Over and over again I receive letters from people who want to know why the Cassiopaeans won't just answer every question and give them all the inside scoop on the nature of the universe.

Well, at this point, we have a pretty good idea that all the sources that do exactly that may have an agenda that is not necessarily inclusive of our free will! Yes, they may give truth about the cosmos and describe for us the many planes and realities and laws and so on and so forth. But, it seems that many of them have done so in such a way as to not only obscure the real things we need to be applying ourselves to here at our level, but in ways designed to actually keep us at this level. What good does it do us to know that, at seventh density, *all is one*, when the lesson of this density is to choose one or the other polarity? It is rather like teaching a child the theory of flying a jet plane when, in actual fact, that child has no access to a jet, and even if he did, would not fit into the seat, would not reach the controls, and would have no practical experience to guide him even if he could overcome those difficulties, so that at the first sign of any variable he would end up in a fiery heap at the end of the runway.

Michael Topper, who uses the nom de plume "Marshall Telemachus" or sometimes "Mother Terasu", among others, has some interesting things to say on the subject. The following is drawn from a series of articles he wrote. After producing a great deal of material, most of which was published by Val Valerian in his series of *Matrix* books, he more or less disappeared from the scene. The series is long and complex, and the complex language usage makes it almost inaccessible to the average reader. I am sure that this was intended, because it is hard work to read it. There is no free lunch in the universe. In this series, he gives away incredible secrets of reality; but you still have to work to get it.

I have here synopsized and condensed a portion of one section of this series with great effort to assure that I have retained the content intact.[3]

---

[3] Topper, Michael, *The Positive/Negative Realms of Higher Densities*, reproduced at http://www.cassiopaea.org/cass/stalking.htm

THE POSITIVE/NEGATIVE REALMS OF HIGHER DENSITIES

In the higher densities, the name of the game is consciousness. This simply means that the higher densities of existence, whether positive or negative in orientation, all recognize that the business of being and existence everywhere is consciousness. Becoming more and more aware.

The difference is that the positive guys recognize consciousness as being an integrative activity of mutual networking and interdependence because they view all others as self, and therefore seek to help and assist because the others are self, in an absolute sense. In this way, absolute consciousness or God is glorified, if you wish to put it in those terms.

The control system, on the other hand, play the game in terms of domination, subjugation and absorption of other consciousness. But they too understand that the rules of the game posit that in order for them to truly consume into their being another consciousness, that this other must choose to become part of this self-aggrandizement. An unwilling food source is not as nutritious. If the consciousness does not choose, it becomes a poison to the consciousness that seeks to consume it.

So, we have to understand here that the true agenda of the negative realm is to consume consciousness. So, this actually prevents an overt take-over in literal, physical terms. If an invasion were detected, this would mean the veil would be lifted and all would see the "man behind the curtain", would be disgusted and would turn away. Just as in the *Wizard of Oz*, those ruby slippers must be obtained very carefully!

Gathering the essence is an art of great subtlety. The agenda of the negative realm is in its purest sense *stalking*.

The aim of stalking is to create a completely controlled artificial environment composed of thoroughly predictable human behaviors. Behaviors made predictable because the humans have been programmed to respond to cues of conditioning, inculcated through centuries of lies and obfuscations presented in the form of religions. And all of this revolves around a story that is actually untrue, and wholly misrepresentative of the actual negative aim.

For centuries these programming signals have been being set up – either because of time travel capabilities, or because of actual historical presence. Various prophets or religious leaders have been influenced to preach, teach, or prophesy philosophies designed to lay a foundation for later take-over – possibly in our present time. When people begin to wisen up, those in the negative realm simply go back into the past, add something to the soup to adjust for the new awareness. This then acts as a domino effect and influences our present. Time loops and all that. A lot of people think that the alien invasion scenario is a ruse concocted by the government to create the impression that there is a forming "threat," thereby enabling the institution of a New World Order. But, this idea is based on a misrepresentation of the process just described.

The important thing to remember is this: there is not a unified conspiratorial activity going on here in the hierarchy of government. The divide and conquer effect has also manifested at this level and suits the alien purposes to a tee. Such activity at all levels is consistent with their program of stalking, in which confusion and cross-purpose prevent a clear perception on the part of the stalkees.

Yet, at some deep level there may be a direct conspiratorial interaction between the secret government and the negative aliens ... but it is unlikely that any name of those involved would be recognized by anyone, no matter how in the know they are regarding the subject. These secret superiors are just that: secret. Any organization you can name, or about which you are aware, are merely outer circles.

What is the designed objective of this stalking? It is two-fold. First, the effect of stalking is sort of like stampeding a herd of cattle. Bit by bit, they are consolidated into a negative mode that consists of the idea of "us vs. them". Even though on the surface it may seem that this mode is positive or STO, (i.e., save the world because it is wrong or flawed, or blighted with original sin or whatever) the very fact that it is formed in the dominator mode of perceiving salvation outside, means that it can more easily be taken over in body, mind, and soul, at a level that is unseen and imperceptible. In other words: Satan can and most often does appear as an angel of light!

It is only at the lower levels of the power structure that many still believe they are playing out the basic antagonism and self-protection roles. They believe that sending love and light to those in need is appropriate, without realizing that this activity is predicated upon a deep belief that there is something wrong, in error, in rebellion, and thus becomes again, "us vs. them".

There is evidence that extensive implant technology may be used to ensure influenced obedience; yet a degree of freedom must be conserved through the consciousness due to the essential fact that the valued commodity *is* consciousness. A completely drugged, surgically altered and thoroughly programmed psyche is only good for robotic service (and this may also be taking place, by the way). It is in this understanding that we find our way out of the trap. It isn't easy, but it is a way.

The primary object of negative stalking is to persuade through strongly influenced but not robotic behavior pattern. For the free choice of the targeted consciousness to align with negative higher-density existence. Because, in the long run, the object is the eating of functioning units of consciousness by the negative hierarchy, with free will intact. Otherwise, it is not good food.

And this is where physics comes in again ... because the conserved element of true consciousness is the irreducible value of free will. The mind of the subject must retain free will, which distinguishes consciousness as such.

The instant the negative polarization is chosen as a result of true prerogative of free will, the subject functionally becomes a part of the higher-density negative entity responsible for having induced the choice in the first place. And this is regardless of the deceptive means employed, or the persuasive misrepresentations used in conditioning the terms through which the fateful choice is made. In other words, confusion, physical, emotional and mental pain, exhaustion, blackmail, and even forms of torture are legitimate modes of persuasion. Of course, the more subtle the means used, the more value is retained.

A tortured consciousness is the equivalent to being overcooked. Many higher-density negative entities are veritable connoisseurs. They particularly relish the subversion of those who are truly pure and strong willed.

There's an immediate psychic bond in this relationship to the higher-density negative entity; the handler of the human agent who is now a functional part of his new master, and, the negative hierarchy is proportionately enhanced with each induction of an additional member.

In other words: the negative hierarchy is a pyramidal food chain. The apex of the pyramid is comprised of the most persistent of negative graduates, the one who has stuck it out against every evidence of diminishment, and is the ultimate example of wishful thinking.

This ultimate wishful thinking means they cannot see that they do not become God by assimilation and control of others but that the real result is a gradual compaction, implosion, and dissolution into primal matter and Non-being.

And here is where physics comes in again to help us get a handle on this conflict: without duality, there would be no existence to discuss.

From the One there is bilateral emergence. Exactly one half joyfully seek life, creation, play, and exploration ... a love of adventure of sorts. The other half expresses a fundamental fear of losing self in this play and exploration. This causes it to recoil upon itself and thus establishes the tension of polarization. This is the stuff of which the cosmos are constructed.

This can be more easily understood as "love of God through others," i.e., by loving others unconditionally as God, since all are one, even though differentiated; as opposed to "Love of God through self", i.e., believing that love of himself *is* love of God, therefore others must love him too.

The former view sees all others as self, and loves all and seeks to serve others. The latter sees *only* self and seeks to appropriate all others to self so as to restore equilibrium; to go back to the cosmic sleep of Oneness.

One analogy would be the difference between a free and adventurous child who is full of the sense of adventure as opposed to a child who wishes to own the mother and cling to her and incorporate her to himself, i.e., jealousy.

The love of God through self is in fact a state of consciousness that has existed from the very beginning of individuation and which covets attention for itself alone. This consciousness hates, fears and deeply distrusts creation, and just wants to effectively roll over and go back to sleep in eternal union with the One.

An important point here is: this negative consciousness arises from the self viewing self at the instant of creation and is therefore an integral part of creation. It cannot be separated from creation because it exists only due to positive creative inception. Neither can exist without the other. It's that simple.

Negative consciousness – or darkness – is the selfness of creation. The gravity that draws all that exists back to itself. It is the aspect of the One involved in contemplation and rejection of creativity in its own heart. Frozen in that moment of vertigo; experienced at the outrush of creative energy.

And, because this state of consciousness occurs in conjunction with and precisely because of creative potential, and is in fact identified through that factor, it cannot be done away with without all returning to the One and just going back to sleep. Thus we see that the efforts to save the world via punishment of the wicked, or conversion to the light or spiritualizing matter with love, are all expressions of the fundamental desire to undo creation itself; to kill God. Through the idea that darkness is a rebellion, a fault, a thing to be done away with, the twist is introduced that lays the groundwork for domination and absorption. This is why, even though promulgated "Christian principles" seem to be good and uplifting and in fact can be, the fundamental *raison* is flawed and also expresses itself throughout Christian history in such ways as the many slaughters that have been instituted in the name of Christianity.

So the bottom line is: this other half of the all, this darkness born along with the creative upsurge, becomes focused on actualizing its own impulse. To undo creation. For it realizes that only then can it be at peace.

The only way it can achieve this ideal narcissistic withdrawal into itself in infinite self-contemplation is through reclaiming all attention and consciousness. This is in effect borrowed against the inconceivable magnitude of consciousness in cosmic sleep.

Darkness becomes, in effect, an incurable insomniac.

The consciousness of darkness feels that it must tear apart the creative fabric of existence, thereby liberating the units of energy involved in the creative functions and swallow them back into itself, erasing their differential properties and powers so as to restore the One *as One*.

Itself.

However, this is not clearly seen at the lower densities until the masks are stripped away. The deepest implications of this are hidden by many veils. And even fourth and fifth-density participants do not necessarily comprehend this ultimate dissolution. Much like the ultimate light eater preaching the gospel of devolution as though it were salvation.

~

The important thing in the above article that I want to draw your attention to is:

> The control system, on the other hand, play the game in terms of domination, subjugation and absorption of other consciousness. But they too understand that the rules of the game posit that in order for them to truly consume into their being another consciousness, that this other must choose to become part of this self-aggrandizement. An unwilling food source is not as nutritious. If the consciousness does not choose, it becomes a poison to the consciousness that seeks to consume it.

Note the key term: choose. In some way or manner the individual must be induced to choose to become part of their food. How are you going to make somebody choose to be your food? Well, clearly it is not going to happen by saying, "Hey! Ya wanna be lunch?" Nope.

Won't work. If it were that obvious, clearly they would starve to death over at fourth-density STS HQ!

So, what to do? Well, the first step in the grand deception began many thousands of years ago with what we today call our standard religions. It was fairly easy at that time to bring people under subjection via these myths and dramas, to induce servitude to the one true God, and other similar nonsense.

One of the main clues that these religions are indeed cults is the fact that it has been forbidden for almost two thousand years to even question the dogmas of the various faiths. In fact, tens of thousands of people who did ask a few reasonable questions were burned at the stake.

Now, I ask you: is truth so fragile a thing that it must be protected against honest doubt? If it is truth, all the questions in the world will only serve to establish this more securely. Somebody (and it is now thought by many analysts to have been the scribe Ezra during the Babylonian captivity, or even propagandists during the Maccabean revolt) assembled a great deal of stories in many variations, and tried to make it a continuous historical thread by adding in a completely fictional genealogy, and that is what came to be known as the Bible.

The fact is, when we are talking about such fuzzy things as religion and history, we immediately come up against a certain problem. As the reader might know, I spent many years as a hypnotherapist as part of my search for answers within the realm of mind. This work gave me a unique perspective on just about every other branch of study I have since followed. The main thing I learned from this is that most if not all human perspective is rooted in emotional thinking. Emotions have a curious tendency to frame and color what we see, experience, and remember so that what we think becomes, very often, a matter of wishful thinking.

In doing good science, a researcher must be aware of this tendency to be fooled by one's own mind – one's own wishes. A good scientist, because he is aware of this, must scrutinize things he wishes to accept as fact in a more or less unemotional state, as far as is possible. Things must be challenged, taken apart, compared, tested for their ability to explain other things of a like nature, and if a flaw is found, no matter how small, if it is firmly established as a flaw, the hypothesis must be killed.

The problem with the subject of the Bible and history is that there are so many fields that can contribute data – archaeology, paleontology, geology, linguistics, and so forth. On the other side we have mythology and history. They are unfortunately quite similar because, as it is well known, the victors write history. And people are prone to do many evil deeds in difficult situations, which they later wish to cover up to present themselves in a more positive light for posterity.

Now, in terms of the Bible as history, one needs to ask a very simple set of questions: who wrote the Bible and why?

I had a long conversation once with an individual who spent many years in military intelligence and who told me, "One of the primary rules of intelligence is to see the situation clearly ... to observe what *is*, as it is, and then extrapolate to who might benefit, and there you will find why." In terms of the Bible, we really ought to look at it in these terms when we are trying to discover things. Because, it might be thought, in the end what we want is the truth, right? And if that is the case, we have to do things to our hypotheses with the data plugged in that is very much like what is done to a new car ... put it on a rack and try to wear it out with stress testers to see what the tolerances are.

In terms of ideas about what may or may not have happened in the past, when we form a working hypothesis we have to challenge our assumptions – assuming that we have put them together in the first place with as little wishful thinking as we can muster. The problem with using the Bible as history is the lack of secondary sources. There are tons of materials from the various ancient libraries prior to the 10th century BCE, grist for the historian's mill, but they fall silent almost completely at the close of the 20th dynasty in Egypt. Thus, the Bible, being pretty much the only alleged source about this particular period, becomes quite seductive.

But, might there be a reason for this silence?

The person who is using the Bible as history is forced, when all emotion is taken out of the picture, to admit that he has no means of checking the historical veracity of the biblical texts. Wishful thinking generally results in such statements as, "nevertheless materials relevant for the historian can be gathered from the narratives ... [and] the work appears to be rich in materials of high value to the historian," and, "There seems no reason to question the general reliability and the substantial accuracy of [the account's] chronological sequence," and, "There seems to be no good reason to doubt the existence of a historical kernel."

Then, the same writer will say, "Our sources are the products of later working and editing, so that the original elements, more often than not, cannot be isolated with any exactitude." And then he will turn around and do exactly that, stamping one passage as "a rather realistic report of what actually happened," another as "legendary," and another as "non-controversial matters of fact," and others as "impossible to consider ... a historical record." As Donald Redford was compelled to say:

> The standard scholarly approach to the history of Israel during the United Monarchy amounts to nothing more than a bad attack of academic 'wishful thinking'. The scholars who admit, when pressed, that rigorous historical criticism forces us to discard the Biblical narratives, nevertheless will use them saying 'what else do we have?' (Redford 1992)

Again, I ask: *why?*

In older times, we know that the many books written about the Bible as history were inspired from a fundamentalist motivation to confirm the religious rightness of Western civilization. In the present time, there is less of this factor involved in Biblical Historical studies. Nevertheless, there is still a tendency to treat these sources at face value by folks who ought to know better.

I could go on about this in some detail, but I think everyone reading this is with me in having a clue about what I'm saying, even if they don't agree. But, the point is, again, "Who wrote the Bible and *why?*"

I came across a curious remark by the medieval Jewish commentator Rashi saying, in effect, that the Genesis narrative *was written to justify what we now call genocide.* The God of Israel, who gave his people the "promised land", had to be unequivocally supreme so that no one, not even the dispossessed, could appeal against his decrees (Isserlin 1998).

In Umberto Eco's *The Search for the Perfect Language*, the idea is suggested, though subtly, that the development of the Hebrew Bible, even if there were some ancient texts involved (though not nearly as ancient as most believers suppose), was primarily *a promotion to validate Judaism.* This validation was necessary in order to then validate Christianity as the one true religion. In other words, the rights of the Jews, the unappealable decrees of Jehovah/Yahweh, could be inherited by the Christian Church as instituted for political reasons by Constantine.

Again, during this period, we have the Dark Ages where very little secondary sources survived. Could there be a reason?

So, what we observe is a monotheistic system put in place over most of the globe. It is the well from which much in our society – our mores, ethics, judgments, etc. – are drawn. It has been the justification for the greatest series of bloodbaths in recorded history. Could there be a reason for this?

Now we have people here and there performing amazing feats of cerebral gymnastics with this material and other supposedly adjunct confirmation to their various hypotheses ... all focused on a very strange thing: bloodlines. Now, what could be the reason for that?

When I think about this puzzle, the thing that occurs to me over and over again is this: the Bible was written to create a history for a group who possessed a particular commodity that was useful. This history was integral to the commodity. The commodity was a direct bloodline from Jesus back to Adam; and Adam, of course, was created by God. So, a concomitant element of the bloodline is authority. Domination. Service-to-Self.

There are certain particulars about the Bible that prompt the response, "methinks they protest too much." That is, the genealogies mentioned above. I have taken the time and trouble to enter these things into a genealogy program just so I can have a really good handle on who is who. The problem is, they break off just when they ought not, and continue only when it is politic to create a link. Not only that, but the numbers involved don't make sense in genealogical terms.

So, when I thought about it, it just seemed to me that there were a lot of what we call in genealogy (my hobby, by the way) "placeholders." Now, suppose that this whole genealogy thing was created just as a ruse to give the impression of a long period of existence as a national entity.

Maybe the long history of the Jews was not, in fact, a fact. In all the sources I have studied, there are virtually no references to Israel, its founders or associates prior to the twelfth century BCE. From that point, and for 400 years onwards, only a scarce few allusions can be derived. Half a dozen or so. But, the Bible has this extensive history of doings and folks doing this and that. Something is very fishy here. The Bible talks about big shots, Shepherd Kings with slews of critters and bevies of wives and children, stomping all over Canaan, striking terror into the hearts of those vile others.

When you study the Biblical references themselves, you find an absence of detail about the surrounding countries, including Egypt, that were dominant during the 2nd millennium. So dominant, in fact, that it would have been only a deliberate act at the time to *not* talk about it; or the result of somebody writing the stuff much later when Egypt was no longer a power to contend with.

Then, there are all the anomalies of the scriptures that reveal a real ignorance, not just silence. I'm sure all of you are familiar with these lists of contradictions, places out of time, and all that. Then, there are the peculiar duplications of stories. You are probably also familiar with that. You know, Abram and Sarai with the "she's my sister, don't kill me" routine. Then, the same story is told with Isaac and

Rebekah in the starring roles. Most peculiar. The dates that are claimed don't add up; the genealogies don't make sense; the ignorance of the milieu of the time; the lack of many things that ought to be there; and the presence of things that ought not to be there. All these things are data.

What does this data tell us? It suggests a hypothesis that somebody made up a history out of various stories that were known and common to an amalgamated group, but may have all occurred within a much shorter period of time.

John Rhys and others went around collecting Celtic and Manx folk tales to write them down. When you read these tales, you see that there are any number of versions of the same story, some closer than others, some with name changes, place changes, time changes, and all of this from the same general culture. Then, when a hero accomplishes a different deed, you find that his name has been changed, though you know from certain clues that it is the same guy. This is true in other folk tales and mythologies.

Now, it is pretty well established that the Pentateuch was composed by combining four different source documents into one continuous history. That's data. It is also clear that whoever did this clearly assembled them to make one continuous history. But, the dissonances in the document indicate that it was not. And, judging by comparing it to other collections of folk tales, if you leave out the genealogies that have been put in to create the impression that it is a long history, you have the same thing. Different stories about the deeds of a small handful of people who probably interacted within a very short period of time.

Okay, so suppose this is the case. What happens then? Well, it opens up the whole field in an incredible way. If this is the case, we can look for and find the points of commonality of the different characters that are presented as ancestors or descendants and merge them into a more likely event sequence. On the one hand, we have the historical traditions of Genesis, Exodus, Numbers, Joshua and Judges and then we have the archaeological evidence and very minimal extra-Biblical textual evidence.

For centuries, to even ask who wrote the Bible could get you burned at the stake. That raises questions of its own, but even in the last century and the present, people are still trying to make it all fit. But, the plain fact is, it doesn't. Unless you telescope it and find the right slot for it.

The data tells us that some time during the last part of the thirteenth century BCE, Egypt knew of a group or political entity called

Israel that had never merited mention before. From the Ramesside age, literary descriptions of upland Palestine reveal to us a group of pastoralists in the process of settling down. These guys, far from being kings were headmen of small pastoral communities – often destitute, lacking such essentials as transport and in constant danger of having their property confiscated by the Egyptians. It is a wild exaggeration to term these impoverished people "an agrarian elite of shepherd kings." It is an unassailable fact that the culture of Iron Age Palestine, that is from 1200 to 1000 BCE (when the Bible alleges such great things taking place with their cultural expansion), show no archaeological evidence of anything at all but a late Canaanite culture. Nothing "Israelite" can be discerned at all.

So, again, the hypothesis is this: that the Bible was put together deliberately to create a continuous, long history that didn't actually exist. Available stories – factual, semi-factual, or "borrowed" – were used to make up this "history". If the stories of the Bible are factual yet mythicized, as occurs in other mythologies, the names can change with the telling of specific incidents, though they may be talking about the same person as is named otherwise in a different story about a different incident. Add to that the deliberate fabrication of the compiler who had something to hide, and an agenda. The bottom line is that *it was all used to produce a mind program that held sway for about two thousand years.* With a little help from the Inquisition, and other strong-arm tactics.

But, in terms of who inspired the Bible and the resulting control system, we have to remember our friendly time travel guys. Remember what Ann Haywood said about her "travels with the demon lady": "One night the Lady took me back in time. ... The Lady took on the appearance of a beautiful woman in a blue robe. She performed miracles for them ..." How many religions, cults, New Age teachings and philosophies have been started thusly?

Friedrich Nietzsche wrote:

> The Jews are the most remarkable nation of world history because, faced with the question of being or not being, they preferred, with a perfectly uncanny conviction, being at any price; the price they had to pay was the radical falsification of all nature, all naturalness, all reality, the entire inner world as well as the outer. They defined themselves counter to all those conditions under which a nation was previously able to live, was permitted to live; they made of themselves an antithesis of natural conditions – they inverted religion, religious worship, morality, history, psychology, one after the other, in an irreparable way into the contradiction of their natural values. (Aphorism 24, *The Anti-Christ*, 1888)

Our present Western world view is based upon the New Covenant of Jesus the Jew and the early progenitors of Christianity sought to validate Judaism in order to validate the lineage of Jesus right back to Adam so they could make the claim to the one, true God and religion, thereby establishing a control system so vast and far reaching that the entire world has been dominated by it ever since. In actual fact, the Christian community only continues to exist because the critical examinations of the Bible are mostly kept from them. Or, they are so programmed into the 11th Commandment, "Thou shalt not question," that any attempt to discuss it in a rational way is met with the circular excuse: "For the believer an explanation is unnecessary, for the non-believer an explanation is impossible." Talk about specious reasoning.

But this is not the place to talk extensively about the origins and background of the Bible and related monotheistic mind programs. The point is: in the past few hundred years, the old programming of the standard religions, wherein people were duped into choosing to be absorbed through the assembled myths and outright lies that came to be known as Holy Writ, has declined due to the advance of scientific research in the many fields that reveal to us a broader picture of the nature of the cosmos in which we live.

This, of course, led to many new questions being asked about the validity of the Old-Time Religion, and many answers were found that challenged the old faith and glory concepts. People were beginning to wake up a little bit here and there. Thus, it was necessary for the controllers of humankind to invent something new.

I have described above just how this proceeded through the last few decades of the New Age leap into consciousness exploration that has in many cases ended tragically. In other cases, however, it has certainly done its intended job. There are dozens of new sources that promote this or that cosmology, far more subtle and elaborate, to replace the archaic and now mostly outgrown fundamentalism of the past. In other words, we have a whole new program.

Surprisingly, with the help of the Neoconservatives and the theories of Leo Straus, even the Old-Time Religion made a big comeback, with George W. Bush as its nominal messiah.

As we have discussed, only those who have learned the lessons of third density will be ready to graduate to fourth density. There are many who do not choose to graduate. They like third density just fine. Even if it is suggested to them that an entire cycle in this density consists of the perception of 300,000 years or so, with many incarnations of varying sorts, they are perfectly willing to take the good with the bad. And that is a perfectly valid choice. But, for those who do wish to move from this classroom, so to speak, the new mind programs seem to be a concerted effort to prevent this.

What is so special about fourth density, you might ask? Well, apparently we cannot fully grasp the state as yet, just as a dog cannot grasp what it is like to be a human, but the Cassiopaeans have given us some intriguing clues, such as:

> Remember, most all power necessary for altering reality and physicality is contained within the belief center of the mind. This is something you will understand more closely when you reach 4th density reality where physicality is no longer a prison, but is instead, your home, for you to alter as you please. (08-12-95)

From this remark, it seems clear that there is some distortion in the teaching, "you create your own reality by what you think and believe." Yes, the Cassiopaeans are saying that the power to do this is contained within the belief center of the mind, but its activation seems only to be possible *after* one is in the fourth-density state. This state is described as that of awareness, and awareness is based on knowledge of the environment and what actually *is* behind the symbol set of our reality.

So we return to the simple understandings we must achieve in order to graduate with the coming of the Wave.[4] It is in this context that I am sharing these experiences and excerpts from the Cassiopaeans on the subject of mind programming. It is only in waking up that one has any hope of becoming sufficiently aware to become a fourth-density candidate and in order to wake up, as we have seen in the above example, one must begin to use the mind; one must extract oneself from the illusions; one must begin to think; one must be deprogrammed.

From this idea we begin to understand the difference between the Cassiopaean method of stimulating us to think by leading us through various exercises and frustrating periods of excruciatingly tedious questions and answers. It is almost precisely the method described above as that which works to deprogram.

Over and over again the Cassiopaeans have said, "Think! Use your mind! Discover!" or have given only maddening hints, and then refused to give any more data until we have gone out and done our homework.

---

[4] Volumes five and six of *The Wave* (*Petty Tyrants*, and *Facing the Unknown*) continue the discussion of these understandings, specifically in the domain of interpersonal relationships and life conditions as "symbol sets" of deeper reality.

September 16, 1995

A: Questions that prompt reflection, reflection prompts analysis, analysis prompts conclusions, which builds knowledge, which fosters protection!!!

A: Learning builds spiritual growth, and awareness "solidifies" knowledge.

Q: (L) Mike Lindeman has proposed that we submit the channeling to "rigorous testing".

A: Mike Lindeman does not channel, now does he? What sort of rigorous testing does he propose?

Q: (L) He didn't say. I guess they want short-term predictions and all sorts of little tests ...

A: Precisely, now what does this tell you?

Q: (L) It tells us that he wants proof.

A: Third density "proof" does not apply, as we have explained again and again. Now, listen very carefully: if proof of that type were possible, what do you suppose would happen to free will, and thusly to learning, Karmic Directive Level One?

Q: (L) Well, I guess that if there is proof, you are believing in the proof and not the spirit of the thing. You are placing your reliance upon a material thing. You have lost your free will. Someone has violated your free will by the act of *proving* something to you.

A: If anyone *chooses* to believe, that is their prerogative! And what would constitute proof?

Q: (L) Predictions that came true, answers that were verifiable about a number of things.

A: Those would still be dismissed by a great many as mere coincidences. We have already given predictions, will continue to do so, but remember, "time" does not exist. This is a 3rd density illusion. We do not play in that sandbox and cannot and never will. *The primary reason for our communication is to help you to learn by teaching yourselves to learn, thereby strengthening your soul energy, and assisting your advancement.*

April 18, 1998

Q: (A) I was exchanging email with a Spanish guy, and this Spanish guy was a funny guy; he was very interested in this Cassiopaean business. But, he wanted to have a proof of some kind. I was trying to explain to him that it was impossible to have proof. So, I was asking myself why I couldn't ask even a simple mathematical question. I am sure I would not get an answer, and I would like to know why?

A: Because, as you know, mathematics is a concrete field of study, as opposed to an abstract one. Oh yes, there is theoretical mathematics, and some types of mathematics involve variable interpretation. But ... in general terms, we are speaking of a scientific field, which connects concepts in order to uncover truths. Therefore, to employ mathematical communication in this conduit would likely rob one of the free will initiatives in respect to learning.

Q: (A) I don't understand. For instance, if I ask for the square root of seven, why can't you answer? Don't you know or don't you want to tell me?

A: Do you know it?

Q: (A) I don't know it right off hand, but I can compute it in two minutes. Then I will know it.

A: Then there is no need to tell you, is there? We wish to reiterate something further on this subject, Arkadiusz, and for anyone else in need of the following message: we are not communicating with you in order to "prove" our existence. If one has faith and is willing to learn, to explore new realms and to discover what will one "day" be commonplace awareness profile, then no "proof" is necessary. If, on the other hand, one is of the opposite psychic orientation, then no amount of proof is adequate.

Q: (A) Yes, I think it is like the story of the crocodile skin where you can make wishes, and with every wish it becomes smaller. And, you are told that when it becomes too small, then you die. And, of course, you try, and say "let me do one more wish ..." and that is it. *Once you make the choice to ask and not do the work, then it becomes easier and easier and you want more and more ... and your own will and force becomes smaller and smaller ...* (L) I think that the most important thing that has come out of this channeling is that sometimes the Cs sort of trick me into trying something and they pique my curiosity and I go out and *do* something that results in a learning experience that is truly awesome. And the important thing is, getting out and doing the work actually makes you stronger. And, like you just said, *each time you make the choice to not go after the answer yourself, to try and get it the easy way, it makes you weaker and lessens who you are.* (F) Yes, and the crucial point is the robbing of free will *initiative*.

April 15, 1995

Q: (L) Is there anything you wish to tell us before we shut down for the night?

A: Reread information given about attack warning and discuss amongst yourselves for strengthening of learning and knowledge base for purposes of protection and ultimately, survival!!

June 10, 1995

A: You are still asking a question. What we are asking you to do instead is ask yourselves, discuss and come up with the answer. ... This is the correct way to go about discovering the answer to this question rather than demanding all of the answers of us. You have the capabilities to pull the answers from within. We are more than happy to assist, but *our goal is to help you strengthen yourselves for future use*, if you will. It all helps one to advance and progress. All there is is lessons. It's all learning. *Therefore, the quickest, the strongest way to learn is to use your own capabilities to that end.* Asking us questions is certainly permitted, and helpful, but trying to seek all of the information from this particular source, in the long run, may be detrimental. Now, if you will continue, please ...

January 20, 1996
Q: (L) Does acquiring knowledge in a spiritual sense assist in the development of knowledge in other areas, such as communication?
A: Correctness in all areas, as agreed upon by convention, can only serve to help or improve or strengthen all processes.

June 19, 1999
A: Knowledge is power. If we give it to you like Halloween candy, it is diffused.

The most interesting thing to me about the Cassiopaean communication has been the exponential growth in my awareness, my life force, and my ability to truly discern and navigate through dangers that previously would have devastated me (and did) physically, mentally, and emotionally. And it seems that it is because they are, in effect, deprogramming our minds through their often frustrating interactions that challenge our minds, break down our illusions and delusions, and more than anything, make us think.

The Cs are here to help us break free of the programming we have been under for the past many thousands of years. Yes, sometimes what they say is shocking, uncomfortable, controversial, or just plain infuriating. I have been so upset with them on occasions that I refused to talk to them for weeks on end. One correspondent even said they were "arrogant." They have been called "cold and cruel" because they wouldn't coddle anyone. Many people have thought, "Oh! Goody! A new channeled source where I can go and get confirmation of my ideas or the teachings of so and so that I like so much!" And the Cassiopaeans will gently inform them they need to get rid of their assumptions and open their minds. Of course, such people always think that they *do* have open minds because they have escaped the Old-Time Religion and are now on the right track with Swami So-and-so or Lord Sandyanda of the Galactic Federation or whoever.

So they drag all their assumptions and elaborate castles in the air to the session and, when they don't get the answers they want, they run back to the warmth and comfort of other sources that will give them the answer to every question they ask – even if the answer is later proven to be wrong or simply does not hold up to rational review or simple research. The most classic example of this is in the following exchange:

> September 16, 1995
> Q: (L) Any other questions? (RC) I'm not going to ask because they didn't really answer what I wanted to hear.

Go figure.

Let's just have one last look at what Mr. Patrick, "Black Lightning" had to say about deprogramming before we move on to the next, final section on mind programming:

> "Deprogramming is like taking a car out of the garage that hasn't been driven for a year. The battery has gone down, and in order to start it up you've got to put jumper cables on it. It will start up then, but if you turn the key off right away it will go dead again. So you keep the motor running until it builds up its own power. This is what rehabilitation is. Once we get the mind working, we keep it working long enough so that the person gets in the habit of thinking and making decisions again." (Ted Patrick in Conway and Siegelman 1978)

And that is, in essence, the purpose of the Cassiopaeans as they have stated over and over again. If you are looking for a new prophet or a new system of belief, you might as well look elsewhere right now. Take the blue pill and be done with it!

> Men fear thought as they fear nothing else on earth – more than death. Thought is subversive, and revolutionary, destructive and terrible; thought is merciless to privilege, established institutions, and comfortable habits; thought is anarchic and lawless, indifferent to authority, careless to the well-tried wisdom of the ages. Thought looks into the pit of hell and is not afraid ... Thought is great and swift and free, the light of the world, and the chief glory of man.
>
> But if thought is to become the possession of the many, and not the privilege of the few, we must have done with fear. It is fear that holds men back – fear that their cherished beliefs should prove delusions, fear lest the institutions by which they live should prove harmful, fear lest they themselves prove less worthy to the respect than they have supposed themselves to be.
>
> —Bertrand Russell, 1926

CHAPTER 21
ROSWELL REVISITED
OR SHADES OF THE X-FILES

A recent correspondent wrote:

> In May, this year, I met Cathy O'Brien and Mark Phillips in Sydney. If what they said in their book and the two tons of material they possess cannot prove their story, what can? But for Cassiopeians that is not credible. What sort of reason they would [O'Brien and Phillips] have in spreading lies?

As we have already seen, there are a lot of reasons for the spreading of lies, though I doubt that conscious, deliberate lying on the part of the individual involved is the most frequent. But, before we say anything else, let's go back over what the Cassiopaeans really *did* say about the Cathy O'Brien case. In order to have the questions and answers in context, I am going to insert the particular quote from *Trance Formation of America* by Cathy O'Brien and Mark Phillips. I did not include it in the original transcript (for obvious reasons), but feel that the reader will have a better grasp of what is being said by reading for him/herself.

> ... Using standard Jesuit hand signals and cryptic language, he triggered/switched me and accessed a previously programmed message. 'Senator Johnston sent me to give this to you.' I handed [governor] Clinton a thin, large brown envelope. 'And I have some fairy dust guaranteed to make you fly high.' I took the personal stash of cocaine that Johnston was sharing with Clinton from my pocket. Clinton snorted two lines of the coke immediately. He smiled. 'Tell Ben I'm impressed.' He showed me to the door. The severe torture and mind-control programming that I was enduring at Tinker Air Force Base had prepared me for this simple 'mission' and many others. Although Cox's out-of control occult serial killings polyfragmented my multiple personalities as intended by [Senator] Byrd, it was Johnston's alien theme mind conditioning that locked me into absolute robotic helplessness. After all, had I been capable of rationalizing, I would have found that the thought of inter-dimensional travel and aliens was no more bizarre to me that Cox's

murderous actions or having found out pornography king Jerry Ford held the office of President. ...

(President) Clinton added to what Houston said, talking in local colloquialisms. 'Bottom line is, we've got control of the (drug) industry, therefore we've got control of them (suppliers and buyers). You control the guy underneath ya' and Uncle (Sam) has ya' covered. What have ya' got to lose? No risk. No one's gonna hang ya' out to dry. And whatever spills off the truck as it passes through (he laughed and snorted another line of coke) you get to clean up.' Hall smiled at his friend, which was apparently interpreted as consent. Clinton motioned for his aide to get his ledger. Overstreet began pulling out his paperwork, and Hall neatly cleared the table of the remaining coke lines. Clinton gestured to me and told Houston, 'Get her out of here.' Houston didn't move and laughed. 'She's a Presidential Model. She's kept secrets bigger than yours.' Hall's wife led me away and locked me in a back bedroom.

After an indeterminate period of time, I heard her telephone Hillary at the guest villa. She then drove me up the mountain through the dark to meet with Hillary. Although I had previously met Hillary we had very little to say to each other – particularly since I was still dazed and tranced from the tortures I had endured at the CIA Near Death Trauma Center in Lampe. Hillary knew I was a mind-controlled slave, and, like Bill Clinton, just took it in stride as a 'normal' part of life in politics.

Hillary was fully clothed and stretched out on the bed sleeping when Hall's wife and I arrived. 'Hillary, I brought you something you'll really enjoy. Kind of an unexpected surprise. Bill ordered her out of the meeting and I took her to my bedroom and made an interesting discovery. She is literally a two-faced (referring to my vaginal mutilation carving) bitch.'

'Hmm?' Hillary opened her eyes and sleepily roused herself. 'Show me.' Hall's wife ordered me to take my clothes off while Hillary watched. 'Is she clean?' Hillary asked, meaning disease free. 'Of course, she's Byrd's,' she responded, continuing the conversation as though I were not there. 'Plus, I heard Houston say something about her being a Presidential Model, whatever the hell that's supposed to mean.'

'It means she's clean,' Hillary said matter-of-factly as she stood up. I was not capable of giving thought to such things back then, but I am aware in retrospect that all Presidential Model slaves I knew seemed to have an immunity to social diseases. It was a well-known fact in the circles I was sexually passed around in that government level mind-controlled sex slaves were 'clean' to the degree that none of my abusers took precautions such as wearing condoms.

Hall's wife patted the bed and instructed me to display the mutilation. Hillary exclaimed, 'God!' and immediately began performing oral sex on me. Apparently aroused by the carving in my vagina.

> Hillary stood up and quickly peeled out of her matronly nylon panties and pantyhose. Uninhibited ... Hillary had resumed examining my hideous mutilation and performing oral sex on me when Bill Clinton walked in. Hillary lifted her head to ask, 'How'd it go?' Clinton appeared totally unaffected by what he walked into, tossed his jacket on a chair and said, 'It's official. I'm exhausted. I'm going to bed.' (O'Brien and Phillips 1995, 107, 155)

That was certainly edifying, won't you agree? And now you may understand why I didn't want to either read it into the record, much less have to retype it from the tape! So, let's look at what the Cassiopaeans *did* say about it:

> September 19, 1998
>
> Q: (L) I have several things from the little mail list that I would like to get to first because I think they may go fairly quick. The first is this book called *Trance Formation of America; The True-Life Story of a CIA Slave* by Cathy O'Brien with Mark Phillips. There is a rather lengthy quote from this book here that we have all read. I certainly am not going to read it out loud because I don't want to have to type such a thing myself, so I won't read it, but I am sure you are aware of what it says. What I would like to know is: what is the motivation behind the authors of this book?
>
> A: Disruption.
>
> Q: (L) Disruption of what?
>
> A: Anyone disruptable.
>
> Q: (L) It specifically seems to be aimed at the Clintons or the power structure. Are any of these descriptions of the behaviors of Hillary and Bill Clinton as explicated in this extract anywhere near close to reality?
>
> A: Anywhere near? *Well maybe, but not as described.*
>
> Q: (L) Is there such a thing as this girl describes? These CIA slaves that are sexually mutilated and programmed with this mind control programming that she has described?
>
> A: *Any such experiment would be handled by the cellular structure of pseudo-governmental satellite, not normally by CIA.*
>
> Q: (L) So, what you seem to be implying is that *what is described here is taking place?*
>
> A: To an extent, *but the story as related is fictional.*

So we see that the Cassiopaeans are not precisely saying that these folks are spreading lies. In fact, in a funny sort of way, they confirmed what O'Brien and Phillips are saying, but added that the story itself is fictional. On another occasion, the Cassiopaeans said, "As you know ... fiction is often the guise for the deliverance of the deepest of truths."

So, when the Cassiopaeans said above that the purpose of the book was disruption, it may very well be that the efforts of these people, using whatever guise for the message they felt necessary to protect the genuine source of the information, is to disrupt such programs and to inform the public. And, if even half of it is accurate in any terms at all, honey, we are in deep trouble!

We must also consider the idea that the defamatory claims made about the Clinton family, may very well be the work of COINTELPRO. Obviously, if there is a network set up to satisfy presidential lusts, Billy Boy wouldn't have gotten caught with Monica's cigar. In retrospect, we might even think that the backing for Cathy and Mark was the same backing that put George W. Bush in the White House.

From the proliferation of books and websites about mind programming, it is beginning to sound like everybody has been kidnapped and messed with. Is it really that bad?

> May 25, 1996
> Q: (S) I don't want to sound paranoid, but all the reports about mind programming ... is it as widespread as we have been lead to believe? That it could be the guy next door, and a certain color, or word or sound could set them off? What is the percentage of programmed people?
> A: 2 out of every 100.
> Q: (L) How many are programmed by human means?
> A: 12 per cent of the 2 per cent.
> Q: (L) So, out of every 10,000 people, there are 200 that are programmed, and 24 of these are programmed by humans which leaves 176 programmed by aliens, as in fourth-density STS?
> A: Understand that 4th density is physical, indeed. You are drifting further and further toward an ethereal only perception/theoretical position.
> Q: (L) You are saying that the humans working on these kinds of things ... and ...
> A: No, Laura, we are saying that there is really a very strong "nuts and bolts" reality to this phenomenon, and don't ignore it!

Now, those figures are frightening! Two percent of the population of the United States, the last time I read a population figure of 275 million, would be 5.5 million individuals. That means that something like 660,000 of them are programmed by human agencies. That number is pretty hard to believe. What are the logistics of mind programming that many people? If there is any possibility that this number is anything close to accurate, we have to conceive of a very large and extraordinary bureaucratic machine that handles the coordination and tracking of such a project. And trying to think of that – well, I suppose it is not so difficult when you are dealing with mind-progammed people as it might be if it were a simple government agency where people spend as much time complaining and demanding service as anything else. Maybe mind-programmed people don't do that? Maybe they are easier to deal with than the people in the local welfare waiting rooms?

But still, we are left with two people out of every hundred. That means that in any large gathering, there is likely to be one or more programmed individuals present, and that is not a pleasant thought. But I think that for the most part we are talking about people in the public eye or who have a public presence in politics or the arts and education and so forth. Yes, there are probably the "Manchurian Candidate" types who are programmed for special needs, such as causing riots, mass killings, assassinations, or special missions, and maybe a sex slave or two just for variety. But for everybody to get paranoid about their neighbors and family members is going to an inadvisable extreme.

It also points out the fact that out of that 100 people, if there *are* two who have been messed with and the programs have glitches, and they begin to be deprogrammed, there is not likely to be much support or understanding from the majority who have no experience with such a reality and will certainly find it difficult to believe, much less relate to. Yet, they too are programmed – only in a different sense.

For the most part, the other 98 people are programmed as we have discussed in the previous section – via religion and related popular belief systems, including scientific materialism. Most of these never merit further programming efforts because the easy, environmental methods and assorted Master Programmers work just fine, thank you very much!

In addition to the more overt programming efforts, we have another item to consider here: past life programming. We have to remember that, with the time travel capabilities, with the presence in our reality of the control system, for some considerable time there have been programming influences throughout many incarnations. This becomes a very real program that one must overcome. The following exchange highlights this aspect:

December 21, 1996

Q: (AM) So many things have happened to me, that I am wondering if something happened to my brain in this life or another that would explain my thinking. Did anything happen in another life that has caused me problems in this life?

A: The answer is yes, as with all others.

Q: (L) What happened to cause these mental problems?

A: Not mental, emotional.

Q: (L) Can you tell us a little bit about it?

A: Death of a twin in the last lifetime. Farming accident in 1880s. Fell off of the ox-driven combine, driven by father. Was decapitated.

Q: (L) And what were their names?

A: Lucas and Lawrence. Lucas was the one that died.

Q: (L) Where was Lawrence, at the time?

A: In the house.

Q: (L) And what kind of emotion has carried over into this lifetime?

A: Her longing is insatiable as she is always "looking for love" due to her loss.

Q: (L) How old was Lucas when this happened?

A: 8 years old.

Q: (L) How many years after this accident did Lawrence live?

A: 22 years.

Q: (L) Have any of the persons of that lifetime returned to interact with her in this life?

A: No.

Q: (L) Not even the twin?

A: Correct.

Q: (AM) Emotions are not mental, there is a difference? So, my problems now are emotional and not mental?

A: Your problems are due to maladjustment.

Q: (L) From life to life or just this life?

A: They are the same.

Q: (L) Was there any sense of blame or resentment directed toward her by the parents of that time?

A: No.

Q: (L) Was there any mental or emotional abuse that took place in that lifetime?

A: Maybe some, but it is not significant.

Q: (L) What steps can she take to resolve this maladjustment?

A: Awareness of the root of the problem.

Q: (AM) So, all the problems that I had as a child were the result of this?

A: Some seek an environment of "punishment" in an attempt to resolve leftover issues.

Q: (L) Did she have feelings of guilt that her twin had died and she was still alive?

A: Yes, but this was not imposed by others.

Q: (L) Okay, she felt guilt, and sought an environment that would punish her?

A: Close enough for hand grenades.

Q: (AM) Let me ask this: all of the experiences that I had as a child were caused by this emotion where I was trying to punish myself. I have spent my lifetime trying to punish myself. Is that right?

A: Close. But remember, the point is, you sought out an environment that you perceived to be restrictive and unforgiving. Especially with your father.

January 10, 1997

Q: (AM) Since you told me about the past life experience, and that all of my problems have been emotional, have all the mistakes that I have made been because that is what I *intended* to do in this life? Were all the mistakes I have made in this life part of a plan?

A: No. Mistakes are made by choice, plan is merely "blueprint".

Q: (L) So, she had a blueprint, and the mistakes were made by choice because she made the wrong choices?

A: Yes.

Q: (L) Well, I think that what she is trying to deal with here is her guilt. She wants to know why she has lived her whole life making these mistakes and messing everything up every time she made a choice to do something?

A: Must be specific as to mistakes, always!

Q: (AM) Well, I am not prepared to do that.

A: Not prepared due to "shyness". Remember, we told you about the unfulfilled quest for love, acceptance, approval, and to be "needed". The reason for the failure of the quest is being hasty, impatient, and stubborn.

Q: (L) Can I help her to get to the issue here?

A: She must do this on her own.

Q: (AM) Why have I been so hasty, impatient and stubborn?

A: Because of past life programming. You see this is the challenge for all those in third density existences. Some learn in any given lifetime, and some do not!

Q: (AM) But, I had never heard of it!

A: Not necessary. Just follow "the signs".

Q: (AM) Is it that I am so stubborn that I cannot see?

A: Have been; less so now.

Q: (AM) Well, I've never *seen* any signs.

A: That is part of the lesson, but it really should be obvious.

Q: (AM) Well, I can't think how to ask any more questions ...

So we see that in this case an individual had a past life experience that was so traumatic it colored her emotions into this life. At every point where she made a choice, she *could* have used her mind to think, but was so deeply stubborn and impatient that she consistently made decisions based on these deeply programmed emotions, which led further and further into disaster after disaster. She was so afraid of loving, living in a state of emotional paralysis, that this had caused her to rationalize that she was thinking logically when she avoided emotional involvement. And she stubbornly resisted anything that suggested that the real problem was *fear*. Because of course she was denying emotions, right? Therefore, she didn't feel fear, right? So, she would be impatient and jump into situations to prove she was not fearful, all the while the underlying dynamic was *fear of love*.

Then, when she started to feel in any relationship, her mind would freeze her emotional response, and she would begin to create negative dramas wherein her demands and behaviors were so completely unloving as to drive away a saint. And, when normal human beings finally rejected her, she was able to proclaim triumphantly, "See! I predicted it was not love, and now I am proven right!" And of course in each of these dramas she created, she chose to believe that everything was done to her by others because she had let her emotional guard down, and this just further justified her logical approach to life, eliminating love from the picture altogether. So, at a deep level she believed she deserved to be punished and so clung stubbornly to this concept. It was and is a tragic situation because this individual is now advanced in years and struggling to come to terms with a lifetime of hurt and harm to both herself and others due to this past life programming.

Another interesting result of some of the mind programming efforts is a recent proliferation of books by "Pro-Reptoid Experiencers" trying to implement damage control in response to the many revelations about the Reptilian control system, possibly even including our own material. The following is an exchange where we were discussing just such a volume, which curiously admits to the programming and genetic engineering of human beings, but giving the ostensible purposes as being highly benevolent. This author, who claims to be a "new Reptoid hybrid", also remarks that Bill Clinton is also a Reptoid hybrid. The title of the book is *The Ultimate Alien Agenda.* You might enjoy reading my review of it at Amazon.com.

> January 2, 1999
>
> Q: (L) Okay, now, onto this alien book. It seems to be almost a point-by-point refutation of some of the things you have told us. At the same time, it is very revealing. This guy says that "alien scientists have developed an array of human programs or life orientations

which they use to create human hybrids. I was programmed to serve others, and most of my life has been devoted to service as a public official, educator, and psychic counselor. My life exemplifies one category of alien programming." Is it a fact that the Reptoid aliens [4D STS] are making a bunch of hybrids to serve others?

A: No.

Q: (L) Another thing he talks about is the underground laboratory, and he has a terrible time trying to speak about it because of the pains in his head. He finally gets to the point where he admits that part of the "human engineering project", part of what they are doing with the embryos they create by harvesting human eggs and sperm, is that they use them for nourishment. Naturally, he is aghast at this admission from his own memory. And somehow he just glosses over it. Is this true? That some human embryos are being created to provide nourishment for aliens?

A: In a sense.

Q: (L) He never comes back to this specifically, except to vaguely state that the vats and body parts and all that which are reported by many eyewitnesses, are merely symbolic imagery to teach us how unimportant the body is ... Can you comment?

A: Not necessary. We have already stated that the vats do exist and what they are for. [See *High Strangeness.*]

Q: (L) He further says that the Reptoid aliens [4D STS] have been increasing human intelligence for these many thousands of years with the intention of letting go and leaving us on our own. The Reptoids are going to pull out soon, because they just came to "help us evolve," and now we are at the stage we can take charge of things ourselves ... Have the Reptoids been increasing human intelligence? Is this part of their agenda?

A: Perhaps, but the agenda is not as stated.

Q: (L) Okay, he says, "I wonder if the current relationship between humans and aliens may be analogous to the abolition of slavery in America. Freedom arises when people accept others rather than being afraid of them or trying to control them. We may be learning to accept a technologically advanced interdimensional race, and the aliens may be trying to transform us into compatible neighbors. Perhaps humans and aliens will become more alike as time passes and our two dimensions will become increasingly integrated. They are now allowing us to discover this information. I believe the aliens are getting ready to reveal who they are, but first they are helping us to discover who we are. Aliens may be programming human hybrids like myself to learn through self-discovery and self-acceptance, and we are likely to learn more about them as we discover ourselves. Important information about them may be archived in our minds or implanted in our bodies. To retrieve the information, we must learn to express the interdimensional aspects of our being. In other words, we must integrate our human and interdimensional selves and learn to function in both worlds. I believe this is how we will eventually establish two-way communication with our alien creators, and learn to coexist with them." Blah blah blah. Then he says that he was created from the genetic material, and soul essences of three separate individuals. Comments please.

A: No need.

Q: (L) Well, yeah. All of these things have already been covered, which is why it was so interesting to see such different explanations for the same observations. He says that his "image is being used to tell people: wake up human hybrids! It's time to accept your interdimensional identity. It's time to discover your Reptilian heritage and fulfill your mission!" Yuck! Then he talks about the sexual aspect of abduction. He wondered why it occurs so frequently. He thinks there is a link between the frequency of human sexuality and Reptilian intelligence ... He thinks that "this could explain why people so often perceive aliens and their messengers in sexual roles. So many abductees report having sexual experiences, in fact sexuality is a common theme of all alien abduction experiences. Could sexual stimulation be part of the methodology of alien intelligence?" Could it?

A: And the "Playboy Channel" originates on Zeta Reticuli!

In another session the following exchange took place:

January 10, 1995

Q: (L) The whole point of this article [by Lyssa Royal] is to say that ETs who abduct people are here to help us evolve and that it is only us, if we have dark and dirty unconscious minds, who perceive them as negative.

A: Wrong, you do not need "help" evolving, nor does anything else.

I guess this guy is the equivalent of a Madison Avenue adman for the control system. I do find curious the reference he makes to slavery. He said, "I wonder if the current relationship between humans and aliens may be analogous to the abolition of slavery in America." How does that even relate? Unless of course he is freely admitting that we are slaves and the aliens are slave masters. On the other hand, does he mean to imply that the aliens are slaves and *we* are the slave masters who are afraid of and trying to control the aliens? Most peculiar. His mixed metaphors are just further evidence of the confusion factor of these kinds of communications where the programmed individuals seem to be talking out of both sides of their mouths at once.

Speaking of those lively Lizzies and their libidinous appetites, we have still another factor of our reality that is possibly a side effect of some singularly distasteful programming (no pun intended!).

As I wrote in my book *Amazing Grace,* it was as a result of looking into a local murder case that I became so ill that I was bedridden. During this time, I began to read about the alien reality when Frank, a friend at the time who participated in most of the early sessions, brought over a bag full of books on the subject. On the first day I was out of the house after this opening of the doors of perception, or, at the very least, asking the question, I encountered "Pat", who was my first abduction case. And, of course, as I have said, I was pretty determined to demonstrate that it was not an alien abduction – and failed. This is chronicled in the *St. Petersburg Times* article pretty well, so I won't repeat it here.[5]

Nevertheless, there was this strange connection between my looking into the case of the murdered girl and the woman who was lying on my sofa the night the Flying Black Boomerangs were seen all over the three county area.

Later, as I have written in the last volume, *Soul Hackers,* I ran into the same woman running a print shop when I was looking for a printer for the nascent *Aurora Journal.* Now, what I haven't talked about are some of the details behind that event.

At a time prior to this when I was working with Candy, another abductee who had what may have been physical evidence of her experiences,[6] I had been down at the local Private Investigator's office one day talking about Candy's situation and we started talking about the above mentioned murder investigation, which had pretty much been the beginning of the relationship between the PI and myself. I asked him if anything new had come up, and he said, "No, they were just waiting to see." It was the opinion of several of the law enforcement officials that the guy would "go off" and "do another".

I thought about it and said I was pretty sure it was a one-time thing. Unless something really unusual came up, this guy would never kill again. But the PI felt that he would. As I left that day, his parting words were, "All we can do is wait until the pressure builds up and he has to kill again!" His words stuck in my head.

So, time went by and there I was in the print shop talking to this woman who had been my first abductee two and a half years earlier.

---

[5] French, Thomas, "The Exorcist in Love: A Tale of Possibilities," (*St. Petersburg Times.* St. Petersburg, Fla.: Feb 13, 2000).

[6] I tell more of her story in *High Strangeness* (although I used the pseudonym Maryann) and *Soul Hackers.*

The very next day after this very strange renewal of our acquaintance, another girl went missing from the same general area as the first girl who had been murdered. I picked up the newspaper and saw the photo of the second girl and nearly dropped my teeth. She was almost the spitting image of the first girl. My blood ran cold. I remembered what I had said about the guy never committing a murder again unless something really unusual came up. What if that unusual thing was another girl who looked exactly like the first?

At the same time this happened, I was reading a book about UFOs and cattle mutilations that talked about some cases where lights in the sky had been linked with the cattle mutilations on the ground. I noted that this particular series of mutilations had occurred in the very same area of the country that Ted Bundy lived in at the very time many researchers conjectured that something happened to him to turn him from an ordinary mild pervert to a cold-blooded killer. And, of course the reason these two ideas connected was because I had just finished reading several books about Bundy which endeavored to explain what is now called the psychopathic personality. I had read these books because of the idea that serial killers such as Bundy might be attached or possessed by one or more discarnate entities, and I was looking for clues that this was a possible factor in this particular psychological disorder.[7]

In the book about Bundy, a pretty long section had been devoted to trying to figure out exactly what it was that happened at a certain point in his life when he just "switched", as the author put it. He had the whole world in front of him; he was a smart guy with charm and looks and wit. He was on a track to success and then, suddenly, he just snapped. And no one knew why because Bundy himself never could adequately explain it.

So the date of Bundy's switch was in my head when I read about these lights in the sky associated with cattle mutilations in the same area where he had disposed of many of the bodies of his victims. I had already wondered about the possibility that cannibalistic murders, such as those of Jeffrey Dahmer, might not be influenced by aliens, even if only by example and exposure to their own appetites. Now, a whole different connection suggested itself to me. I began to think about the connection of the murder investigation that occurred just prior to the UFO flap in my own area, and could it be possible that the individual who had committed *that* murder had been abducted and programmed to respond to a certain type of individual? Could

---

[7] See volume seven, *Almost Human*, for a more in-depth analysis of psychopathy.

that be the link between the two girls? Not only that, but the fact that looking into this case resulted in a situation wherein I was brought face to face with the alien reality had a curious effect on me. From looking into the murder I was then looking into a deeper level of the control system. Was there a connection?

I knew I was stretching it, but I brought it up at the next session.

January 9, 1996

Q: (L) It has become increasingly obvious to me that there is some sort of connection where MG [an unsolved murder of a local 13-year-old girl] was concerned, some synchronous connections between that murder and the appearance of the Black Boomerang UFOs in this area. And I also noticed a connection between the life pattern, or change in life pattern, of Ted Bundy and certain UFO sightings, and cattle mutilations that were in his area of the country. At that time, I first met Pat and experienced my own awakening to the other reality. Now, we have another girl who has come up missing *at the same time Pat and I reconnected and was actually discussing the MG case!* It is just too bizarre! This new case has a lot of things that seem to be common to that case. I see that there is an issue here that I would like to explore. Did my involvement with the MG case have anything to do with opening the door of my mind to other phenomena, particularly UFOs and aliens?

A: Possible.

Q: (L) You can't give me a clear answer on that?

A: Learn!

Q: (L) Okay. I had dreams about it. The work that I did on the case, the dreams I had about it, as well as certain impressions I received, convinced me that a particular individual was the killer. Was that an opening of my instinctual awareness in some way?

A: Maybe.

Q: (L) Was there some soul connection between MG and myself?

A: No.

Q: (L) Was there some connection between MG's murder and alien activity?

A: *There is always this connection in one way or another, at one plane convergence or another.*

Q: (L) So, the murder of MG was a mini-plane convergence. Can this mini-plane convergence be described as a point where one person's individual plane of reality converges with another person's plane of reality, and one or the other gets annihilated?

A: 4th, 5th and 3rd density is involved.

Q: (L) So it is sort of a plane convergence of those three densities. Is this true with all murders?

A: Discover and yes.

> Q: (L) Was my interaction into that reality a sort of entering into a point of plane convergence?
> A: *Flirting with the edges.*
> Q: (L) So, when a person is working on a murder investigation, or thinking about it, or applying thoughts, talents, instincts or whatever to the solving of this kind of puzzle, they are interacting with a plane convergence?
> A: This represents one manifestation of the always-present desire to return "home" to 5th density.
> Q: (L) Okay. Well. Now, I want to get to the 64,000 dollar question. In the MG case, was my conclusion correct?
> A: "Correctness" takes many forms and provides a window to many conventions. We recall advising a cautious approach, in order to insure that your lessons are learned not only accurately, but painlessly as well.

It was true, and I understood it clearly, that my awareness of the killer did place me in some danger. But it seemed that the Cassiopaeans were implying greater danger than just that.

> Q: (L) Could you suggest, just to get me on track here, a form of question that would be a cautious question? Then I can frame subsequent questions on that model?
> A: The issue here is not how to "frame" a question in such a way as to lure us into answering in the way you desire, but for you to learn most effectively. Do not have prejudice that there is only one thing to be learned from each response. "You never know what there is to be learned when you inquire with innocence and freedom from supposition."

At this point, since Frank and I were working alone, I played the tape back to find out what the Cassiopaeans had said in that long delivery. The tape was full of static and sound anomalies that had never occurred to us before.

> Q: (L) I just played the tape back and it is all muddy. Could you tell us why we are having this problem with the tape?
> A: Telekinetic wave transfer.
> Q: (L) What is this telekinetic wave transferring?
> A: Evolving energy.
> Q: (L) Given off by us?
> A: Both to and from.
> Q: (L) From us to you?
> A: You and others, not us.
> Q: (L) Who are these others?
> A: 4th density eavesdroppers, Pat's involvement should "heat things up". Expect anomalies.

That one went right past me!

> Q: (L) Okay. Back to the issue. Was there something about Ted Bundy, and the fact that his life seemed to disintegrate at the same time a lot of UFOs were sighted, related to this kind of activity?
> A: Yes.
> Q: (L) Was Ted Bundy abducted?
> A: Yes.
> Q: (L) Was Ted Bundy programmed to do what he did?
> A: Yes.
> Q: (L) What was the purpose behind that programming?
> A: We must withhold answer for the present.
> Q: (L) Okay. Bundy described his murdering urges as a "pressure building inside" him that he couldn't overcome, and it seemed to cause him to stop being human, as we think of it. That seems to me to be an example of a program being able to overcome a person's social behavior, or controls over antisocial tendencies. Is this also what happened to the person who killed MG?
> A: Maybe.
> Q: (L) Is there a connection between the newly missing girl and MG?
> A: You are doing well in your probing of the knowledge within on this issue, we suggest continuance, and after all, learning is fun!
> Q: (L) So, it seems to me that there was a connection between the physical looks of the new missing girl and MG. Could it be that the individual who killed one or both of them was programmed to respond to this particular type [of] facial characteristic? Could that be part of the programming?
> A: End subject.
> Q: (L) What do you mean?
> A: We have helped you all that is necessary for now on this matter. It is beneficial for you to continue on your own for growth.
> Q: (L) Can I ask just one or two more little questions in a different direction? I mean, this is like walking away and leaving me in the dark!
> A: No it is not! Why don't you trust your incredible abilities? If we answer for you now, you will be helpless when it becomes necessary for you to perform this function on a regular basis, as it will be!!!!
> Q: (L) Well, frankly, I don't want to be involved in any more murder investigations. It is too upsetting. Am I supposed to do this sort of thing regularly?
> A: Not same arena.
> Q: (L) Well, then how do you mean, "perform this function"?
> A: No, *seeing the unseen!*

So, it seems now, in retrospect, that I was getting very close to some matters that are essential to know, but must be learned on one's own. The Cassiopaeans almost seemed desperate to prevent me from following this track too directly, or in an improper way, and their particular remark about "learning lessons painlessly" was certainly a hint that this was a sensitive subject.

When we look at the questions and answers above, we discover some very interesting things. The first one is of course the idea of a mini-plane convergence. I am reminded of the fact that the Cassiopaeans have referred to the earth as a "convergence point" of the Wave. That's one thing to think about. But the fact that a murder or murders are evidence of a convergence of fifth, fourth, and third densities opened up a whole new area of speculation.

Another thing is the idea that an interest in such matters is not necessarily prurient, but, "This represents one manifestation of the always present desire to return 'home' to fifth density."

But the clue about the face being a sort of trigger apparently really was close to home, and deserves some consideration. Can it be that no murder is really a random event? Can it be that murderers are programmed, even if at fifth density and prior to incarnation, with some sort of seed to murder that individual who has a certain facial likeness? And, if that is the case, how else can facial likeness be used to trigger programs?

Are some people programmed to choose their mates based on this type of trigger? Whether for good or bad, using those terms loosely, what can this suggest? What if the "right" person is kept away, and the "wrong" person with the "right" facial characteristics is then brought in to trigger the love program to run, thereby causing a serious setback in incarnate plans and missions? Is that another means the Control System uses to interfere with our purposes? And if so, it is indeed important to be able to "see the unseen". To see behind the facade, as it were … the face.

But, there was still another interesting series of remarks in the above session:

January 9, 1996
Q: (L) I just played the tape back and it is all muddy. Could you tell us why we are having this problem with the tape?
A: Telekinetic wave transfer.
Q: (L) What is this telekinetic wave transferring?
A: Evolving energy.
Q: (L) Given off by us?
A: Both to and from.

Q: (L) From us to you?
A: You and others, not us.
Q: (L) Who are these others?
A: 4th density eavesdroppers, Pat's involvement should "heat things up". Expect anomalies.

I had spent the day in the company of Pat, talking about this murder and the new missing person case, as well as negotiating for the printing of the new magazine, but I really had no idea how interesting this was going to become.

When I had first met Pat, at the time of the first session described by Tom French in the *St. Petersburg Times* article, she had introduced herself as a real estate agent caring for a sick husband who was retired from government service. As we became reacquainted after the passage of over two years, I learned a lot more about her background. Pat's husband was in fact a physicist who had been employed by the government for many years and had even worked on the Mars Observer project in the field of pattern recognition.

Humans have the ability to recognize letters. Whatever fonts are used, no matter what size, color, style, or whatever, we are able to say, "this is A", or "this is B". If we are asked how we know this is "A", it is very difficult to give an answer. We would say that "A" consists of three straight lines. But, if they are not straight, but wavy, we still have no problem discerning that it is "A". If they are not lines, but a series of dots, our mind will convert it into an "A" and tell us that it is an "A" made of dots. Even if the "A" is upside down, we still know that it is an "A".

Now, the idea of pattern recognition is to try to teach a computer to do the same. A computer that is taught pattern recognition for the purposes of going to Mars would be one that should be able to observe a rock formation and to be able to tell if it is natural or artificial. It should also be able to tell if a series of signals of any kind is random or intelligently contrived.

Clearly, the purpose also includes the ability to note that stars are stars; asteroids are asteroids, determining their shape or illumination, and other environmental conditions.

But, the most significant idea is this: to be able to note and determine the presence of an object near or far, for the simple purpose of avoidance in terms of survival, does not require pattern recognition. It only requires sensory input. The idea that pattern recognition is a project for computers launched into space may suggest that something else is being looked for, i.e., artificially constructed objects.

So, Pat's husband worked for the space program in the field of pattern recognition. That was a very interesting revelation when you consider the UFOs that suddenly appeared all over the area the night I had her under hypnosis on my living room sofa. But it became more interesting when I discovered that Pat, herself, had held a security clearance and had worked in some sort of government installation out West.

Well, that certainly explained why something or somebody was very interested in keeping her quiet.

Pat was very interested in our communications with the Cassiopaeans and asked to attend a session. After what they had said about her interaction heating things up a bit, I didn't see any reason why she couldn't. It certainly did not sound like a negative thing that was being suggested, so I agreed.

January 7, 1996
Q: (L) We have Pat with us tonight ...
A: Hello Pat.
Q: (L) Now, with all of us here, we would like to ask why the black, flying boomerangs showed up on the night Pat first came for hypnosis?
A: Examine issue carefully.
Q: (L) The first thing we thought about it was that this was a, if not necessarily rare, at least somewhat rarely observed type of craft, and the event itself was rare ... Is this correct?
A: It is rare.
Q: (L) If it is rare for such a "UFO flap" to occur in response to a hypnosis session, which person were the UFO occupants particularly interested in?
A: It was not a person, but information that is hidden in the subconscious memory of Pat.
Q: (L) Were they wanting to get this information?
A: No. To monitor what would be revealed.
Q: (L) Does this mean that Pat has information programmed into her before birth that she needs to access as you have suggested about others?
A: No. Abductions.
Q: (L) They wanted to see if anything would be revealed about their abductions of her?
A: Yes.
Q: (L) Okay, since she is here, can we ask who abducted her?
A: Grays.
Q: (L) How many times has she been abducted?

A: 4. Snow scene was only 3rd density abduction. Abduction, which occurred there was strictly physical.

Q: (L) Okay, the abduction that occurred in the snow was a physical abduction. Perhaps the others were not? Were they physical also?

A: The others were 4th density. 3rd density abduction only occurs rarely, and is of great import.

Q: (P) Was my son abducted also?

A: Frozen.

Q: (L) Why did they want Pat so bad that they would take her physically?

A: Do you have any ideas?

Q: (L) Yes, I have ideas. Maybe Pat has ideas and knowledge that she could access to use against these beings?

A: But real reason is more fundamental: Exposure. Government proximities!

Q: (L) What we were talking about earlier; about people who have a family member working for the government, and that such people tend to be abducted more often. But, just because Pat was married to a scientist who worked at JPL doesn't mean she knew anything herself. I don't get it.

A: Not what she knew. Because of proximity to Consortium [secret government] activity. Pat was implanted for possible future activation.

Q: (P) Was this related to what was going on under the mountain? (L) What mountain? What's under the mountain? (P) Just ask.

A: Not locator, personnel are factored.

Q: (L) It was not so much where she was as who she was in contact with?

A: Yes.

Q: (L) Was it her husband?

A: Perhaps.

Q: (L) Maybe that is why there is a higher rate of abduction among family members of government employees, so that they can be activated or controlled? (P) But my husband wasn't really working on anything secret that I know of. Yes, he had a security clearance but ...

A: He had access to sensitive facilities.

Q: (P) I had a security clearance, too. (L) So, Pat had an implant put in. An actual, physical implant. Where is it?

A: Behind sinus cavity.

Q: (L) What is this implant designed to do?

A: Activate behavioral control reflex and thought pattern generation and alteration.

Q: (P) Is that why I can't remember anything?

A: Some.

Q: (P) I do have this memory problem in a big way. (L) So, can I say that this UFO appeared over my house on the night Pat was under hypnosis, to reinforce the implant so that she would ...
A: To monitor.
Q: (L) If Pat had revealed the details of her abduction, would there have been any repercussions?
A: Not in this case.
Q: (L) Are there cases when persons reveal details of their abductions, that there are repercussions?
A: Varied.
Q: (L) So, if Pat had gone to anyone at all for hypnosis, these craft would have appeared?
A: Yes.
Q: (L) You have already told us that this is extremely rare. (P) Does this have anything to do with Camp David?
A: Not the issue, its personnel!
Q: (L) Was it that she knew someone or interacted with someone in particular?
A: Many others!
Q: (P) Do the planes have anything to do with it?
A: It is up to Pat, the extent she wishes to retrieve and divulge, the many unusual experiences that were met, by Pat, with unusual indifference.
Q: (P) The first thing unusual was the geographic location of our house. Directly West of us was the mountain that housed all the communications to be used in the event of nuclear war. We were 13 miles North of Camp David. And, while we lived there, many, many things took place at Camp David that were of global significance. And, we built a barn in 1982. We had bought the house in 1976, and never, in all the years that I lived there, did I ever notice these planes until we built the barn. If I had a stick in my hand, I could have touched them, that's how low they flew. Right over my barn. The same days every week. And there were always two of them, and they never had a single marking on them. And, they were propeller planes. And I wondered: what in the hell is this country doing flying planes, unmarked, propeller driven, and so low, over this area? This continued until we moved from that house. So, these planes came twice a week from 1982 until 1989. (L) What were these planes?
A: Search to learn.
Q: (P) Well, after the first couple of times, I sort of just said, "Well, there are the planes." So, what else is new?
A: Indifference.
Q: (P) I thought the planes had something to do with the mountain. We knew they were flying under radar. Now, that I am thinking about this, nobody else ever talked about these planes. It was like we

were the only people that ever saw them, or just the people who were at our house saw them too. My best friend who lived right up the road never saw them. I asked her, "Did you see the planes?" and she said, "What planes?" I mean, she was seven acres away and nothing in between!

A: Unusual experiences mount!

Q: (P) My husband also noticed these things and he would always say – he was less indifferent than I was – he would say, "What in the hell are those planes, and what are they doing?" (L) Why was Pat so indifferent? (P) Well, it didn't affect *my* life, except that I was damn mad that it upset my horses. But then, the horses got used to them too, and they became indifferent! [Laughter] Well, they came so often, twice a week – "It's Wednesday, the planes will be here!"

A: More ... continue probing ...

Q: (P) The planes came from East to West, and in the West was the mountain ...

A: Catoctin.

Q: (P) That is the name of the mountain! (L) What is it? (P) The tunnel where all these facilities were ... under Catoctin Mountain. Camp David is near, too.

A: And MUCH ELSE! Mount Weather, Virginia. And why did you live in area ... helicopters? What brought you to Maryland?

Q: (P) Fort Detrick. (L) What does Mount Weather mean? (P) The underground tunnel – everybody in town called it The Tunnel – but there was nothing around there to ever give anybody the slightest clue as to what it was. In fact, I lived there for quite a long time before I knew it existed. And, on top of the mountain there was a weather station ... My husband was doing electron microscopy – cancer research.

A: REALLY? Helicopters, Pat? We are asking you!

Q: (P) Well, the helicopters in Fredrick went over our house every time the president was at Camp David. But, that was our house in Walkersville not in Emmitsburg. When we first moved to Maryland. Sometimes the helicopters were unmarked ...

A: You see, Pat is resistant due to experiences, things don't "phase" her easily, programming, etc.

Q: (L) So, all of these things happening around her, the planes, the mountain, the helicopters ... (P) But the helicopters, I knew it was the President either going to or coming from Camp David.

A: Resistant, not resisting.

Q: (L) Is the term "resistant" a clue?

A: All is a clue here!

Q: (P) Isn't that just my personality, that if it doesn't affect me I don't bother with it?

A: Yes. Shoot somebody in front of Pat, and she says: "Oh well, that's life" so, to discover spectacular things, one must be patient and probe carefully, no hasty assumptions, please!! There is much to be retrieved, revealed, studied. Let Pat digest it, and report back later.

Q: (L) At the time we had all those sightings around here on the night we did that session with Pat, why did so many other people see them?

A: Window was "blast".

Q: (P) I would like to know about the apparitions of the Virgin Mary at Conyers, GA, as well as this book *Mary's Message to the World* and all the other messages about the End Times that are coming out all over?

A: The forces at work here are far too clever to be accurately anticipated so easily. You never know what twists and turns will follow, and they are aware of prophetic and philosophical patternings and usually shift course to fool and discourage those who believe in fixed futures.

January 13, 1996

Q: (P) One last question: How could I be used to monitor personnel when I never noticed anything as being unusual?

A: Very complex, in fact, parallel subject. Pat is a "locator probe" for the purpose of monitoring those in her midst. Telling is not important, reading is. Besides, most of the work performed did not involve conscious awareness.

Q: (L) Is this still going on?

A: Partly, but also, Pat could be used as a probe to monitor all events taking place at JPL and other laboratories by examining aural imprints of her husband and others with whom she was acquainted. All events leave permanent imprints upon aural energy fields. This explains, for example, some sightings and apparitions. "Ghosts" are sometimes merely spontaneous activations of the aural records of the natural surroundings.

Interestingly, every session Pat attended was plagued by extreme static on the tape recorder. This also occurred if I had simply been in her presence for any period of time on the same day as the session was held. This had never happened with our tape recorder before, and every effort to solve the problem failed. We even tried using a back up recorder, and it failed to record at all.

But, note the most interesting remark above that "Pat is a 'locator probe' for the purpose of monitoring those in her midst. Telling is not important, reading is. Besides, most of the work performed did not involve conscious awareness."

That tells us a bit about how people can be used without their conscious awareness. Apparently, a person can be implanted with a particular device that simply is read at a distance by either human or alien personnel.

What is even more interesting is, "Pat could be used as a probe to monitor all events taking place at JPL and other laboratories by examining aural imprints of her husband and others with whom she was acquainted. All events leave permanent imprints upon aural energy fields." This seems to be saying that there is some sort of fourth-density technology that can read the aural imprints of other people in such precise terms that it even knows where they were and what they were doing.

Now, that's creepy! It made me realize a very important thing: even if I like or love someone, even if they are totally innocent in conscious terms, they can be used to monitor me or even vector energy in my environment that is harmful. That opens a wide door to manipulation and control in our lives. We can be manipulated to invite someone into our lives who is nothing but a tool to be used against us. And the tragedy is, they can be totally and completely innocent. That hurts!

And, I would like to add another thing about the above case: there is more or less independent corroboration of what the Cassiopaeans were saying about Pat. Clearly, there was extreme interest in her from some other levels of reality, as was evidenced by the numerous sightings of Flying Black Boomerangs that began at exactly the time she was under hypnosis on my sofa. That is an incontrovertible fact, reported by numerous witnesses, and written up in the *St. Petersburg Times*. Thomas French wrote about it in his article saying:

> The newspaper and TV were reporting multiple sightings of UFOs in the area. From mid to late April in 1993, more than a dozen people in Pasco, Hernando and Pinellas counties said they had seen a large, boomerang shaped craft moving across the sky. One of the witnesses, a Hernando County sheriff's deputy, said the craft carried no markings, was adorned with blue lights and had a wingspan of at least 200 feet. He watched it for several minutes, he said, before it accelerated away from him at a speed that would have been impossible for any human-made craft.
>
> 'Based on what I know now, no, I don't think it's from this planet,' the deputy told a St. Petersburg Times reporter. 'Nothing on Earth could hover and haul ass like that.'
>
> ... The first alleged sighting of the boomerang-shaped craft had been made in New Port Richey on the evening of Thursday, April 15, the same night she [Laura] was conducting her hypnosis session

[with Pat]. The person who had seen the object that night lived only six blocks or so from Laura's house; she said she had seen the craft through her bedroom window after 10 p.m. that evening, after L.A. Law came on. ... The witness claimed that she had seen the giant boomerang at the exact time Laura was deep into her session; in fact, she said she'd seen it hovering over Laura's own neighborhood.[8]

So we have a certain form of validation. But, of course, as I have said, at the time I had no idea of the significance since I did not know of the government connections of my subject. My feeling at the time was that the boomerang craft appeared just to scare me away from the subject matter of UFOs, or to get my attention. That was a little bit egotistical, in retrospect. And after learning of Pat's background, the whole incident, including the accompanying UFO flap, made more sense. Indeed, it does seem that Pat had information that somebody, or some thing, did not want me to access. And, we are left with the problem of how such knowledge was communicated to these unknown beings.

As I pointed out to another researcher, futurist Mike Lindemann, the kind of surveillance that was implied by the knowledge that I was going to do that hypnosis session, particularly when nothing about aliens or abductions was ever mentioned, would be predicated upon mind reading. If we are going to postulate that it is some sort of secret government that is behind the UFO phenomenon, then we must allow for this mind reading technology. And, if our government possesses and uses it, we are all screwed. Which is, of course, a distinct possibility.

But there is another kind of tool in the alien bag of tricks: robots. This is a subject that was mentioned briefly in *The Ra Material*, though that group never came back to the subject as far as I can tell:

> Q: Is an entity in the fourth density normally invisible to us?
> Ra: ... The fourth density is, by choice, not visible to third density. It is possible for fourth density to be visible. However, it is not the choice of the fourth density entity to be visible due to the necessity for concentration upon a rather difficult vibrational complex, which is the third density you experience.
> Q: Are there a Confederation or Orion [STS] entities living upon the Earth and operating visibly among us in our society at this time?
> Ra: There are no entities of either group walking among you at this time. However, the crusaders of Orion [STS] use two types of enti-

---

[8] French, Thomas, "The Exorcist in Love: A Tale of Possibilities," (*St. Petersburg Times*, St. Petersburg, Fla.: Feb 13, 2000).

ties to do their bidding, shall we say. The first type is the thought-form; the second, a kind of robot.

Q: Could you describe the robot?

Ra: The robot may look like any other being. It is a construct.

Q: Is the robot what is normally called the "Men in Black"?

Ra: This is incorrect.

Q: Who are the "Men in Black"?

Ra: The "Men in Black" are a thought-form type of entity, which have some beingness to their make-up. They have certain physical characteristics given them. However, their true vibrational nature is without third density vibrational characteristics and, therefore, they are able to materialize and dematerialize when necessary.

Unfortunately, no further questions were asked about "robots". However, the Cassiopaeans did expound on this subject to some extent. We already have talked about the Grays being cybergenetic probes of the Reptoid beings, and there is a great deal of discussion of this aspect in my book, *High Strangeness*. What we want to talk about here is something a bit different.

The subject of robots was brought up in response to some questions about Roswell and the alien autopsy video. It is not the time or place to engage in a lengthy debate about either Roswell or the much contested video. However, I do intend to cover the Roswell subject more thoroughly at another time. For the moment, just let me make a few comments.

I recently had a conversation with an individual who is fairly certain that all of the so-called alien activities are merely planted memories or perceptions devised by any number of secret government mind control projects somewhat akin to what was revealed in the Greenbaum lecture. It is thought by many who take this view that Nikola Tesla and Andrija Puharich were the brains behind the technology that could produce the effects I have described above in my own experience with the abductee and the black boomerangs.

I had researched the black boomerangs and discovered that they were not all that usual, but at the same time, they did have a history that made me give the matter some thought. As I pointed out in *High Strangeness* in relation to the black boomerangs, the earlier sightings and relationships were so similar to my own as to suggest something altogether different. They were sighted as far back as 27 years before my own experience with seemingly no change in model and design. So, as I suggested there, if it is a secret government project, those boys in black ops have no imagination at all. Still using the same model!

But, more seriously, how does one relate the idea of a secret government project based on Tesla and Puharich technology to all the many sightings of UFOs and clearly alien-type beings throughout the past two millennia or more? It seems that some of such interpreters want to make a distinction between those incidents of the distant past, and everything that has occurred since Kenneth Arnold followed by Roswell. My contention is that it is the same phenomenon wearing a new suit of clothes as I have explicated in *High Strangeness.*

History did not begin with Tesla, Puharich, or the secret government, and I could cite many cases from the past here that would demonstrate clearly we are dealing with the same phenomenon.

Now, of course, I say to those individuals who claim that the whole scenario of the present day is part of some mind control project that has evolved from technology discovered in this century, if that is the case then they must also permit time travel capabilities for this same secret government to explain many of the related or similar historical events. And if they do that then we are really in not much different shape than if it *were* alien beings who can come in and out of our reality via hyperdimensional space. And the argument becomes moot.

There are many problems with the Roswell story, which are touched on by the following excerpts, not to mention the many arguments against the alien autopsy film revealed to the world by Ray Santilli.[9] One of the rather naive arguments against the autopsy film was that, if the government had really captured alien beings, they would have engaged a competent camera man, or would have engaged the finest scientific minds and done the autopsy in the dissection theater of some large university, and certainly would not have had such inept hands handling something of such great, scientific and historic import.

Well, let's get real here. If you are a small group of power-mad control freaks functioning in the darkness of secrecy, who are you going to get to do this kind of work? Somebody with an international reputation and no fear of you, who would go to the press first thing next morning, or somebody over whom you have considerable control by intimidation?

---

[9] The Alien Autopsy film is steeped in severe controversy. It alleges that the US government undertook and filmed an autopsy of an alien that had crashed in the Roswell vicinity on June 2, 1947. The 50-year-old film canisters came into the possession of Ray Santilli from a freelance photographer of the 1950s.
(http://www.mufor.org/gehrman1.htm)

I vote for the latter, myself. And, if that is the case, then your options are limited. Obviously, such a group did not plan to have a crashed UFO with bodies, or they would have been prepared with proper personnel and equipment in advance. But, once the event was in their hands, the best and only option would be to involve only those people who could be relied upon to keep their mouths shut for any number of reasons, including the fact that some life shattering secret about their lives could be held over their heads to keep them in line.

And, if that is the criteria for selecting the person to do the autopsy and the film, then obviously you don't have a wide selection that matches the requirements. So we can dispose of the idea of the camera man even being a competent handler of the equipment he had available, and can also conjecture that the whole camera man story was a deliberate ruse from the very beginning. Therefore, those who have pursued that avenue of potential revelation are following a red herring from the start.

As to the competence of the autopsy itself, the crude handling and procedures, the same rule would apply. If you are part of a secret organization that was not really prepared for such an occurrence, then you just do the best you have with what you've got. So, you don't have a great surgeon or anatomist handy to do the autopsy of the millennium. Maybe all you have is a mad scientist who you have rescued from Nuremberg, and who spent the war butchering little children. Well, that's what you've got. You find the best secured location you can get, gather your little team of guys who you know you can control because they have some really dark secrets of their own, and send 'em in to do it.

Now just suppose, some years later, a few members of this secret government who thought they were in charge of the whole situation, discover that they are not at the top of the food chain. And maybe they discover that things are much further out of control than they ever imagined it could be, and they get really scared. Well, what are they going to do? They have to figure out some way to set the situation up so that when the doo doo hits the oscillating vector, there just might be an out for them. So, they hatch a plan to release information via various doorways. Suppose Ray Santilli is one of those doorways?

Under such circumstances, dealing with such hidden controllers, do you think for a minute that Ray is going to cave in and say anything other than the story cooked up by the black ops guys? Nope.

Don't count on it. In such a case, he would behave exactly as he has behaved. He cannot do otherwise. I repeat: cannot.

Having said all of this, let's have a look at some of the Cassiopaeans' comments about Roswell and the alien autopsy film:

> May 27, 2000
>
> Q: (L) Now, we have a problem here with Roswell. I just finished reading Kal Korff's book *Roswell: What They Don't Want You to Know*, and it is pretty much a bashing expose of lies and confusions spread, supposedly, by the many witnesses who have come forward over the years. He takes Jesse Marcel apart, he takes the fireman's daughter's story apart; he rips the undertaker's story to pieces; he takes Phil Corso's story apart; you name it, he bashes it to bits. Pretty effectively, too, in my opinion.
>
> He seems to have located the origin of the "little sticks with hieroglyphics on them" seen by several of the so-called witnesses. This is a serious problem with this whole story. The problem is that, despite the fact that this guy has dissected all the stories so effectively, there are things he cannot account for, and explanations that he makes that simply don't fit his thesis. On the one hand, he claims that the Roswell base people instituted a cover-up of a top-secret balloon project, and on the other hand, he says that the Roswell base did not know about the top-secret balloon project because it was so secret. That is completely irreconcilable. Then he quotes a general's written statement that something was going on that had something to do with alien interactions, and dismisses this signed statement as "hearsay."
>
> The thing that occurs to me is that a) either we have somebody going back and forth in time, tweaking the facts, such as Marcel's military records and such things including any records of the nurse that the undertaker claims to have talked to; or b) we have something that did happen and either they went back in time to set a situation up so that people would start remembering something other than what happened, so as to cover up the real event with more or less "false memories" that could be not stand scrutiny; or c) they are just feeding disinformation through all of these people, and have produced a whole scenario with all kinds of witnesses and weird stuff to cover up something that happened. Could you comment on this?
>
> A: Try scenario 3.
>
> Q: (L) So, they are feeding disinformation through all the so-called "Roswell witnesses"?
>
> A: Close.
>
> Q: (L) To cover up something that really did happen?
>
> A: Yes.

Q: (L) And they are feeding the disinformation through the people so that they will come out with this whole story, make all this big splash, so that it can then be proven false, so that everybody will think that the whole thing was a crock of kaflooey. Is that it?

A: Not quite. Confusing stories and fabrications are used to muddy the waters in anticipation of future disclosures. And beware of authors who cast one stone and hit multiple targets. As with any conspiratorial mystery, keep focused on the earliest entries in the evidentiary train, i.e., "RAAF recovers flying disk in Roswell region."

Q: (L) Oh, the newspaper headlines. Yes. Hmm ... Terry was saying that he thought the Roswell business was a cover-up for space-time travel by some secret U.S. group.

A: No. Roswell did involve evidence of non-human intelligence.

Q: (L) I just can't understand some things. When these researchers get out there and they start digging into things, and this happens over and over again, they don't dig deep enough ...

A: Kennedy was assassinated by everyone ... according to the myriad researchers, so called.

Q: (L) So true. You read one "carefully researched" book, and there is one candidate for the assassin. You read another "carefully researched" book and there is another candidate. By the time you get done reading all the books, everybody in the country is implicated. At the very least, everyone present in Dealey Plaza had the opportunity. (F) They keep on searching. But, if you go back to the very beginning, that is where the clues are. Right away, there were reports of shooters on the "grassy knoll." The very early evidence gathered from those present was completely ignored and washed away as "irrelevant" or "misperception." (B) There were people ducking and diving for cover because of their awareness of the source of the bullets! (L) Yes, but all that is just brushed away as panic or whatever because, of course, Oswald did it! And, handily, Oswald gets blown away by Jack Ruby so he can never talk, for sure. (F) And Jack Ruby died of cancer without talking to anyone except Dorothy Kilgallen, who then decided that it was the best time to commit suicide, right after interviewing Jack Ruby ... naturally, before she ever wrote a word about it. (L) Is there any trail we could follow that would enable us to obtain a more definite indication of what really did go on in the Roswell case?

A: There is no "proof" or evidence unless the perceiver is willing.

Q: (F) Yeah. It's the same story with the abduction experience. They have now discovered that if you put somebody in a sensory deprivation chamber and subject them to EM waves of some sort, they will report the same thing. So, let's just ignore the physical traces of alien interaction, not to mention history! Let's forget all that and pronounce that, "See? We have tested these other people in tanks, under waves, and that proves that this is the only thing going on here!"

July 15, 2000

Q: (L) Now, in regards to Kal Korff's book, you have said that my scenario about the different stories, the various witnesses, whoever is behind the cover-up is just feeding disinformation through all of these people and have produced a whole scenario with all kinds of witnesses and weird stuff to cover up something that happened, and that this is the closest to being correct. I would like to know how close, and just how they are feeding disinformation through all of these witnesses. Obviously, these people believe what they are saying.

A: They do.

Q: (L) Why do they believe?

A: They are telling what they remember, but it is soaked in twisting parallels.

Q: (L) Are the people doing this themselves?

A: No. Event mixture. There was more than one "crash in the vicinity" of Roswell, and at different times. The four-body scenario refers to the incident most frequently cited.

Q: (L) How many were there?

A: Three.

Q: (L) There were three in the July period?

A: June/July. June 4th, July 1st, and July 4th. This explains the famous news release because the base was abuzz due to all these occurrences.

Q: (L) It seems to me that if the base were already abuzz with these occurrences, they would already have had their cover organized and their stories straight! In such a case, the famous news release would never have happened.

A: No.

Q: (L) But they all seem to remember this July 4th crash, or so they say.

A: Yes. But events were intertwined.

Q: (L) So, some may have witnessed different events?

A: Parts of ...

Q: (L) Have they also been tampered with in terms of abduction or having implanted memories or screen memories?

A: No.

Q: (L) Have they, in any way, been exposed to something that was falsely staged by the government in order to make them think ...?

A: No.

Q: (L) So, they are all sincere and honest witnesses, but they are witnesses to different events, and they all think that they are witnesses to the same event?

A: The so-called suspicious circumstances are merely a patchwork, cleverly used by those who wish to conceal.

Q: (L) For example: did the fireman actually go to a crash site and witness what his daughter claims he witnessed?

A: Yes.

Q: (L) Was it an alien craft crash site?

A: Yes.

Q: (L) Did Jesse Marcel witness a crashed UFO?

A: Pieces of one.

Q: (L) Did Glenn Dennis really talk with a nurse who later disappeared?

A: Yes.

Q: (L) How did this woman disappear? Kal Korff could find no record of her existence.

A: Transferred, discharged, records expunged.

Q: (L) Is she dead?

A: Yes.

Q: (L) Did she die under suspicious circumstances?

A: No.

Q: (L) Did the little balsa wood pieces actually come from a toy company as Korff suggests?

A: No. Kal Korff was paid to mislead, but it is now moot as the military changed its story yet again after his book was published.

Q: (L) One of the things that Kal Korff did was to dig into Jesse Marcel's background, and he claims that Marcel never had any of the background that he claimed, and that Jesse Marcel is basically a liar. He has the military records to back him up on this. Were Marcel's records altered?

A: Jesse did not lie.

Now that we have an idea that there is more to Roswell than we might have initially thought, let's see about the alien autopsy and how it may relate.

August 12, 1995

Q: (L) Earlier today, at the MUFON meeting in Clearwater, there was a speaker who proposed that the Vedic idea of who and what the Lizard beings [4D STS] were is that this is the activation of the sexual principle, or kundalini within us. Any kind of UFO or alien activity is merely the reflection of what is inside all of us. Is this a correct assessment?

A: In truth, the best way to most adequately answer those questions is to ask yourself what do you believe, based on the knowledge that you have collected and have been given.

Q: (L) Well, I sometimes wonder if they are not part of ourselves, in a parallel universe, and they emerge into our world and interact with us in a negative way. And, that the historical stories of alien/human interaction are really just stories of human performance of mechanical operations, guided by negative aspects of their own being in another dimension or density. Would this not be a distinct possibility?

A: Not in the sense that you are thinking. Remember, it is always wise to review ALL of the previously gathered information whenever any new ideas appear before you. This is true not only in this particular instance, but also all others as well. For example, how often would mere thought patterns, or realities emerging from a parallel universe, appear in desert locations and be retrieved by third density beings for study in the third density realm?

Now, if indeed you believe that this has happened, and it HAS, one must contemplate the meaning of such and how it relates to one's proposal that the whole issue involves much higher levels of density on the etheric plane, and, or, inter-dimensional capabilities that cannot be measured within the realm of third density. These theories, certainly, are part of the answer, but merely a part of the answer, and none of them represents the entire answer. And we caution very strongly that you avoid falling into the trap of believing too strongly in any one explanation that appears, as this too, is a form of attack which can lead to destructive consequences.

Q: (L) So, there are actual, material, alien craft that have been captured or retrieved by the government and studied?

A: Do you have any doubt of this?

Q: (L) Well, sometimes I wonder if the whole thing is cooked up by the government just to make us all crazy!

A: Well that's an interesting concept, but we can assure you, that that is not, in any way, correct.

Q: (L) Well, if these craft emerge into our reality from fourth density, as I assume some of them do, how do they stay here? Do they become absolutely physically material and do they remain here?

A: If they malfunction in third density, they then become frozen in third density. Very simple.

Q: (L) And, does the same hold true for the beings?

A: Precisely.

Q: (L) So, they are very real and physical ...

A: They are very real and physical in fourth density, too. The difference is that fourth density physicality is not the same as third density physicality. But that is not to say that there is no physicality in fourth density. In order to completely remove all attachment to physicality, one must reach sixth density or higher.

Everything below that involves some aspect of physicality or attachment to physicality; as in fifth density, the contemplation zone, which is simply a recycling of those from 1st through 4th densities, in the etheric plane. They are brought back down and recycled into one of the physical realms. Each density level one through four, involves lesser and lesser physicality, as you know it, but nevertheless there still is physicality.

Third density physicality, however, remains constant on third density. When a being or a craft or an instrument of any kind manufactured or conceived in fourth density arrives in third density, it is able to navigate through third density in fourth density reality. However, when it malfunctions, whatever is left of it remains in third density. Those reports of objects or of any physical structure whatsoever, be it a being or a construct, disappearing from third density to fourth density, in each and every case, involves an object or a being, or a construct, which is not in the process of malfunctioning. It is still fully operational at its fourth density realm. It is merely visiting third density which has a limited capacity, as you measure time in its passage, therefore it does, indeed, remove itself naturally, at some point, to fourth density. However, if it malfunctions or is in any way broken or altered, it will remain in third density.

Q: (L) So, if someone removes an implant, the best way to keep it here would be to smash it?

A: If someone removes an implant it is no longer functioning as it was designed to function.

Q: (L) Okay. So we have some real things happening, and a possibility that a film was taken of this interaction with these malfunctioning fourth-density beings and craft. And, supposedly, this film is going to be shown on television. Is this film of this autopsy, and examination of craft remains, a true filming of same, or is it a fake, or fraud?

A: Well, one would suggest that for the maximum amount of learning, that the film be witnessed by those seeking the truth, in order to determine for themselves whether or not it is factual, as such will be possible upon viewing.

We took a break to watch the alien autopsy film.

September 2, 1995

Q: (L) Well, on the subject of abduction: we watched the film on television, Monday the 28th, that was a purported video of an alien autopsy, or, more correctly, an autopsy on an alien body. Was this, in fact, an alien?

A: How do you define "alien"?

Q: (L) Was it a being other than a naturally born human on this planet, as we know human beings?

A: That is correct.

Q: (L) It was other than a naturally born human? In other words, it was not a deformed human?

A: Correct.

Q: (L) Okay. What kind of a being was this?

A: Hybrid.

Q: (L) What was it a hybrid of – combining what elements?

A: Cybergenetic creatures you refer to as "Grays", and earth human such as yourself, third density. So, in essence, it was a hybridization of a 3rd density and 4th density being. It was a 3rd and 4th density being.

Q: (L) How can a being be both third and fourth density?

A: It is the environmental surroundings that count, not the structure of the individual. The same is true, for you. After all, you have read literature stating that your world or planet is in the process of ascending from 3rd to 4th density. Have you not?

Q: (L) Yes.

A: And this literature has also stated that this is an ongoing process, has it not?

Q: (L) Yes.

A: Then, one must wonder, if it is an ongoing process, how would it be possible, if it is not possible, for a being to be in both 3rd and 4th density at one time ... Also, if you will recall from review material, you are currently living in the same environment as 2nd and 1st density level beings. Is this not true?

Q: (L) Yes.

A: At least that is what you have been told. So, therefore, it is possible for a being to be in 3rd and 4th density. And as we have also told you, when 4th density beings visit 3rd density environment, they are, in effect, 3rd density beings, and vice versa. The so-called abduction takes place, especially if it is a physical abduction, the subject becomes temporarily 4th density, because it is the environment that counts. And the key factor there is awareness, not physical or material structure.

Q: (L) I have a paper here that talks about the Grays and says that they have two brains: an anterior brain and a posterior brain; and that if you shoot one – this is what it says, I am not suggesting that I want to shoot anybody – that if you shoot one, and only shoot one part of the brain, that it does not die; that you have to shoot it in a special way and get both brains in order to kill one. Is this a correct concept?

A: Well, it is rather puzzling. Brings up a lot of questions. One question that comes to mind is: why would one seek to shoot anything?

Q: (L) Well, I didn't suggest that I wished to, this is just what this paper says here.

A: The physical description is accurate in terms one variety of what is referred to as the Grays. It does have an anterior brain. However, this is secondary to all other issues. And, also we would suggest that it would not be advisable to seek to cause physical harm to any particular species. Therefore, it may be advisable to disregard the information contained in the work that you are describing.

Q: (L) It also says that the Grays have to be very close to a person to telepathically link with that person. Is this correct?

A: Close? No, as we have described to you before, there are technological processes involved, which do not require close physical proximity as you measure it.

Q: (L) It also says that they implant some sort of crystal on the optic nerve of humans that is 2 to 4 microns in diameter and that this crystal is tuned to the frequency of the individuals implanting it, which allows them to establish a mental frequency for communication. Is that anywhere along the line of what you are talking about?

A: Physical implantations do occur. The precise locations vary according to the desired effects. And when it comes to the interactions between the human species in 3rd density, and other STS issues in 4th density, there are a variety of mechanisms in use as well as a variety of directives and objectives. For example, some implants are used merely for tracking. Others are used to alter consciousness, and still others are designed to be mind altering or motor altering mechanisms.

Each of these has a different structure and a different material content according to which is being employed and for what purpose. The particular function you are describing there has been used, or, rather, something similar, though we are not completely familiar with that which you have described; so, we suggest that this may be fabrication to some extent, or expansion of accurate information. But, in any case, it is true that implants do get implanted for various reasons.

Q: (L) Shifting gears back to the alien autopsy: can you access the information and indicate whether this hybrid being was one that was obtained from a crash that occurred at Roswell, New Mexico in 1947?

A: The crash did not occur at Roswell. It was in a desert area, approximately 157 miles to the West by Northwest, of the Roswell location. The Roswell location that you are familiar with did not include either a craft or any bodies or living beings. It was merely a debris field. The craft, which had malfunctioned over Roswell, thus leaving behind the debris field, had, in fact crashed some distance away. This is where the bodies and living beings were recovered along with what was remaining of the craft. And, yes, the being in the film you have seen DID come from there.

December 2, 1995
Q: (L) Now, switching gears: while watching the alien autopsy film, we saw a massive organ that occupies the whole center of the abdominal cavity. What was that?
A: Heart/liver.
Q: (L) (S) A combination of both in one?
A: Yes.

Q: (L) They also carefully removed a solid or hard object that they then put in a small container. What was this object?
A: Crystal transceiver.
Q: (L) What was all the loose matter?
A: Organic tissue. Not important.
Q: (L) Was it a female or a male?
A: Both and neither.
Q: (L) Was it a being that could reproduce sexually?
A: No.
Q: (L) What kind of nourishment was required by that being?
A: Saline gelatin globules. Applications using biological microforms to metastasize through primary glandular channels.
Q: (L) Did that being use oxygen as in breathing?
A: Yes.
Q: (L) Where were the lungs?
A: Side of torsal cavity.

We obtained a copy of the British TV version of the autopsy film and watched it numerous times, after which we came back and asked more questions.

October 21, 1995
Q: (L) I want to talk about the Roswell [autopsy] video that we've all watched. Now T continues to insist that it was not Roswell, that it's a phony video. He just can't get into it. This is also the consensus of the UFO community at large, due to the lack of cooperation of Ray Santilli. I would like to know if that video is of alien beings that were retrieved from the crash referred to as "Roswell" even if we know it did not take place precisely *at* Roswell?
A: Yes.
Q: (L) Okay. Why did so many people report seeing aliens that had only four fingers and [toes], you know, like the standard grays? The being in the film had six fingers and toes.
A: Multiple subjects.
Q: (L) Okay, so there were more than one type of alien on that one craft?
A: Yes.
Q: (L) Okay, the story that came from the camera man who shot the video was that there were these four beings outside the craft. One was dead, and three were standing outside the craft, crying and clutching boxes to their chests. What were those boxes?
A: Storage of translation matrix group to individual; emotion stabilization units.
Q: (L) What is a translation matrix?

A: Translates foreign thought patterns, not needed except in emergency loss of electromagnetic grid wave.

Q: (L) Okay, what is an emotion stabilization unit used for?

A: Variety of uses, mostly for survival by neutralizing thoughts of harm by emotionally charged beings, not accustomed to shocking turn of events.

Q: (L) Were the harmful thoughts that they were designed to neutralize, thoughts emanating from other beings?

A: Yes.

Q: (L) Well, they didn't work very well, did they?

A: Did not have chance to activate.

Q: (L) Okay, so if they had had the opportunity to activate these boxes, they would have been more or less able to extricate themselves from this unpleasant situation?

A: Not extricate, lessen negative aspects.

Q: (L) Okay, how many beings were in this particular craft that crashed?

A: 21.

Q: (L) How come the reports say there were only four?

A: Reports are suppressed and fragmented, as far fewer individuals witnessed interior of craft!! Also, some reports are of other incident.

Q: (L) Okay, now of the 21 that were in the craft that was captured, so to speak, there were four outside the craft when it was approached, is that correct?

A: Yes.

Q: (L) Then that would mean that there were 17 inside ... Of these 21 beings, how many were grays, the standard gray lizzie-probe type being?

A: Most.

Q: (L) Were there other kinds of beings in there?

A: Human.

Q: (L) There was one human in there also?

A: 5.

Q: (L) There were 5 humans inside, so we have ... Why were those humans in the craft?

A: Retrieval and study specimens, two big foot types.

Q: (L) Does that mean that the humans that they had in there were retrieval and study specimens, or otherwise known as abductees?

A: Deceased.

Q: (L) Oh, they were dead humans. Wonderful! It just gets uglier and uglier! Did they abduct them dead? Or did they abduct them alive?

A: No.

Q: (L) Did they abduct them alive and then kill them?

A: No.

Q: (L) Were they dead as a result of the crash?
A: No.
Q: (L) Well, then, what's the story here, I mean, what other choices do I have?
A: Retrieved. Picked up after expiration.
Q: (L) Okay, so they picked up dead bodies, is that it?
A: Yes.
Q: (L) You said that there were two big foot types: were the big foot types also dead?
A: Yes.
Q: (L) You said that there were five dead humans inside that were retrieval and study specimens. Where did they get these bodies?
A: Mexico and South America.

Now, let's insert here a segment from another session wherein a particularly bizarre series of remarks were made, which prompted me to ask a certain question that we will come back to shortly. In the following excerpt, we had a guest, TK, who was retired from the Navy:

October 14, 1995
Q: (L) TK does have a couple of questions he would like to ask, and one of the questions is: has he himself ever been abducted by aliens?
A: Complex. Ships are vulnerable to ELF and "Zero Time Transfer".
Q: (L) So, are you suggesting that any abductions that took place, took place while he was on board a ship?
A: Maybe.
Q: (T): What did you serve on, what kind of ships? (TK) AEGIS Cruiser, I was just on one ship, that was just the last five years or so ... (T) Were his abductions ... did they take place while he was on the ship, on the cruiser?
A: We see "Bahrain".
Q: (TK) We were only in Bahrain one night.
A: Examine. You must remember, different branches of your military services have underlying code mechanisms to determine their classification status for "secret" duty, including study of personnel, this is all very complex ... Now, "U.S. Navy is status 2", which means among other things, that it is married to a class 2 "Cooperation Agency", the O.N.I. All technical personnel are approached during their service, and asked to perform tasks for Secret Government. If they accept, they are "brought under classified management".
Q: (L) That was the answer to the question, why was he abducted? (J) Or was he abducted at all?
A: Examined, as with all others on ship.

Q: (T) Was the Navy aware of what was happening?
A: Segmented. Some know and some don't. Some in Navy are cooks.
Q: (T) That's what Steven Seagal said in [the film] *Under Siege* – "I'm just the cook, you know!" He wasn't really a cook. (TK) The funny thing is, I *was* a cook in the Navy in the beginning ... (T) Okay, you gave us some information about Navy being connected to Navy Intelligence. (L) Are all military personnel routinely abducted and studied by aliens?
A: No.
Q: (L) Are all military personnel routinely abducted and studied by the military itself?
A: No.
Q: (L) What is the classification that the person has to fall into in order to be abducted and studied by the military?
A: What makes you think "classifications" correlates with abductions?
Q: (TK) It's not the classification, it's ... it's gotta be the type of person ...
A: Yes.
Q: (TK) And how easy it would be to influence ...
A: Of course. And many other factors.
Q: (TK) It would have to have something to do with what they could do for the abductors. I mean, they have to be in a position to help them ...
A: Yes. STS vibrational frequency.
Q: (T) Okay, that's a factor. There's more than one agenda involved with abductions. Are the military personnel that are being abducted; is that a specific agenda that is being followed?
A: Artificial classifications, such as military designations, are important to human groups only.
Q: (J) I've got a question. Isn't it true that in order to become part of the military, you have to go through boot camp, the indoctrination to the point where you're going to follow orders without questioning, and that that mindset would lend itself more towards? (TK) The Marines are about the only ones that even try to get people to follow orders without question any more. The Navy has all but given up on that. It's not a time of war so it's not necessary right now.
A: Yes. Some have always "faked" such blind allegiance anyway.
Q: (TK) I basically faked it, I ...
A: You were not alone.
Q: (TK) Oh, yeah! There were a bunch of us. "Yeah, sure, tell us what to do. If it's in our interest, if we're going to stay alive, we'll do it; if you're going to kill us, forget it!" I used to tell them on the ship, that if I ever got captured, I'm going to tell them everything I know. I said, they aren't going to have to torture me long ... (T) Be-

sides, when you torture me, I tend to scream a lot and not tell you too much, so I'll just tell you and let's skip the torture. (TK) So when I refused to go up for ESWS, I was kind of an outcast, I wasn't in the club anymore ... Enlisted Surface Warfare Specialist. (T) Aha, that's when you were asked! (J) That's where they separate the men from the boys ... (TK) This captain put it in such a way, he said, "Well, if you'll work on your ESWS and get that pin, I'll see to it that you get good marks and make chief ..." which to me was like saying, well, if you don't do it, you're not going to make chief. I said, "Sorry, bud! I'm not going to do it. I don't respond to that kind of bribery/intimidation stuff!" (F) You would have set the service back a number of years. (TK) That's when I became an outcast from the club.

A: Not correct concept, not outcast, just deemed not SG material.

Q: (L) What's SG?

A: Secret Government.

Q: (TK) Darn! (J) You had your chance Tom, and you blew it! (TK) Was FRW initiated? Was he one of the Secret Government agents?

A: No. Was a "conduit". There are several steps that must be followed to become part of the Secret Government.

Q: (J) You have to know the handshake ... (T) I can't get my foot in my ear, I'm sorry! [Laughter]

A: Vietnam MIA's, where do you suppose they are now?

Q: (TK) Have they been abducted? (T) Some of them got blown up so badly that they couldn't be found, so they were listed as MIAs, because they couldn't mark them as KIAs. Some of them are deserters, some of them ... well, deserters would fall into several classifications, which I won't bother getting into. Some of them went into the drug trade. (TK) Some of them just decided they liked it better over there. (T) Yeah, there's that, and some of them, I would imagine, have been either abducted or swapped, moved into the Secret Government. (L) Is all of this correct?

A: Yes.

Q: (TK) Are we supposed to still be on the military subject?

A: KIAs ... are a separate subject!! KIAs, how many really were?

Q: (T) How many of the 60,000 really were killed? How many of them are listed as dead when they're not? (TK) Tell you what, there were so many different kinds of people that went over there, the Secret Government could have recruited a bunch ... (L) Are these some of the people working in these underground places we are always hearing stories about?

A: Yes ... Yes ... Yes.

Q: (L) That's where those personnel are coming from ...

A: And many other places, times, etc.

Q: (TK) Wars all through the ages. How many are we talking about?

A: Since your imagination center is on low frequency tonight, suppose we have to spell it all out for you ...

Q: (L) Go ahead, spell it out for us. How many are we talking about here?

A: W.W.II, 72,355, still alive where????

Q: (T) Now, wait a minute ... That's how many people the Secret Government has snatched up? (J) From W.W.II? (TK) That's out of something like 40 million ... (F) Total People killed in W.W.II was 70 to 80 million ... (TK) Military casualties ... We're not talking about just US military, either, we're talking about total, anybody's army ... (T) That was supposedly killed in action ...

A: Yes.

Q: (T) ... from all branches of the service?

A: Yes.

Q: (TK) These people aren't aging; they're still in action and ready to go ...

A: Precisely, my friends!!!

Q: (TK) How about Korea, Vietnam, etc.

A: Korea: 6,734.

Q: (T) Yeah, there were about 55 thousand casualties in Korea, in the four years of Korea. Really it was 3 1/2 years in Korea. So 6,000, about a little over 10% of them aren't really dead.

A: Vietnam: 23,469.

Q: (T) 23,000 of the 66,000 ...

A: Yes.

Q: (T) ... are still alive?

A: Yes. Some are body duplicate soul receptacle replacements.

[Change in tape sides; first few sentences were lost.]

Q: (J) They have just around 100,000 with those three figures they gave us. (TK) They've got a military force right now, and it's not just a military, these are elite. I mean, they've been recruited. (J) They've been asked the question, and they said yes! (T) Yes, this is not some guy hunking a gun in a foxhole just for the heck of it. These are specialists. (TK) The CIA was siphoning people off in 'Nam right and left.

Q: (L) Are there any Civil War KIAs involved in this scenario?

A: A few.

Q: (T): Well, the farther back you go, the specialties weren't developed. But a specialist is a specialist, no matter what the war.

A: Not point.

Q: (L) I think the point is *who* they are. Now, in the *Matrix* material, there's a section that talks about technical abilities to jerk people's souls out of their bodies, insert other souls, reprogram the memories, essentially that there is no congruency ...

A: False.

Q: (L) Okay, so the jerking out and the manipulating of souls as described are false? In a general sense?

A: Yes.

Q: (L) Okay, now, you said a moment ago that some of these bodies were used as receptacles, soul receptacles. When you say soul receptacles, do you mean soul receptacles for whom?

A: Replacements for dead bodies, i.e., duplicated.

Q: (L) So, in other words, they make replacements for dead people and put their souls in a replacement body, so that they can continue living on, is that it?

A: Yes.

Q: (L) Do they ever use dead bodies and reanimate them and then put other souls in them?

A: No. For example: a soldier is KIA, his body is duplicated, his soul is replaced into new body, then he is "reprogrammed for service" to aliens and S.G.

Q: (L) Where does the new body coming from?

A: It is duplicate of old body. TDARM. [Trans Dimensional Atomic ReMolecularization]

Q: (T) Otherwise known in Star Trek as a "replicator". (TK) Does somebody have to die in a certain way before they can do this?

A: No.

Q: (TK) Is there a time limit on how long they can be dead?

A: No. Zero time.

Q: (L) They use the frequency vibration of the soul pattern, they take it into another density, use their TDARM technology to cause a molecular re-assembly; in other words, the atoms begin to assemble around it in the pattern that it had before, and then it is a full-fledged body, and then they insert it back through the time doorway into 3D again. Is that correct?

A: Close.

Q: (T) Okay, you said ... Let's use Vietnam. You said there were 23,000 KIAs of the 60,000 that actually were not killed in action. True? Yes?

A: Were killed, then reanimated.

Q: (L) We're not talking about physical bodies here, are we?

A: Yes.

Q: (L) Okay, there are some that were killed in action that the actual bodies were reanimated? (J) As long as they weren't blown up in a land mine, yeah. (L) There were actually bodies that were actually reanimated, is that correct?

A: Some, but *most were duplicated*. War makes covert actions so easy.

Q: (T) It's just that the cover of a war, is easier to take the bodies. (TK) They do not want people to realize ... They do not want to just take them out of the graves, because if you did, it would be more noticed. (L) Were some of these bodies taken ... Were the bodies picked up, taken into another density for this remolecularization patterning?

A: Yes.

Q: (L) Okay, so they had to have an actual body for the pattern. Were the original bodies returned once the duplication was done?

A: More than one type of situation.

Q: (L) So, in other words, it could be sometimes, yeah, they were, and sometimes, no, they weren't. (T) Were some of these supposed 'killed in action's actually not killed? Were they still alive when they were removed?

A: All possibilities.

Q: (L) So this is in a sense a "crime of opportunity". (J) War is a supermarket of opportunities! (T) Some were just taken by the Secret Government when they were alive, some were dead and brought back in new bodies to continue on, and they were considered dead, but they're all considered dead.

A: Taken by aliens, not SG. Secret Government is aware to some extent, but not in control of operation.

Q: (L) Okay, now this brings up the question about ... We were told that there was, and this was ... last week we asked about this thing about the death ... and we were told that there was an impenetrable triple veil that prevents some of this type of activity, that he describes happening. How can this be reconciled? Well, the explanation that I see is that it happens that they do this before they go into the tunnel, into the light. They catch them in the transition before they go to 5D. Is that correct?

A: Time adjustment.

Q: (L) Does that mean that they know that they're going to die, and they go back in time to just before they die, or just at the moment of death, or ...?

A: Close.

Q: (T): Now, what are the aliens doing with these bodies? With the humans that they replicate and duplicate and reanimate? What are they doing with them?

A: Serve them. Workers.

So, now that you know what was in my head when we were talking about Roswell, you will understand why I asked the next question in the session we broke away from to insert the above segment about KIAs.

October 21, 1995
Q: (L) Okay, did they plan to reanimate these corpses?
A: Open.
Q: (L) Do they ever pick up dead bodies, you know, right after, and reanimate them?
A: Yes.
Q: (L) When they pick them up and reanimate them, do they reanimate them with the souls that left them? Do they like, catch the soul and put it back in?
A: No.
Q: (L) When they reanimate them, do they reanimate them with an alien soul?
A: Multiple possibilities.
Q: (L) If they reanimate them, is it possible to reanimate them with no soul?
A: Yes.
Q: (L) Okay, when they reanimate them with no soul, do they have kind of like a zombie-like situation?
A: No.
Q: (L) Well, could you give us a little more information on this particular aspect? If they reanimate them with no soul, what is the animating force or energy?
A: Indistinguishable from other humans.
Q: (L) How is that possible?
A: Technology makes all things possible!!!
Q: (L) Of course, you are talking about fourth-density technology?
A: Yes.
Q: (L) Now, a reanimated corpse that has been animated by infusion of some form of an energy pattern ... (SV) Is it "chi" energy, maybe? (L) What if the reanimated corpse dies again, I mean, you have got to understand here, that we perceive the soul as being the animating force of the physical body, and when the soul is gone, the body dies. Is that correct?
A: You are making assumptions based on limited data.
Q: (L) Okay, well, will you expand my database by telling me how a corpse can be reanimated if not done by a ... if not with a soul?
A: Complex technology, using electronic biogeneration frequency matching, combined with extremely high frequency radio beacon transmitters for tracking and control of all functions, including thought pattern mimic and emotional frequency vibrational rate modulation!!!!
Q: (L) If they're doing this, does it make the physical body do all normal physical functions?
A: Yes.

Q: (L) The blood, the heartbeat and everything ...

A: All functions, including cellular, are duplicated.

Q: (SV) What about the aura? (L) Would a being such as this still have an aura?

A: Projected. This is method used for subjects discussed in "Matrix Material" instead of "Robots", as suggested.

Q: (L) Is there any way that a normal person would be able to identify such a being?

A: No.

Q: (L) Approximately how many of this type of being are walking around on our planet, acting like normal people?

A: 2,000,000.

Q: (L) Approximately 2 million?

A: Yes. You, Laura, have come in contact with 7 of them!

Q: (L) Who are they?

A: Discover.

Q: (L) Can you give me a clue, has it been within the last ...

A: Open. All it takes is a "hospital visit".

Q: (LM) Then what happens? Does this mean if one goes into a hospital for surgery, that it's possible for them to die and be reanimated in this manner? Without anybody being aware of what happened via time/space manipulation?

A: Yes.

Q: (L) Is it up to me to figure out what characteristics these individuals have, in order to ...

A: Based upon data given, yes.

Q: (L) Okay, is one of the characteristics I think, that these kind of individuals might have, since they have this projected emotional frequency, would be a repeating emotional pattern, that they just simply, in spite of seeming intelligence, do not seem to learn from anything; that it just repeats over and over again, is that a clue?

A: Yes.

Q: (L) Okay, then, this same inability to get a clue about what's going on ... Okay, that's a clue, right there. Is there any kind of instinctual sensation that one would get about these types of individuals?

A: Bland.

Q: (L) That they're bland in some way? Is that it, that these individuals are bland individuals?

A: Spend inordinate amounts of "time" in solitude. Bland is not universal in this situation, just a clue for you to identify individual.

Q: (L) Okay, bland is just part of it.

A: Not key component, more likely to be spreading of disinformation.

Q: (L) Okay, well, there are people I have noticed, that if you tell them something logically, it's almost like they have a preset program that runs, and the minute you get to the point where you think that they just *have* to be getting it ... then it just shuts down and they repeat the program, almost word for word! And it just amazes me that people can be that way. Okay, do these beings know what they are?

A: Not conscious beings! Are being remote controlled.

Q: (SV) So, if you told one of them what they were, they'd agree with you? (L) No, they'd probably disagree with you. Whoever is in charge would not want you to know it, so they'd naturally deny it vehemently. (L) Now, what is the purpose of putting 2 million of these kinds of critters on the planet? Can you give us a clue?

A: Wait and see.

April 28, 1996

Q: (L) Okay, if a person were, say, a robot person, when a person becomes a robot person, what happens to the soul of the robot person?

A: Same process: Death.

Q: (L) So, a person can die and leave their body, their body can be taken over and reanimated and controlled to function, and do a lot of things for a long time? Meanwhile, the original soul has completely departed to fifth density ready to recycle?

A: Yes, but body is replaced, not reanimated. We caution that, even though you have met 7 "robots", in your entire lifetime, not to "see" them under every bush or around every corner. You have met so many people in your life. We gave you one, and only one!! [One was identified for me as part of the clue system.]

Q: (L) Well, there are two million of them on the planet, and I have been told that I have encountered seven. I did think that this was a pretty high ratio of robot people for one person to encounter ...

A: Yes, but your life path has been unusual.

Q: (L) Can you tell me in what sense it is unusual?

A: Can't you?

Q: (L) Well, I thought I would trick you into telling me ...

A: No tricks, we only treat.

So it seems that, in addition to "green bombs", in several varieties, mind controlled individuals manipulated by the secret government, we also have a handful of "robots" wandering around on the Big Blue Marble just waiting to do *something*. Or, even doing it all along, seeming to be ordinary folks like you and me except for a particular blandness that is not universal to them, and a propensity for spending a lot of time alone.

But, two million is really a pretty small number, considering the population of the planet, taken as a whole, so these must be pretty specialized individuals. That they are servants and workers for the control system is pretty clear, and that many of them are supposedly drawn from a military pool is also pretty clear, but the possibilities are wide open in terms of where and how they might be placed.

We came back to the subject at one point, with more interesting revelations:

May 4, 1996

Q: (L) One of the things we talked about the last time TK was here was about the underground bases and military interference in civilian affairs and civilian interface with military affairs. One of the questions we were dealing with was the use of warfare to create situations in which bodies could be taken ...

A: Warfare has many "uses". Generation of environment to facilitate inconspicuous replacement of gene pool. Factors in paradigm shift through stimulation of conception activity, *replacement of key personnel* according to frequency vibration pre-readings ...

Q: (L) "Replacement of key personnel according to frequency vibration pre-readings ..." Okay, do you mean to say that war ...

A: Creates "environment" for unnoticed genetic modifications because of greatly heightened exchange of both physical and ethereal factors.

Q: (L) What do you mean by "replacement of key personnel"? Key personnel according to whose definition?

A: 4th density STS.

Q: (L) Are these key personnel human?

A: Yes.

Q: (L) When you say replacement, do you mean something as simple as someone dying, such as a head of state, and being replaced by another person who comes to power? That would be the simplest scenario that would fit this explanation.

A: Your scenario is not simple.

Q: (L) I mean simple in terms of the logistics ...

A: Both.

Q: (L) Would it also be that key personnel could also be replaced as in duplication?

A: Yes. And removing to secret activity realm. Enough wars have taken place to effectively create entire new "underground race" of humans, both from direct capture followed by "re-education", and spawning activity using these persons and others.

Q: (L) What do you mean by spawning activity?

A: Those captured have reproduced offspring, these never having seen your world.

Q: (L) Are you saying ... (TK) They have given birth and these children have never seen our world ... (L) How can an entire race of people, or groups of people, live under the surface of this planet, without the whole 6 billion of the rest of us on top, or at least a large number, realizing that there is anything going on? This is so wild an idea ...

A: No. How much space exists underground, as opposed to that on the surface?

Q: (L) A lot, I suppose. You aren't saying that the earth is hollow, are you?

A: No, not exactly.

Q: (L) Well, how deep is the deepest of these underground cities?

A: 3,108 miles.

Q: (L) That's pretty deep! But wouldn't it be too hot at that depth?

A: No. Temperature averages 68 degrees F. [20 degrees C.]

Q: (TK) That's pretty comfortable! (L) How do they have light?

A: Magnetic resonance.

Q: (L) Well, aren't they subject to being crushed by earthquakes?

A: No, earthquakes are not felt deep underground!!

Q: (TK) Is any of this under the ocean?

A: Yes.

Q: (TK) Well, we'll never explore all of what is under the ocean. (L) It just staggers the mind to think about it. What do they want these people for?

A: To replace you.

Q: (TK) And why? Because they can control them better?

A: Completely.

Q: (L) Do these people being bred and raised in these underground cities have souls?

A: Yes, most.

Q: (TK) Are they just like us only raised differently?

A: More complicated than that.

Q: (L) How long have they been doing this?

A: 14,000 years, approximately.

Q: (L) If they have been doing it that long, obviously the ones they have taken at the beginning have croaked and are of no use to replace anybody on the earth unless they have been replacing people from time to time for various reasons ...

A: No, their technology makes yours look like Neanderthal by comparison! Hibernation tubes ... One heartbeat per hour, for example.

Q: (TH) That means that for every year we live, they would live 4200 years ... (L) How do we fit into all of this? (TK) We don't!

A: You have been the "preparation committee".

Q: (L) What have we been doing? Is it part of the plan for us to destroy the planet, destroy the ozone layer, pollute the seas, and so forth, to make it more habitable for them?

A: Those things are inconsequential and easily repaired.

Q: (TK) With their technology, they can fix all of that. (L) This is really horrible, you know! To think of all this ... (TK) Apparently, from what I am understanding, they can't just come in and wipe us out and replace us, because the "rules" won't allow it.

A: Yet the natural cycles within the framework of the natural order of things will allow all these things to fall into place.

Q: (L) Is there some law within the realm of these beings, sort of like the law of gravity that prevents them from just coming in and taking over?

A: No.

Q: (TK) I don't think it is like the law of gravity ...

A: What "law" is there that inhibits you from manipulating 2nd density beings at will?!?

Q: (L) Well, I don't go out and deliberately hurt or manipulate anything or anybody. (TK) Of course, in our handling of these "critters", we are conserving them in some ways so that we will have an ongoing food supply ... I think there are rules to the game. It's like a chess game. They can't just come in and change things, it has to progress in some way. But, there are loopholes and they can sneak in and manipulate and get away with some things ... (TH) Then, those aren't rules – there are just guidelines.

A: Two important points there: 1) When we said "you", we meant 3rd density collectively. 2) You missed our statement about the natural cycle and order of things almost completely. We suggest you reread and ponder ... Also, what if your race is manipulated to destroy yourselves, or, just hang around until the next natural cataclysm?

Q: (TK) Well, it seems like there is another side that is trying to prevent them from gaining control. (L) Well, from what I understand, the only thing the good guys are able to do is, because of free will, they have to wait to be asked for help, and the only thing they can really do is give information. (F) Well, this is valuable if used by the right people at the right time. (TK) You have to come up with the right questions, too. You have to have enough information to be able to come up with the right questions. I am sure the information is there. You have one group with all these people underground and they want to take over the planet. This group likes being fourth density – they don't want to advance. They want to block advancement. Then, you have the group that wants to advance; they want the natural order to proceed. This negative group wants to stay there and keep everyone they can there. Obviously we have the information, but we haven't really dug deep enough so that we don't know the questions that we need to ask. Is this true?

A: No.

Q: (TK) Is what I was saying close to the truth?

A: Yes. Total truth is elusive.

Q: (TK) So, what I said was the gist of what is going on here. So, we have to figure out what we are supposed to do so that the earth can be maintained ...
A: You will do what you will do.
Q: (TK) This is true.
A: Do you, in general, control 2nd density beings on earth?
Q: (L) Yes.
A: So, what is "fair" about that?
Q: (L) Nothing.
A: Okay, so what is the difference?!?!???
Q: (TK) So, basically, we control second density, and fourth density controls us. There are the good guys and bad guys. (L) And we will do what we will do. Either we choose to align ourselves with the good guys, or with the bad guys.
A: It's up to you.
Q: (TK) However, if too many people align themselves with the bad guys, then the balance tips in their favor, and there is no more advancement, so there has to be education so that people will know ...
A: TK, you are close, but you are missing the point.
Q: (L) What is the point?
A: The point is, there "has to be" nothing. You will do what you will do. You choose. We have told you this repeatedly, but you still suffer from self-centered perspective.
Q: (TK) Everybody is worried about themselves. They all want to be saved and not worry about others.
A: More to the point, everybody in an STS realm views themselves as somehow "special, chosen, or protected". This is simply not so!!
Q: (L) So, in other words, by having knowledge of the situation, what we do with it is our choice?
A: Yes.
Q: (TK) The point is it's going to happen ...
A: But, nobody is there to intervene on your behalf as many would like to believe.
Q: (L) So, we are here on this planet, and we will either make it or we won't, just like Dorothy and Toto in Oz, based on our own ability to figure it out, to overcome the odds, the witch, monkeys and soldiers ... (TK) Maybe what they are trying to do is give people the information, or make the information available so that people can make the choice, do they want to stay ...
A: We are not "trying" to do anything. We are here to answer questions if asked. We cannot interfere.
Q: (TK) Yes, the noninterference idea is pretty clear and understandable. So, they cannot interfere ...
A: And, even when we answer, you may not believe, it is up to you!

Q: (L) So, we are really on our own!

A: You always have been, and so have we, and all others, too!!

Q: (TK) I guess then, it is a matter of asking the right questions so that you will know what course of action to take. I mean, do you want to advance? Do you want to go to fourth density? Or do you want to go higher? Or do you want to stay here? How can you make an informed choice if you don't know the true conditions and what your options are? (L) Is it that the religions that have been generated and foisted on the human race, have been designed to give people a feeling of complacency or faith in something outside themselves, and that this prevents them from seeking knowledge, opening their eyes, facing the facts of their existence, and therefore keeps them in bondage?

A: Its just obstacles, as always. You employ those too, for your 2nd density friends!!

Q: (TK) What state of mind do you have to have to want to advance? (F) Well, you know you are on the path when you can see that the words don't match the facts of life. Think of all the people you have met with whom you may have had a philosophical conversation. How many will say, "Oh, all I need is the Bible. That's all I pay any attention to."

(TK) I don't have many philosophical conversations with people because I rarely agree with anything that is said.

(F) Well, you must have decided on this because you tried it and found it didn't work.

(TK) I have a real problem ... yes, the Bible has been around for a long time, and religion has been around for a long time ... but I have a real problem believing something that is so obviously produced by humans with agendas of their own!

(F) But most people that you tell that to will say, "Oh, no! People didn't write the Bible, God did!" Or, they could be a complete atheist and believe only in the religion of science.

TK) I believe that a person is supposed to live by rules and treat people with respect and honor life ... and some of the ideas of religion are good ... but they just go over the edge.

(F) That is how they suck people in. Mix lies with the truth.

(L) Yes, a lie sandwiched between two truths makes it easier to swallow.

(F) Yes, if it were all false, the vast majority of people would have figured it out immediately. Or, very quickly.

(TK) The vast majority doesn't care. They just want to be led like sheep. They don't want any responsibility.

(F) And what happens to the vast majority of cattle? They munch away in their pasture until time to get in the truck to go to the butcher. And, if you talk to the religious types, they will say, "Oh, I don't have any answers ... I just follow the Bible."

(L) Not only do they not have any answers, they don't have any questions, either. And, I think that is the clue. The people who are still asking questions after wading through all the religions and mystical mumbo-jumbo as opposed to the ones who think they have found the ultimate answer ...

(TK) The whole purpose of life, it seems to me, is to obtain knowledge and advance. You are stuck on this level until you figure it out. But what are you supposed to figure out?

(L) I think that the knowing is the doing.

(TH) "Ye shall know the truth and the truth shall set you free." It's in the Bible!

(L) Is the knowing the key?

A: Yes.

Q: (L) I think that knowing changes your frequency. Is that true?

A: Yes.

Q: (L) The acknowledging and the seeing?

A: Yes.

Q: (L) What did they tell us once ... it's not where you are, but who you are and what you see that counts? (TK) So, we aren't gonna change what happens. There is no way we can have any appreciable effect on the underground armies ... it is just a matter of changing ourselves and whoever else we can share with.

A: Correct, the cow has no effect on the health of the livestock industry ...

Q: (TK) The cow has no effect on the herd. One cow doesn't ... or even a lot of cows. (F) But there might be a few cows that follow the one that breaks out of the herd. (TK) Yes, you might be able to affect somebody else's life, but not the whole group.

A: First, some blockbuster stuff for the Knighted ones ... Look upon a detailed map, and reflect, remember lonely journeys from long ago, and begin to unlock shattering mysteries, which will lead to revelations opening the door to the greatest learning burst yet!!

Q: (L) Well, what I really want to know is why have we had all of these crazy things happen in our lives, and all of these people ranged all around us seemingly placed there, or manipulated deliberately to affect us negatively. I mean, am I wrong, or is this not a very unusual and crazy situation?

A: Why do you think?

Q: (L) Well, I have no idea!

A: Because you are of the extremely rare and few who have the abilities to put the puzzle together.

Q: (L) So, what are we supposed to do? (TK) Discover.

A: Yes.

Let's go over those most important remarks above one more time:

> The point is, there 'has to be' nothing. You will do what you will do. You choose. We have told you this repeatedly, but you still suffer from self-centered perspective. More to the point, everybody in an STS realm views himself or herself as somehow 'special, chosen, or protected'. This is simply not so!! Nobody is there to intervene on your behalf as many would like to believe. We are not 'trying' to do anything. We are here to answer questions if asked. We cannot interfere. And even when we answer, you may not believe. It is up to you!

It seems that we are in a quandary. What can all of this rather bleak perspective possibly mean? Well, we were given a clue:

> You will do what you will do. Do you, in general, control 2nd density beings on earth? So, what is 'fair' about that? ... What is the difference?!?!???

Let me remind you that the Cassiopaeans do all their own punctuating. In this last remark above, I counted the exclamations and question marks that were indicated, and the group above represents the actual given sequence. The Cassiopaeans often use such devices as part of the clue system. Yes, they cannot violate free will by even suggesting what we ought to choose or do, but they have said so often that "you will do what you will do" in such a context as to make it absolutely clear that the information they are giving us can either be acted on or not. It depends on how it affects the individual hearing or reading it.

We have traversed ideas in these pages that are utterly fantastic. We have talked about things that, if true, could scare the chrome off of a car bumper! And yet, I look outside the window and see the blue sky, clouds and sunshine, birds and squirrels; I hear my children moving about the house engaged in their little pursuits; traffic passes on the street carrying people to and from their myriad destinations, engaged upon their personal lives and enterprises, and the world seems to be spinning normally in the velvet blackness of space. Billions of suns spewing forth unimaginable energy, twinkling slyly at night, while the tropical moon glides across the sky. And the Bible asks, "What is man that thou art mindful of him?"

I hope to be able to answer this question in the next chapters. I may not satisfy everyone, because there are many who still suffer from a self-centered perspective. More to the point, everybody in an STS realm views themselves as somehow special, chosen, or protected.

To give you just a hint, however, let me say this: to be special, chosen or protected is a choice. And that is the biggest clue the Cassiopaeans have given us. It is up to us as to how we interpret it, and what we then do with that realization.

CHAPTER 22
THE NEXUS SEVEN MEET THE CASSIOPAEANS

Why? That's the big question I am asked over and over again. Why? Why do the Cassiopaeans tell us that we live in a prison? Why do the Sufis teach that we are in a prison? Why did Gurdjieff, influenced by the Sufi teachings, or even older mystery schools, tell us that we are living in a prison? Why did Castaneda write about the prison of reality (whether or not don Juan was even real or merely a literary device to convey something he had learned in the course of his studies)? Why did the Gnostics, and later the Bogomils and Cathars, teach that we are living in a prison, and then why did the Catholic Church institute the Inquisition to deal with this "deadly heresy"? And why is this Heresy received with the most heated umbrage by every promulgator of love and light, whether from the standard religious mode or from the New Age mode grafted onto the Old-Time Religion? Further, why does this prison seem to be designed to foil our every attempt to break free?

Why? What a monstrous thing to say about this wonderful, beautiful, God-created and divinely inspired world in which we live.

Of course, the *why* goes much deeper than this. Not only do we wish to know why in practical terms, we want to know why in ontological terms. Even if we have a reasonable explanation for the practical why, how do we explain our place in the universe, and in the care of a Divine being who loves us, if he allows such a condition to exist! Such a God must hate his children.

Well, let's begin by addressing the practical side of the issue, because only then can we even hope to approach the ontological issues with any clarity. What the Cassiopaeans have said about our reality happens to be the explanation that fits the facts of which can be observed and gleaned by anyone who is sufficiently motivated to dig through the many fields of study as suggested by the topics covered in these pages. The fact that the Cassiopaeans' remarks are repeatedly supported by research, observation, and experience has given me no pleasure, only a desperate drive to find the solution, the way out;

not only for myself, but for anyone who takes the time and effort to read what I am sharing, and to then do their own research and experimentation.

There have been many conjectures as to why the alien faction of the Control System has not revealed his face in a public and definitive way on Earth. It seems that they have chosen to interact only with individuals and small groups in situations that are subject to denial at official levels. If they were so anxious to be accepted, why would this be so?

Why hasn't ET (the extraterrestrial) landed on the White House lawn and emerged from his craft saying, "Take me to your leader!" The fact that the aliens have not done so, that they have not interacted with anyone of sufficient power and importance (when clearly, they could) has led to a great deal of speculation. And, if they have interacted with anyone in the higher echelons of power, what is the reason for the maintenance of institutional silence about their presence on this planet?

No matter which way you look at it, warning bells go off all over the place, and it is because such instinctive warnings *do* exist that we are subjected to such massive use of mind control efforts. In case the institutional mind control efforts don't work, there are added brainwashing elements pouring forth daily in the form of channeled teachings and "revealed truths" extracted from standard religious teachings. All of these combine to talk us out of our instinctive knowledge that a great cosmic shell game is going on, and we are the suckers being fattened up for the kill.

One of the disinformation ploys claims that the reason the world governments keep the lid on the so-called ET situation (keeping in mind that the reality is more likely hyperdimensional and not simply "extraterrestrial") is because human acceptance on a mass scale might be taken as an invitation by ET to just move in and take over.

> August 5, 2000
>
> Q: (L) It says here in this "Top Secret"[10] document penned by the so-called Nexus Seven: "The bottom line is, ARC [Alien Response Consortium] has discovered that it is very possible that confirmation, validation and consensus scientific acceptance equals an open invitation to invasion. Think about it. Denial may be one of the most powerful measures we have at our disposal to prevent the overt acceptance of the reality of advanced alien presence into the consensus

---

[10] The Nexus Seven, "Top Secret/Demon, (Ancient and Future Custodial Alien Races and the HyperDimensional Symbolic Cryptographic Munitions Conspiracy)," 1999, (http://psychicspy.com/demon.txt).

consciousness. Denial is a munition." They are saying that as long as the whole idea of alien presence "remains in the realm of the fantastic and kooky, the implausible and mentally ill" that it is a line of defense against aliens. They see this as just a little "guided free will" to protect consensus belief using "popular deployable psychological munitions of belief." They are saying that denial is a psychological weapon, a "deterrent of aliens into mainstream reality since the aliens seem to respect the stance of individual and group consciousness and acculturation free will more than military might and power. Therefore, we can, by accepting alien presence and existence above board in enough mainstream public, unwittingly turn off the restrictions against overt contact the aliens are following. The overt invasion trigger is our general human acceptance." Could you comment on the idea that denial of the reality is protection? Is that, in fact, so?

A: No. Protection comes from awareness, not the other way around.

This, of course, leads to the line of thought that ET has interacted with individuals in power and that either they are conspiring together, or the secret government has taken a position of opposition to ET. This latter option could be for one of two reasons: either ET is very evil and the secret government is an association of good guys just trying to protect us; or ET is good and the secret government are the bad guys, seeking to control the whole world, and with plans to fight ET at some point in the future when ET tires of playing cat-and-mouse. On the other hand, the secret government may be spoiling our big chance to join an intergalactic community because ET will just get tired altogether and go home, taking all their toys and technology, leaving us to wait on another chance for advancement.

The idea that ET is obeying the free will choice of humanity in not stepping out from behind the curtain, whether this is due to their goodness or evil, and the many variations of possibilities revolving around their relations with the power echelons, is pretty much based on some of the explanations given by assorted channeled sources when their prophesied mass landings and rapturous reunions do not take place on schedule. The explanation goes along the line of: "Well, your governments did not roll out the red carpet and acknowledge us, so we, being sticklers for honoring free will, must regretfully decline to show ourselves, and that means that you poor, miserable humans have to continue to muddle along on your own without our munificent assistance."

This slick sidestepping of the big revelation, (after months and months of buildup to the mass landing that is guaranteed to happen), is usually followed by instructions that the recipients of said information must lobby their representatives more in the coming days and months, in order to garner acceptance for ET in the public sphere. Meanwhile, of course, all ET can really do is just keep talking to his or her favored prophet, giving sage and wonderful advice and insight and dire warnings of the awful things that are going to happen, and how much humanity is going to need ET to help them out of the mess they are in.

Meanwhile, abductions are explained in dozens of ways including the idea that some aliens are actually ourselves physically time traveling back from the future and working with yet other helper aliens to effect modifications on their own past genetic line. In other words, some of the ETs are us coming back to remake a future that went wrong.

Some of these sources say that the military re-abduction of abductees soon after alien contacts is to try to discover the ET agenda or technological data, which the ET may have shared with the abductees. It is also claimed that some of these MILABs or military abductions are by those humans who are working with the aliens and are helping them to treat their ancestors with evolutionary adjustments.

Once people began to notice there was an awful lot of abduction activity going on – far more than would be needed to just sample or preserve the genetics of Earth – another explanation about the phenomena was forthcoming. It was suggested that something truly terrible was in our future and that, if the aliens did not fix some of us up, there would be no survivors of the coming catastrophe. This is just a variation on the "something went terribly wrong in the future and they are coming back to fix it" scenario.

Certain contactees say that their ET informants (or channeled information) have outlined the main reasons for abduction and that it is "for your good". They claim to be upgrading the genetics and even the soul energies. There are endless variations of these positive explanations for abduction, and it always includes, either implicitly or explicitly, the idea that the abductee has given permission for the activity at another time and place including the higher self, the future self, the past self, or whatever.

One very popular source of the present time, Anna Hayes, writes:

> The large amount of ET intervention with Earth that is now taking place is due to our planet's position within its present time cycle. Presently humans have little understanding of these processes and so could not possibly remove themselves from harm's way without the assistance of more advanced stellar races who do possess this knowledge. But the Guardians need humanity's assistance to accomplish this task in a way that would insure human survival during

these changes. Abductions and ET contact with Guardian groups are carried out in order to educate and biologically prepare certain humans to assist in this forthcoming process. Humans selected to assist in this endeavor are those who possess specific genetic codes that allow for more flexibility of the biological structure. Not everyone has these codes, and those who do have a responsibility toward the planet and toward the populations who do not have the needed genetic imprint. What the code carriers do with this hidden genetic propensity will determine the overall outcome of the Doreadeshi for the remaining populations.[11]

Now, we see the agenda of the man behind the curtain, who Anna Hayes designates as "the Wizard" and which is her analogy of the source of her information. Curious that she didn't notice that the Wizard, even when he did emerge from behind the curtain, was still a humbug – giving out fake hearts, phony degrees, and useless testimonials.

Yes, indeed ... "Abductions and ET contact with Guardian groups are carried out in order to educate and biologically prepare certain humans to assist in this forthcoming process." Just another elaborate hoax to justify abductions and helping those poor humans to evolve or survive.

> There is no time left for squabbling over truth or fiction. Though it may require a large leap of faith for most humans to accept the truth of what the Guardians are saying, if that leap is not made and appropriate actions taken, humans will have no one but themselves to blame for the consequences of their choices. If Earth changes of severity do occur at the Doreadeshi, it will be due to the failure of the human populace in fulfilling its responsibility as the Guardian race of planet Earth. For those who make this leap of faith, Guardian education and assistance will be provided, either consciously or on a subconscious level and through dreams and intuitive guidance.[12]

This reminded me of a vacuum cleaner salesman who once came to my house and told me how sorry I would be if I didn't take advantage of this "great sale" right now because tomorrow, the chance would be gone.

But, haven't the Cassiopaeans said that they are us in the future? And haven't we speculated on the sending of messages back in time as being a possible source of true channeled material? What is the difference between that, and genetic tweaking of bodies by aliens abducting human beings who say they are doing it for our good?

---

[11] Anna Hayes, 1998, from *Contact Forum*, Volume 6, No. 1, Jan-Feb 1998.
[12] Ibid.

July 22, 2000

Q: (LC) I feel like all of us here have been drawn together for a reason. We had a hell of a time getting here, every one of us, but we did, and I'm just wondering what is this all about? Why did all of us feel so drawn that we just had to be here?

A: You are not wondering so much as you are seeking confirmation. Every one here thinks on more than one level. This already puts everyone into a different category than the status quo. You all have quite well developed senses; a more difficult task is learning to trust the messages. Remember, you all have received negative programming at the third density level, which is designed to derail your higher psychic awareness. You by now know that this is false programming, but we realize that the subconscious centers are more difficult for you to overcome. Patience will pay off for you big time!!!

Q: (P) This is my feeling about the whole thing: us coming together, the energy created by each of us being in each other's presence is a key; it's unlocking something that we agreed to come together at this time, though it may not be apparent now, it's going to be. That's the way I have felt about this whole meeting we are having. (I) Yes. I had to come. No matter what. (P) Yes. (LC) I guess I wanted confirmation of why I felt I had to come! (L) And they are telling us "patience will pay off big time!" (A) What kind of programming do we all have? I know it's negative, but what kind in specific?

A: You receive programming daily from many sources, but the ultimate root is essentially the same.

Q: (I) Yes, TV, cell phone towers, all of that, I guess ...

A: Childhood training, etc.

Q: (LC) Okay, another question, and this is a kind of selfish one I am thinking about ...

A: Wait a minute, remember, your plane of existence is STS by its very nature and that is okay, because you're all where you are for a reason ... Now LC, fire away and be just as selfish as you please, dear. [Laughter.]

Q: (LC) Well, if that's the case! I want to ask about past life relations between us. I'm sure there is. Are there any specific past life connections between any of the women in this room?

A: Before we answer that, we wish to hear from you what you perceive a past life circumstance to be. How do you perceive the reincarnation process to be?

Q: (LC) I perceive it as you come back with people you choose to come back with, and that you choose people that you are karmically connected to. (I) I see it a little bit differently than that ...

A: Aha! We have a variance!

Q: (I) I think that when we die and go to fifth density, that we make pacts with people in each incarnation, so when you come back, it is coming back to fulfill that pact. (LC) Yes, that is the way my line of thinking is going. But, when they asked that question, I was thinking that you have people you come back with because of closeness. Somebody may be your mother in one life, and there is a love bond, and then there are other people that you come back with because you have to resolve something to let go of that person rather than to get closer.

A: This is partially correct. But, there is more to it than this. For example, one can incarnate on various planes of existence, not just the one you perceive currently. And, one may actually reincarnate on more than one plane concurrently, if one is advanced enough to do this.

Q: (L) Are you suggesting that ...

A: Yes, we are!

Q: (L) I was thinking it, but they didn't let me finish. For the record, I was thinking that we are all part of the same soul unit here.

A: To an extent, but you may not yet understand what exactly a "soul unit" is in that sense. And of course, there is more than one sense for this as well. The "trick" that 3rd density STS life forms will learn, either prior to transition to 4th density, or at the exact juncture, is to think in absolutely limitless terms. The first and most solid step in this process is to not anticipate at all. This is most difficult for you. We understand this, but this as also why we keep reiterating this point. For example, imagine if one of your past lives is also a future life?

Q: (P) Now, I just want to say that I think that we have all of us here traveled back in time to change the way things are now. We inserted ourselves into this time period to wake up and see what is really happening. This is third-density thinking, I know, but it is the only way I can describe it. We looked back on the way things happened, the way the world is now, and we have come back to change things. We have come from the future, to wake up now, because we didn't wake up before. (C) Maybe that's our "past life/future life" connection here? (P) Right, we all agreed to insert ourselves in this time line ... (L) So, we *are* from the future ... (P) Because the world is going in this direction, and *something* had to be done. That's what I see.

A: Yes. That is close to being totally correct!

Q: (P) The Cs say that they are *us* in the future. So, we, being *them* in the future, some of who they are in the future, have come back as us, to do what we are doing, to undo what is happening on Earth ...

A: Close, but more complex than that. It would be difficult for you to completely understand at this point, but let us just say that you are close.

Q: (P) I think we are creating a possibility that would not have existed if we had *not* come together here.

A: Yes, but that is generally true in most similar circumstances. The question is the degree to which there is significance.

Q: (I) How significant a possibility are we creating here now?
A: That is for you to see.
Q: (I) So, we don't know. We sense something very important about changing the universe.
(L) I think that it is also up to us, individually and as a group, to choose how we respond to the upcoming events. The saying "many are called, few are chosen" should be rephrased to say, "Many are called, but few choose to answer the call."
(P) Everyone is called!
(L) Yes. But so many succumb to the attacks, can't overcome the blocks and barriers, and choose to continue to view life in mundane, surface terms. When push comes to shove, how many really do answer. It is a very subtle thing to read the signs and "see the unseen" in the morass of conflicting signals that the third-density reality sends to block our vision.
(P) Yes. Animals have an abundance of young in order that some will survive. I think there is an abundance of us so that some *will* wake up. The odds are against it, so there has to be an abundance of us that have come back for this reason.
(L) Getting back to the programming, I had a call from BV who thinks that the UFO phenomenon, the alien abduction phenomenon, and the many and varied other things we talk about and study and discuss, are a product of super advanced technological, human controlled mind programming projects using the technology of Puharich and Tesla. Yes, it is supposed to be so advanced that they can not only read minds and can control minds, but that it is, in the end, merely human engineered programming. Is he, even in part, correct?
A: Well, there are elements of the phenomenon, which may be connected to human, 3rd density STS engineering, but by and large, this is not the case.
Q: (L) He also said that the area we are living is the center of a particular programming experiment, something like Nazi/Black magick cultists or something like that.
A: Better not to get too carried away. Remember, the root of all "negative" energies directed at 3rd density STS subjects, coming from 4th density, is essentially the same. Suggest a review of the transcripts relating to the situation in Nazi Germany for better understanding here. The concept of a "master race" put forward by the Nazis was merely a 4th density STS effort to create a physical vehicle with the correct frequency resonance vibration for 4th density STS souls to occupy in 3rd density. It was also a "trial run" for planned events in what you perceive to be your future.
Q: (L) You mean with a strong STS frequency so they can have a "vehicle" in third density, so to speak?
A: Correct. Frequency resonance vibration! Very important.

Q: (L) So, that is why they are abducting, programming and experimenting? And all these folks running around who some think are programmed, or chosen abductees could be individuals who are raising their nastiness levels high enough to accommodate the truly negative STS fourth density – sort of like walk-ins or something, only not nice ones?

A: You do not have very many of those present yet, but that was, and still is, the plan of some of the 4th density STS types.

August 5, 2000

Q: (L) Okay, last session you brought up the subject of Frequency Resonance Vibration. You suggested that there are certain STS forces who are developing or creating or managing physical bodies that they are trying to increase the frequency in so that they will have bodies that are wired so that they can manifest directly into third density, since not being able to hold the frequency in third density seems to be the real barrier that prevents an all-out invasion from fourth density ... the fact that we are in third density and they are in fourth. *Now, I assumed that the same function could be true for STO individuals.* It seems that many individuals who have come into this time period from the future, coming back into the past via the incarnational cycle so as not to violate free will, have carefully selected bodies with particular DNA, which they are, little by little, activating so that their fourth-density selves, or higher, can manifest in this reality. Is it possible for those energies to manifest into such bodies, which have been awakened or tuned in third density?

A: *STO tends to do the process within the natural flow of things. STS seeks to alter creation processes to fit their ends.*

Q: (L) This "Top Secret" document talks about many abductions being "ourselves from the future" who have come back to the past, or what is for us, the present, to abduct their own bodies to make genetic adjustments so that they can advance and not make the mistakes they made in another timeline. Is that, in fact, part of the scenario?

A: Very close to the truth!

Q: (L) Can you abduct yourself in an STO manner and help yourself in this way? Can that be STO?

A: It is not, because that is not STO.

Q: (L) So, when that is happening, and if it is happening, it is occurring in the STS parameter?

A: Yes.

Q: (L) How do the STO manage?

A: They do not concern themselves with such things.

Q: (L) Well, if the STS guys are genetically tweaking themselves to have some kind of different outcome for some reason that we do not perceive, don't you think there should be a balancing action on the STO side of some sort?

A: You are thinking in STS terms. But that is natural, since human 3rd density is STS.

Q: (L) You say they don't concern themselves with that. What do STO individuals, coming back from the future into the past, concern themselves with?

A: Answering calls for assistance with knowledge.

Q: (L) What do these STS individuals coming back into the past hope to do by genetically tweaking their ancestors? What happened that they want to have happen differently?

A: Infinite number of possible answers to that question.

Q: (L) So, they are coming from all different timelines with all different kinds of agendas – all designed to serve themselves.

When information about the flat emotional condition of the aliens began to be discussed, a new explanation was offered. The aliens now claimed they were trying to save humanity from a dreadful mistake of evolution where we lost the capacity for the full range of emotions and spontaneity. Naturally, this was also tied up with some sort of cataclysm that most people did not survive. It was again claimed that to aid the abduction process is to save ourselves in the future. Thus, support for abductions was presented as a matter of human species future security. One source said:

> Those of us in the future who followed the path that deserted the Heart, we evolved into abnormal extremes, we of such interspecies genetic masteries and technological power.
>
> We limited our brain chemistry for passion and feelings in ways to promote group harmonies, and help in our species upgrade at the time. In time, the human enhancement program upgrades were discovered to have been more of a loss of vital function. The cost-benefit was miserable to development of certain qualities of spirituality and spiritual energies.
>
> This was partly by choice, partly out of survival circumstances at the time. We eventually lost our way, but by universal grace we found means to travel back in time and encode the best of our future life streams with the best of your present life streams, and thus move on to grow again in ways we had lost.
>
> We leave you in peace to grow into a future that will be new and different than the one we ourselves have come from. That future is the undiscovered country, and don't worry, in the end we are all together anyway you slice it. But our genetic uplift influence is not necessary at all if you merely don't resist the coming wave of cosmic energies and influences.

Just weather this time of momentous change in human history. Find the small ways you can assist present human evolution in important personal and social ways, and develop your ability to give and receive love.

But be careful with whom you ally in the spiritual world. Follow all your sacred faith tests, and or sacred science tests, for revealing false prophets and then some.[13]

The only problem is, as we have seen, the so-called sacred faith tests and sacred science tests are very often a load of hooey. From all the reports that come in from every direction, it seems that there are ETs of all levels and temperament. They can be angels or devils. The problem is: they all seem to be converging on Earth in massive covert contact and influence strategies, including genetic experimentation and possible religious takeover plans.

December 3, 1994
A: UFOs dramatic increase and Gulf Breeze gets swarmed, becomes massive "Mecca". Laura sees much more UFO activity. Huge wave of UFO activity. All manner and origins. Just you wait, it will give you chills and that feeling in the pit of your stomach. Many aliens will appear and we will be visible too. Think of it as a convention. All must awaken to this. It is happening right now. The whole populace will play individual roles *according to their individual frequencies.* This is only the beginning. Just you wait "Henry Higgins," just you wait!
Q: (L) Well, why is all this activity happening now?
A: The grand cycle is about to close presenting a unique opportunity.
Q: (L) Does this mean that this is a unique opportunity to change the future?
A: Future, past and present.
Q: (L) Well, that sort of makes me think that if things are not changed somewhat at this point on the grand cycle that things could get really direfully screwed up, is that correct?
A: But they won't. You have not grasped concept.
Q: (L) Yeah I have, I got you, I understand. It's just part of the cycle. It's all a cycle. I mean their being here is part of us being here ...
A: You do??? [Inscribed giant question mark on board]
Q: (L) Do what?
A: You said you understood concept. Really? Learn. Convention is because of realm border crossing.

---

[13] 21st Century Progressive Psionic Awareness Study, Reply #65 (November 8, 2004), (http://vancouverbc.proboards21.com/index.cgi?board=progressive&action=display&thread=1099966131&page=5).

Q: (L) And why is there a convention attending this realm border crossing? I mean, is it just a "really big shew!"
A: It is an opportunity.

Q: (V) As in the windows are all opening at one time so that all these beings can get in at one time?
A: As in an opportunity to affect whole universe. Picture cosmic playing of "Pomp and Circumstance" AKA "Hope and Glory".

Q: (L) How can a convention with a slew of different kinds and races of beings, converging on a single little pinpoint planet on the outer edges of an insignificant galaxy, at the farthest reaches of this enormous universe, affect the whole thing?
A: That is your perception.

Q: (L) Well, what is the correct perception? Are the planet Earth and the people thereon, and the things that are going on in this spot, the Earth specifically, more important than maybe we would ordinarily have thought?
A: The Earth is a convergence point.

Q: (L) Was it designed to be a convergence point from the beginning?
A: Natural function.

Q: (L) Has it been a convergence point all along? Is that why so many weird things happen here?
A: That is difficult to answer because you have no understanding of "time".

Q: (V) Has this type of convention thing happened on other planets with other groups of beings?
A: Has, is, and will.

Q: (L) If these convergence points are scattered around the universe, is the convergence of this realm border crossing going to occur simultaneously at all points in the universe that are convergence points?
A: No.

Q: (L) It only happens at say one, or selected, convergence points at any given point?
A: Close.

Q: (L) So, do realm borders have something to do with location?
A: Realm borders ride waves.

Q: (L) And where do these waves come from?
A: They constantly cycle.

Q: (L) Does it have something to do with the movement of the planet Earth into it or does it move onto us?
A: Either or.

Q: (F) Does this convention or convergence have something to do with the fact that there are living beings on the Earth?
A: Yes. And because you are at critical juncture in development.

Q: (L) In the book *Mass Dreams of the Future* [by Chet B. Snow], there are four scenarios described regarding the future of our planet; are all of these scenarios accurate in terms of general experience?
A: Possible futures.
Q: (L) So, when a person does a future progression, they are seeing a possible future and not necessarily ...
A: Depends on quality of channel.
Q: (L) In talking about the new level of being after transition to fourth density, will this be something like what is described in the book *Celestine Prophecy* [by James Redfield]?
A: Close.
Q: (L) When was the last time a realm border crossed as far as the earth is concerned?
A: As you measure, on Earth, 309,000 years ago.
Q: (L) What does this wave consist of in terms of energy?
A: Feeling. Hyperkinetic sensate.
Q: (L) What does that mean?
A: All
Q: (L) Okay. How many times has the Wave come and involved the Earth, as we know it?
A: Infinite number.

The idea of denial being munition, as quoted above, is from a recently propagated document, "Top Secret" written by individual(s) calling themselves *The Nexus Seven*. This piece of writing attempts to put together many fragments of both third-density analytical assessment of the current situation regarding the ET reality, and apparently channeled material from a variety of sources. I was very interested to read this document because it usefully creates a platform from which to discuss some of these issues more thoroughly. They write:

> The idea is that as long as the idea of an alien presence remains in the realm of "the fantastic and kooky, the implausible and the mentally ill," this is just a little "guided Free Will" to protect consensus belief using popular deployable psychological munitions of belief.

What is "a little guided Free Will"? Can it really mean that certain enclaves of higher echelon humans have decided what humanity, as a whole, needs? As the Cs said, "An STS vehicle does not learn to be an STO candidate by determining the needs of another (Sept. 19, 1998)."

> The Alien Response Consortium deploys domestic and worldwide counter-intel measures thwarting consensus verification of the alien presence and reality just like any well-honed counterintelligence propaganda machine, and the technological compliment of tools at hand in the psi-ops theater is staggering ...

> Denial is a psychological weapon, a deterrent to alien incursion of mainstream reality, since the aliens appear to respect the stance of individual and group consciousness and acculturation free will more than even military power. Therefore, we can, by accepting alien presence and existence above board in enough mainstream public [ways], unwittingly turn off the restrictions against overt contact the aliens are following.
>
> The overt invasion trigger is our general human acceptance. Especially if they invade parading as holy hosts.

But is that really the case? Is denial of the reality the thing that is preventing ET from coming in the front door? Or, is this a misreading of the true state of affairs, a misunderstanding of the nature of the realities?

> November 16, 1994
>
> Q: (L) If the Lizzies have been feeding off of us frequently and are planning to come and take over our planet, why, when they achieved their domination 300,000 years ago, did they not just move here and take up residence and be in charge?
>
> A: No desire to inhabit same realm.
>
> Q: (L) Why was this?
>
> A: You are 3rd level they are 4th level.
>
> Q: (L) Why are they planning to now?
>
> A: They want to rule you in 4th density.

From the above, we see that there actually may be an entirely different reason for the fact that ET has not emerged from behind the curtain: they cannot. They are fourth density, and as long as we are third density, the contact will continue to be covert and spotty. Thus, the fears of the secret government, as well as their reactions to the current state of affairs is not only based on erroneous thinking, it may actually be detrimental to humanity, and even their own objectives.

> The covert public alien presence admittance and education program, is exactly that: largely covert, and will remain so. *Part of the program is to keep the true reality of aliens forever in question* and so they will still maintain psychological suppression and intimidation of any confirming evidence or highly credible witnesses.
>
> This way, the existence of the pervasive, technologically far advanced, spiritually questionable, and possibly hostile alien presence, is kept under the lid as long as humanly possible. For once the alien presence comes out from under the fringe lid into broad consensus scientific verification, the majority of human institutions and people will have a severe identity crisis and coping crisis.
>
> When that happens, God and religion, military power, and confidence in the economic systems, ethics, all go absolutely haywire and

need to have a response plan, an accommodation plan, an assimilation plan, a social adaptation plan. But most religions, military brain cases, and insider scientists don't have a plan, except to try to escape if invasion is inevitable, or even ally themselves with ET devils or angels or just plain Joes, as they may end up being.

The problem is, this sort of control of society has been part of the alien arsenal, effected through human agents and agencies down through the millennia and the Nexus Seven are exactly correct when they note the fact that the ET, as far as religious institutions are concerned, are the Gods of Holy Writ.

November 7, 1994

Q: (L) What was the Ark of the Covenant?

A: Power cell.

Q: (L) What was the origin of this power cell?

A: *Lizards given to the Jews to use for manipulation of others.*

Q: (L) Why was it that if you came close to this object or touched it you would die?

A: Energy overload; scrambling by reverse electromagnetism.

Q: (L) What is reverse electromagnetism?

A: Turned inward. Liquefaction of matter.

Q: (L) Well, that is pleasant. This cell was kept in an ornate box of some sort, is that correct?

A: Yes.

Q: (L) Why was it only the priests who could handle it?

A: Only those who would not try to use for selfish reasons.

Q: (L) But then did just coming near it injure a person?

A: Yes.

Q: (L) Well why were these individuals able to come near it?

A: Non-selfish energy field.

Q: (L) So it could tune into thought fields?

A: Yes. Patternings.

April 11, 1998

Q: (L) In reading *Fingerprints of the Gods* [by Graham Hancock], I discovered that there is the tradition of the Ark of the Covenant being in Ethiopia. This guy did a bunch of research on it, and it seems possible that it is there, and that it may even be active. Is it, in fact, in the church of St. Mary of Zion in Ethiopia?

A: No.

Q: (L) Where is it?

A: If we were to reveal this to you, it would be akin to giving a hand grenade to a baby!!

October 21, 1994

Q: (L) Okay, where is the Ark of the Covenant currently located?

A: Alternative 3.

Q: (L) Alternative 3 is the plan to take all the people, all the smart guys, and all the elite, off the planet and leave everybody else here to blow up, isn't it?

A: Maybe. Maybe not. Discover. Study Alternative 3 to find answer!

This remark was a puzzle to me until I read the remark in the "Top Secret" document: "But most religions, military brain-cases, and insider scientists don't have a plan, except to try to escape if invasion is inevitable, or even ally themselves with ET devils or angels or just plain Joes, as they may end up being."

Then, it made perfect sense. Obviously, the movie about Indiana Jones rescuing the Ark of the Covenant from the Germans was not altogether fantasy. It is very likely that either somebody knows where it is, or they are desperately looking for it. (Fortunately, I don't have a clue where it is, so all you guys in the three-piece suits with dark glasses can get some rest!)

Nevertheless, in lieu of the Ark of the Covenant, the so-called HAARP (High Frequency Active Aural Research Program) project could be involved with the idea that there is an above top secret group planning to save their own hides while sacrificing the rest of humanity to some sort of ET takeover. It is also possible that the HAARP project is being built at the direction of certain ET factions with planned uses that exceed our ability to conceptualize. In *UFOs and the National Security State: The Cover-up Revealed*, historian Richard M. Dolan writes:

> In 1985, Bernard J. Eastlund, a physicist for ARCO Power Tehnologies, applied for the patent "Method and Apparatus for Altering a Region in the Earth's Atmosphere, Ionosphere and/or Magnetosphere." The idea was to use high-frequency radio waves to beam unprecedented amounts of power into the ionosphere, more than 100 miles above the planet's surface. The beam would energize and heat the ionosphere ... (Dolan, 2009)

This project later morphed into HAARP, which could:

> ... disrupt satellites and communication systems. It could also use *Earth-penetrating tomography* to search for natural gas or petroleum deposits, or even artificial structures like underground military bases. (Dolan, 2009)

We asked the Cs about HAARP:

February 17, 1996

Q: (L) Some people have written asking me to ask about this HAARP thing ... seems to be some sort of antennae thing ...

A: Disguise for something else.

Q: (L) What is that something else?

A: Project to apply EM wave theories to the *transference of perimeters.*

Q: (L) What does that mean?

A: If utilized as designed, will allow for controlled invisibility and easy movement between density levels *on surface of planet as well as subterrannially.*

Q: (L) Can you tell us if this is a human organization or aliens, or a combination?

A: Human at surface level.

Q: (L) Is there more you can tell us about this?

A: It has nothing to do with weather or climate. These things are emanating from 4th density, as we have told you before.

Q: (L) So, HAARP has nothing to do with the weather?

A: And also EM associated with same as reported.

Q: (L) So, when is this HAARP thing scheduled to go into operation?

A: Open.

Q: (L) Is it currently in operation?

A: Experimental.

Q: (L) How long have they been working on this thing?

A: Since the 1920s.

May 4, 1996

Q: (L) You said that HAARP was something that was to be used to "transfer perimeters." I am assuming that this means to manipulate space, time and density.

A: Yes.

Q: (L) Is it possible that they are planning to use this to bring up the Atlantean crystals to utilize.

A: Not so much to "bring up," as to utilize.

February 22, 1997

A: "HAARP" is being designated for capturing and modulating electromagnetic fields for the purpose of total control of brainwave patterns in order to establish a system of complete "order on the surface of the planet" in either 3rd or 4th density.

Q: (L) Is HAARP in operation at the present time?

A: Yes, in its early experimental stages.

Q: (T) Is the spreading of all these communication towers out across the country the equivalent of a HAARP program on a continental scale?

A: Back up system. Towers serve dual and lateral purposes.

The Nexus Seven repeat the idea that the secret government, in some ways, may have humanity's best interests at heart, but I think that is a baseless assumption. Denial is never acceptable. It seems that their own denial is being imposed on the masses. And, the consequences could be disastrous.

> November 19, 1994
>
> Q: (T) Is the government planning to stage an invasion by aliens to cause the populace of the world to go into such a fear state that they will accept total control and domination?
>
> A: Open. But if so, will "flop".
>
> Q: (T) Why?
>
> A: Many reasons: 1. Visual effects will be inadequate and will have "glitches". 2. Real invasion may take place first. 3. Other events may intercede.
>
> Q: (T) Such as what?
>
> A: Earth changes.
>
> Q: (T) Am I correct in assuming that some of these hotshot, bigwig guys in the government who have plans for taking over the whole world and making everything all happy and hunky-dory with them in charge, are just simply not in synch with the fact that there are some definite earth changes on the agenda? Are they missing something here?
>
> A: Close. *They are aware but in denial.*
>
> Q: (T) Are these earth changes going to occur prior to the arrival of the cometary cluster?
>
> A: No. But "time" frame is, as of yet, undetermined.
>
> Q: (T) Am I correct in saying that if they knew what was really going to happen that they would still continue with their stupid little plans to make money and try to control the world?
>
> A: Yes. Greed is a sickness.

On the other hand, sharing knowledge and awareness might have an altogether different outcome:

> July 18, 1998
>
> Q: (L) Now, one question that we were discussing earlier is: how can the close approach of the theorized companion star cause an increase in the Sun's gravity when there is no reason why it should change anything since gravity is a function of mass?
>
> A: But do you really know all there is to know about gravity?
>
> Q: (A) No, we don't know. But, does this mean that this will be an effect that does not follow from the theory of gravity that we know already?
>
> A: Gravity is the life force that binds all realities as one. In order to understand this, you would need a reworking of the theorem.

Q: (A) We have Einstein's theory of gravity, and the question is whether the effect of increasing the Sun's gravity is something that goes beyond Einstein's equations or not?

A: You must see the wave.

Q: (A) What wave, a gravitational wave, or an electromagnetic wave, or some other wave? What wave?

A: Arkadiusz, how do these intersect?

Q: (A) Gravity and electromagnetic?

A: Yes. And others.

Q: (A) How they are described within a theory, or how they intersect in space when they come together?

A: Both.

Q: (A) Okay, why does this increase in the Sun's gravity have anything to do with electromagnetism? We were told that the brown star will not radiate any radiation, so, in particular, no electromagnetic radiation. So, where does electromagnetics come in? I do not understand ...

A: *Gravitational pull incites electromagnetic impulse.*

Q: (A) Okay, that means we go beyond gravitational theory, and this is part of Unified Field Theory?

A: Yes, exactly!! The complete UFT was withheld from you!

Q: (T) So, the complete UFT is known to someone here on the planet?

A: Yes.

Q: (T) And they are not making it available ...

A: Oh no, because "The Truth Will Set You Free!" You may access hyperspatial truths with UFT.

Q: (A) Well, we started with the increased mass of the Sun, and we came to UFT, which is hidden from us because it would make us free; there is this tendency in me to follow this road because it is science and would open a new road. The question is whether such activity or knowing such things will lead to other densities? Is it just for satisfaction, or is there real value in knowing more in this direction?

A: Well, the Unified Field Theory unlocks the door completely to the higher densities ... Grids.

Q: (L) What kind of grids ...

A: The planet has been enshrouded with EM grid.

Q: (T) Are these the ley lines?

A: No.

Q: (L) Are they artificially generated?

A: Contoured.

Q: (L) They are artificially contoured. What is the result of this shrouding?

A: Manipulated for use by 3rd/4th Consortium.

Q: (A) What kind of EM grid? (L) The natural EM grid is being contoured ...

A: Like a gently waving geometric "blanket".

Q: (T) Is it on the surface of the planet, through the planet, or where?

A: Above.

Q: (T) The gravity waves, whether they exist or not, are a controversy, yet they are part of the UFT, and someone already knows how it works. Therefore, it is only controversy to those who don't know what the answer is, and it is not a controversy to those who know. They know what it is and how to measure it and how to use it.

A: Of course.

Q: (A) Some power is used to sustain this grid. What is it?

A: Land and space based generators.

Q: (T) What can it be used for?

A: Multiple uses. Net. Calculates ... You are dancing on the 3rd density ballroom floor. "Alice likes to go through the looking glass" at the Crystal Palace. Atlantean reincarnation surge brings on the urge to have a repeat performance.

Q: (T) The Atlanteans who have reincarnated are getting ready to do the same thing they did before with the crystals. So, this is an Atlantean type thing that is being done now? Different equipment, but the same type of thing?

A: All lessons must be learned before you can move onto bigger and better things.

Q: (L) Is that a general statement about the Atlanteans repeating the lessons, or that once we learn this lesson, we can move onto bigger and better things in counteracting this grid?

A: All that is present and future too.

Q: (A) I want to ask if there is something that we can and should do about this grid for ourselves?

A: Why? To know was all you need.

Q: (A) Well, it was said that this was for the purpose of control and manipulation. So, knowing is all that we need. Or, we could try to shield ... (L) But, to know *is* the shield. I don't know how that works, but it seems to be so.

A: Yes.

Q: (A) Now, how did we come to this grid from UFT?

A: Grid construction represents application of ...

Q: (L) Somehow we went from the increased gravity of the Sun, to UFT, to the grid ...

A: UFT explains the "increased" gravity of Sol. But, is there not something in UFT about increase/decrease???

Q: (A) There is no reason for it to increase or decrease ... but this is Einstein's theory, which we were told is incorrect ...

(L) Well, maybe it is speed? When two things are rotating in tandem, when they come together, wouldn't it increase their speed, and doesn't speed increase gravity?

(A) No, we were told that there is some interaction between gravity and EM wave, and this is what UFT is about … If we use other dimensions, which we are supposed to use in this UFT, going with Kaluza-Klein, then the very concept of mass is something, which is not so clear, and mass can be variable …

A: Yes, variability of physicality.

Q: (T) Fourth density. (A) We were told earlier that this UFT opens the door to other densities …

A: Yes.

Q: (A) Can we have a UFT that unifies EM and gravity and does not include the concept of other densities? In other words, can we put in a textbook all about the gravity and electromagnetics, and a student could learn all of this and still know nothing about other densities?

A: No. Other densities become apparent when …

Q: (A) So, it means that Einstein and Von Neumann knew about these other densities?

A: Yes, oh yes!!!

Q: (T) Just a thought: having UFT and being able to manipulate different fields within it, creates different effects. So, as we understand it in the apparent present state of science, we have to spin something in space in order to create gravity. But, with the UFT, one small offshoot is that one could create real gravity without spinning anything. So, the problem of weightlessness is really already solved …

A: Elementary my dear T, elementary.

Q: (T) So, this whole thing with the space station and all the trouble they are having readapting to gravity when they come back, is all a game …

A: When you "let the cat out of the bag," you create an entire feline "nation".

Q: (T) So, we are capable of *Star Trek* right now?

A: In a sense, but there is so much more than that.

Q: (T) Of course. Most people would say that cutting edge science is 25 years ahead of what we see, and I say it is more like a hundred years, and I am even off? Cutting edge science on this planet is more like three or four hundred years ahead?

A: More like 30 to 40,000 years "ahead"!

Q: (L) Is that because of fourth-density influence and information?

A: Yes.

Q: (T) 30 to 40 thousand years? Let me get that number right …

A: Yes, at least.

So, it seems that the secret government is not really protecting anything but their own interests. Of course, one of their interests is the control that is exercised via religion. The "Top Secret" document continues:

> ... If the ETs are connected to key religious characters of our history, then ET intervention and active culturing of their human 'experiment' on earth have been going on since ancient times. That is hard to swallow. The idea of angels and devils was always a magical subjective world of beings and powers of myth and lore, not a hard nuts and bolts physical ET race with weapons and all. To find out many heavenly religious benefactors of history and the ancients were just cloned, dickless bio-drones, carrying out orders in a heavenly hierarchy of hardware and alien super-science, is plainly a scary thought to just about anyone in power on earth. More likely, there are aliens who Do have big dicks so the question is – are they our friends or not?
>
> These are questions technophallic, top dog centric worshipping, economic-warrior captains and lieutenants would naturally ask. Abductions have involved lots of sex and reproduction related genetic control activities, after all, and this makes military dicks go limp. And they are not alone. It makes the kings of power and influence all need Viagra. They want to stop ET, but they don't even really know who to hate, or how to stop them, and they feel awfully impotent in the face of ETs' incredibly advanced technology and powerful telepathy. All our thoughts may already be under the microscope.

I would like to suggest that the secret government is neither ignorant of the above nor having "limp dick syndrome," (excuse the vulgarity). There is evidence that some human members of this Control System have been engaged in the human management part of this conspiracy for many thousands of years.

March 7, 1995
Q: (L) Who were the Elohim of the Bible?
A: Transdefinitive. And variable entities. First manifestation was human, then non-human.
Q: (L) Well, what brought about their transformation from human to non-human?
A: Pact or covenant made with 4th density STS.
Q: (L) Well, that is not good! Are you saying that the Elohim are STS? Who were these STS beings they made a pact with?
A: Rosteem, now manifests as Rosicrucians.
Q: (L) What is their purpose?
A: As yet unrevealable to you.

October 4, 1997

Q: (L) In the book *The Orion Mystery* [by Robert Bauval and Adrian Gilbert], the author talks about the fact that Giza was formerly known as RosTau, which is Rose Cross. I would like to understand the symbology of the Rose affixed to the Cross. It seems to me that the imagery of Jesus nailed to the Cross is actually the Rose affixed to the Cross. How does Jesus relate to the Rose?

A: No, it is from the Rose arose the Cross.

Q: (L) Oh ... I see ...

A: Said the blind man.

Q: (L) Elaborate, please. It is from the Rose that the Cross arose ... and, therefore, the cross symbolizes ... What does the cross symbolize?

A: The symbology is not the issue. It is the effect.

Q: (L) What is the effect of the cross?

A: All that has followed it.

December 21, 1996

Q: (L) In other words, control of the masses via religion. Who or what brought about the end of the Knights of the Temple?

A: Rosicrucians move as a "thief in the night".

Q: (L) But, as I understand it, the Rosicrucians did not come into being until after the end of the Templars ... Many people think that the Rosicrucians *are* the Templars ...

A: No.

Q: (L) Do you mean that the information that came out, that Pamphlet about Christian Rosenkreutz, that is a purported fable, might be correct?

A: Yes.

Q: (L) Well, goodness sake! The Rosicrucians advertise in magazines! Is this worldwide organization that promotes itself so blatantly ...

A: Well, the "worldwide" order is not all-inclusive.

Q: (L) Is there an inner circle of this order that is unknown?

A: Yes.

Q: (L) Are the Rosicrucians connected to the Masons?

A: In a roundabout away.

Q: (L) Are the Illuminati connected to the Rosicrucians in any way?

A: Same.

Q: (L) The Priory of Zion, that has been purported to be the progenitor or inheritor of the Templar tradition, is that a mystical organization of great secrecy and import?

A: It is a cover for.

Q: (L) Another smokescreen.

A: Yes.

THE NEXUS SEVEN MEET THE CASSIOPAEANS

May 7, 1997

Q: (L) You mentioned that the "Rosicrucians act as a thief in the night."

A: Connect the Rosicrucians to your favorite island by the "beech." Horticulturally, please, and family.

Q: (L) Oak Island?

A: Yup! Then, connect the Pyrenees to the Canaries. Research the history of the Canary Islands for clue.

May 31, 1997

Q: (L) In the information I now have on the Canaries, I found that a strange icon appeared on the island long before the conquest, and long before any missionaries or Europeans arrived. The original natives were said to be giants, some of them over 14 feet tall, with 80 teeth. They said that the natives, even when they knew nothing about Christianity, knew this icon was divine because following its appearance, there were processions of angels, or divine beings, up and down the beach where it appeared; lights, smells, chanting and singing and so forth. How did the statue of the Virgin of Candelaria arrive on the beach at Tenerife?

A: Teleportation.

Q: (L) Who teleported it there?

A: The "Celts".

Q: (L) Celts in the sense of the Druids?

A: Or in the sense of Atlanteans. "Celts, Druids," etc. are merely latter day designations.

Q: (L) Well, I came to the conclusion that the Rosicrucians are just the new incarnation of the Druids. I mean, the Druids disappeared and the Rosicrucians appeared not too long afterward.

A: Partially.

Q: (L) Julius Caesar had a standard policy of religious toleration. The only exception seems to have been the Druids. He was determined to stamp them out. Why?

A: Their mysterious powers.

Q: (L) Where did they get these mysterious powers?

A: Knowledge passed down.

Q: (L) Were the angelic beings that appeared on the Canaries Druids or Rosicrucians?

A: They were 4th density.

Q: (L) Were they STS of STO?

A: Both.

Q: (L) Do the STS and STO hang out together?

A: Do you hang out with all types of your realm?

Q: (L) Well, in these processions of beings that the Guanches of the island saw, were they STS or STO?
A: Both.
Q: (L) You mean they would see one and then another?
A: Close.

October 4, 1997
Q: (L) In the little book on the Canary Islands, written by a friar of the Order of Preachers back in 1590, and later published by the Hakluyt society, it specifically mentions spiders. I looked up any references to this in the Bible, looking for clues, and found a truly bizarre thing in Proverbs 30:28. In the King James Version, it is given as a spider, and the context is completely different from the actual intent of the original Hebrew, which designates a lizard instead of a spider. Then, there is the spider image of the information that has been propagated by the Priory of Zion, which seems to be a sort of signature of this super secret organization. The crazy thing is, when you reverse the numbers of this Biblical quote, you actually have 28:30, and when you look at this line of latitude on the planet, you find that it passes just south of Mount Everest, the Pyramids of Giza, through the Canary Islands, and just north of my house right here.

When thinking about all this, I have noticed that there are only two classes of arachnids. There are scorpions and there are spiders. The zodiac was changed by taking the pincers away from the Scorpion and creating out of them the sign of Libra. This image was one of a woman holding a balance scales, usually blindfolded. This was done within recorded history, but was probably formalized through the occult traditions of Kaballah. Now, in trying to figure out who has on what color hat, if there is such a thing, I have come to a tentative conclusion that the spider, or spinner of webs, is the Rosicrucian encampment, and that the Scorpion represents the seeker of wisdom ... because, in fact, the word for Scorpio comes from the same root as that which means to pierce or unveil. Therefore, the Scorpion is also Perseus, per Ziu, or "for God". And the Rosicrucians are the other side, so to speak. Can you elaborate on this for me? Or comment?
A: What a tangled web we spin, when we must not let you in.
Q: (L) So, the Rose is the Spider?
A: Different objective.
Q: (L) So, the Rose, with its thorns ... Can you help me with this Rose image ... Is the Rose the Scorpion?
A: No. Different objective ... Rose is a stand-alone symbol.
Q: (L) So, the Rose can be used by either side, is that it?
A: Maybe.

Q: (L) Another derivation of the word root of Scorpio is "skopos", or "to see". You once said that the human race was seeded on a planet in the constellation Scorpio, and, therefore, when the zodiac was set up and the clues were laid out, it seems to me that the insertion of the sign of Libra was designed to take power away from human beings, to take their hands away, to prevent them from seeing, to make them defenseless. Is this imagery close?

A: On track.

September 16, 1995

Q: (L) Okay, change of subject. Back when we were talking about the pit on Oak Island, and you asked me to do some research on it, the answers I came up with were that the responsible group were alchemists. Is this correct.

A: Yes.

Q: (L) Was one of the alchemists involved Nicholas Flamel?

A: Yes.

Q: (L) Is it true that there is an enclave of alchemists that live somewhere in the Pyrenees ...

A: Yes.

Q: (L) Do these alchemists use this powder as talked about by David Hudson to enhance their longevity and their physical health?

A: And to control.

September 24, 1995

A: ... Monoatomic gold is but one minor issue here. Why get lead astray by focusing upon it solely. Alchemy is but one minor piece of the puzzle.

Q: (L) Okay, I understand. But, understanding the alchemical connection, and its potential for extending life and opening certain abilities, makes it more feasible to think of a group that has been present steadily and consistently for many thousands of years on earth.

A: They are not the only ones!

Returning to the Nexus Seven:

The complexity of having both good and bad ET's makes the whole situation intolerable. Even certain global poison pill strategies have been on the table as a means to persuade ET against overt contact. That is, not a mutually assured destruction doctrine with the aliens, but instead *an individually assured destruction pill to the ET human experiment.* Any preemptive counter-threat against the aliens is worthwhile to prevent disclosure that we are in a fishbowl. Disclosure can cause the downfall of modern civilization and an integration and assimilation into an advanced ET custodial racial culture. Do we want that?

So the answer seems to be to both prepare for contact without the preparation tipping off the authoritative public institutions that are at risk. This means *flooding the social consciousness with the existence an[d] eventually, the plausibility of ET is already here, all without any verifiable genuine acknowledgment.*

Aliens bait; we make the switch. All in a day's work to save us from assimilation on ET's terms, not ours. What we cannot stop, we must delay. What we cannot delay, we must distort and debunk. What we cannot distort and debunk, we distract from and focus elsewhere. There is no other choice in the matter. *ARC would rather start a worldwide nuclear war than welcome ET with open arms. Scorched Earth is an option, unfortunately the least desirable.*

Unfortunately, if the Nexus Seven assessment is anywhere near accurate in terms of what those in the higher echelons of power really think or plan, such ideas are completely impotent. We are talking about hyperdimensional beings here that can repeatedly go back in time and change things to suit their own ends. But, indeed, the secret government is so terrified of the public getting wind of any of this that they do, indeed, make the switch – but for their own reasons – not to "help" the aliens.

January 21, 1995

Q: (L) Back in the 1970s in the Central United States there were quite a number of cases of animal mutilation. There has been a lot of publicity about this at some point and then it died down and was covered up, and there were a lot of ideas and theories about it. What I would like to know is who was doing the animal mutilations?

A: Many.

Q: (L) Okay, who was doing most of the animal mutilations?

A: Not applicable.

Q: (L) Okay. Was some of the animal mutilation done by the U.S. Government, or entities within the government?

A: Was?

Q: (L) In other words, it is still going on. Okay, so they are still doing it. Was, or is, some of this activity being conducted by alien individuals?

A: Yes.

Q: (T) Were they acting for the same reasons?

A: No.

Q: (L) Why did the government do animal mutilations?

A: *Copy, in order to throw off investigation.*

Q: (L) So they copied this activity to throw off investigations. Did they do this as an act to protect the aliens who were doing animal mutilations for their own purposes?

A: No.

Q: (L) Were they doing it to protect themselves from the public knowing that they were engaged in alien interactions?

A: *They do it to protect the public from knowing that which would explode society if discovered.*

Q: (L) What is this item that they were protecting so that society or the public wouldn't know about it. What activity is this?

A: *Humans eat cattle; aliens eat you.*

Q: (T) They've said that before. (L) Okay, yeah, we eat second level; they eat third. Did aliens do some of the cattle mutilations?

A: Yes.

Q: (L) What do aliens do to cattle?

A: Blood.

Q: (L) They take the blood out of them?

A: Yes.

Q: (J) What do they use this blood for?

A: Nourishment.

Q: (L) Okay, but you just said that aliens eat humans, and humans eat cattle. Why were the aliens being nourished by cattle, if that's not their normal bill of fare? (T) A cow's blood is a lot like human blood.

A: Do you not ever consume facsimile? Facsimile is less controversial, obviously!

Q: (L) So in other words, they were eating cattle just to keep from having to eat so many humans, that would have just upset people a lot, is that it?

A: Yes. Some of their human "food" is merely emotions; think of flesh as being the equal of "filet mignon".

Q: (T) Some of their food is merely emotions. Okay, when we're talking about these aliens, are we talking about the Grays?

A: No.

Q: (T) We're talking about the Lizards.

A: Yes.

Q: (T) Okay, what do the Grays feed on?

A: Plasma.

Q: (T) Okay, the Grays feed on plasma, blood plasmas of some kind, is this what you are saying?

A: Yes.

Q: (T) Okay, so that's why they want the blood. So, do the Grays feed on emotions?

A: No. They send them to Lizards. Transfer energy through technology. *Lizards and Grays only need physical nourishment while "visiting" 3rd level, not when in natural realm, 4th density, there they feed on emotions only.*

Q: (L) There have been very frequently associated with the phenomenon of cattle mutilations, sightings of black, unmarked helicopters, who or what are these helicopters?

A: Variable.

Q: (L) Are some of these helicopters disguised alien craft? Are some of these helicopters the property of the U.S. Government?

A: Yes to both.

Q: (T) Are some of these helicopters private enterprise?

A: Yes. Some too, are projections, this phenomenon is multifaceted.

Q: (L) Who are the oriental-appearing personnel that have been seen manning the helicopters and the white vans that have been sighted all over the country?

A: MIB. And government copycats.

Q: (L) How many alien craft, actual alien craft, are in the hands of the government or this consortium?

A: 36.

Q: (L) And were these captured craft? Or gifted?

A: And recovered.

Q: (T) Were the gift ones not what we would really consider gifts, but they were given to us in return for something else, some other kind of payment? Barter?

A: No. Because all sought return favors were already achieved.

Q: (L) So it was all just a farce. *They weren't payment; they weren't gifts. They were distractions?*

A: *Closer.*

Q: (T) Okay, so there are a lot of different categories of how these ships got into the hands of the federal government?

A: Yes. Multidimensional

Q: (L) Who is "O. H. Krll"?

A: No one. Symbolism. For documentary purposes only, your government likes code names.

Q: (L) Are you implying that this piece of work was put out by the government for dissemination of the subject matter? (J) Is it disinformation?

A: Complex.

Q: (L) Give us a percentage of factual information in this document.[14]

---

[14] The O.H. Krll document (http://pdharris0.tripod.com/krill.htm#Krill%20Papers) was written by John Grace (AKA Valdamar Valerian, author of *The Matrix* material). According to Richard Dolan, Grace wrote the document "shortly after John Lear's hypothesis [on the UFO/alien conspiracy] was published in December 1987…" Grace, who was still on active USAF duty at the time, used the name "Krll", suggested to him by John Lear, while Grace added "O.H." Dolan writes: "Among the Krill document's many conclusions were that the U.S. government had a longstanding working relationship with aliens with the goal of perfecting gravitational propulsion, beam weaponry, and mind control. Advances in these and other areas vastly ex-

A: 43%

Q: (L) Okay, so, in other words, this has been planted by the government.

A: No. Planted? No.

Q: (T) It was leaked purposely?

A: Your government is operating on many cross-purposes, very complicated! On purpose!

Q: (T) Very true. Question: The government, our government, the U.S. government, is holding 36 craft of one kind or another that they gotten in one way or another. How many other governments have craft?

A: All is one.

Q: (L) *We already have a one-world government is what they're saying.* (T) Yes, they're just waiting to make it official somehow.

A: *Has been so for long time, as you measure time.*

Q: (L) What is the "ultimate secret" being protected by the Consortium?

A: You are not in control of yourselves, you are an experiment.

Q: (T) When you say this is the ultimate secret, that we're being "protected" from by the government, are we talking about the ultimate secret of humans only here?

A: Basically.

Q: (T) The ultimate secret of the human race is that we are an experiment that other humans are conducting on the rest of us?

A: Part.

Q: (T) Okay, does the other part have to do with the Lizards?

A: Yes.

Q: (L) Other aliens also?

A: Yes.

Q: (T) Okay, so, are the humans, who are running the experiment, do they know that they are part of the experiment also?

A: Yes.

Q: (T) And they're doing this willingly?

A: They have no choice. Already in progress.

Q: (T) Okay, is this part of ... Is this about the experiment the Lizzies are doing of dominating us and sucking us dry?

---

ceeded anything the public knew about, and the space program was a public relations cover for more serious space operations. Live aliens had been "hostage" to the U.S. government, alien autopsies had been conducted, and abductions, murder, and mutilation had all occurred in connection with the UFO situation. ... The aliens ... had intervened in human genetic development and religion, had bases on the Earth and Moon, and actively controlled elements of human society. ...[H]umans inhabited a multi-dimensional world visited by a large number of hostile and friendly entities from other dimensions." (Dolan, 2009)

A: Yes, but there's much more than that, you will understand at level 4.

Q: (L) Okay, in this Krll document there was a statement made that the Grays and other aliens use glandular substances extracted during physical exams of human beings, what they would call the gynecological and the sperm extraction exams, that they used these glandular substances to get high or to feed on, that they are addicted to these, is this a correct assessment?

A: No.

Q: (L) Do they use glandular substances at all?

A: Yes.

Q: (L) What do they use glandular substances for?

A: Medicine.

Q: (L) And what or who do they use this medicine on?

A: Themselves.

Q: (L) And what does this medicine do for them?

A: Helps them cope with 3rd density.

Q: (T) Is this something that they use to help them stay in the 3rd density?

A: Close.

Q: (L) Does it help them to manifest in a more solid physical manner?

A: Yes.

Q: (L) So, in other words, they draw glandular substances. Do they also use sexual energy given off by individuals to maintain their status in 3 dimensions?

A: No. That feeds them in 4D, as we told you before.

Q: (L) Yes. Okay. How "long", and I put long in quotes, because we know, as you say, there is no time, but how long, as we measure it, have the Grays been interacting with our race? The Grays, not the Lizards, the Grays, the cybergenetic probes?

A: No. Time travelers, therefore, "Time is ongoing." Do you understand the gravity of last response?

Q: (L) They are time travelers, they can move forward and backward in time, they can play games with our heads ... (T) They can set up the past to create a future they want. (D) They can organize things so that they can create the energy that they need ... (L) They can also make things look good, make them feel good, make them seem good, they can make you have an idea one minute, and then the next minute, create some sort of situation that confirms that idea ...

A: When you asked how long, of course it is totally unlimited, is it not?

Q: (L) That's not good. *If they were to move back through space-time and alter an event in our past, would that alteration in the past instantaneously alter our present as well?*

A: *Has over and over and over.*

Q: (D) So they do it over and over and over, constantly?

A: You just are not yet aware, and have no idea of the ramifications!!!

Q: (L) We're getting a little glimmer! Yeah, I do, a little! (T) The ramifications of being able to move in and out of time and manipulate it the way you want. (J) And the ramifications of what they are doing to us and what they will do to us, over and over. (L) So, in other words, our only real prayer in this whole damn situation is to get out of this density level. That's what they're saying, that's what it sounds like to me.

A: Close.

Q: (L) Because, otherwise, we're just literally, as in that book, stuck in the replay over and over and over, and the Holocaust could happen over and over, and we could just, you know ... Ghengis Khan, Attila the Hun ... over and over and over again. (T) We're stuck in a time loop; they're putting us in a time loop. (J) Are we in a time loop?

A: Yes.

Q: (D) Mankind has found it necessary for some reason or other to appoint time for some reason or other. The only reason I can see is to have a means of telling, like in verbal or written communications ...

A: Control mechanism.

Q: (T) Is there a way for us to break the control mechanism? Besides moving to fourth density? (D) That was part ...

A: Nope.

The Nexus Seven define the policy of the Secret Government rather succinctly:

> The covert nature of alien-human contact programs already in progress does not vouch for ET's operating without deceit and hidden agenda. These are hidden agenda that could be threatening to human freedom – physically and spiritually – we don't know. And until we do, the word is "aliens don't exist".

However, considering what the Cassiopaeans have told us, and it certainly fits the consensus of evidence, even if most of it is circumstantial due to the nature of the control of the secret government, then *not knowing is the greatest danger to humanity imaginable.* Knowledge does protect!

> And whoever does say that aliens do exist is in serious need of meds. That's the word from the conditioned authorities and experts. ... A large daylight UFO sighting could happen over a major city for an extended period, and many would change the channel thinking it is just another Independence day rip-off. In other words, until the Internet came along, the whole enchilada was kept under much tighter wraps.

> The more people who are holding the line of denial and mainstream academic and scientific refusal of aliens existing, the greater the zone of exclusion we maintain humanity from overt alien integration, and as it looks to some, prevent a monstrous invasion.

This is a baseless assumption born out of supreme wishful thinking. It is also clever disinformation because, as we can surmise, the secret government knows exactly what it is doing.

> ... To avoid massive social breakdowns, the alien presence must be suppressed. Otherwise kiss your normal human life good-bye as we enter the science fiction world of living on a planet invaded by some of it's original experimental caretakers, with a new identity of being kept animals in some giant laboratory, with all our spiritual and physical authority and power usurped by non-human aliens calling themselves our divine benefactors.

This should actually say, "To avoid loss of power, for as long as they can maintain it, the secret government suppresses knowledge of the alien presence for their own benefit." It could also be that they have been promised some exalted position in the coming fourth-density hierarchy. Too bad they don't study history or they would realize that the betrayers and double agents who assist the conquerors are generally the first to be eliminated in any kind of coup.

> The controlling secret societies have no interest in fame, only power and influence, and influence only comes in terms of capital (economic), force (military), or belief (religious) as root resources for control amongst the incognito power elite. So the leaders of capital systems, military might, and religious influence would naturally secrete and accrete themselves into well-funded, well-insulated, well-connected institutions of secrecy, inside the very systems that are vaguely aware of their presence, but unaware of their intent. It's all just business, don't forget.

Indeed, and it seems that their intent is to retain this position in the coming "New World Order" conceived to be instituted when the planet transitions to fourth density. However, there is something they have not considered in their linear, third-density brains, and that is the nature of fourth-density reality. It may not be as simple to stay on top as they think. In fact, they may find themselves on the absolute bottom.

November 11, 1995
Q: (L) I wanted to ask about is the references I come across in tons of reading, that the number 33 is somehow significant. Could you tell us the significance, in esoteric terms, or in terms of secret societies, of the number 33?

A: As usual, we do not just give you the answers; we help you to teach yourself!! Now, take 11 and contemplate ...

Q: (L) Well, three times eleven is thirty-three.

A: Yes, but what about 11?

Q: (L) Well, eleven is supposed to be one of the prime, or divine power numbers. In Kaballah, 11 is the power number ...

A: Yes ...

Q: (L) Eleven is 10 plus 1; it is divisible only by itself and by 1. I can't think of anything else.

A: Astrology.

Q: (L) Well, in astrology, the eleventh sign is Aquarius. The eleventh house is friends, hopes, dreams and wishes, and also adopted children. Aquarius is the Waterbearer, the dispenser of knowledge. Does 11 have something to do with dispensing of knowledge?

A: Now, 3rd house.

Q: (L) Gemini. Okay. Gemini and Aquarius. Third house is how the mind works, communication, relations with neighbors and siblings, education, local travel, how one speaks. Gemini is known as the "consummate man". Somewhat shallow and interested in the things of material life. It is also the divine number of creation. So, what's the connection here?

A: Matrix.

Q: (L) The third house and the eleventh house create a matrix?

A: Foundation.

Q: (L) In terms of cosmic things, Gemini is in June, Aquarius is in February ... Gemini is the physical man, and Aquarius is the spiritual man?

A: Yin-Yang.

Q: (L) So Gemini is the physical man and Aquarius is the spiritual man ... Yin-Yang ... is that the ...

A: Yes ... Medusa 11.

Q: (L) Medusa 11? What does Medusa have to do with it?

A: Heads.

Q: (L) Heads. Medusa. 11. This is really obscure ... You need to help me out here.

A: We are. 11 squared divided by phi. 1 times 1; 5 minus 3.

Q: (L) I don't get it. A math genius I am not. What is the concept here?

A: Look: 353535. Is code.

Q: (L) What does this code relate to?

A: Infinite power.

Q: (L) How is infinite power acquired by knowing this code? If you don't know the correspondences, how can you use a numerical code?

A: Lord of Serpent promises its followers infinite power which they must seek infinite knowledge to gain, for which they pledge allegiance infinitely for which they possess for all eternity, so long as they find infinite wisdom, for which they search for all infinity.

Q: (L) And that is the meaning of the number 33? Well, that is a round robin ... a circle you can't get out of!

A: And therein you have the deception! Remember, *those who seek to serve self with supreme power, are doomed only to serve others who seek to serve self, and can only see that which they want to see.*

Q: (L) The thought that occurs to me, as we are talking here, is that the STS pathway consists of an individual who wants to serve themselves – they are selfish and egocentric – they want to impel others to serve them; they want to enslave others; and they find ways to manipulate others to serve them.

But, they end up being impelled by some higher being than they are. Because they have been tricked into believing that by so doing, they are actually drawing power to themselves through the teachings, including the popular religions, which promote being saved by simply believing and giving up your power.

And then you have a whole pyramid of people taking by trickery and deception, from others. The taker gets taken from in the end. A pyramid where all those on the bottom, the majority, have no one to take from, so they get absorbed into the next level higher, until you get to the apex and everything disappears in a black hole.

But, in the STO mode, you have those who only give. And, if they are involved with other STO persons, everyone has and no one is at the bottom or at the top, in a void. In the end, it seems like everyone ends up serving someone else anyway, and the principle is the intent. But in STO, it is more like a circle, a balance; no one is left without.

A: Balance, yin-yang.

Q: (L) Obviously the 33 represent the Serpent, the Medusa, and so forth ...

A: You mentioned pyramid, interesting ... And what is the geometric one-dimensional figure that corresponds?

Q: (L) Well, the triangle. And then, if you have a triangle point up you have 3, joined to a triangle pointing down, you have 3, and you have a 33. Is that something like what we are getting at here?

A: Yes.

Q: (L) Is there a connection between the number 33 and the Great Pyramid in Egypt?

A: Yes.

Q: (L) And what is that connection? Is it that the builders of the pyramid participated in this secret society activity?

A: Yes. And what symbol did you see in "Matrix", for Serpents and Grays?

Q: (L) You are talking about the triangle with the Serpent's head in it?
A: Yes.
Q: (L) Are we talking in terms of this 33 relating to a group of aliens, or a group of humans with advanced knowledge and abilities?
A: Either/or.
Q: (L) Is this what has been referred to in the Bramley book, as the Brotherhood of the Serpent or Snake?
A: Yes.
Q: (L) So, we have a bunch of people who are playing with mathematics, sacred geometry, and playing with higher knowledge, basically as a keep busy activity to distract them at the human level from the fact that they are being manipulated at a higher level. Is this what is going on? Or, do they consciously know what they are doing? Is it a distraction or a conscious choice?
A: Both.
Q: (L) If I were to name some names, could you identify if named individuals were involved in this secret group?
A: It would not be in your best interests.

Let me again make a note to some of our more "spooky" readers that the Cassiopaeans simply won't give answers to questions that it would be dangerous to know. So, y'all can get some rest now! Back to "Top Secret":

> To find the secret beneficiaries of greatest power, just take the backbone of key leaders in the non-appointed multi-generational custodial infrastructure of government and religious infrastructure. These are individual people in military intelligence, economic cartels and global Mafia, and secret religious security orders, though quite compartmentalized. Here you have a pretty good set of true candidates for who the actual "controlling elite" are. The very top of the pyramid in America is a group that is comprised partly of leading ex-Nazis and their next generation brethren, the multinational anti-alien global security apparatus who want to prevent alien invasion and world breakdown, so they themselves can pick at their oyster with traditional impunity. They will even ally themselves to certain aliens that can help them escape the intentions of other aliens, if necessary. Think Faust.

Better yet, think Machiavelli. Make people think that the enemy is over there or outside or at least not me, and you can plunder with impunity in the guise of being a savior.

> *The issue is conflict, conflict between secret elements that have come to different conclusions, created alliances, and instigated different strategies.* The most powerful rogue elements are unfortunately the most highly placed in the above-legal system. All

critical intelligence in the entire global ET-related intel gathering apparatus is diverted to these elements. Other less rogue elements almost as highly placed realize the Faustian bargain problem going on, and are attempting appropriate counterbalancing counterintelligence and seeding potentials for mass psych-ops operations that help. The two opposed parties are both in the need-to-know above-the-law rarified echelon levels.

Bad Rogues: engage social resistance processes, denial, and fight contact at all cost, except as useful for gaining alien technology for military use.

Good Rogues: engage social assimilation processes, tacit acceptance, and encourage human-alien awareness.

The bad rogue's strategies worked too well. So the good rogues are seeding selected human capital with staged deniable information disclosure to counterbalance. This is becoming increasingly hard data. The thresholds of social assimilation, and resistance to assimilation are being tested to keep things from going runaway. Pullback into fail-safe deniability is always included in any surreptitious disclosure program equation. The conflict generates a wide range of inconsistent activities on the part of the elite power circles, deriving from their opposing allegiances.

In the Nexus Seven diatribe, much is made of the seven echelons of Secret and Above Top Secret, and Above Top, Top Secret groups (and so on.) He/they attempt to define some of them as benevolent because they are the lesser of the evils in terms of their STS behaviors. I would like to suggest that it is not that there are good rogues, so much as there are simply circles within circles of the STS hierarchy, and that those at the lower levels simply are not sufficiently polarized to the STS pathway to be let in on the deeper secrets of negativity. They still have some STO potential, but it is being gradually purged from them by engaging them in the ongoing controls and deception. At some point, some of them may be faced with stupendous choices that will force their allegiances out into the open. But, that subject properly belongs to our coming ontological discussion, so we will leave it for now.

> The deeper essence of the conflict between a bunch of very macho intelligence folks is just the same age-old conflict continuing to be reflected. The God-based religions decimated or appropriated Goddess religion … There are competing celestial forces. Intelligent beings traveling in craft and between spaces even seem to somehow "live" in parallel space. These alien beings are assumed beyond the terrestrial worldliness. But yet some are quite physical. Some of these crafty critters claim divinity. They say if we hold persons A, B, or C in our history as divine, then that is saying these ET are divine too

– and they can prove it. They were there. They made it happen ... The authentic real McCoy [creator gods] may crash our image of what we held spirituality and God to be. We thought beyond biological, beyond physical, as religion had always assumed, [to be good and holy and loving.] The doctrine of the human soul, the holy trinity and Nature.

May 31, 1997

Q: (L) Cayce talks about the division in Atlantis between the Sons of One and the Sons of Belial. Was this a racial division or a philosophical/religious division?

A: It was the latter two, and before that, the former one.

Q: (L) When it was a racial division, which group was it?

A: *The Sons of Belial were the Kantekkians.*[15]

Q: (L) Well! That is not good!

A: Subjective ... you are not bodies; you are souls.

07-19-97

Q: (L) Now, from putting the information about religions together throughout the centuries, I am coming to a rather difficult realization that the whole monotheistic idea, which is obviously the basic concept of the Sons of the Law of One, is the most clever and devious and cunning means of control I have ever encountered in my life. No matter where it comes from, the religionists/priests say, "We have the one god, we are his agents, you pay us your money, and we'll tell him to be nice to you in the next world!"

A: Clever if one is deceived. Silly truffle if one is not.

Q: (L) Well, I know! But, uncovering this deception, this lie that the power is out there is unbelievable. So, the Kantekkians were the Sons of Belial, which is not a negative thing, necessarily. So the Sons of the Law of One was perverted to the monotheistic Judaism, which then was then transformed into the Christian religious myths, and has been an ongoing theme since Atlantean times.

A: Woven of those who portray the lights.

Q: (L) And that is always the way it has been. They appear as angels of light. And, essentially, everything in history has been rewritten by this group.

---

[15] According to the Cs, Kantek was the fifth planet of the solar system, destroyed over 80,000 years ago and leaving in its orbit what we now know as the asteroid belt. Its inhabitants were transported to Earth prior to the destruction using 4D technology. They "landed" in the Caucasus and surrounding areas, the cradle of the Caucasian/Aryan race. The many myths of tall Aryan types traveling around to places as far as India, China and South America, often with knowledge quite advanced in relation to the local populations, refer to this advanced racial group entering the world stage.

A: Under the influence of others. And whom do you suppose?
Q: (L) Well, the Orion STS.
A: Sending pillars of light and chariots of fire to deliver the message.

The curious thing is that if the original Kantekkians were the Goddess worshippers, then that means the purer Orion genetics belongs to that camp. Yet in the present day there are those who twist this in the most unbelievable ways to make it seem that the ancient Goddess religions were demonic and reptilian. Study of the ancient symbols will show that the oldest form of the Goddess worship was associated with stars, birds, vases, spirals and the partnership mode of society. It was only in the early stages of reptilian inversion that the Divine Son was introduced as heir to his murdered father, and displaced the feminine potentials. And, it is at precisely that point that the serpent image was introduced. But, again, that is a subject for ontology, not necessarily the practical issue of why there is so much in the way of lies and deception running rampant on the planet at the present time. Nexus Seven write:

> But if it's true more than one custodial alien civilization has returned, there may be a little crowding going on, and a lot of stuff coming through the cracks. ... If any Earthly catastrophe of human or natural geospheric or cosmic magnitude happens, then the playing field of general populace conscious permeability to alien contact becomes much, much lower, meaning, much more "Mommy, they're here, and they want more than milk and cookies! I'm scared."

Q: (L) In trying to picture this upcoming wave in my mind, this thing you call the Grand Cycle Transformation, the cycle moves out, in dispersion, begins to accrete and return to the source. It looks like a yin-yan toroid composed of infinite fibers of being, all at different points of the cycle individually and collectively. Is this a close approximation?
A: Close.
Q: (L) Is this representative of the fact that exactly half of all that exists, is moving into imbalance, while the other half is moving into balance at any given, excuse the term, "time"?
A: Close.
Q: (L) All the cosmos? All that exists?
A: Yes.
Q: (L) Is it possible that one area of the cosmos has more of the balance seeking energy while another has more of that which is seeking imbalance?
A: Oh yes!
Q: (L) Is the Earth one of those areas that is more imbalanced than balanced at the present time?

A: Yes, but rapidly moving back toward balance.

Q: (L) Is the realm border, or Wave, part of this balancing?

A: Yes.

Q: (L) Okay, speaking of the balancing of Earth. How can this be done? The "buckets of love and light" group say that it is going to be balanced because everyone is going to think nice thoughts, surround everything with light, see, hear and think only good and positive thoughts, and all of their buckets of love and light are going to eventually reach a critical mass and spill over onto all the rest of humanity and all of the negative things are going to be transformed into positive things. This is the standard version. Is this what you mean?

A: No.

Q: (L) Isn't the energy that is being manifested in the positive, in love and light on and around the planet, going to reduce the level of negativity in the beings existing on the planet?

A: This is not the point. *When "Earth" becomes a 4th density realm, all the forces, both STS and STO shall be in direct contact with one another ... It will be a "level playing field", thus, balanced.*

A curious thing about this Nexus Seven document is its mention of the Wave. After I had first shared some of the Wave ideas with some discussion groups and Val Valerian back in '94 and '95, I began to get some questions from various sources about some sort of Wave that was going to destroy the earth that was on its way. I tracked this information down at the time and discovered that it was originating with me! The only problem was that by the time it got back to me it had been so distorted and twisted that it was almost unrecognizable.

But then of course the Nexus Seven may have had access to the Cassiopaean passage on the "Convention" as quoted at the beginning of this segment, which was originally delivered in December of '94. From "Top Secret":

> Think about the coming wave, the coming convergence of diverse human and alien and cosmic influences. Who are the essential usurper players in the game? *Who in power has the most to lose in facing the prospect of a voluntary evolutionary uplift and paradigm change from Patriarchy to balance between [feminine and masculine forces]?* Who indeed. ... Here is the gum in the works: supposedly, divine beings, in religious terms, were always considered above the flesh, above the worldliness of physical impediment, above the limitations of a physical cosmos. And now they are not? They are slimy bugs, lizards and other Dr. Moreau morphs out of our animal kingdom, and they are the heavenly hosts, angels and Olympian man-gods of history and myth.

Hide this fact and throw away the key! This has driven many mad. If some intelligent and powerful men (in the realm of the power centers of the dollar, the soul and the sword), have been driven to drink and eventual psychosis over this, one can understand the fear of War of the Worlds mass hysteria. ... The line between psychotic belief and religious belief is thin, and mass psychosis is something that can really happen. Before Dr. Mack, and maybe even still after Dr. Mack, the American Psychiatric Association is more than ready to declare just about every maven related to the UFO, NWO, and religious conspiracy worlds as nuts. These mavens and contactee and abductee people are all victims of mass hysteria cults, brain disorders, or they are sociopathic predators or hate crime suspects, or people exhibiting dangerous forms of psychosis, promoting paranoia, schizophrenia, inciting mass hysteria, mass delusion, and other conditionally arrestable hate crime offenses for those rogues that get too close to the public trust.

In other words, if it could, in a well-structured world, the science establishment would consign all ET telepathic contact to insanity. There would be mandatory ordered drugging to "cure" people of having 'insane spiritual experiences' and of promoting insanity in the population at large. It is not pop culture anymore; it is a social hysteria response, a response system that must be stopped. But we haven't got laws like that yet ...

... Physical ET stakeholders being part of "divine" history is a difficult assimilation and will our institutions survive the full disclosure day? ... Now the institutions have discovered to their great dismay, that the divinities and deviltries of history are just readily and easily bypassing them. The last thing these institutions want humankind to generally believe is that ETs are the real heavenly masters of spiritual history. And in turn, *they don't wish to have the populace educated in knowing how to spot a false master when they see one.*

Who is the false master? The ETs that helped to create the Messiahs, or the human institutions that represent the Messianic divinities of history?

Now you can get an idea of how sticky the wicket gets. ... Since we even have to ask the question if the bug is nice or not, reveals our principal strategic vulnerability! We are unable to tell what some alien agendas are because we can't read the ET mind, and ET is not telling. These entities are deft at communicating and contacting us using advanced subconscious subliminal techniques, which for the most part seem harmless and sometimes even beneficial for the involved parties. But the larger unknown agenda can still spell invasion, and we are in an early phase – a covert alien incursion on a marginal scale.

... *But forces other than our conception of God are at work, heavenly hosts, both innocent and all too knowing, hosts friendly yet threatening, hosts alien and somehow all too familiar. We are being cultivated, and they do not want to spoil the broth.*

The question shall remain and always be debated, even if their presence seems to recede, "We, humanity, are being cultivated for what?" The simple idea is that sparks and fragments of God, called souls, invested in humanity, may be cultivated into something different and somehow beyond (not necessarily better than) their creators. The harvest rights to that bounty are probably the real endgame. If the harvest is indeed a misnomer by it being really a voluntary free will choosing kind of deal, then the human populace might benefit from a physical brochure and/or a psychic travel brochure or two.

Maybe free will with spiritual empowerment is more likely at its new beginning and we have a choice in the matter far more than meets the eye.

The coming wave has already happened negatively, as evidenced by the existence of many time travelers – future humans – coming from distant futures long after disaster had already happened. They had advanced enough to migrate their souls back to catch a different part of the big wave that is about to happen, still in our future, but almost upon us. The soul migration back from into the "past", our present, is to redirect the human "future" spiritual evolution from what futurally ostensibly happened. Therefore the present "real future" is engaged in counter-phasing itself into a better outcome. Humanity is hitchhiking back into human genetics and our current time registration to catch a new direction on the coming wave. Cosmic surf's up!

... *The coming resonance wave in the next decade* is in many ways, hyper-dimensional and beyond our current ability to comprehend. To some need-to-know ARC elements, this smacks of hyperdimensional invasion, yet to other need-to-know ARC elements it is the chance for apotheosis. The question is, is it a false or genuine apotheosis? Is it spiritual liberation or entrapment?

... Could it be the soul substance we were endowed with is meant to develop new evolutionary factors for the universe? Is the grander plan one of humanity ultimately spreading out amongst the stars, seeding it's consciousness and propensity to cause change, something most ultra-stable ET civilizations are rather afraid of, and few are welcoming? Does humanity have the right stuff?

Some humans and aliens believe we do not and should be just used and herded as a hyper-dimensional power base commodity. Some humans and aliens believe humanity does have the right stuff to break free of their bonds and survive, but will take a long time getting it right. Do we repeat future bad history currently on schedule or do we phase tunnel into a new future history?

Does the snake eat its tail, where the Omega is game over and starts over as the Alpha once again, or do we graduate to a new level

Alpha, beyond the historical pattern loop? The loop is the harvest being plowed under. Can Ouroboros stop eating its tail and move into the next spiral position of evolution? If it happens well and goes positively, the loop will be broken and the new unpredicted, virgin future will occur. In that future, certain negative power enclaves do not survive, being obsolesced by spiritual evolution in humanity. If it goes negatively, again, the loop will stay locked, and the ancient future will happen again.

August 9, 1997

A: Here is something for you to digest: Why is it that your scientists have overlooked the obvious when they insist that alien beings cannot travel to earth from a distant system???

Q: (L) And what is this obvious thing?

A: Even if speed of light travel, or "faster", were not possible, and it is, of course, there is no reason why an alien race could not construct a space "ark", living for many generations on it. They could travel great distances through time and space, looking for a suitable world for conquest. Upon finding such, they could then install this ark in a distant orbit, build bases upon various solid planes in that solar system, and proceed to patiently manipulate the chosen civilizations to develop a suitable technological infrastructure. And then, after the instituting of a long, slow, and grand mind programming project, simply step in and take it over once the situation was suitable.

Q: (L) Is this, in fact, what has happened, or is happening?

A: It could well be, and maybe now it is the time for you to learn about the details.

Q: (L) Well, would such a race be third or fourth density in orientation?

A: Why not elements of both?

Q: (L) What is the most likely place that such a race would have originated from?

A: Oh, maybe Orion, for example?

Q: (L) Okay. If such a race did, in fact, travel to this location in space-time, how many generations have come and gone on their space ark during this period of travel, assuming, of course, that such a thing has happened?

A: Maybe 12.

Q: (L) Okay, that implies that they have rather extended life spans ...

A: Yes ...

Q: (L) Assuming this to be the case, what are their life spans?

A: 2,000 of your years.

Q: (L) Okay, assuming such a bunch have traveled ...

A: When in space, that is ...

Q: (L) And what is the span when on terra firma?

A: 800 years.

Q: (L) Well, has it not occurred to them that staying in space might not be better?

A: No. Planets are much more "comfortable".

Q: (L) Okay ... imagining that such a group has traveled here ...

A: We told you of upcoming conflicts ... Maybe we meant the same as your Bible, and other references. Speak of ... The "final" battle between "good and evil ..." Sounds a bit cosmic, when you think of it, does it not?

Q: (L) Does this mean that there is more than one group that has traveled here in their space arks?

A: Could well be another approaching, as well as "reinforcements" for either/or, as well as non-involved, but interested observers of various types who appreciate history from the sidelines.

Q: (L) Well, swell! There goes my peaceful life!

A: You never had one!

Q: (L) Well, I was planning on one!

A: You chose to be incarnated now, with some foreknowledge of what was to come. Reference your dreams of space attack.

Q: (L) Okay, what racial types are we talking about relating to these hypothetical aliens?

A: Three basic constructs. Nordic, Reptilian, and Grays. Many variations of type 3, and 3 variations of type 1 and 2.

Q: (L) Well, what racial types are the good guys?

A: Nordics, in affiliation with 6th density "guides".

Q: (L) And that's the only good guys?

A: That's all you need.

Q: (L) Wonderful! So, if it is a Grey or Lizzie, you know they aren't the nice guys. But, if it is tall and blond, you need to ask questions!

A: All is subjective when it comes to nice and not nice. Some on 2nd density would think of you as "not nice", to say the least!!!

Q: (L) That's for sure! Especially the roaches! Maybe we ought to get in touch with some of these good guys ...

A: When the "time" is right.

Q: (L) Now, there is a lot being said about the sightings out in the Southwest area. They are saying that this is the new imminent invasion or mass landing. Can you comment on this activity?

A: Prelude to the biggest "flap" ever.

Q: (L) And where will this flap be located?

A: Earth.

Q: (L) When is it going to begin?

A: Starting already.

Q: (L) Is this biggest flap going to be just a flap, or is it going to be an invasion?

A: Not yet an invasion. Invasion happens when programming is complete ...

Q: (L) What programming?

A: See Bible, Lucid book, Matrix material, Bringers of the Dawn, and many other sources, then cross reference ...

Q: (L) Well, if something is fairly imminent, we are not going to have time to do all the things you have suggested that we do!

A: Yes you will, most likely.

Q: (L) Well, we are supposed to do a lot of things here ... This just sort of takes the heart right out of me!

A: Not so!

Q: (L) Well, are we going to have time to do all these things?

A: All these things were suggested for this reason, among others.

Q: (L) So, all the things you have suggested are to get us ready for this event?

A: Yes.

Q: (L) Well, we better get moving! We don't have time to mess around!

A: You will proceed as needed; you cannot force these events or alter the Grand Destiny.

Q: (L) I do not like the sound of that! I want to go home!

A: The alternative is less appetizing.

Q: (L) Sure! I don't want to be lunch!

A: Reincarnation on a 3rd density earth as a "cave person" amidst rubble and a glowing red sky, as the perpetual cold wind whistles ...

Q: (L) Why is the sky glowing red?

A: Contemplate.

Q: (L) Of course! Comet dust! Sure, everybody knows that! Wonderful!

The important remark above is that there *is* a "Grand Destiny" that includes certain preparations for a cosmic "battle between good and evil." Further that, not getting ready for this event, going home early or avoiding the issues would lead to a less appetizing result, i.e., reincarnation on a planet that has suffered mass destruction. Not only that, but one of the reasons for setting up the pieces on the board has a far more insidious intent:

January 11, 1997

Q: (L) We once talked about the fact that significant, conscious choices made at certain junctures in one's life, can literally create a new, or branching universe. Later, I had an idea that when we think with awareness, meditate and make conscious STO choices, then more universes are created along this path, than along the STS pathways, so that you're balancing the mindless, thoughtless, just-choosing-because-you-don't-know-any-better universes ... (T) Well, isn't that what the lizards are doing? (L) Yes, it is ... (T) They're manipulating it to make negative. But, they can never make more than there is – more negative than positive – because the universe is constantly seeking balance. So, every place they make a negative branch, there's some place else that becomes a positive. You can never make more. You can try.

A: True.

Q: (T) Although, they're working on the false premise that they can do this. (L) Wishful thinking.

A: No, they are working on that false premise that they can seal realms into "4th" density and 3rd, 2nd, 1st STS for eternity.

Q: (L) They want to seal all of creation into physicality?

A: No, not physicality through all densities, just 4th through 1st density STS.

Q: (L) Oh! (T) They don't care if it's physical or not. They're in fourth. They just want to seal them off and keep them STS to feed off of them.

A: "Eternity" is the key word there. It is where the wishful thinking comes into play.

October 22, 1994

A: ... Now, as you advance to the fourth level of density which is coming up for you, you must now make a choice as to whether to progress to Service-to-Others or to remain at the level of Service-to-Self. This will be the decision which will take quite some time for you to adjust to. This is what is referred to as the "thousand year period". This is the period as measured in your calendar terms that will determine whether or not you will advance to Service-to-Others or remain at the level of Service-to-Self.

And those who are described as the Lizards have chosen to firmly lock themselves into Service-to-Self. And, since they are at the highest level of density where this is possible, they must continually draw large amounts of negative energy from those at the third level, second level, and so on, which is why they do what they do. This also explains why their race is dying, because they have not been able to learn for themselves how to remove themselves from this particular form of expression to that of Service-to-Others.

And, since they have such, as you would measure it, a long period of time, remained at this level and, in fact, become firmly entrenched in it, and, in fact, have increased themselves in it, this is why they are dying and desperately trying to take as much energy from you as possible and also to recreate their race metabolically.

Q: (L) Well, if we are sources of food and labor for them, why don't they just breed us in pens on their own planet?

A: They do.

Q: (L) Well, since there is so many of us here, why don't they just move in and take over?

A: *That is their intention. That has been their intention for quite some time. They have been traveling back and forth through time as you know it, to set things up so that they can absorb a maximum amount of negative energy with the transference from third level to fourth level that this planet is going to experience, in the hopes that they can overtake you on the fourth level and thereby accomplish several things:*

1. Retaining their race as a viable species

2. Increasing their numbers

3. Increasing their power

4. Expanding their race throughout the realm of fourth density.

To do all of this they have been interfering with events for what you would measure on your calendar as approximately 74 thousand years. And they have been doing so in a completely still state of space-time traveling backward and forward at will during this work. Interestingly enough, though, all of this will fail.

Q: (L) How can you be so sure it will fail?

A: Because we see it. We are able to see all, not just what we want to see. Their failing is that they see only what they want to see. In other words, it's the highest manifestation possible of that which you would refer to as wishful thinking. And, wishful thinking represented on the fourth level of density becomes reality for that level. You know how you wishfully think? Well, it isn't quite reality for you because you are on the third level, but if you are on the fourth level and you were to perform the same function, it would indeed be your awareness of reality. Therefore they cannot see what we can see since we serve others as opposed to self, and since we are on sixth level, we can see all that is at all points as is, not as we would want it to be.

July 31, 1997

Q: (L) Now, a reader asks: "The Cassiopaeans have said that there are 16 groups of good guys and 16 groups of bad guys. Have they ever mentioned the names of any?"

A: Excuse us?

Q: (L) Well, they want you to name the different groups since you did make this remark at one point. Are you going to give a list of the participants on each side?

A: No, we are not.

Q: (L) So this is one of the things we have to learn to figure out ourselves.

A: Yes.

The reader may note that there are endless sources that name names in terms of who are the good guys and who are the bad guys. If you stop and think about this and the nature of free will, you will immediately realize that such sources, even if they are telling you the truth, have deprived you of your free will. And it seems that everything is about free will. But, again, we are getting ahead of ourselves; so let's leave that for the moment.

July 31, 1999

Q: (L) Here is another question from a reader who wants to know if there is a possibility that the effects of the Wave are reflected in physiological phenomena, such as elevation in blood pressure and other things?

A: In some cases.

Q: (L) Okay, L & E sent a question. A correspondent wrote to them as follows: "L, I am getting some strange reports about the Pacific UFO. What have you heard? One thing, there is more and more effort being put into finding it or getting it, or however you put it. If you will look into it, the Navy has just launched a deep-sea rescue submersible and they announced that they are going to test it in the Pacific. Another thing, ASTAT announced about a week ago, maybe two, that there is an unidentified sonic source from the deep Pacific." So, L added: "It appears to me that the Lizzies are constructing an underwater base in anticipation of the arrival of more than 36 million Lizards due to arrive soon. Could this be so?"

A: The problem with these questions is that they attempt to construct the beginning at the middle: presumptuous!! If one truly wishes to learn, one must be open to all possibilities.

Q: (L) Okay, I guess that you are saying that there is some assuming going on here. So, let me ask this: are there 36 million Lizards on their way here?

A: The Lizard beings occupy 4th density.

Q: (L) Are you saying that because they occupy fourth density, they don't have to *come* here because they *are* here?

A: Close.

Q: (L) Now, you have told us that there are 36 million Nephilim on the way.

A: Nephilim are 3rd density. Big difference.

Q: (L) So, the third-density Nephilim have to utilize some physical means of travel, even if it does include warping space-time, but the Lizards and other fourth-density beings have no such constraints. Is an underwater base being constructed in the Pacific in anticipation of something?

A: No need to construct that which already exists.

Q: (L) Is there any truth to the idea that the U.S. Navy is trying to find or get something out in the Pacific?

A: Maybe, but all governmental stuff is compartmentalized, so it is pointless.

Q: (L) Okay, he also writes: "the photon belt energy is almost upon us according to our channels." I guess he means the wave energy, or the interpretation of this according to these various channels. Is a "photon belt" or wave energy almost upon us?

A: Laura, you know how to deal with this.

Q: (L) I know. This purported photon belt has been "almost upon us" so many times that it is becoming boring. Now, you told us that the Montauk experiment was something that began in the 1920s. All of the stories say that the Navy was trying to make ships invisible to radar for defensive purposes. That's the story. My question is: is that just a cover story?

A: No.

Q: (L) Is that, in fact, what they were attempting to do?

A: Close.

Q: (L) Can you get me any closer to it? What were their intentions?

A: Convergence of interests: US Navy, Secret Government, Esteemed physicists.

Q: (L) Did they actually, even accidentally, discover through this work something about time travel?

A: Yes, but it was more an accident for the Navy than for others involved.

Q: (L) Okay, was the accident and following fiasco fairly accurately represented in the various books about it?

A: Fairly.

Q: (L) After all of this, did they bring the project to a halt, even if only temporarily?

A: No.

Q: (L) Did they decide that, "Oh, we have discovered something really fantastic; let's see what we can do with it?"

A: Closer.

Q: (L) Did this actually take place at Montauk?

A: Some.

Q: (L) Were Russians and/or Germans working on similar projects at the same time, or even a little later?

A: Germans earlier, Russians later.

Q: (L) Are the efforts of the Germans, Russians, and the Americans combined at the present time?

A: At some levels they are combined, yes.

Q: (L) Would you be able to evaluate the efforts of the three and say which one, at the present time, is the most advanced?

A: Does not work that way.

Q: (L) Why does it not work that way?

A: Advanced goes to Consortium.

Q: (L) Are you saying that when work of this kind gets to a certain level, it gets absorbed into the Consortium?

A: Close.

Q: (L) Back to Montauk: the Montauk project continued. Did they ever, at any point in time, produce monsters as some of these stories I have heard relate?

A: Maybe.

Q: (L) Was this a result of opening portals between densities or dimensions and having cross-density window fallers dropping in, so to speak?

A: Partly.

Q: (L) Were any of these supposed monsters that they were supposed to have created, productions or creations of their minds?

A: Other densities afford a degree of one and the same thing.

Q: (L) Okay. You previously have said that the HAARP project is a continuation of the Montauk project.

A: Partly. You must remember compartments.

Q: (L) So, the right hand often doesn't know what the left is doing. You also once said that the HAARP project was partly operational. Are some of these wildly extravagant shootings of recent times, or people going off the deep end, a result of some of the HAARP experimentation in mind control, or testing?

A: This is a result of many forces.

Q: (L) Is Montauk connected in any way with this Alternative Three idea of transferring groups or perimeters in the event of a cataclysm or disaster?

A: Too complex, but be careful of what you read. Disinformation. This is most of what you hear and read.

Q: (A) Okay, you have mentioned the Navy and the physicists, and then there were these people who simply were producing monsters, which does not seem to be anything that the Navy would want to do, much less physicists!

A: You are confusing subjects and time frames.

Q: (A) Somebody had to plan this experiment, yes?

A: But that was the Philadelphia Experiment.

Q: (L) How did this business of producing monsters and all that even come into this project?

A: Experiments in mind programming and psy-warfare.

Q: (L) So, these were separate experiments. But, did they fall under the Montauk project ...

A: Yes. But the monsters were long after the Eldridge.

Q: (L) When did the experiments with the monsters occur?
A: Late 70s.
Q: (L) Have they continued on with this monster producing business?
A: No need to get hung up on "monsters". There were other materializations. Not just monsters.
Q: (L) What other kinds of materializations did they have?
A: You name it!
Q: (L) Were they able to materialize money for themselves?
A: No need.
Q: (L) Were they able to materialize people from the past or the future?
A: Temporarily.
Q: (L) Did they, in fact, do this?
A: Yes.
Q: (L) Did they ask people from the future what kinds of events have occurred between then and now in order to refine their plans and activities?
A: No such.
Q: (L) Why?
A: Variable futures.
Q: (L) So, they could materialize somebody from the future, but it was only as potential, or probable future, so therefore, it meant very little, or was useless?
A: One of 329 decillion.
Q: (L) Probable futures?
A: Yes. Up to a point ...
Q: (L) Could they select whom they materialized, or was it random?
A: The materialization was really a duality. Review texts re: abductions between densities for idea.
Q: (L) Could it be possible that, using this technology, the U.S. Government, or secret government, has been doing abductions on human beings that the victims think is an alien abduction?
A: Maybe in some cases, but the technology is not comparable.
Q: (L) Other than people from the past and future, what other kinds of things did they materialize in the Montauk experiments? What kinds of things were they interested in materializing more than anything else? (A) Probably technological devices. (L) Did they materialize technology from the future?
A: This is more complex than your questions indicate.
Q: (L) I realize this. I am struggling with this whole idea. When they were doing this materializing, did they not have direct intent? Were they just experimenting to see what would materialize at various settings?
A: Their knowledge brought them to a level different than your current imaginings.

Q: (L) Well, help me out here! What do you mean?

A: No use comparing apples to oranges.

Q: (L) At any point did their knowledge and materializations incline them toward benevolent acts and tendencies regarding the rest of the human population?

A: This is not working because you are thinking one way and they do not.

Q: (L) Can you give me a word or two that will clue me as to how to change my thinking?

A: Sure. Try to explain calculus to a kindergartner!!

Q: (L) You are saying that this Consortium, these Montauk folks, have a level of knowledge, and a way of thinking, that makes my thinking, and our thinking, seem like ...

A: Poppycock.

Q: (L) My thinking is poppycock relative to theirs?

A: Close.

Q: (A) But this is only because we do not have this knowledge!

A: Right!!!!

Q: (L) And we are trying to get it!

A: You cannot get it without an enormous amount of patience! These experiments have been conducted over a time period you would recognize as about 93 years and have involved thousands of humans and a few hundred NHIs (Non-Human Intelligences).

Q: (L) Are the people involved in these experiments STS or STO?

A: All "people" are STS.

Q: (L) Well, the people who are working in the direction of STO, what chance do they have of access to this knowledge?

A: They do not need it.

Q: (L) Why don't they need it?

A: They will have it when the elevator reaches "floor number 4".

Q: (L) Are you saying that it is not essential for us to struggle to know these things to that level because it will come naturally because we are linked in a network?

A: Close.

Q: (L) Well, gosh! You had me worried there! So, these guys are working and digging for knowledge to control others?

A: Close.

Q: (L) Are they trying to develop technology to lock the planet into third density so that it won't go to fourth density?

A: Some may be.

Q: (L) Do they see the moving to fourth density as a threat to their plans and projects?

A: Perhaps.

Q: (A) I believe that there is a lot of this knowledge that would be useful for me to know before I go to fourth density, assuming I will go. I mean, knowledge is knowledge, and I am sure I would make good use of this. Why did you say that this knowledge is not needed for us?
A: We did not say that. You are misreading what we said!!!! Your line of questioning bespoke a level of knowledge not on the same level as those directly engaged in the vast experimentation, which in part, was conducted at Montauk. If you were to review the transcripts extensively, you would find that you possess much more knowledge on this sort of thing than you apparently have remembered for tonight's session. You have put forth so much energy toward building the website that you have drained some of your conscious recall ability for the moment. And no, we are not criticizing your efforts; we applaud them!!! But, you could use a thoughtful, meditative review!

Well, it is indeed true that I could use a long rest, but as long as there are questions being asked of me, I will attempt to share what little I have managed to experience over the past 40 some years, and there are other more pressing questions to which we must proceed. So, in closing, let us just deal with one last bit of possible disinformation:

August 5, 2000
Q: (L) In this Nexus Seven document it says: "What is the final ontological matrix of hidden truth? What elucidates all the aspects of the true-to-life UFO phantasm in our past, present and future? What are the critical goals of Echelon beyond information suppression and technological catch-up? What are the hyper-intelligence focal points for the future? The sun, our sun, is dying, and too soon. This was caused by regional dimensional vortex shutdown some 90,000 years ago. Solar instability can cause much life on Earth to be unsustainable in 40 years. Ancient astro-theology calendars all end around now. There are also dangerous interplanetary bodies, with civilization threatening capability due to cause more serious damage to Earth in another 150 years. One way or the other we are slated to leave Earth, sooner or later, or else. This is a prevailing secret truth. Those in control would rather save themselves and a few elite than worry about the whole of mankind, despite the presence of a few well meaning but deluded true human patriots amongst the bunch."
Is, in fact, our sun dying?
A: Yes, and so is everything else.
Q: (L) Is it going to do it in 40 years?
A: You do not understand our attempted allusion. What is not dying?
Q: (L) Well, I know that, but they are saying that our sun is dying too soon.
A: No. What is "too soon"?

Q: (L) Well ... (A) Forty years is certainly too soon!
A: Why?
Q: (A) Because scientists would normally give the sun much longer ...
A: But do "scientists" really know?!?
Q: (L) You are not helping here! Are you saying this guy is right?
A: Be patient, Laura, this is a lesson.
Q: (A) Well, no, scientists don't really know; but they conjecture.
A: Ah hah! Conjecture!
Q: (L) So, what's your point?
A: Our point is: what is too soon and why?
Q: (L) Too soon would be ... well, I guess that in completely objective terms, there is no such thing as too soon. When things happen, it is exactly the right time for it to happen. When something happens, everything is perfect.
A: Okay.
Q: (L) So, in the deepest sense, nothing is ever too soon ... however ... (C) What situations would have to be in place for this to happen within forty years?
A: There are unlimited numbers of situations ... Some of those possibilities are always present, especially when combined with multitudinal external factors.
Q: (L) What would the external factors be?
A: Energies, or cosmic forces present in space at various locators, which the sun would pass through in its journey through space, for one example.
Q: (L) Are we slated to pass through any of those energies or forces?
A: Wait and see.
Q: (L) Well, let me ask the next question on that subject. Does any of this have to do with dimensional vortices that were shut down 90 thousand years ago in the area of Sirius?
A: We are interested in knowing the "dimensional shutdown of vortex process." Could you explain, please?
Q: (L) Well, no. I don't think anyone else could either. It's just a term here. Is there such a thing as a dimensional vortex?
A: Semantics.
Q: (L) What would you call a dimensional vortex?
A: Once again, this is not flowing because you are navigating haphazardly through subjective proclamations.
Q: (L) So, you are saying that all of this analysis of what the deep ontological truths are is just subjective proclamations. Was there ever something that happened that might have been perceived by the person who wrote this material, as a dimensional vortex shutdown 90 thousand years ago?

A: What is that?!?

Q: (L) So, basically, you are trying to point out that there is no such thing as a dimensional vortex shutdown. But, you have said that the planet Kantek exploded between 70 and 80 thousand years ago, right?

A: If so, that is not what the writer is attempting to portray.

Q: (L) Could it have been a supernova?

A: Look here! This is pointless.

Q: (L) So, all of this stuff is nonsense? I am really missing the point here. Okay. What I am getting from what you are and are not saying, is that this person is clearly trying to portray something, and that there *is* something behind what he is saying, but I am just too dense to figure out the right question so you can download the answer.

A: Dense? No my dear! You are just learning, as are we all.

Q: (L) Now, I did have a thought that this 90-thousand-year cycle could be the period of the companion brown star you have said is on it's way into the solar system. Is that what they might be talking about?

A: Closer.

Q: (L) So, what they are really talking about, or may have seen in some way, is the companion star, rather than the death of our own sun. (A) Let me just ask a simple question. Can you estimate the likelihood that the sun will die in 40 years?

A: That is unlikely.

Q: (L) Well, what a relief! (A) We are done! How unlikely?

A: There is one chance in 189 million.

I think I will go and buy some lottery tickets. I have a really good chance of winning – one in thirteen million!

July 22, 2000

Q: (I) I was writing something in my journal about supernovae being steps toward the Big Bang, in the sense that each supernova represents a reflection of ourselves.

A: *In a more physiological sense, supernovae present cosmic energies, which "up the ante" of awareness, when one is in close enough proximity.*

Q: (I) Now, this supernova that happened in fairly recent times – the Cassiopia A supernova of 1658, or thereabouts – does that have anything to do with our awareness thing going on right now?

A: It has some to do with this conduit.

Q: (I) I had that feeling. I went back and read *Supernovae, Vehicle of Ascension?*[16] Did whatever happen with that supernova, is it affecting us?

---

[16] Laura Knight-Jadczyk, "Supernovae, Vehicle of Ascension?" November 29, 1999, (http://www.cassiopaea.org/cass/supernovae.htm).

A: The more interesting question would be, what about the NEXT supernova?!?

Q: (I) There is one coming up, and that's going to be the Wave? Or ...

A: No, no, no. No anticipation, please.

Q: (L) Well, that's pretty hard when you said "what about the *next* one"!

A: Reflection, yes, but anticipation? No!

In short, in terms of the practicalities of our 3D prison, we have learned that the ETs apparently visiting our planet are actually 4D STS beings. They have been interacting with humanity for its entire recorded existence, tending to humanity as a cattle farmer tends to his herd. They want to lock 1D to 3D in place so as to secure a permanent physical living space and feeding ground. Some are preparing new bodies in which to incarnate in 3D, and in the case that they are unable to lock humanity at this level, they prepare to control us in 4D, thereby increasing their numbers and power.

They have been interacting with a select human consortium for millennia, the human component of the Control System. In short, some humans have always known the alien agenda, and have actively collaborated toward it. They have steered world events to desired ends not in the interest of humanity at large, and they are connected with groups such as the Freemasons, Rosicrucians, Illuminati, etc. though it is clear that they work very much through mainstream religions in their efforts to keep humanity deaf, dumb and blind. Aware of some of the possibilities facing our future, they plan to escape, or have been promised safety by their 4D masters, leaving the rest of us to our fate. In order to keep control, they must keep the public from learning the truth about ETs at all costs. But, given the nature of secrecy and compartmentalization, there are some who wish to let the truth out, and this has been done through controlled leaks of information with plausible deniability. The humans in league with 4D STS have an array of technologies for mind control and disinformation at their disposal.

CHAPTER 23
LUCIFER AND THE POT OF GOLD
OR
THE QUEST FOR THE HOLY GRAIL OF NO ANTICIPATION

We are still asking "why?" We have peeled the onion, layer by layer, and have come to the center and found nothing there. Or, is that altogether true? It may take a little time to put the puzzle back together, and I hope the reader will bear with me because it would be completely useless for me to give the answer in twenty-five words or less. Following the trail of clues, however, will provide many opportunities for comparison, for assimilation, and for points of further investigation.

We know that this question of why is one that we don't like to face, but when we awaken late at night, alone in our thoughts, with no distractions of daily life to fill the void, we are face to face with our existential dilemma. And it is a terrible silence. In those moments of cold clarity, the bleakness and futility of our existence in cosmic terms rises up to confront us as it has confronted all of humanity throughout millennia.

We have seen that, to escape this monstrous dark night of the soul we will accept any answer that may be offered because the cold, abyssal silence that follows the question must be filled at any cost. And the sad fact is there are plenty of people willing to try to convince us that they have the answer to all our questions. But these answers generally consist of confusing the discernment of reality with personal opinion, which results in a judgment upon reality by refusing to acknowledge it. And we have seen that those parts of reality which are refused or judged as wrong or evil have a way of manifesting in our face, demanding to be witnessed.

On the one hand, we have the Cassiopaeans telling us that the conditions of our reality are exactly like what Gurdjieff spoke about in the Tale of the Magician that we recounted in book 1. We have found similar witnesses to this version of the great question in very ancient traditions such as Sufism, Gnosticism, and perhaps even

Catharism, as well as the more contemporary treatments such as the writings of Carlos Castaneda.

On the other hand we have the myriad imaginary beliefs of humankind. These beliefs are dearly held, as we can see by this note from one of our readers:

> Dear friends Laura & Ark
>
> I have read many of your C messages, the final feeling is always a sad tone of despair. Finally, I begin to question how can be gathered so many misfortunes on a little planet like earth if the universe is so big? ... All the message of Cs is of the same: we are damned whatever we can do. However please think: the human race is far better than all those beings from 6D, 4D and all others dimensions, if we can have Mozart, Bach; Music and poets, mothers that care for their children and loving fathers. We are far better than all these silly things. Believe me, they are trying to confound you, and with a message as of the good guys, some truth with many lies between, and at the end we are all damned. Do not waste your time and your soul.

Whenever I receive correspondence of this sort, I do not just automatically reject it as something from someone who is not getting it. I always use it as an opportunity to reexamine everything I think in order to discover if, by some chance, they could be absolutely right and I could be wrong, and the Cassiopaean information could be just another in an endless series of disinformation campaigns designed to get humanity under the control of some dark forces by the act of making them believe in them.

In the first part of the last volume, we discussed how information could be corrupted by the biases of the receiver or ignorance of the source, even if that source is discarnate. But, we still need to deal with the deeper question suggested above. How do we do this?

As the reader probably knows by now, we don't just take everything the Cassiopaeans say as truth without a lot of checking and crosschecking and experimentation. We don't now, nor did we ever, take it as true believer material. It sure is interesting because of the many areas that have independent corroboration, but some of it is by its very nature unverifiable.

As I have already written, there are many things we have learned, and not just from being informed, but also by having a suggestion given to us, which we then observed, experimented with, and developed more fully on our own. This is one of the keys to the Cassiopaeans: they don't just hand it out. As I have noted before, they give clues, but not road maps. Their position is that if we don't do something, work for it as it were, it is useless like candy: empty calories. Clearly, this approach is designed to make the practice of channeling unnecessary and obsolete. We will eventually become them. Repeatedly they tell us that leading us by the hand is detrimental; they have laid the groundwork, given us the boost because we asked (and did so repeatedly, consistently, and with dedication for over two years before the contact initiated), but that the real purpose is to get us to learn to walk on our own, aware, protected and free of fear and ignorance. Hopefully, I will be able to convey this to the reader as well. It has taken many words and hundreds of pages to get us to this point, to the moment where we ask the question, and I would like to devote an equal amount of space to building the foundation for the answer.

> A: Subtle answers that require effort to dissect promote intensified learning. Learning is an exploration followed by the affirmation of knowing through discovery. Learning is necessary for progress of soul ... this is how you are building your power center ... Patience serves the questor of hidden knowledge ... Search your "files". ... Learning is sometimes best accomplished by study and exploration ... There are other clues that you can discover by your own study ...

This is going to become an important point, this building your power center, so hang on to that idea.

Getting back to our reader who suggests that the Cassiopaeans are "trying to confound you, and with a message as of the good guys, some truth with many lies between ... All the message of Cs is of the same: we are damned whatever we can do".

It is a logical inconsistency to teach awareness and defense against dark forces as a means of fostering control by these very same forces. This issue has been brought up many times in the past, the most significant treatment of it being expounded by Jesus:

> Then a blind and dumb man, under the power of a demon, was brought to Jesus, and He cured him, so that the blind and dumb man both spoke and saw. ... But the Pharisees hearing it said, 'This Man drives out demons only by and with the help of Beelzebub, the prince of demons'. And knowing their thoughts, He said to them, "Any kingdom that is divided against itself is being brought to desolation and laid waste, and no city or house divided against itself will last or continue to stand. And if Satan drives out Satan, he has become divided against himself and disunited; how then will his kingdom last or continue to stand? And if I drive out the demons by Beelzebub by whose help do your sons drive them out? ... Or how can a person go into a strong man's house and carry off his goods without first binding the strong man? Then indeed he may plunder his house. ... Either make the tree sound, and its fruit sound, or make the tree rotten and its fruit rotten; for *the tree is known and recognized and judged by its fruit.*" (Matthew 12:22-33, Amplified, Zondervan)

Curiously, the effect of the demons was the condition of being blind and dumb. The analogy also included the idea of a strong man being bound up so that a thief could come in and plunder his possessions, which is pretty much what we are finding to be the case. But, the main point was the issue of the Kingdom of Satan being brought to waste and desolation by division. "If Satan drives out Satan, he has become divided against himself and disunited: how then will his kingdom last or continue to stand?" Jesus was pointing out to the Pharisees that it was completely illogical to accuse him (Jesus) of working in concert with darkness since the effect of his work was to free the man of his demonic attack, which enabled the man to both see and speak.

In actual fact, the greatest deception of all is the teaching that there are no real negative forces. And if there are, we needn't worry about them because if we just think nice thoughts, meditate regularly, and use our warm and fuzzy affirmations, nothing icky will ever enter our reality.

I can assure you that evil insinuates itself into our lives in the guise of goodness and truth. The difficulty in talking about evil nowadays lies not in the weird or bizarre, but rather from the insistence by our culture that religious views of good and evil are outdated. The New Age teaching that evil simply does not exist unless an individual creates it in their reality further exacerbates the problem. This is an important point because the process of evil follows the line of erosion of our spirituality through the erosion of knowledge. What better way to protect evil activities than to deny that they exist? The fact is, the "selves" who create evil and wish to perpetuate it are those at higher density levels and against whom we have no defense *except through knowledge of who they are and how they work.* We must learn about the lies in order to perceive the truth.

There are those who speak of fallen angels who have become the minions of Satan. However, many ancient teachings describe this attitude, this essence of evil, as existing from the beginning. This implies there has always been a pathway of darkness or Service-to-Self since the instant of creation. This means that on one side of the coin, loving all others as the mode of loving God and self exists; and on the other, the opposing philosophy of loving oneself as God and manipulating others to perpetuate this love of self is equally valid. It might even be said that without this tension of opposition, nothing could or would exist.

If we remove the terms light and dark or good and evil, we are left with the clinical terms positive and negative polarities. But even here, we have a judgment that may not be appropriate. Nevertheless, using these words as a convention, we can observe that there is a pinnacle of negative polarity and there are those entities from many realms who follow this pathway. We must understand that it *is* a path. It has validity in the realm of creation. If it were intended to be destroyed, could not God ease all our problems and reach out and return this energy to himself?

There are those who believe that putting one's attention on these ideas gives them energy. This is true only if one focuses in this way with the intention of participation, even if vicariously. However, *a comprehensive understanding of these forces is absolutely necessary in order to know how to give them less energy.*

"The only thing necessary for the triumph of evil is for good men to do nothing."

But, what should good men do? What are we supposed to derive or understand about the Cosmos from all the Cassiopaeans have told us? Clearly, they are not going to give us all the answers on a silver platter; we have to figure it out! I am working on it and these pages are the result.

I am not saying that my interpretation or understanding of any of it is in any way final or absolute. And, with new information, some of my ideas may change. But for now, I am sharing what I think I have learned. If it finds resonance in the reader, if it provides a platform for his or her experiments or seeking, then it has served its purpose.

The Cassiopaeans have said that one should not "act against" the forces of darkness, but that rather one should "act *for*" one's own destiny. In a very practical sense this can even include physically extricating oneself from any number of unpleasant situations, even with force if necessary. If someone is trying to kill you or someone you love, and it is your perception of your destiny, or you feel it is your responsibility to prevent that, then it is entirely within the parameters of acting for one's own destiny to do whatever is necessary to save your life or the lives of others.

But, we are talking about this in many further subtle ways. How can one act *for* one's own destiny if one has been deceived and hypnotized to think that what is good is actually evil or vice versa? And, it is not always that simple. The analogy of the Evil Magician and his flock suggests to us that, in a certain sense, the flock is being cared for. But this care has an objective: occasionally the Evil Magician comes and takes one or more of the flock for its "flesh and skin".

We can certainly see that there seems to be a certain amount of "care" manifested for humanity by some of these forces and beings that have been proposed or identified throughout the ages. But there are certain issues about this that we need to consider with cold logic. We have the ancient legends of the Fish Gods and the Dragon cultures, the Serpent Gods and the Sumerian Annunaki and so forth, all identified as civilizing influences on humanity. But, as we have already discussed, these benefits may have a different agenda than just to assist humankind.

> Q: (L) This book [Graham Hancock's *Fingerprints of the Gods*] says that on this pyramid, at the time of the spring and autumn equinoxes, patterns of light and dark combine to create the illusion of a giant serpent undulating on the northern staircase. On each occasion the illusion lasts for 3 hours and 22 minutes exactly. What was this optical illusion created to convey?
>
> A: Worship of serpentine deity.
>
> Q: (L) Was it created to convey or produce any other effect other than worship?
>
> A: The key is in the reading of the geometric cycle.
>
> Q: (L) On page 80, the book talks about these statues at Tiahuanaco on Lake Titicaca. It says: "Carved in red sandstone, worn and ancient beyond reckoning, the statue stand about 6 feet high and portrays a humanoid, androgynous being with massive eyes and lips. In its right hand it clutches something resembling a knife with a wavy blade like an Indonesian kris. In its left hand is an object like a hinged and case-bound book. From the top of this book, however, protruded a device which had been inserted into it as though into a sheath. From the waist down, the figure seemed to be *clad in a garment of fish scales.*" Okay, there is another statue with an object in its left hand that is like a case bound book, but from it protruded a forked handle. The right hand object was roughly cylindrical, narrow in the center and bigger at each end. It appeared to have several different parts. I would like to know what these objects, or devices, carved into these ancient statues represented?
>
> A: Conductor for Quartzine energy from atmospheric source.
>
> Q: (L) What was this energy used for?
>
> A: All. When one harnesses free energy, no limitations need apply.
>
> Q: (L) Why were these beings depicted with these fish-like garments?
>
> A: *Reptoids* [4D STS Lizards] *have that genetic profile to varying degrees.*
>
> Q: (L) According to the Sumerian traditions, this was like the god Oannes. In the night time, he would plunge back into the sea, but in the daytime he would converse with men, giving them insight into letters and sciences and every kind of art. But, it was noted that he

was never observed to eat. It says that he taught men how to construct houses, temples, to compile laws, and explained to them the principles of geometric knowledge. He made them distinguish the seeds of the earth and made them gather fruits. In short, he instructed them in everything that would tend to soften manners and humanize mankind. From that time, so universal were his instructions, that nothing has been added materially in the way of improvement. The surviving images of Oannes on Babylonian and Assyrian reliefs clearly portray him as a fish man. Is this another similar profile?

A: "El legato."

Q: (L) Was this Oannes fish man similar to the Quinotaur that was supposedly the half-father of the Merovingian royal line?

A: Only if one considers losses in the translative quarry.

Q: (L) Here it says: "The Spanish Conquistadors and missionaries destroyed nearly everything that we could possibly use to learn about the South American civilizations. A sixteenth century eyewitness says that there was an emerald idol that was completely fantastic. Father Benito took this idol and had it ground up, stirred the powder in water, poured it on the ground and stomped on it.

"Cortez was given two circular calendars, one of gold and the other silver, as big as wagon wheels, with all kinds of hieroglyphs on them, which he immediately had melted down and cast into ingots. All over Central America, vast repositories of knowledge, accumulated since ancient times, were painstakingly gathered, heaped up, and burned by the zealous Catholic missionaries.

"In July 1562, for example, in the main square of Monte, in the Yucatan, Father Diego de Landa burned thousands of Maya manuscripts, paintings and hieroglyphs inscribed on rolled up deerskins." He said: "We found great numbers of books written in the characters of the Indians, but since they contained nothing but superstitions of the Devil, we burned them all, which the natives took most grievously, and gave them great pain."

Hancock says: "Not only the natives should have felt this pain, but anyone and everyone then and now who would like to know the truth about the past. Diego de Landa participated in Spain's satanic mission to wipe clear the memory banks of Central America. In the marketplace at Texcoco, they built a vast bonfire of astronomical documents, paintings, manuscripts, and hieroglyphic texts, which the Conquistadors had forcibly extracted from the Aztecs during the previous eleven years. As this irreplaceable storehouse of knowledge and history went up in flames, a chance to shake off some of the collective amnesia that clouds our understanding was lost to mankind forever."

So, having read this sickening description about "Spain's Satanic Mission" to destroy the past, I would like to have a comment on what was motivating the Catholic Church, the Catholic Missionaries, and Spain itself. Could you comment?

A: You should not need commentary, as *we have told you much about the desires of 4th density STS to obscure truth by manipulating 3rd density STS.*

Q: (L) Well, yes. But Lord have mercy! It just makes a person sick to think about it ... all of this and the Library at Alexandria too! Was this the kind of stuff that was being done in Europe during the so-called Dark Ages?

A: Yes.

Q: (L) And that is why the Dark Ages are dark. The Catholic Church destroyed everything that did not sharpen their axe.

As William Bramley noted in his book, *The Gods of Eden,* when we consider history, we can clearly see that the drive of human beings to have peace is as strong, if not stronger, than the drive to have war. But, when the issue of war is examined, one realizes that most often the trigger for war and related inhumanity to man is that the drive for spiritual freedom is twisted by manipulation.

It's easy to look back on history and see where this or that group was misled in their beliefs and thereby fell into errors of thinking that led to the perpetration of unspeakable horrors. We can point to the genocide advocated by the God of the Hebrews, or the religious-zeal-run-amok of the Catholic Church when it instituted the Inquisition. We can see the twisted version of the genetic superman that led to the holocaust. It's easy to discern these errors of the past, because we know more now. Well, isn't that an interesting thing? We know more now. How much more can we learn?

It almost seems as if the game has just gotten more and more complex, but the same essential errors keep being repeated. What is at the root? (Aside from the fact that we notice the above examples all relate to monotheistic exclusivity.)

Human beings have a sort of built in drive for spiritual knowledge. And over and over again we can see that this drive is what is being manipulated. When genuine spiritual knowledge is distorted while, at the same time, the inner desire for salvation is constantly being stimulated by various religious teachings, a great many people can be led into doing a lot of cruel and stupid things. The need to save souls is a prime example of how such a seemingly positive polarization can be *suddenly shifted to do the exact opposite of what the religious teachings explicated.* And this is an important point to remember.

Zecharia Sitchin and William Bramley, following Von Däniken, have postulated that the ancient evidence demonstrates the actual, physical presence of an extraterrestrial race who came to earth to implement controls over humanity, with possible plans to return and harvest the fruits of their efforts. In both cases, their studies have indicated strongly that this extraterrestrial race does not have humanity's best interests at heart! These guys did a lot of work, gathered a lot of facts, and were not listening to some bug-eyed Gray alien who was trying to convince them that "this is for you! We are here to help!"

But, those same aliens we find today, zipping about, sliding in and out of our reality like slippery eels, gazing and probing and communicating all kinds of excuses and scenarios to explain what they are doing based on how gullible or ignorant their victims are, this must be considered also. In other words, what Sitchin and Bramley fail to factor into their arguments is the continuing evidence of interaction and domination from another realm of existence.

The Annunaki, as defined by Sitchin, and the "Custodians" as defined by Bramley, did not come as physical beings (in our terms) to occupy, dominate, and then leave for some obscure reason. The evidence of those, now numbering in the multiples of thousands, claiming alien abduction and contact with aliens and even visions of the Virgin and other miracles throughout history, contradicts this view. It seems far more likely that the ancient stories indicate a cultural openness that permitted perception of such beings, acknowledged their reality, and merely made the distinction between them and ordinary human beings by referring to them as "gods".

William Bramley also chronicled considerable historical evidence of a relation between the sightings of UFOs and the sudden onslaught of deadly diseases or plagues. We have similar concerns in the present time, which indicates that this is not a new thing, but merely part of a cycle. *The Annunaki (4D STS) have never left, and the Brotherhood of the Serpent (the secret government or Consortium) is still with us, active and growing stronger by the day.*

As noted, a number of modern contactees and abductees claim the aliens are here to help humankind, to eradicate disease, to bring us health and happiness. The historical evidence does not support this. Though in some individual cases it may be true, wouldn't it make sense for those of the darkness to care for their agents?

In their attempts to warn us, to educate us, to wake us up, the Cassiopaeans have told us many dreadful things. Why?

The above reader sees this as "we are all damned in the end". But is that what the Cassiopaeans are saying? Are they not really saying that we need to wake up to what is under the surface of our very contradictory reality? That we need to become aware and alert and see the unseen? Are they not telling us "Satan can appear as an angel of light"? Are they not telling us that we are "strong men" who have been "bound" so that what is ours can be stolen? Are they not telling us to "drive out the demons" and open our eyes and begin to speak?

It's a little bit curious that just those two terms were used, omitting the "ears" as something that might be opened by the casting out of demons. The fact is, most of the distortions of our reality come to us by listening rather than observing. Deception and error of perception would have far less influence on us, and we would have no illusions if we would look at the face value of objects and see things for what they really are. Most of humankind's illusions are the children of the ear and hearsay. My beloved grandmother always told me to "believe none of what you hear and only half of what you see". This is very good advice. If we open our eyes and look at the problem as objectively as we can, forgetting all our beliefs and assumptions, and all the things we have been told we might be able to draw some conclusions.

A problem is defined in terms of two categories: *objects* and *operations*. The objects are the things that the problem-solver has to manipulate. They may be people, things, or situations. The operations are the steps by which object A is transformed into object B. Solving a problem is a process of understanding the sequence of transformation. To do this, we try to understand the differences between object A and object B. These understandings lead us to the choice of operations. Those operations, which will add to the transformation process, will be retained; those that will diminish the process will be eliminated.

I believe that we can come to some understanding of our reality problem in this way. I would suggest that the alien Control System demonstrate adherence to the process described above, but with time travel capabilities, it is possible for them to effect their manipulations in such a way that we have great difficulty perceiving them. With a broad historical perspective, careful examination of the cycles and events within the cycles, we can see the fingerprints of these elusive controllers of our reality. We can see human beings as the objects, and the events of history as the "operations". When we observe these things, the events of history and how they have affected humanity, and where humanity is today as opposed to yesterday, we begin to have a clue that we certainly are not in Kansas anymore!

What is even more interesting is that we come across some of those very strange periods in history where a great darkness descends. And before this darkness humankind was going in one direction, and after this period, humankind is going in an altogether different direction. You probe into these periods, and you discover that very strange things were going on. Not only that, you discover that a seemingly concerted effort was made afterward to assure that documentation of the period was destroyed to as great an extent as possible. In other words, somebody was busy on a global scale, and whatever they were doing, they definitely did not want it made public. Two of these historical periods really stand out. The first is the time in which the national history of the Jews was supposedly in full development. The second is the period of the transition from Paganism to Christianity. Both of these periods are called Dark Ages. Maybe that should give us pause! The idea that humankind is being manipulated and controlled like an experiment then becomes not merely what the Cassiopaeans are telling us, but also what we can see ourselves if we exert the effort and care to look.

The point of all this is that it seems the only criteria we may have by which to judge any phenomenon is the fruit it bears, since it is possible for things to be represented as positive and not be so, in fact. But in this case, the fruit can only be seen in a very broad historical perspective.

To synopsize: an alien presence has been noted at many points in history of great disaster or mass death and cultural darkness. Examination of the few records and documents has led some scholars and researchers to conjecture that many of history's darkest hours have been created by this alien presence. The laws of probability tell us that, without any intelligent control, fifty percent of the time events would occur leading to great good and benefit. Factoring in intelligent decisions to do well would bring this average up to about seventy percent Yet we can clearly see that this is not reflected in our reality. Why not? Who or what is influencing things to the negative?

One answer that we are given is the ever popular New Age channeled teaching that the reason things are so bad is because we were an experiment in free will that went bad. We have screwed things up so badly that now we need help to haul ourselves out of the soup. And the aliens, in their infinite wisdom and mercy, are going to do that for us if we will just let them! Further, if we just think nice thoughts, nothing bad will ever enter our reality. And we must not look at evil because it just doesn't exist unless we believe in it. This is a dangerous and cunning lie. What better way to protect the forces of darkness at higher levels than to deny their very existence?

My work as a hypnotherapist has shown me that the vast majority of people want to do good, to experience good things, think good thoughts, and make decisions with good results. And they try with all their might to do so. With the majority of people having this internal desire, why the hell isn't it happening? In my experience, when the surface or screen memories of an individual who has had abductions has been probed in a competent way, this individual reveals memories of events so chilling in their implications that the "love and light" interpretation must be looked at carefully. Yet, the aliens somehow convince the experiencer that it is for their good or for the good of the planet or the enhancement of the human race.

> Q: (L) The whole point of this article is to say that ETs who abduct people are here to help us evolve and that it is only us, if we have dark and dirty unconscious minds, who perceive them as negative.
> A: Wrong, you do not need "help" evolving, nor does anything else.

What does this mean for us in practical terms here on Earth today? It means that alien intelligences throughout history have very possibly controlled and influenced the leaders of our societies to guide us down a particular chosen pathway, chosen by them. They are here; they are playing cat-and-mouse with us to keep us confused and off balance. They are feeding philosophical lies and distortions into our culture to lead as many astray as possible. They control many of the lions of industry, government and culture so that what exists in our world is perverted by a twist, a peculiar upside-down, disjointed, askew perspective governed by deception and falsehood.

We are living in a frightful, topsy-turvy world where everything we instinctively cherish as good, noble, honest and right has been disrupted, soiled, deformed and made ugly. And, more horrible than this, we accept it as normal.

This control system, this infrastructure, is a subtle, goal-seeking phenomenon and it is our purpose here to discover that goal. The Cassiopaeans have given us many clues, but the answers are up to us to figure out. And we are not just interested in finding out the goal, we are interested in finding out our proper response to it.

If what the Cassiopaeans are saying is not true, will we lose anything by entertaining the possibility? Is truth so fragile that it cannot withstand scrutiny? And if what the Cassiopaeans are saying is true, what might we lose if we don't consider the possibility?

On the one hand, the correspondent quoted at the beginning of this chapter is clearly saying he believes there are dark forces that seek to deceive and bind us. But, would those very dark forces do this by telling us that there are dark forces seeking to deceive and bind us, warning us to check things out ourselves, even them? As noted, that is logically inconsistent.

On the other hand, what must we think about the many forces of light who say there are no dark forces except in our minds, that we create them by believing in them? Which naturally puts the onus for the creation of darkness on humankind. They say that if we cease our participation in the belief of darkness, it will be overcome and made null and void. One New Age writer put it this way: "Evil is energy out of sync with the creator."

Logic tells us that anything out of sync with the Creator would, of necessity, imply error on the part of the Creator that would lead to the conclusion that the Creator is, itself, limited in omniscience or omnipotence, which then leaves us in an even worse ontological dilemma than before.

This writer goes on to say that evil is:

> ... energy that was cast off from humankind's energy when we first learned how to establish ourselves as spiritually apart from the all-life. It is an accidental creation. ... The energy of evil ... comes from the human race.

Well, heck! Let's just blame it on Eve, why don't we?

I repeat: it is logically inconsistent to posit an all-knowing, all-loving omnipotent Creator, and then to suggest either accident or rebellion. But how else can we explain it?

How can we understand the apparent fact that we are in an environment of which seems designed to imprison us; to make us little more than cattle kept in a pen to feed ravening monsters from hyper-dimensional space that we can't even comprehend, much less resist? If we don't call it a mistake or a fault or an error, what are we going to do with it?

By seeing it as a mistake, we at least give ourselves the hope of changing it, or believing in some Messiah who has taken the fault away from us, so we don't have to bear the guilt for the aeons of suffering of humankind that we observe. But that is a costly solution in the long run because it leads to ontological answers which are unbearable. But if we have arrived at the point where we can no longer support the inconsistencies of such a view, we are left with the deeper question of how can we understand the ontological existence of such a state?

In other words, if what we perceive to be darkness and evil or Service-to-Self is not a mistake, is not an error, is not something that can or should be fixed in the realm of creation, then what is it? How can we ontologically justify it? Or, leaving aside justification, how can we just simply understand it?

One thing we note at the beginning here is that the Cassiopaeans have said human beings chose to experience this reality for a reason.

> Q: (L) Are human beings entrapped in physical matter?
>
> A: By choice.
>
> Q: (L) Why did they make this choice?
>
> A: To experience physical sensations. It was a *group mind* decision.
>
> Q: (L) Who was in charge of the group?
>
> A: The group. [...] It must also be mentioned here that everything that exists in all realms of the universe can experience existence in one of only two ways. That would be defined as a long wave cycle and a short wave cycle. Going back to your previous question about why humans are "entrapped" in physical existence, which, of course, is voluntary and chosen, this was due to the desire to change from the long wave cycle experience of completely what you would call ethereal or spiritual existence, to the short wave cycle of what you call physical existence. The difference is that a long wave cycle involves only very gradual change in evolution in a cyclical manner. Whereas a short wave cycle involves a duality. [...] *The necessity to form the short wave cycle was brought about through nature through the natural bounds of the universe when the group mind of souls chose to experience physicality as opposed to a completely ethereal existence.* [...] The positive byproduct is an increase in relative energy, which speeds up the learning process of the soul and all of its one-dimensional and two-dimensional interactive partners, in other words, flora and fauna, minerals, etc. *All experience growth and movement towards reunion at a faster rate on the cycle through this short wave cycle physical/ethereal transfer.*

In our overview of the conditions of the reality in which we live, we are forced to think in new ways about purpose. How can it be good to live in such an environment? Sure, it's fine and dandy to say that "all experience growth ... at a faster rate" and all that, but what does that really mean when we are faced with some of the factors we have been discussing in these pages?

And remember, we have not been talking about just channeled material – we have been collecting facts and observations throughout this examination of our reality. And, because of the many letters I receive from readers, I can assure you that it is not just my reality, or even just a minority reality. It's a fact, and, as don Juan would say, "a damn scary one"!

Many individuals in the present time are convinced that the New Age paradigm is going to unite all of humanity into one big happy family with the amalgamation of the common threads of belief that run through all the great religions. They point to the messages from this or that source that claim this is the great plan put into place by higher beings millennia ago, so that all different types of human beings could grow to maturity, each in their own ideal environment, much as different areas of a garden are more or less suitable for different types of plants.

Very often, such people cite the "great new research" that supports this view, that man is creating a new reality. Paul von Ward writes in *The Solarian Legacy:*

> Patterns are created by consciousness that have the power to shape apparent nothingness into tiny quanta of something. ... The use of conscious intent is a more effective route to human participation in a creative life process, including maintaining health, than purely mechanical manipulation. ... Modern research evidence has been found to support the conclusions of many cultural traditions that human consciousness communicates with and influences the behavior of other life forms. ... Assuming there is an ongoing, reciprocal flow of such behavior-influencing communications among local concentrations of mind (animals, plants, and individual cells), how does the conscious being deliberately intervene in the natural flow to bring about a desired end? The answer – at this point an intuitive one – involves clarity of focus grounded in definite emotions. The process appears to work in a manner analogous to the progression from "gas" through "liquids" to "solids", i.e., from "amorphous" through "evolving" to "definite". (von Ward, 2001)

So far, so good, right? We can see (though this is greatly abbreviated) that there seems to be a real principle behind the idea that "you create your own reality". So, let's keep going here:

> After someone had the first "clear" idea of a candle, it entered the "potential" phase as soon as there was real intent to create. The movement to gather materials placed the pattern in the "becoming" phase. The "actualization" phase of the idea was ignited by fire. The same sequential process applies to all fields of human life: agriculture, food preparation, health, psychokinesis, sports, politics, or economics. The idea of democracy first starts with clarity about a few basic assumptions. Only when a number of individuals attach emotional support to the ideas does democracy have real potential.

> That emotional energy translated to action results in the practice of democracy. A vision of health must be underpinned by emotional commitment in order for the cells to get the message to do their part and for the individual to eat appropriately. To facilitate the bending of metal through conscious intent, one focuses the idea on the metal, the metal's atoms become agitated, and when as a result the material softens, only a slight pressure will bend it.
>
> Recognizing the power of this natural process, it is foolish to assume specific limits to creative powers exist in natural law until they have been tested and re-tested. Currently perceived constraints may actually be due to false or limited interpretations of cosmic law. If a clearly focused thought is more than a fleeting mind game, emotionally energized to a level of potential, will it be realized? Or, are there certain thoughts that cannot be actualized in space-time? When we learn the answers to these questions, we will realize our fuller power as cosmic beings. ... Given the research highlighted here, and similar work, it is now justifiable for a prudent person to accept that mind does communicate with and influence matter at the subatomic and cellular levels. Through the mechanism of thought, consciousness or mind likely shapes reality in more ways than we can currently conceive. (von Ward, 2001)

Well, Mr. Ward certainly has synopsized the popular view of the "new thought" movement incepted during the nineteenth century. But, he has also pointed out certain problems that most people who hear the basic idea of "you create your own reality" do not notice. They hear an idea, which appeals to their emotions, and don't pay much attention to the caveats. Mr. von Ward continues:

> It is important to remember, however, that human consciousness – individually and collectively – can shape microcosmic reality *only within limits, due to certain characteristics of our phenomenal realm.* One of these limits appears to be the direction of the stream of arrow of time. ... *This seems to indicate that we cannot arbitrarily change the nature of a phenomenon while a particular directionality is maintained.* To change a vector (velocity combined with magnitude and direction) of anything requires the application of a greater force. ... *Only a power beyond our universe can mitigate the influence of its inherent arrow of time.* (von Ward, 2001)

Hmm. Have we discovered something here? Let's go back to a clue the Cassiopaeans gave:

> The necessity to form the short wave cycle was brought about through nature through the natural bounds of the universe when the group mind of souls chose to experience physicality as opposed to a completely ethereal existence. It was a *group mind* decision.

Right here we have some clue to the restrictions on "creating your own reality". If an individual seeks to do so in opposition to the "natural bounds of the universe", *which is a manifestation of the "group mind" decision,* they are going to run into some serious problems.

> Q: (L) At one point we were told that time was an illusion that came into being at the time of the Fall in Eden, and this was said in such a way that I inferred that there were other illusions put into place at that time.
>
> A: Time is an illusion that works for you because of your altered DNA state.
>
> Q: (L) Okay, what other illusions?
>
> A: Monotheism, the belief in one separate, all-powerful entity.
>
> Q: (T) Is separate the key word in regard to Monotheism?
>
> A: Yes.
>
> Q: (L) What is another one of the illusions?
>
> A: The need for physical aggrandizement.
>
> Q: (L) What is another of the illusions?
>
> A: Linear focus.
>
> Q: (L) Anything else at this time?
>
> A: Unidimensionality.
>
> Q: (L) The veil ... (J) The perception of only one dimension ... (L) Were these illusions programmed into us genetically through our DNA?
>
> A: Close.
>
> Q: (L) Can you tell us a little bit about how these illusions are enforced on us, how they are perceived by us?
>
> A: If someone opens a door, and behind it you see a pot of gold, do you worry whether there is a poisonous snake behind the door hidden from view, before you reach for the pot of gold?
>
> Q: (L) What does the gold represent?
>
> A: Temptation to limitation.
>
> Q: (L) Was limitation presented as a pot of gold when, in fact, it was not?
>
> A: What is snake?
>
> Q: (T) The Lizards?
>
> A: Result of giving into temptation without caution, i.e., leaping before looking.
>
> Q: (L) So what you are saying to us is that the story of the temptation in Eden was the story of Humankind being led into this reality as a result of being tempted. So, the eating of the fruit of the Tree of Knowledge of Good and Evil was ...
>
> A: Giving into temptation.

Q: (L) And this was a trick.

A: No! Tricks don't exist!

Q: (T) Okay, no trick, a trap?

A: No! Traps don't exist either. *Free will could not be abridged if you had not obliged.*

Q: (T) Now wait a minute. I am losing the whole train here. What were we before the Fall?

A: 3rd density STO.

Q: (T) We were third-density STO at this time. Was this after the battle that had transpired?

A: Was battle.

Q: (L) The battle was in us?

A: Through you.

Q: (T) Okay, we were STO at that point. You have said before that on this density we have the choice of being STS or STO.

A: Oh T, *the battle is always there, it's "when" you choose that counts!*

Q: (T) This must tie into why the Lizards and other aliens keep telling people that they have given their consent for abduction and so forth. We were STO and now we are STS.

A: Yes, continue.

Q: (T) We are working with the analogy. The gold was an illusion. The gold was not what we perceived it to be. It was a temptation ...

A: No temptation, it was always there. Remember Dorothy and the Ruby slippers?

Q: (T) Okay, we were STO at that time, before we stepped through. We didn't have to step through. It's always there ... (J) It's there now ... (T) The Lizards ...

A: Yes, think of the Ruby slippers. What did Glenda tell Dorothy???

Q: (L) You have always had the power to go home ...

A: Yes.

Q: (L) So, we always have the power to return to being STO? Even in third density?

A: Yes.

Q: (T) *The door has always been there.* The temptation has always been there ... (J) Is there ... (T) Has, is, will be ... is always.

A: "When" you went for the gold, you said "Hello" to the Lizards and all that that implies.

Q: (T) So, the concept is that, as STO beings we had the choice of either going for the gold or not. By going for the gold, we became STS beings because going for the gold was STS.

A: Yes.

Q: (T) And, in doing so, we ended up aligning ourselves with the fourth-density Lizard beings.

A: Yes.

Q: (T) Because they are fourth-density beings and they have a lot more abilities than we at third density.
A: You used to be aligned with 4th density STO.
Q: (T) But, by going for the gold we aligned ourselves with fourth-density STS.
A: Yes.
Q: (T) And by doing so we gave fourth-density STS permission to do whatever they wish with us?
A: Close.
Q: (T) So, when they tell us that we gave them permission to abduct us, it is this they are referring to?
A: Close.
Q: (J) Go back to what they said before: "Free will could not be abridged if you had not obliged." (T) We, as the human race, used our free will to switch from STO to STS. (L) So, at some level, at some point, we have chosen the mess we are in. We fell by falling into that door, so to speak, going after the pot of gold, and when we fell through the door, the serpent bit us!
A: But this is a repeating syndrome.
Q: (L) Is it a repeating syndrome just for the human race or is it a repeating syndrome throughout all of creation?
A: It is the latter.
Q: (L) Is this a repeating syndrome throughout all of creation simply because it is the cyclic nature of things? Or is it as the Indians call it, Maya?
A: Either or.

So, again we come up against the issue of the constraints against creating our reality. We have chosen the school we wished to enter, and the natural bounds of this school is the STS Control System. As third-density beings aligned with Service-to-Self beings, we have chosen these constraints. We agreed to have our free will abridged.

Q: (D) I have a question about ... Mankind has found it necessary for some reason or other to appoint time ... The only reason I can see is to have a means of telling, like in verbal or written communications.
A: Control mechanism.
Q: (T) Is there a way for us to break the control mechanism? Besides moving to fourth density?
A: Nope.

Now, just exactly what is the "pot of gold" used in the analogy above? What event brought about the Fall from alignment with Service-to-Others to Service-to-Self? Well, the designations STO and STS give us a clue, but there is more. At several points I returned to this issue for clarification, and I hope that my efforts will help to make it clearer for others:

> Q: (L) Where did the souls come from that entered into the bodies on the planet earth? Were they in bodies on other planets before they came here?
> A: Not this group.
> Q: (L) Were they just floating around in the universe somewhere?
> A: In union with the One. Have you heard the super ancient legend of Lucifer, the fallen angel?
> Q: (L) Who is Lucifer?
> A: You. The human race.
> Q: (L) Are the souls of individual humans the parts of a larger soul?
> A: Yes. Close. The One. All who have fallen must learn "the hard way". You are members of a fragmented soul unit.
> Q: (L) Are you saying that the act of wanting to experience physical reality is the act of falling? What is it about wanting to be physical is a fall?
> A: Pleasure for the self.
> Q: (L) Prior to the Fall, did the human race live in an Edenic state, where they were able to use bodies and still have a spiritual connection?
> A: Yes. But not long. No addiction takes long to close the circle.
> Q: (L) So, mankind was addicted to pleasuring the self?
> A: Became quickly.
> Q: (L) How long from the time of the moving of souls into bodies did the Fall in Eden occur?
> A: Not measurable. Remember, Laura, there is no time when this event occurred. Time passage illusion did not exist at that point as well as many other falsehoods.
> Q: (L) So you are saying that the Fall in Eden was also the beginning of time?
> A: Yes.

So, here we have a little bit of a clue. "Pleasure for the self." But this remark does not mean that pleasure in and of itself is strictly Service-to-Self. It became clearer with further questions:

> Q: (L) Does it hurt a plant when we eat it?
> A: Does it hurt you when a "Lizzie" eats you?
> Q: (D) If we hurt plants by eating them like the Lizzies hurt us when they eat us, how are we to survive without eating?
> A: When you no longer crave physicality, you no longer need to "eat".
> Q: (L) So part of the Fall into the physical existence and part of the Fall from Eden story where it says "you shall eat by the sweat of your brow", has to do with being physical and needing to eat?
> A: Lucifer, "the fallen angel". This is you.

Q: (L) So, "falling" means going into physical existence wherein you must feed on other life, other beings, is that it?
A: Yes.

Now, we need to remember the story of Lucifer, that he was an angel of great beauty and glory. The Cassiopaeans have suggested that the legend of Orion is closest to the original version of the story.

> A: In this part of your 3rd and 4th density universe, specifically your "galaxy" it is the region known as Orion that is the one and only indigenous home of human type beings ... reflect on this! Indigenous home base, not sole locator. ... Approximately one half is STO and one half is STS. ... Pay attention to Orion! This is your ancestral home, and your eventual destination. The name "Orion" is the actual native name, and was brought to earth directly. Study the legend of the "god" of Orion for parallels.

I am not going to delve into a full-scale analysis of the Orion legend here, but I will give the fullest account I have been able to put together so that the reader can play with the concepts as we go along. According to Edith Hamilton, it goes like this:

> He was a young man of gigantic stature and great beauty, and a mighty hunter. He fell in love with the daughter of the King of Chios, and for love of her he cleared the island of wild beasts. The spoils of the chase he brought always home to his beloved, whose name is sometimes said to be Aero, sometimes Merope (one of the Pleiades). Her father, Oenopion, agreed to give her to Orion, but he kept putting the marriage off. One day when Orion was drunk he insulted the maiden, and Oenopion appealed to Dionysus to punish him. The god threw him into *a deep sleep* and Oenopion *blinded him*. An oracle told him, however, that *he would be able to see again if he went to the east and let the rays of the rising sun fall on his eyes*. He went as far east as Lemnos and there he recovered his sight. (Emphasis added)

A more complex treatment derived from several ancient sources goes as follows:

> The parentage of Orion has been matter of dispute, but some have said that Orion's father was Hyrieus, son of Poseidon and his mother was Alcyone, one of the Pleiades. It was said that Hyrieus' father, Poseidon, came to visit him, accompanied by Zeus and Hermes. Hyrieus sacrificed a bull for the occasion. To show honor to Hyrieus for his hospitality, the gods offered Hyrieus a gift of his choosing. Hyrieus was a very rich but childless, so he asked his visitors for a child. The gods urinated in the hide of the sacrificed bull, *buried it in the earth* and from it Orion was born. In time Orion grew tall as a

giant, and he was granted by Poseidon, his grandfather, (or father in some versions) the power of walking on water.

Orion fell in love with Merope, the daughter of King Oenopion of Chios, son of Ariadne and Theseus or Dionysus. But her father disliked the idea and he made Orion drunk, put out his eyes as he slept, and then cast him on the beach. Others have said, however, that Orion came to Chios and, having drunk heavily, *raped the girl, this being the reason why he was blinded and expelled from the island.* He then came to Lemnos, where Hephaestus gave him his servant Cedalion to serve him as a guide. Orion set him on his shoulders and bade him lead him to the sunrise, and when they arrived Orion was healed by the sun's rays.

Orion believed himself to be the best of hunters and once said that he was able to kill anything the earth produced. It was then that Gaia (Earth), angered at this boast, sent the Scorpion that killed him. But others have said that Orion was killed by Artemis who was challenged by Apollo to shoot an arrow into a black object in the sea, which she could not see, and that later was discovered to be Orion's head. How the goddess could commit such a mistake has not been explained. Still others say that Orion was killed for challenging Artemis to a match of quoits, or shot by her for raping Opis, one of the maidens who had come from the Hyperboreans. But others have believed that Orion died because the gods were jealous that Orion was the lover of Eos. For this, they allowed Artemis to kill him.

Odysseus saw Orion when he descended to the Underworld. Apparently, down there he had the same occupation as when he was on Earth: "... I marked huge Orion driving together over the Plain of Asphodel wild beasts which himself had slain on the lonely hills, and in his hands he held a club all of bronze, ever unbroken ..." (Odysseus. Homer, *Odyssey* 11.542)

Yet Orion is considered to be immortal since Artemis, who mourned him, placed him among the stars. To prevent him being alone in the sky, the Dog (Canis Major) was later added to the stars to keep Orion company in his hunting.

The proposed parentage of Orion is as follows:

a) Poseidon & Euryale. Euryale was said to be the daughter of King Minos of Crete.

b) Hyrieus & Clonia. Hyrieus owned a treasure inside a building built by Trophonius and Agamedes, which had a stone that they could take away from the outside, thus robbing him, until one of them was caught in a trap made by Hyrieus. Clonia was one of the NYMPHS.

c) Bull's hide

d) Gaia (by herself)

It's easy to see how the legend would be transposed into the Biblical story of Lucifer, and why there would be associations with the Morning Star, or the act of letting the first rays of sunlight, the Goddess Aurora, fall upon his eyes for healing.

But, it is interesting that the same images presented in the allegory given by Jesus about the "strong man" being "bound" or cast into a deep sleep, and "blinded" by demons are also present in the story of Orion. Perhaps it was a deliberate allusion to Orion?

The story of Osiris being tricked into his coffin by Set is another variation of the strong man being bound, though in this case, we have the additional detail of the body being ultimately dismembered which seems to be the allegory of the "fragmented soul unit". The Egyptians know the constellation of Orion as Osiris, and the dog companion is his sister-wife, Isis.

But, the issue here is: how did Orion take the fall? It is said that he got drunk and insulted or raped the maiden of whom he loved. Afterwards, he was then made drunk or was "put into a deep sleep" during which his eyes were put out. Whatever it was, apparently he was not in full possession of his senses as a hunter when he was put out for the operation.

The story also is reflected in the Biblical legend of Samson and Delilah. Samson was a Nazarite with a vow to never cut his hair. Delilah had him "sleep upon her knees" and while he was sleeping, she called a man to come and "shave off the seven braids of his hair". And his strength went from him. He was taken and his eyes were put out. The clear connection of this to the Orion legend makes it altogether likely that this is merely the Hebrew variation of a very ancient story! I was curious about this hair business, so I asked:

> Q: (L) I have an idea relating to the ancient gods and heroes ... They all had these massive amounts of hair, and it seemed that cutting off the hair caused them to lose their strength in some way. Was this totally symbolic, or was it actually believed that they had to grow their hair?
> A: Symbolic.
> Q: (L) What was the hair symbolic of?
> A: Virility.

Samson was deprived of his virility by losing his hair. For all we know, losing one's hair could be an ancient euphemism for having an orgasm. Maybe in the weakened condition after this *petit mort*, one is less aware and therefore more susceptible to being put into a sleep or made drunk again? To be drunk, or intoxicated, is to be in a condition where one has lost control over one's faculties. It is also a term that means overcome by emotion. Do we have another clue here? Well, I asked more questions:

> Q: (L) I have this book, *Confessions of an Intergalactic Anthropologist*, by a woman named Marcia Schafer. One thing she says is: "The snake is associated with the sign of wisdom and higher learning, and is often regarded quite highly in mystical circles." I would like to have a comment on the idea of the snake as a "sign of wisdom and higher learning". Does this, in fact, represent what the snake symbolizes?
>
> A: Snake is/was reported in context of the viewpoint of the observer. Maybe the observer was just "blown away" by the experience. If you were living in the desert, or jungle, about 7,000 years ago, as you measure time, would you not be impressed if these Reptoid "dudes" came down from the heavens in silvery objects and demonstrated techno-wonders from thousands of years in the future, and taught you calculus, geometry and astrophysics to boot?!?
>
> Q: (L) Is that, in fact, what happened?
>
> A: Yup.
>
> Q: (L) As I understand it, or as I am trying to figure it out from the literature, prior to the Fall in Eden, mankind lived in a fourth-density state. Is that correct?
>
> A: Semi/sort of. 4th density in another realm, such as time/space continuum, etc.

Remember that they have already said we were formerly third density aligned with STO fourth density. This suggests that to be third-density STO and in contact with fourth-density STO entails significant positive interaction and bleedthrough between the two densities as suggested above. A very different realm indeed!

> Q: (L) Could you describe to me the true meaning of the Osirian cycle? What was the symbology of the killing of Osiris and the cutting up of the body?
>
> A: Removal of knowledge centers in your DNA.
>
> Q: (L) So, the breaking up of Osiris' body represents the breaking up of the DNA in our bodies?
>
> A: Partly. Also means knowledge capacity reduction.
>
> Q: (L) What was the symbology of the throwing of the phallus into the river and its being eaten by three fishes?
>
> A: Sexual violence energy introduction.
>
> Q: (L) What did Isis searching for her lord Osiris symbolize?
>
> A: Separation of female energy from male energy union.
>
> Q: (L) Does this have anything to do with brain activity?
>
> A: Yes. The separating of the hemispheres of the brain.
>
> Q: (L) Was this achieved through DNA modification?
>
> A: Yes.

Q: (L) What did the son of Isis, Horus, represent?
A: New reality of limitation.
Q: (L) What is the meaning of Horus avenging himself upon Set, the murderer of his father, Osiris?
A: Beginning of perpetual conflict energy to limit humanity.
Q: (L) Who did Set represent?
A: War.
Q: (L) Okay, so this realm changed, as a part of the cycle; various choices were made: the human race went through the door after the gold, so to speak, and became aligned with the fourth-density STS faction after the right-brain/female energy consorted with the wrong side, so to speak. This resulted in a number of effects: the breaking up of the DNA, the burning off of the first ten factors of DNA, the separation of the hemispheres of the brain …
A: Only reason for this: you play in the dirt, you're gonna get dirty.
Q: (L) What was the motivating factor for playing in the dirt? What essential thing occurred? You said once that it was "desire-based imbalance". What was it a desire for?
A: *Increased* physicality.
Q: (L) What was the objective sought for in this desire for increased physicality?
A: Sensate.

Sensate is derived from a Latin word, *sentire*, which means "to feel". This suggests not merely physical sensations, but also emotions. The root of the Latin word is, curiously, the Indo-European root, *sent*, which means, "to cause to go, to find out, to discover".

Q: (L) How was sensate experienced so that these beings had an idea that they could get more if they increased their physicality?
A: Not experienced, demonstrated.
Q: (L) Demonstrated how, by whom? Demonstrated in what way? Did they say, "Here, try this!" Or did they demonstrate by showing or doing?
A: Closer to the latter. More like: "You could have this."
Q: (L) What seemed to be so desirable about this increased physicality when they said, "You can have this"?
A: Use your imagination!
Q: (L) Was there any understanding, or realization of any kind that increased physicality could be like Osiris lured into his own coffin by Set? That they would then slam the lid shut and nail him in?
A: Obviously, such understanding was lacking.
Q: (L) Sounds like a pretty naive bunch! Does the lack of this understanding reflect a lack of knowledge?
A: Of course. But more, it is desire getting in the way of …

Here we have another clue to the ways in which we can be manipulated: desire gets in the way of knowledge. But, we will come back to this.

> Q: (L) Okay. The Fall occurred. It seems like, and some of the archaeological studies indicate, that for many thousands of years, there was a peaceful existence and a nice agrarian society where the goddess or female creative forces were worshipped. At least, this is what a lot of present-day books are proposing ...
>
> A: No. These events took place 309000 years ago, as you measure it. This is when the first prototype of what you call "modern man" was created. The controllers had the bodies ready; they just needed the right soul matrix to agree to "jump in".

And this brings up a very interesting solution to particular problems in terms of the Reptilians being touted as the bringers of civilization and their association with the Goddess religions, promoted in the present time as being the peaceful partnership way of agricultural paradise. Apparently, that was not exactly the case.

If we remember the story of Cain and Abel, we find the original conflict between the shepherd and the agriculturist. Cain and Abel, being the two sons of Adam and Eve who have been cast out of Eden, merely symbolize the two main forms that the control system took in order to perpetuate conflict. Both ways contain within them implicit ownership of something, either cattle or land, and both suggest the use and manipulation of the earth for their own benefit, and to the detriment of the Great Mother. The only reason Abel was glorified by the Hebrews was because it was *their* way of life. But that leads to another whole line of investigation, so we will leave it for now.

> Q: (L) So, prior to this time, this prior Edenic state ...
>
> A: Was more like 4th density.
>
> Q: (L) But that implies that there was some level of physicality. Was there physicality in the sense of bodies that look like present-day humans?
>
> A: Not quite.
>
> Q: (L) Does this mean that the bodies we possibly would metamorphose into as fourth-density beings, assuming that one does, would also be too complex for us to understand? You are saying that this sort of fourth-density pre-Fall state, or third density aligned with fourth-density STO, in terms of the physical bodies, is too complex to understand. If going back to fourth density is anything like coming from fourth density, does that mean that what we would go back to is something that is still too complex to understand? This variability of physicality that you have described?
>
> A: Yes.

Q: (L) So, was there any kind of worship of God, or religious activity in this pre-Fall state – this Edenic, semi-fourth-density state?
A: No need when one has a clue.
Q: (L) What I am trying to get at here, what I am trying to understand, is the transition from the goddess worship to the god worship; the change from the understanding of cyclical time as expressed in the feminine cycles, and as expressed as the goddess; to the concept of linear time, expressed as the masculine principle.

It seems to me that these were stages of inversion of concepts which gradually led to the ideas that have been imposed on us, and it seems that bringing these ideas to fruition is a project fourth-density STS beings have been working toward for millennia – the dominator experience which expresses as: "Believe in something outside yourself that will save you, otherwise you are damned because the world is going to end, and you are going to get judged." That is the whole monotheistic concept I am trying to deal with here.

Okay, we had these guys; they fell from Eden, but they were still fairly close to the original concepts, in some terms. Once they jumped into the physical bodies, as you put it, what was their level of conceptualization regarding the universe? Did they still retain some understanding at that point?
A: Kind of like the understanding one has after severe head trauma, vis a vis your normal understanding in your current state.
Q: (L) So, they were traumatized; they may have had bits and pieces of ideas and memories, but they may also have lost a great deal altogether. They may have had big gaps. There may have even been a sort of "coma" state of mankind for many millennia. But, after they woke up, with the bits and pieces floating around in their heads, they may have begun to attempt to piece it all together. So, they started putting it all back together. What was the first thing they put together regarding the cosmos around them?
A: Sex.
Q: (L) What did they decide about sex? I mean, sex was there. They were having sex. Is that it? Or, did they understand the cosmos as sex?
A: More like the former. After all, that is what got you guys in this mess in the first place! Just imagine the sales job if you can: "Look how much fun this is! Want to try it?!? Oops, sorry, we forgot to tell you, you cannot go back!"
Q: (L) I really fail to understand – and I know it is a big issue that has been hinted at and alluded to, and outright claims have been made regarding sex in all religions and mythologies – but I fail to understand the mechanics of how this can be the engineering of a fall. What, precisely, are the mechanics of it? What energy is generated? How is it generated? What is the conceptualization of the misuse of this energy, or the use of the energy?

A: It is simply the introduction of the concept of self-gratification of a physical sort.

Q: (L) On many occasions you have said that the ideal thing is to have perfect balance of physicality and spirituality. Now, I don't understand how it can be that gratification of a physical body can be the mechanics by which one is entrapped. Is it not gratifying to look at something beautiful? Is it wrong, sinful, or a form of a fall, to look at beauty, to hear something beautiful such as music, or to touch something that is sensually delightful such as a piece of silk or the skin of a loved one? These various things that the human being derives pleasure from very often elevate them to a spiritual state.

A: *Possession is the key.* In STS, you possess. If you move through the beautiful flowers, the silk, the skin of another, but do not seek to possess ...

Q: (L) It seems to me that it is possible to experience all of these things, including sex, without the need or desire to possess, only to give. In which case, I still don't understand how it can be a mechanism for a fall.

A: If it is desired, then the mechanism is not to give. Do you eat a piece of chocolate cake because it is good to give to the stomach? In STS, which is your realm do not forget, one gives because of the pleasant sensation which results.

Q: (L) Could it not be said that, if everything that exists is part of God, including the flesh, that if one gives to the flesh, without being attached to the giving, that it could be considered a giving to the all?

A: Explain the process.

Q: (L) For example: at one extreme there are some people who like to suffer, because they believe that the flesh is sinful. For centuries the monotheistic religions have made this big deal about sex and anything that might be considered pleasant or desirable, that it should be denied, and that a person should suffer, and revel in their suffering.

A: If one seeks to suffer, they do so in expectation of future reward. *They desire to possess something in the end.*

Q: (L) What I am saying is: if a person can avoid self aggrandizement in either direction, and to simply *be*, in the doing and being of who and what they are, in simplicity; to become involved in doing everything as a meditation, or as a consecration, whether they are walking down the street and being at one with the air, the sunshine, the birds and trees and other people; in this state of oneness, doesn't that constitute a giving to the universe as giving oneself up as a channel for the universe to experience all these things?

A: Not if one is "feeling this oneness" rather than *being* it.

Q: (L) Well, if people would just relax and be who and what they are in honesty, and do what is according to their nature without violating the free will of others, is this a more pure form of being than

doing things out of any feeling of expectation, or desire; to just *be*, not want ... just *be*?
A: Yes, but STS does not do that.

So, we see that the issue is not sex per se, or really anything in specific about the third-density environment so much as it is a certain generation of emotion via physical processes that have to do specifically with possession. What is it about *desire to possess* that brought about a Fall?

Well, let's just have a look at some other ideas here:

> Q: (L) What was the Fruit of the tree of Knowledge of Good and Evil that was supposedly eaten by Eve and then offered to Adam?
> A: Knowledge restriction. Encoding. *Eve is symbolic of Female energy.*
> Q: (L) What did it mean when it said Eve, or the female energy, ate of the fruit of the tree of knowledge. What act was this?
> A: *Consorted with wrong side.*
> Q: (L) What does consorted mean?
> A: Lost some knowledge and power. *Limitation.* Conceptually limited.
> Q: (L) I want you to know that this does not make a whole lot of sense.
> A: Yes it does. Think carefully. Laura you are missing the obvious.
> Q: (L) In what sense would the fruit of the tree of life be limiting?
> A: *Believing that one source contains all knowledge is contradicting reality.*
> Q: (F) If the concept was the eating of the Fruit of the Tree of Knowledge provides all knowledge, then one is being deceived, because no one particular source can provide all knowledge. Therefore, when one believes in the deception, one has now trapped oneself within parameters. And, forevermore, the human race, will be poisoned by the very same problem which is reflected in several different ways: one is always seeking the truth through one pathway instead of seeking it through a myriad of pathways; and also believing in simplistic answers to very complex issues and questions.
> Q: (L) Where was Eden?
> A: Earth.
> Q: (L) The entire Earth was Eden?
> A: Yes.

Now, we are getting somewhere. "Believing that one source contains all knowledge is contradicting reality." It is "conceptually limited".

Over the years, many scientists have studied the effects of head and brain injuries. These studies were aimed at understanding the physiological and psychological effects and used a number of experiments to map the brain. The results have led to theories about two different modes of thinking or styles of thought, which are generally attributed to the left and right hemispheres of the brain.

In general, the left side of the brain controls the right side of the body, and the right side of the brain controls the left side of the body. According to the test results and the developing theory, the right brain is most often associated with direct sensual experience of the five sense organs as well as the sixth sense of intuitive thinking. Feelings are also associated with this side of the brain, and these feelings are often observed to be the result of the person's sensation of the environment. This sensation of the environment can be the external world or the internal state of being. Also, we must note that the right brain, as the observer of the external and internal environment, only perceives *now*.

The left brain is associated with the process of conceptualization and imagination in its many forms, including the powers of symbolic imagination and those functions related to the symbols we know as language such as labeling, categorizing, following verbal rules and rules in general. The left hemisphere mode of operation is much like a computer screen on which the whole range of concepts of the mind are portrayed and manipulated in the mind's eye. One of the main concepts we utilize is time as in time-future and time-past. Have a look at the chart below to see how the different hemispheres seem to operate.

Left Hemisphere Consciousness	Right Hemisphere Consciousness
Conceptualization, imagination, dogma, time-future, time-past.	Sensing, perceiving directly via observation, empiricism, *now* (no time).
Theoretical imagination.	Physical connection.
Linear logic.	Nonlinear logic.
Ritual, habit, fixed roles, repetition, fixation.	Creativity, spontaneity.
Morality, judgment.	Compassion, acceptance.
Superstition derived from imagination; often misuses limited direct observation and experience.	Science based on collecting of data, direct observation; can create theories with proper use of theoretical imagination.
Asceticism, sense deprivation.	Celebration.
Theology: Confucianism, Hinduism, Buddhism, Greco-Roman Religion, Judaism, Christianity, Islam.	Mysticism: Taoism, Tantrism, Yoga, the "Mystery Traditions," Gnosticism, Alchemy.

Now, this is enormously important to grasp: religions, philosophies, beliefs in general, through which we view the world and by which we interact with the world also fall to one hemisphere or the other in terms of how they activate our consciousness. There are teachings that place emphasis on the sensual right brain, and there are teachings that place emphasis on the abstract, imaginative left brain. Belief systems organically reflect one or the other of the two kinds of human consciousness.

The sense-oriented traditions encourage direct interaction with the physical environment. This has been often corrupted to gala sensuality of physical pleasure. Nevertheless, the pure mystical traditions tend to identify spirituality with the Cosmos itself and urges its followers to seek their unity with God through the physical world.

On the other hand, concept bound theologies tend to forbid sensual experience and observation, relying instead on imagination to support certain beliefs. In this mode, spirituality is equated with conceptual constructs, images, symbols and words that must be pictured in the mind's eye, or upheld in an abstract thought of imaginary belief so that the person is effectively attempting to impose an imaginary construct on reality rather than observing reality and allowing the observations to form the abstraction.

This is why the central issue in Christianity, to use just one example, is whether or not one believes in Jesus Christ. What one is being asked to do is to imaginatively support the church's conception of Jesus: that he was the son of God, that he died for remission of sins, and so on.

Each theological construct has its own cast of characters and its own plot, and each one demands that the followers believe in these imaginations. But the point is: the various symbols themselves are less important than the fact that the common act of conceptualizing, or imagining and making real that is central to theologies, is the left hemisphere mode of thought.

Left hemisphere thought also tends to assign religious authority to different writings or permanent scriptures and words. It also has a hierarchy of clergymen and priests who are designated to administer or interpret those words.

The left hemisphere mode of consciousness is opposed to direct observation, scientific progress, and discovery. It focuses on ritual repetition of established ideas and traditions. The words of the scriptures and the traditions of the interpreters of these words are given more authority than the natural world itself. The Cassiopaeans have often commented on ritual.

Q: (L) What ritual do you want us to do?
A: None.
Q: (L) Does ritual enhance or prevent communication?
A: They constrict energy flow.
Q: (L) Are there any rituals that can be performed to provide protection for one against intrusion by the Lizzies?
A: Rituals are self-defeating. Ritual drains directly to Lizard beings. Why do you think organized religion is obsessed with rituals?

Pure universal knowledge includes everything, and if you establish a ritual, that means you are adhering to one line of thought, one mode of thinking, one idea structure, and excluding all others. As noted, mystic traditions identify spirit with the Cosmos itself. They have no sacred traditions or priesthood. The authority to discover God is suggested to be within the power of each individual and they are encouraged to make direct and personal observations.

Q: (L) Are there any technological means we can use [for protection]?
A: The only defense needed is knowledge. Knowledge defends you against every possible form of harm in existence. The more knowledge you have, the less fear you have, the less pain you have, the less stress you feel, the less anguish you feel, and the less danger you experience of any form or sort. Think of this very carefully now for this is very important: Where is there any limitation in the concept behind the word "knowledge"? Being that there is no limitation, what is the value of that word? Infinite. Can you conceive of how that one concept, that one meaning frees you from all limitation? Use your sixth sense to conceive of how the word, the term, the meaning of knowledge can provide with all that you could possibly ever need. If you think carefully you will begin to see glimpses of how this is true in its greatest possible form.
Q: (L) Does this include knowledge learned from books?
A: This includes all possible meanings of the concept of the word. Can you think of how it would be that simply with one term, this one word could carry so much meaning? ... You can have glimpses of illumination and illumination comes from knowledge.

If you strive perpetually to gain and gather knowledge, you provide yourself with protection from every possible negative occurrence that could ever happen. Do you know why this is? The more knowledge you have, the more awareness you have as to how to protect yourself. Eventually this awareness becomes so powerful and so all encompassing that you do not even have to perform tasks or rituals, if you prefer, to protect yourself. The protection simply comes naturally with the awareness.

Knowledge has all substance. It goes to the core of all existence. [...] It includes adding everything to one's being that is desirable.

And also, when you keep invoking the light, as you do, truly understand that the light is knowledge. That is the knowledge which is at the core of all existence. And being at the core of all existence it provides protection from every form of negativity in existence. Light is everything and everything is knowledge and knowledge is everything.

... If you simply have faith, no knowledge that you could possibly acquire could possibly be false because there is no such thing. Anyone or anything that tries to give you false knowledge, false information, will fail. The very material substance that the knowledge takes on, since it is at the root of all existence, will protect you from absorption of false information that is not knowledge. There is no need to fear the absorption of false information when you are simply openly seeking to acquire knowledge. And knowledge forms the protection – all the protection you could ever need.

Q: (L) There are an awful lot of people who are being open and trusting and having faith that are getting zapped and knocked on their rears.

A: No. That is simply your perception. What you are failing to perceive is that these people are not really gathering knowledge. These people are stuck at some point in their pathway to progress and they are undergoing a hidden manifestation of what is referred to in your terms as obsession. Obsession is not knowledge; obsession is stagnation. So, when one becomes obsessed, one actually closes off the absorption and the growth and the progress of soul development which comes with the gaining of true knowledge. For when one becomes obsessed one deteriorates the protection, therefore one is open to problems, to tragedies, to all sorts of difficulties. Therefore one experiences same.

This is why all major scientific progress has been associated with mysticism. What we call modern science was derived directly from the alchemists of the European Renaissance, such as Newton and Paracelsus who were part of the historical attitude of empirical scientific inquiry fostered by the earlier mystical traditions. Mircea Eliade writes:

> Everywhere we find alchemy, it is always intimately related to a "mystical" tradition: in China with Taoism, in India with Yoga and Tantrism, in Hellenicism, and Gnosis in Egypt, in Islamic countries with hermetic and esoteric mystical schools, in the Western Middle Ages and Renaissance with Hermeticism, Christian and sectarian mysticism, and Cabala. (Eliade 1978)

It is not just science that is the child of mysticism, but creativity in general:

> The great periods of art and culture are always connected with an erotic-mystical revival. (Daniélou 1992)

So how are we to interpret this seeming contradiction that a sensual experience led to the Fall, and yet the right hemisphere, which relates to sensual experience, seems to be the mode of consciousness that is concerned with gathering knowledge and seeing things as they are? How do we interpret the fact that the left hemisphere–patriarchal–dominator theologies point to this sexual fault repeatedly, which the Cassiopaeans have also confirmed, and then the Cassiopaeans then go on to say that this fault was the actual door for the imposition of the monotheistic left brain domination?

I think that we may find some clues in the comparison of the legend of Orion to the stories of King Arthur and the Quest for the Holy Grail. What does Orion have to do with the Grail Quest? A great deal, I think. The similarities between the stories of Orion and Arthur, in essential terms, are many.

The Arthur of the Grail Quest is not, in a certain sense, a real flesh and blood man, but an archetypal complex of images. Arthur is other and more than the sum of his appearances in literature, and he is present in myths, stories and images that have no direct mention of him.

Arthur is present in the myths of all the sacrificial kings, dying saviors, and heroic slayers of dragons from time immemorial. His story grows with every episode we study, and after a time, we realize that Arthur himself is only a clue. He is a clue to the mythology of Fall and Redemption: The Once and Future King. He is the symbol of the lost Eden and his story has branches that reach out to embrace all the ideas of cyclical changes and power over the environment.

The Myth of the Golden Age: a period when the pole was oriented differently; when the seasons were different; the year was different – a primordial paradise where time had no meaning. Joscelyn Godwin writes:

> The memory or imagination of a Golden Age seems to be a particularity of the cultures that cover the area from India to Northern Europe. In the Americas, the most fully developed mythologies of history were those of the Mayas and Aztecs, *for whom there was no past era unclouded by the threat of cyclical destruction by fire of flood.* Nor does the philosophy of Buddhism have any place for nostalgia, although in practice it absorbed the idea of declining ages from its Indian surroundings. But in the ancient Middle East there is an obvious relic of the Golden Age in Genesis, as the Garden of Eden where humanity walked with the gods before the Fall. The Egyptians spoke of past epochs ruled by god-kings. Babylonian mythology, as reported by Berosus, had a scheme of three ages, each lasting while the vernal equinox precessed through four signs of the zodiac; the first of these, under the dominion of Anu, was a Golden

Age, ended by the Flood. The Iranian Avesta texts tell of the thousand-year Golden Reign of Yima, the first man and the first king, under whose rule cold and heat, old age, death and sickness were unknown.

The most fully developed theory of this kind, and probably the oldest one, is the Hindu doctrine of the Four Yugas. A modern scholar describes the first of these ages:

"In the first Krita Yuga, after the creation of the earth, Brahman created a thousand pairs of twins from his mouth, breast, thighs, and feet, respectively. They lived without houses; *all desires that they conceived were directly fulfilled*; and the earth produced of itself delicious food for them, since animals and plants were not yet in existence. Each pair of twins brought forth at the end of their life a pair exactly like them. As everybody did his duty and nothing else, there was no distinction between good and bad acts.

"After the Krita or Satya Yuga, things get progressively worse: each successive yuga sees the human race falling into increasing unhappiness and evil, until at the end of the Kali Yuga, the world is set on fire, deluged with water, and then reborn." (Godwin 1996)

In order to see the relation of Arthur to Orion, and their respective quests, we need to understand at the outset that stories can be translated both linguistically and culturally to provide meaning to their new owners. There is a story found in the History of Herodotus, which is an exact copy of an original tale of Indian origin except for the fact that in the original it was an animal fable and in Herodotus' version all the characters had become human. In every other detail, the stories are identical. As R. E. Meagher, professor of humanities and translator of Greek classics remarks: "Clearly, if characters change species, they may change their names and practically anything else about themselves."

The truth of the Holy Grail, the quest of the Arthurian knights, the finding of which would restore Arthur to the throne is the same as Orion's quest for the cure for his blindness. Arthur represents something other than just a British Dux Bellorum; he represents a long ago Golden Age, a time of social harmony and wise government, a time of ethics and morality, a time of the way of former kings. The theme of the lost Golden Age is so potent that when Geoffrey made Arthur a sort of Messiah, combining Welsh myth and tradition with genuine history, he touched something so deep in the human psyche that the Medieval Soul took flight in hopes of the restoration of the Kingdom on Earth which could only be restored by the discovery of the Grail.

The story of the Grail is the story of the creative potential of the human race in very real, though esoteric terms – the power to re-create the Golden Age – a pathway to knowledge of an ancient technology that gave rise to the great megalithic monuments for which no rational explanation exists – a power that has been hidden from us for ages past.

In discovering the true Grail we may also find the source of the Control System that has operated on our planet for the past many thousands of years, keeping humankind in bondage to time, history, misery, decay and suffering.

We note above that the left brain rules by conceptualization, imagination, and dogma. We then note that the right brain rules by sensing, perceiving directly via observation.

When the story says that Orion raped his love, the meaning is clear: the left-brain took over the function of the right brain, which was the direct conduit to universal powers of creation within the individual. Eve consorted with the wrong side.

In the prologue to Chrétien de Troyes' romance on Perceval, *Le Conte du Graal*, we are informed that there was once a paradise on Earth. There were two aspects of reality: an inner and an outer nature. Events took place not only in a real location in the material world; they also simultaneously had an existence at another level of being, a realm of archetypes. The everyday world and the twin otherworld were twin universes running parallel to one another.

In this paradise, maidens lived by sacred grottos, wells and springs. It was at these points that the two worlds were believed to meet, overlap, or bridge; that one could cross over to the other side. This is a symbol of the feminine potential, or the functions of the right hemisphere of the brain.

The Maidens of the Sacred Wells would feed wanderers and travelers from golden bowls and cups. This symbolized the creative potential of the right hemisphere, and that it was through this wellspring of creativity that one could literally create reality and all that was needed – plenitude, abundance.

The maidens served all wayfarers and the realm was at peace and fertile until one day an evil king, Amangons, ravished one of the maidens, held her in captivity and stole her sacred bowl. Amangons' followers took example from their king and began finding and raping the well maidens. Soon, there were no maidens serving at the wells. From that time onward, earth was the wasteland. The wells and waters dried up and the land became infertile. The barren wasteland was the condition of the loss of contact with the otherworld.

Now, this happened so long ago that we can only put together what it must have been like by comparing it to other mind rapes of more recent historical times. Regina Schwartz writes in *The Curse of Cain* about the relationship between monotheism and violence, positing that monotheism itself is the root of violence. In her chapter on covenants, she states that collective identity, which is a result of a monotheistic covenant explicitly narrated in the Bible, is:

> An invention, *a radical break with nature* and with the past. A transcendent deity breaks into history with the demand that the people he constitutes obey the law he institutes, and first and foremost among those laws is the requirement that they pledge allegiance to him, and him alone. (Schwartz 1997, 18)

This is what makes them a unified people as opposed to the "other" (as in all other people), which leads to violence. For the sake of these covenants, "in the "Old Testament," vast numbers of [the "other"] are obliterated, while in the "New Testament," vast numbers are colonized (converted)" (Schwartz 1997, 19).

She also talks about the idea of the provisional nature of a covenant, and that this means that it is conditional. "Believe in me and obey me or else I will destroy you." That's all fine and good, and the chief thing that occurs to me is that this belief business in religions or whatever constitutes a sort of permission, if you will, to take the vengeful action if the agreement is broken. The Hebrew phrase for "he made a covenant", is *karat berit*, or literally, he *cut a covenant*. In the covenant with Abraham in Genesis, animals are cut in two and a fire passes between them in a mysterious ritual. Then, there is the cutting of the flesh at circumcision, and the Sinai covenant where the laws were cut into stone. So, these covenants are apparently what constituted Israel as a nation. The entire foundational frame of Israel, which is the basis of Christianity, is framed by the severed pieces of animals, it seems.

> In ancient Near Eastern rituals, the cut made to the animal is symbolically made to the inferior who enters into the covenant with a superior. (Schwartz 1997, 22)

At the making of the Covenant at Mt. Sinai, there were a bunch of sacrificed animals. Moses took the blood and, dividing it in half, he cast one half on the altar. Taking the book of the covenant, he read it to the people, and they said, "We will observe all that Yahweh has decreed. We will obey". And then Moses took the blood and cast it on the people saying, "This is the blood of the covenant that Yahweh has made with you containing all these rules".

> We are ... heirs of a long tradition in which monotheism is regarded as the great achievement of "Judeo-Christian" thought ... [M]onotheism is entangled with particularism, with the assertion that this God, and not any other gods must be worshipped, a particularism so virulent that it reduces all other gods to idols and so violent that it reduces all other worshippers to abominations. ... The danger of a universal monotheism is asserting that its truth is *the* Truth, its system of knowledge *the* System of knowledge, its ethics *the* Ethics – not because ... any other option must be rejected, but because there simply is no other option. ... [They] presuppose a kind of metaphysical scarcity ... a hoarding belief, hoarding allegiance, and even hoarding identity. Because there is a finite supply – of whatever – it must be either contained in whole or protected as a part. ... [It] suggests limit and boundaries. (Schwartz 1997, 33)

What they are doing is developing mental boundaries. They are creating an image of the world in the left hemisphere mode of thinking. It is fixed, limited, and most of all, prevents discovery, change and spiritual evolution. Worse than that, it blocks creativity in a cosmic sense; it is the desire to possess knowledge in a limited form; to own what cannot be owned and place limits on something that is in reality infinite.

The Christian church is the triumph of monotheism/left-brain domination. At that point in time, there were still adherents of the true mystical tradition, and it is very likely that Jesus was an initiate of the Grail and the only hints we can find to his true work are in the Gnostic writings and sects that continued to exist. At the very heart of Gnosticism lies an essentially feminine right brain view of the cosmos and this was the inspiration of the Cathars and alchemists.

The patriarchal priests of Rome, probably as agents of the Control System at fourth density, unleashed a horrendous persecution of the Gnostics and Cathars and any others that did not adhere to their dogma. It has been estimated that the cost of bringing Europe under the domination of Christianity was about ten million innocent lives.

By their fruits, you shall know them.

The Grail Hero, who can be anyone, is one who must discover the meeting place between the worlds where he can reestablish the links between feminine creative sovereignty and the kingship of the material realm. The loss of communion between the divine feminine rulership of the inner land and the rightful kingship of the outer realm is what we are concerned with here. The right brain rules the land or the material reality only by right of his true union with the feminine principle and championship of her freedom.

Springs and wells are symbols of the most powerful outward expression of life-giving abundance. Finding the Grail is the reestablishing of this creative power. In the Grail stories, we find that our hero, Parzival, has to go through three stages on his quest. The first is innocent and unquestioning acceptance of what others tell him. This is a state of unconsciousness of actions. The second is doubt. Parzival rebels against all he has been told because he has seen that it only causes him more trouble. The third stage is when he begins to believe in nothing but the love of a woman. This only means that he finally sees that what is natural and real is more trustworthy than a God who is an unreal, supernatural construct of the left brain. And it is at this point that magic begins to happen.

> Central to the Grail legend is that renewal must be preceded by a ceremonial cleansing, a purging, rather than just a purification. There must be a radical departure from what was past. The old world dies in order for the new one to be born. The principle is "The King is dead, long live the King".
>
> The essential theme of the Grail, repeated in all the Celtic accounts, is that of a union of the two principles of the Goddess and the Hero King. This is the foundational condition of paradise.
>
> But man wishes to create paradise to his own specifications which contains all the desirable elements and none of the undesirable. Yet, every time Parzival lets the reins of his horse loose and relaxes into the saddle, accepting that wherever he goes is fine, it turns out for the best. But, the moment he tries to take control and "change things", to impose his "superior vision" upon the natural order, he promptly becomes lost in the Wasteland.
>
> When we come to the Lovers in the Tarot, the whole underlying message of the Gnostics, the Cathars, and the Grail finally fits into place. The Lovers is the card of *balance* and *harmony* and wholeness reflected in its twin card: Temperance.
>
> And the path to the Light in the little landscape at the bottom left of the card lies between the two peaks – Perce a Val. Parzival has remained loyal to his true love, true to the quest to find something bigger than himself and to find his way out of the habits of being unable to truly see our true predicament in life. He has trusted in the natural order of things and has learned to observe and think for himself. He has stopped dividing life into Black and White and trying to change one to the other and he has learned to accept life as a seamless whole of nature including himself as both a spiritual being and a man of flesh with a family.
>
> The new metaphysical age in the West has become a supermarket place for spiritual wares. All seekers are desperately trying to transform themselves. Every guru, therapist and preacher tells us that with only a little more effort, sending a little more love and light, we

can attain whatever particular goal we desire, be it Moksha, Liberation, return to God, Higher Consciousness, Psychic Enhancement, or Enlightenment. (Godwin 1994)

What is wrong with efforts to send love and light, the achieving of the goals of world peace or personal prosperity? What is wrong with wanting a return to God, or higher consciousness or any of the touted experiences that are guaranteed to initiate a person to whatever they desire? The problem is *anticipation*. When you seek any of these things by holding the thoughts in the left-brain in anticipation of making it real, you are raping the maiden of the well.

What if you are just trying to believe it is now? Belief is a function of the left brain; it blocks the manifestation of creativity because the creative right brain is also the empirical half of the brain that observes the dichotomy between the belief and the reality.

Desire is anticipation. Anticipation is read by the right brain as in the future, therefore not right now, and the right brain can only create now. When we desire, we have a future object in mind. The right brain only knows now.

If we desire to love God, we have a concept (left brain) of the future goal of loving God. It can't exist now. Therefore we experience struggle to constantly love God, against the ongoing now of not loving God.

If we desire to win the lottery, and produce in the left brain future image of money flowing into our life, it isn't now. So now continues moneyless.

If we desire happiness, and create the concept in the left brain, we have future happiness in mind. And the right brain reads it as unhappiness now, and this can manifest in thousands of unhappy experiences.

By the same token, if we send love and light to any directed recipient, we are holding a concept of future fixing that signals a state of brokenness *now* to our right brain, and the repercussions are felt in our life. In a larger sense, we may be signaling the collective right brain that a future state of peace is desired, and therefore, now is not peaceful. And so the right brain creates now. The perception of linear time constantly projects rewards into the future, blocking access to the present, like a donkey chasing a carrot for all eternity.

Q: (L) If someone wanted to win the lottery, for example, what would be the correct approach? What should they do, or be, or think, or say?
A: Completely pure intent, i.e., open. Nonanticipatory.
Q: (L) Anticipation constricts the channels of creativity?
A: Yes.

Q: (L) A person has to be completely uncaring whether they get it or not, so to speak?
A: Happy-go-lucky attitude helps.
Q: (L) So, worry, tension, anticipation, and attachment to the idea, we constricts the flow?
A: Yes.

But you noticed, I hope, that intent is not considered to be anticipation or desire. The words themselves may provide a clue.

> Anticipate: *ante* – before + *capare* – to take. To look forward to; to expect; to make happen earlier, precipitate; to foresee and perform in advance, etc.

We see clearly the connection between anticipation and time.

> Intent: firmly directed or fixed; having the mind or attention firmly directed or fixed; engrossed; strongly resolved; a purpose or objective; will and determination at the time of performing an act.

Do we see a subtle difference? Even if it is somewhat semantically, it is sufficient to make us think about how to deal with our creative potential.

Of course, we see that completely pure intent is a pretty tall order. Thus we see that the key becomes acting now with intent, but no imaginary anticipation for the future. A goal, with applied *will* of action, which necessitates left brain conscious preparing and planning, via the heightened awareness of the right brain, which deals directly with the present conditions, will result in an opening of life changing creative potential.

> Q: (L) Okay, we've been talking earlier this evening about intent, and of course, our own experiences with intent have really been pretty phenomenal. We've come to some kind of an idea that intent, when confirmed repeatedly, actually builds force. Is this a correct concept, and is there anything that you can add to it?
> A: Only until anticipation muddies the picture ... tricky one, huh?
> Q: (L) Is anticipation the act of assuming you know how something is going to happen?
> A: Follows realization, generally, and unfortunately for you, on 3rd density. You see, once anticipation enters the picture, the intent can no longer be STO.
> Q: (L) Anticipation is desire for something for self. Is that it?
> A: Yes.
> Q: (L) Okay, so it's okay to intend something, or to think in an intentional way, or to hope in an intentional way, for something that is to serve another ...

A: And that brings realization. But, realization creates anticipation.

Q: (L) Well, how do we navigate this razor? I mean, this is like walking on a razor's edge. To control your mind to not anticipate, and yet, deal with realization, and yet, still maintain hope …

A: Mental exercises of denial, balanced with pure faith of a nonprejudicial kind.

Q: (L) Okay, so, in other words, to just accept what is at the moment, appreciate it as it is at the moment, and have faith that the universe and things will happen the way they are supposed to happen, without placing any expectation on how that will be, and keep on working?

A: Yes.

Q: (L) We have discussed a lot of concepts about shaping the future. In our discussions, we have hypothesized that it is something like an intentional act of shaping something good, but without defining the moment of measurement. In other words, adding energy to it by intent, but not deciding where, when or how the moment of measurement occurs. Like a quantum jump: you know it is statistically likely, but not definite, so you cannot expect it, but you observe so that you can notice when it occurs on it's own, and in it's own way.

A: Yes. Avoiding anticipation. That is the key to shaping the future … When it hits you, it stops.

Q: (L) When what hits you? The fact that it's happening? That you are doing it?

A: Yes unless you cancel out all anticipation.

Q: (L) Well, this is very tricky.

A: Ah? We have doubts … And yes, you create your own reality!

Q: (L) Well, but you have also said that anticipation messes things up, and so I don't want to have any anticipation.

A: Anticipation is not creating one's own reality.

If *non*-anticipation opens the door to the creativity of the universe, what closes the door to negative occurrences? Can it be that we have a clue here as well?

> Cassiopaeans: "Just remember that anticipation is the "mother of preparation", and defense.
>
> Lesson number 1: always expect attack.
>
> Lesson number 2: know the modes of same.
>
> Lesson number 3: know how to counteract same.
>
> When you are under attack, expect the unexpected, if it is going to cause problems …
>
> But, if you expect it, you learn how to "head it off", thus neutralizing it. This is called vigilance, which is rooted in knowledge. Knowledge protects."

So, it seems that the answer to this part of the problem is that when we are connected to the Cosmos via the right brain, and are not blocking the ability of our Cosmic Connection by limiting the forces with boundary forming imagination or images or illusory concepts, we allow the perfect manifestation of our own frequency resonance to occur. By the same token, when necessary, we can close the door to manipulation of our minds by constantly running a sort of computer scan of possible breaches of our security system in the left brain. We must marry the left brain kingship of the material world to the right brain queen of the inner realm.

Yet, it was only when Parzival rejected *all* of the advice, the exhortations, when he quit seeking to be a great knight on a sacred quest to save the world; only when he rejected God as the pure and good all-father that … it found him.

What is the wasteland? That we cannot accept the world and all within it, including ourselves, as being perfectly natural and perfect just the way it is – with all the good and evil it contains as part of the natural and necessary balance – the whole of existence is natural and as it should be at every moment. When you accept that all is perfect, when you cease holding God hostage by usurping the power of the right brain feminine principle with the images in your left brain, then the world will be perfect and fertile and you will heal the wound of the wasteland in your own heart.

If only we can act spontaneously, without being programmed into someone else's belief system, we can ask the real question of ourselves; ask with no preconceived notion of what the answer will be; ask with no anticipation.

Then, miraculously, for one moment the vessel of the Grail is empty … and in the next it is filled with the wonder and glory of *all* and everything.

> The Spirit of the Valley never dies. It is called the Mystic Female. The Door of the Mystic Female is the root of Heaven and Earth. (Lao Tzu)

And the Mystic Female is the infinite Sea of potential. It is God in the *not* aspect that only can *be* when expectations, anticipations, assumptions and obsessions are completely left at the door.

> Negative existence is the silence behind the sound, the blank canvas beneath the painting, the darkness into which light shines. Emptiness is the stillness against which time moves. Negative existence enables a man to be what he is. It is the mirror of mirrors. Nonanticipation is noninterference, and allows the most perfect reflection of creation. (Lao Tzu)

CHAPTER 24
THE BACCHANTES MEET APOLLO AT STONEHENGE AND PLAY *THE THIRD MAN* THEME

Now, I want to make some little observations and conjectures. Most of the creation myths speak about some sort of ritual fault that occurred to bring about humankind's Fall from Grace. These myths mostly attribute this fault to something having to do with sex. We have already talked about the symbology of this in relation to the hemispheres of the brain, but we still have to deal with the out and out *sex* issue! When it is talked about, it's always rather vague and mysterious and has seldom made much sense, so I am going to try to sort it out here.

In addition to the Fall from the Edenic state, there is also the Flood of Noah and the destruction of Sodom and Gomorrah, which is blamed on sexual excess. In the Sumerian myths, it is said that humans copulating all over the place kept the gods awake and they could get no rest, so they resolved to destroy the whole kit and caboodle.

Putting this ancient mythology together with some of the things the Cassiopaeans have said has caused me no end of exhausting mental gymnastics. On the one hand, they are agreeing that a sex-based event was definitely involved in the Fall, but then they have also said the whole sexual thing was part of the Control System's inducement of increased physicality because the fourth-density STS beings "feed" on orgasmic energy as part of their nourishment:

> Q: (L) Was the story of Noah's flood the story of the breaking up of Atlantis?
> A: Yes. But symbolic.
> Q: (L) How many people were on the planet at that time?
> A: 6 billion.
> Q: (L) Out of this six billion people, how many survived?
> A: 119 million.
> Q: (L) Was Noah's flood caused by the close passage of another celestial body?

A: Yes. Martek. Mars.

Q: (L) Was Martek an inhabited planet at that time?

A: No.

Q: (L) Did it have water or other features?

A: Yes.

Q: (L) When it passed close to the Earth did it, in fact, overload our planet with water we did not have prior to that time?

A: Yes.

Q: (L) Did we, prior to that time, have a water vapor canopy surrounding our planet?

A: Yes.

Q: (L) How was this water vapor canopy suspended?

A: The water vapor canopy was a natural element of the particular composition of your atmosphere at that particular measure point in space-time.

Q: (L) Was the gravity level the same as what it is now?

A: It was somewhat different. But not perceptible to you. That difference is part of the explanation of why that vapor canopy remained suspended.

Q: (L) Did that condition prior to the flood of Noah, the altered gravitational state as well as the water vapor canopy, was that condition more conducive to extended life spans than the conditions that exist on the planet now?

A: Not only those things but all the other conditions that existed on the planet at that particular point in space-time were more conducive to longer life spans. And, by the way, Noah is a symbolic message rather than an historical event.

Q: (L) Do you mean a historical event in the terms of Noah being in an ark or historical event in terms of the flood?

A: First of all, there was no "Noah". Secondly there was no actual real flood as depicted in that story. Thirdly, the whole story was a symbolic message as opposed to an actual event.

Q: (L) What did actually occur and what does the symbolism have to tell us?

A: It is a very broad representation. It simply means that there was a cataclysmic event that did envelop the whole planet at that time and that those that were ready to experience that as part of their soul development without exiting the body, were warned ahead of time. But not by trying to manipulate events, but by simply allowing faith to let them acquire knowledge and being naturally drawn into position to experience what they needed to experience to survive the event.

Q: (L) What was the event a hundred or so years after the flood of Noah that was described as the confusing of languages, or the tower of Babel?

A: Spiritual confluence.

Q: (L) What purpose did the individuals who came together to build the tower intend for said tower?
A: Electromagnetic concentration of all gravity waves.
Q: (L) And what did they intend to do with these concentrated waves?
A: Mind alteration of masses.
Q: (L) What intention did they have in altering the mind of the masses?
A: *Spiritual unification of the masses.*
Q: (L) Who were the "gods" that looked down on the tower of Babel, at those who were building it with the intention of unification, and decided to destroy their works?
A: Lizards.
Q: (L) Okay, so the Lizzies blew up the tower of Babel. What else did they do to the minds of mankind; did they do something causing literal disruption of their understanding of language?
A: Close. Brainwashing of masses.
Q: (L) Did they do this through implants and abduction?
A: Partly.
Q: (L) What is the true meaning, the original meaning, of the Hebrew word "shem"?
A: Purity.
Q: (L) Why was this word related to the obelisks or standing stones later called "shems" by the Hebrews?
A: Symbolic of purity: unification. Uniformity.
Q: (L) How were Sodom and Gomorra destroyed and the other cities of the plain? And by whom?
A: Nuclear; EM pulse. Who else?
Q: (L) The Lizzies?
A: Yes.
Q: (L) Why?
A: To implant fear and obedience.
Q: (L) Weren't the Sodom and Gomorrans really evil and bad doing sodomy and Gomorrahy?
A: That is a deception of history.
Q: (L) What body were the Sumerians talking about when they described the Planet of the crossing or Nibiru?
A: Comets.
Q: (L) This body of comets you have talked about?
A: Yes.
Q: (L) Does this cluster of comets appear to be a single body?
A: Yes.
Q: (L) The planet that was destroyed between Jupiter and Mars, you said was destroyed by psychic energy?
A: Yes.
Q: (L) What was the source of this psychic energy?

A: Beings inhabiting the planet.

Q: (L) Did any of those beings leave that planet and come to earth?

A: Yes. Blond and blue eyed descendants. Eye pigment was because planet was farther from Sol.

Q: (L) How did the people of that planet come to earth? Did they know it was going to be destroyed?

A: Some knew and were taken by Lizzies and they are the Annunaki.

Q: (L) Is there a planet Nibiru?

A: No.

Q: (L) What does Nibiru mean in the Sumerian language?

A: Slave owner.

Now, let's have a look at the Cassiopaean remarks about sex in general:

Q: (L) What happens psychically at the moment of orgasm?

A: For whom?

Q: (L) For anybody. In just a general way. Does anything happen to a person psychically when they have sexual climax?

A: Open.

Q: (L) Is it different for each individual?

A: Close.

Q: (L) Is it different for males from females?

A: Usually.

Q: (L) The reason I ask is because a man named Wayne Cook did some work with dowsing and he found out that the human body, after sexual climax, dowses the same pattern as a dead body. Why is this? (T) Draining of energy.

A: Yes.

Q: (L) Okay, where does the energy drain?

A: To the ether.

Q: (L) Does the energy go to one or the other partner?

A: Maybe.

Q: (L) Is it possible, during this activity, for Lizzies or other beings to be hanging around and be drawing this energy?

A: Yes.

Q: (L) Is that, in a general sense, what often happens?

A: Yes.

Q: (L) Is this one of the reasons that sex has been promoted and promulgated in our society to such an extent ...

A: Yes, yes, yes.

So, on the one hand we have sex bringing us under the control of the alleged Reptoids who supposedly want us to get out there and have sex so they can feed on the orgasmic energy, and on the other hand, we have these stories that tell us that the reptilian gods decided to do away with the whole mess of humanity *because* they couldn't get any rest with all the sex going on! What's the deal here?

Is it possible that there is a kind of sex that is beneficial that might be related to spiritual unification, which would enable them to free themselves from the domination of the Control System?

From the clues above, it seems to me there was something going on prior to the time of the destruction of Atlantis that was dangerous to the Controllers. Not only that, it seems some of the survivors retained this information and were planning on employing it in the Tower of Babel project, the destruction of which has always been presented as an "example" that we should not aspire to be like the gods.

We also recall that the cities of Sodom and Gomorra were presented as being extremely depraved and that they concentrated on sexual excess, which also brought about their destruction.

Well, if it is true that all this sexual stuff is "food of the gods", so to speak, then what can there be about sex that they don't want us to know? Why the big whitewash? And why the big push to take over the whole world with the anti-sex monotheistic religions that made it a sin to make love unless the only objective was to reproduce? If you think about it, such an attitude would naturally tend to make a person finish having sex as quickly as possible with a mental left-brain image at the fore. Hmm ... are we getting a clue here? And nowadays, of course, it is even worse. Sex is a performance oriented sport. How often, how many times, and how high can you "jump"? The confusion between sex and love has also served to further confuse the issue. "If you can't be with the one you love, love the one you're with."

From all I have been able to determine, the ancient civilizations that were in direct contact with fourth-density STO beings were those that were part of the megalithic culture. There are traces of this great age of humankind from China and India to the Atlantic Ocean, and from South America to the middle of the Pacific. According to the most recent research, the very oldest form of religion that can be identified was the worship of the Celestial Mother Goddess by wandering hunter gatherers.

It was thought for a long time that such cultures were very primitive and narrow, but it has since been discovered that this is not the case. New archaeological sites are being excavated at the present time (Jomon in Japan, for example) that show very advanced levels of art and culture among these husbandmen of the Earth. The discernible idea of the religion of these peoples is that of an infinite bounty of the Great Mother. It is thought that they didn't engage in agriculture because the idea of owning land may have been abhorrent to them. The idea of forcing the Earth to yield rather than accepting the natural abundance the Goddess provided was simply not a part of their philosophy. Their Goddess was a "Star Being" rather than the later transmogrification into the Earth Mother/agriculture goddess, and this Star Being was worshipped in Temples that were laid out along Celestial Archetypes.

And, there is also something *very* mysterious about these early people – they seemed to have had the super powers of the Golden Age. Morris K. Jessup wrote:

> We concern ourselves at the moment only with the gigantic stone masonry which remains in almost all parts of the world. Certain characteristics of some of the stonework bespeak origin in a single, widespread civilization, highly developed in some ways, but *not mechanical in the same sense as ours of today*. ... It can be confidently said that the First Civilization had simple and effective methods of working and moving stone which are unused today, and which were more effective than anything which we of the Second Civilization have developed.
>
> In many areas we find evidence of stone blocks of unbelievable weight being quarried, more or less casually moved considerable distances, and then lifted into place. ... Many investigators and thinkers have proposed methods for moving these quarried and dressed blocks. All of the proposals are based on applications of such simple present-day engineering equipment as block-and-tackle or sand ramps. ... No suggestions have been made which really fit all cases, and some of the submissions are so cumbersome and inadequate as to seem ridiculous.
>
> The Fortress (so-called by archaeologists, who admit no types of building other than religious, military, and occasionally residential) of Sacsahuaman is on a mountaintop overlooking modern Cuzco. It is noteworthy as one of the earliest works showing the construction of walls by *grinding and fitting the stones in situ*. These walls are also noted for the very large stones which make up the lower of three tiers, and it is these in which we are more interested.
>
> The stones making up the corners of the reentrant angles of this lower tier appear to be a dark basalt; heavy, hard, and rugged. They are so large that they dwarf a man on horseback standing beside them. Some of them are about twelve feet square at the base, and eighteen to twenty feet high. They are estimated to weigh about two hundred tons each. Other stones in the same walls range from small ones of only a few hundred pounds, through continuous gradations up to the largest. All of them were crudely rough quarried, and were then *ground into their designated niches in the structure by pushing them back and forth, in situ*, until they fitted so closely, completely

and accurately that a knife blade cannot be inserted between them. This is a logical and practical shortcut to effective stone fitting which we have not equaled in modern engineering.

(It is interesting to note in passing, however, that we use this method in what is probably our operation of highest accuracy and precision: lens and mirror grinding for astronomical telescopes. No substitute has been found for this system of grinding pieces of glass together to obtain perfect curvature, and there is no basic difference in the two operations.)

However, there are some startling inferences in the size and mass of the stones. To place the largest of these corner stones in place, so that others could be worked to fit them, required tremendous force. It is unimaginable that sufficient hand labor and crude tackle could be massed around them so that they could be moved and handled.

The intermediate sizes, some of them weighing ten, twenty, and forty tons, or more, had to be picked up, put approximately into place, and pushed back and forth until they ground themselves into their individually fitting contours. This was no mean chore. It is inferred that means of handling must have existed which made it easy, or at any rate possible, to swing these stones up and around, and to shove them to and fro, against terrific friction, while pinched between their adjacent neighbors. Such power would tax any modern machine or power plant and require an installation of generating equipment sufficient to run a city. It seems plainly obvious that some other source of power existed.

It may be that this tremendous power was limited in its application to articles of stone texture only, but this is a little doubtful. Or, *perhaps it was limited to nonmagnetic materials* in general. *Such a limitation would have sidetracked the development of a mechanized culture such as ours of this day, and would partly account for the strange fact that almost all relics of the profound past are nonmetallic.* It does seem possible that the usefulness of that power, whatever it was, may have been limited by its very nature and that it was never developed along industrial lines because of this limitation and even, perhaps, because of a basic difference in values. *This writer cannot see his way to believing that such a power was electrical, magnetic, calorific, or strictly mechanical, else it would have led to industrial developments leaving at least a few traces.* (Jessup 1955; emphasis added)

These last remarks of Morris Jessup's are, to me, the most interesting. It is a fact that the Earth is literally blanketed with megaliths from some sort of ancient civilization. Tens of thousands of them! There are variations in placement and style, but the thing they all have in common is their incredible sizes, and their antiquity. One book on the subject says:

> Looming out of the mists from hillside, moor and forest glade, in a great arc around the coasts of Europe, from Sweden and the Shetland Islands in the north to Spain, Portugal and Malta in the south, stand the megaliths – great gray rocks, roughhewn, streaked with age, often imposing, always mysterious. They range from single natural boulders to grandiose structures, which would have demanded complex architectural planning, and the labour of tens of thousands of men for centuries.
>
> There has never been a systematic census of these monuments, but it is estimated that there are at least 50,000 of them. Even that figure amounts to only a fraction of the total number erected, for countless megaliths have been destroyed by the forces of nature or by man.
>
> The known and lost monuments once formed an enormous blanket of stone extending over Western Europe. Today, often only the skeleton of the original can be seen. The bare gray stones were, in many cases, covered by great mounds of green turf and gleaming white quartz pebbles. Spread by the thousands along the coasts they must have been a dazzling and unparalleled sight.
>
> Unparalleled indeed in human history. For there has never been anything like this rage, almost mania, for megalith building, except perhaps during the centuries after A.D. 1000 when much the same part of Europe was covered with what a monk of the time called a 'white mantle of churches'.
>
> ... The megaliths, then, were raised by some of the earliest Europeans. The reason that this simple fact took so long to be accepted was the peculiar inferiority complex which Western Europeans had about their past. Their religions, their laws, their cultural heritage, their very numerals, all come from the East. The inhabitants, before civilization came flooding in from the Mediterranean, were illiterate; they kept no records, they built no cities. It was easy to assume that they were simply bands of howling half-naked savages who painted their bodies, put bear-grease on their hair and ate their cousins. (Reader's Digest Association 1977)

The whys and wherefores of this megalith mania are still under debate. The fact is, you can't date stones. Yes, you can date organic things found around them or near them, or under them, but you can't date the stones.

The interesting thing is that the peoples who did erect them are still, in most circles, considered to be barbarians because *they did not build cities, engage in agriculture, develop the wheel, or writing.*

Yet, they did something that clearly cannot and was not done by "civilized" peoples who did all of those "civilized" things. They had some sort of "power" that we cannot replicate and do not understand. Yet, this very power may be the answer to our question about why and how sex was implicated in the fall of man, the flood of Noah, and numerous other events that may lead us to some interesting discoveries.

I would like to speculate here for a moment. The first thing that comes to my mind when I consider the problem of the megaliths is that of what I call "payoff". That is, nobody who is human ever does anything without a payoff, or to put it more generally, *for a reason*. What could be the reason for the stones? There were clearly a great deal more of them than would be necessary for simple monumental or worship purposes. They appear to be arranged like the inner workings of some vast machinery whose purpose is an enigma to us.

At the same time, could the overabundant presence of these megaliths have anything to do with the things that are observed to be lacking in these peoples, i.e., the signs of civilization, the wheel, agriculture, writing and cities? Suppose the reason for the stones and the reason for the absence of "civilized standards" are identical?

We have already mentioned the "civilizing influence" of the Consortium and the possible ulterior motives behind it. It is a matter of observation that cities developed in agricultural societies as a central place to manufacture and exchange goods. Agriculture is required to feed stable and static populations. Wheels are needed to both transport people and goods in cities and from agricultural zones to cities and back. Writing is needed to keep records of transactions, as is demonstrated by the clear evidence of the earliest forms of writing: endless lists and tallies of grain and cattle. Writing was also used to record and promulgate the exploits of certain gods and goddesses as well as keeping track of all the goods tithed to the temple and priesthood.

So, suppose none of this was needed? Suppose a civilization existed that did not need cities, agriculture, wheels or writing? That is not to say that they did not produce goods nor that they did not produce food for large groups, or that they did not travel over vast distances or record their exploits. But, suppose they did not do it in the way we would expect? Suppose the stones did it all!

What do I mean? To explain, let me go in a slightly different direction for a moment: one of the things that seems to be almost ubiquitous with these ancient groups and their circles and mighty stone works and "star temples" and all that seems to be the fact that they all just "disappear" with alarming regularity. How many times have you read the following?

"What happened to [ancient group of your choice] is unknown. The site was abandoned and there is no explanation as to what happened or where they went."

Then, such writers go to great lengths explaining all sorts of possible scenarios: plague, war, climate, whatever. Global cataclysm is almost never proposed because it is too scary, and besides, the structures are intact for the most part. But, the single fact remains: the peoples associated with big piles of rocks or megalithic structures have a habit of disappearing. That's an unavoidable observation. Frank Joseph, who has been studying ancient sites in the U.S., their circles of which seem to bear resemblance to the more ancient sites, writes:

> What, then, was responsible for all the loosely connected ceremonial centers scattered from Wisconsin to Georgia [to Mexico, etc.] winding down at the same time? The answer is simple and comprehensively correct: a calendar.
>
> One of the major elements in common among the various walled ceremonial centers was their concurrent function as astronomical observatories ... Above all they worshipped time. They may have felt oppressed by it, or perhaps they strove to live in harmony with its cycles. In either case, *their obvious attention to the movements of the heavens clearly defines an obsession with the regular passage of cycles in nature.*
>
> Here, too, the mound builders compare closely with Tenochitlan's own priest-kings, the Tlatoan, who were likewise self-conscious of time, which they envisioned as the figure of a ferocious sun god. In fact, the chief deity of the Aztecs, the solar Huitzlipochtli, was jointly known as 'the Eagle with Arrows of Fire, the *Lord of Time'*.
>
> The people of Aztalan [the name of the Wisconsin ceremonial center as handed down orally by the local Native Americans] left their ceremonial enclosure, as did the inhabitants of the rest of the walled settlements throughout the Mississippi valley, *because their sacred calendar ordered them to do so. Separated by great distances as they were, their alignment posts of sundial pyramids all told their observers the same thing at the same moment: it was time to go.* (Joseph 1997; emphasis added)

Mr. Joseph is definitely onto something, though it may not be precisely what he is thinking. It is fairly clear, though not precisely proven, that these circles were used as some sort of astronomical observatory. But it is also clear that a simple accounting of time in order to know when to plant the grain, or when to have a ceremony for standard purposes, is all out of proportion to the payoff factor of the megaliths. Smaller and less difficult to build structures would serve the purposes of astronomical observations and ritual activity equally well. It seems as though the circles and other megalithic structures had to be built out of stone for a specific reason, that is, the stones had a function; they *did* something.

Yes, the builders disappeared, group after group. That could imply, as suggested in the previous chapter, an even more interesting phenomenon: the manipulation of space-time. If that is the case, then it is clear why they did not need the accoutrements of so-called civilization. The Stone Movers did not need any of the accoutrements of so-called "civilization" for the simple reason that the *stones did everything*.

There has been some research regarding "recordings" in stones of buildings – of energy fields, earth grids and all that. Certain stones produce electricity under the right conditions, and if the stones were used to amplify mental energies, then they would power not only transport (eliminating the need for the wheel), communication and recording of information (eliminating the need for writing), and perhaps could even manifest anything that was needed in terms of food and other goods (thereby eliminating the need for cities and agriculture).

Tied in to all of this is the ancient alchemical lore about the Philosopher's stone (though I am not so naïve as to think that this is the whole cheese in that regard, but it does make you think a bit). The Holy Grail, the head of Bran the Blessed, and the Philosopher's stone of the alchemists are all connected to the idea of certain powers that have to do with the stopping or manipulating of time, a source of endless abundance (multiplying loaves and fishes), eternal life or the elixir of life, and so forth. Most importantly, they are also connected to the idea of cycles and astronomical placements being necessary to the Work.

It is not entirely out of the question that if such was the case, these stones could have just simply "translated" or transferred the Stone Movers into another dimension at some point when astronomical alignments were right – the "big payoff of going home", so to speak. Remember?

"The people of Aztalan left their ceremonial enclosure ... because their sacred calendar ordered them to do so. ... Their alignment posts of sundial pyramids all told their observers the same thing at the same moment: it was time to go."

Maybe all their careful record keeping in such funny ways (the 19 year moon cycle, for example; the 19th day as a special day of rest for the Assyrians) had to do with the moments in space-time when certain activities were most easily accomplished? Maybe they weren't a bunch of silly, superstitious savages hauling stones around and sweating like crazy just to dance around in the moonlight and discover when to plant the corn?

Getting back to our ideas about sex, what did these ancient peoples think about sex? Do we have a way of figuring it out? Did it, in fact, play a part in their seemingly magical abilities? Did any of these peoples "move to a different reality" of their own volition, or did the Control System destroy them because they were a threat? Are these the types we are talking about when we find stories of sex that "kept the gods awake all night"?

The remark from the Sumerian legends about all of the night long fornicating made me think of another "all night" party I came across in my research.

> And there is also on the island both a magnificent sacred precinct of Apollo and a notable temple, which is adorned with many votive offerings and is spherical in shape. Furthermore, a city is there which is sacred to this god, and the majority of its inhabitants are players on the cithara; and these continually play on this instrument in the temple and sing hymns of praise to the god, glorifying his deeds ...
>
> They say also that the moon, as viewed from this island, appears to be but a little distance from the earth and to have upon it prominences, like those of the earth, which are visible to the eye. The account is also given that the god visits the island every nineteen years, the period in which the return of the stars to the same place in the heavens is accomplished, and for this reason the Greeks call the nineteen-year period the year of Meton.
>
> At the time of this appearance of the god he both plays on the cithara and dances continuously the night through from the vernal equinox until the rising of the Pleiades, expressing in this manner his delight in his successes. And the kings of this city and the supervisors of the sacred precinct are called Boreades, since they are the descendants of Boreas, and the succession to these positions is always kept in their family. (Diodorus, Vol. II, 37-41)

Now, aside from the fact that the only temple that could fit the above description is Stonehenge, which of course, pretty much does away with the modern day version of the Druid hocus pocus, we find the description of the ceremonies to be most interesting in terms of our subject.

From what I have been able to piece together, these ancient peoples of the megaliths were in tune with the Celestial Forces. They were a group apart from the serpent oriented agriculturists, or the serpent hating (though still unwittingly controlled by them in the guise of Yahweh/Jehovah), wandering shepherd king monotheists. They worshipped neither the earth with a pantheon of gods nor a single creator god embodied in a concept. They were, in effect the

"Third Man". At some point in my research, I came across the following in Manly Hall's *The Secret Teachings of All Ages:*

> Jupiter was called Dodonean after the city of Dodona in Epirus. Near this city was a hill thickly covered with oak trees, which from the most ancient times had been sacred to Jupiter. ... From the ancient oaks and beeches were hung many chains of tiny bronze bells, which tinkled day and night as the wind swayed the branches. ... The oracle of Dodona uttered prophecies through oak trees, birds, and vases of brass. The famous oracular dove of Dodona, alighting upon the branches of the sacred oaks, not only discoursed at length in the Greek tongue upon philosophy and religion, but also answered the queries of those who came from distant places to consult it.
>
> Some assert that the celebrated talking dove of Dodona was in reality a woman, because in Thessaly both prophetesses and doves were called Peleiadas. ... Most curious of the oracles of Dodona were the 'talking vases', or kettles. These were made of brass and so carefully fashioned that when struck they gave off the sound for hours. Some writers have described a row of these vases and have *declared that if one of them was struck its vibrations would be communicated to all the others.*
>
> It is supposed that the first temple of Dodona was erected by Deucalion and those who survived the great flood with him. For this reason the oracle at Dodona was considered the oldest in Greece. Many writers have noted the similarities between the rituals of Dodona and those of the Druid priests of Britain and Gaul. ... When the original priests of Dodona – the Selloi – mysteriously vanished, the oracle was served for many centuries by three priestesses called Peleiadas, who interpreted the vases and at midnight interrogated the sacred trees. (Hall 1988; emphasis added)

This written record of a worship that was connected to birds, bells and sounds really struck my curiosity. I had already noted in Marija Gimbutas' comprehensive survey of prehistoric artifacts that the bird goddesses (with their cosmic eggs) antedated the later snake images, so something that seemed to exclude the serpent element seemed to be very significant. Not only that, but these disappearing folks were starting to really pile up in numbers.

> Q: (L) I recently read some things about the Selloi priesthood and the priestesses called Peleiadas. They seem to be involved with urns, birds, tinkling bells, urns that can be struck and which then set up a particular resonance in other urns, oak trees, and some other peculiar references that relate to laurel trees ...
> A: Siren song. Greek mythology.
> Q: (L) What do the sirens represent?

A: Laura, my dear, if you really want to reveal "many beautiful and amazing things", all you need to do is remember the triad, the trilogy, the trinity, and look always for the triplicative connecting clue profile. Connect the threes ... do not rest until you have found three beautifully balancing meanings!! And why? Because it is the realm of the three that you occupy. In order to possess the keys to the next level, just master the Third Man Theme, then move on with grace ... Siren song? What of this? What have we alluded to before about sound?

Q: (L) I was thinking that the "siren song" is probably a mythical representation of antigravity.

A: Close.

Q: (L) Can you give me another clue?

A: No, you do not need one.

So, we are getting "close." But, back to the Third Man, these ancient peoples probably didn't worship anything in the sense we would understand it. Diodorus put his own spin on what he was telling, and it would have been difficult for his Mediterranean mind to grasp people that just simply loved and studied and observed and utilized the principles of Nature.

On the other hand, if Diodorus' description is fairly accurate regarding the dedication of the temple to Apollo alone, it is likely that this was a later inversion of the Celestial worship. Apollo, being a twin to Artemis/Diana, is part of the Divine Twins archetype, which leads us again, to the Third Man.

The divinity in the old religion was not a female or a male figure, but was both male and female. This does not mean that the ancient peoples were hermaphrodites, but rather *it symbolized the balanced right- and left-brain function state prior to the Fall.*

The fact that women were on an equal footing with men, in terms of honor and respect, makes it seem to the modern patriarchal mind that it was a female dominated society. But these were not peoples who were ruled by women. They were cultures in which men and women were in harmony and in which the brain functions were balanced so that they were enabled to "transduce" the cosmic energies into their reality for the purpose of active creation.

Unfortunately, the symbols and their meanings as well as the knowledge of their activation were degenerated into self-serving figments of the prurient imaginations of later redactors. The Matriarchal agriculture oriented societies alongside the Patriarchal Shepherd King societies were the results of the split. Neither of them accurately represented the pre-Fall society that is symbolized by the Androgyne. Mircea Eliade writes:

> The androgyne is understood by decadent writers simply as a hermaphrodite in whom both sexes exist anatomically and physiologically. They are concerned not with a wholeness resulting from the fusion of the sexes but with a superabundance of erotic possibilities. Their subject is not the appearance of a new type of humanity in which the fusion of the sexes produces a new unpolarized consciousness, but a self-styled sensual perfection, resulting from the active presence of both sexes in one ... The decadent writers did not know that the hermaphrodite represented in antiquity an ideal condition which men endeavoured to achieve spiritually by means of imitative rites; but that if a child showed at birth any signs of hermaphroditism, it was killed by its own parents. In other words, the actual, anatomical hermaphrodite was considered an aberration of Nature or a sign of the gods' anger and consequently destroyed out of hand. Only the ritual androgyne provided a model, because it implied not an augmentation of anatomical organs but, symbolically, *the union of the magico-religious powers belonging to both sexes.* (Eliade 1965)

The principles of Nature and the Cosmos that were studied and honored by these ancient peoples were later embodied as Bacchus/Dionysus, which concealed the true meaning and protected the tradition for a time. The Bacchic culture embraced three general principles that were, in modern terms, celebration, creativity and chivalry. Throughout history, whenever the mystic traditions have been revived, these three themes become dominant in the society.

The celebration of the Bacchants has been redacted to drunken revelry. Nothing could be further from the truth of the original meaning, though it is entirely likely that later, ignorant perversions occurred among the followers.

The original principle was that the celebrants achieved elevated states of consciousness by music, singing and dancing, often in processions or highly stylized spiral movements. *The original purpose was to use their bodies as circuitry, or part of the machinery of the megaliths.*

> Q: (L) In many ancient ruins there are found certain symbols, which interest me, specifically the coil or spiral that seems to be ubiquitous throughout the world. This is also very similar to one of the Reiki symbols. What is the origin and meaning of this symbol?
> A: Energy collector translevel; Stonehenge was one. Stonehenge is a coil. The missing stones form a coil arrangement. People have been "zapped" at Stonehenge.
> Q: (L) Who built Stonehenge?
> A: Druids.
> Q: (L) Who were the Druids?

A: Early Aryan group.

Q: (L) How did they move the stones and set them up?

A: Sound wave focusing.

Q: (L) Who taught the Druids to use the sound waves?

A: They knew; handed down.

Q: (L) When was Stonehenge built?

A: 8000 approx. B.C.[17]

Q: (L) What was Stonehenge built to do or be used for?

A: Energy director.

Q: (L) What was this energy to be directed to do?

A: All things.

Q: (L) Was the energy to be directed outward or inward to the center?

A: Both.

Q: (L) Does this sound come from our bodies?

A: Learn. Laura will find answer through discovery.

Q: (L) We've been discussing the crop circles, and would like to know if you have any input on that subject? Do the multiple circles in some of them represent multiple densities?

A: Partly.

Q: (L) Are the crop circles themselves like antennae, or like homing devices for energy or thought patterns?

A: No.

Q: (L) Is the chronology of their appearance important?

A: Semi.

Q: (L) Is their location on the planet, in terms of longitude and latitude, significant?

A: Yes and no. Location, not latitude and longitude ... Those are merely measure markers.

Q: (L) If the location is significant, what is it about the location that is significant?

A: Magnetic generators of bonding frequency portals at those locations.

Q: (L) Okay, location and chronology ...

---

[17] After a great deal of research in an effort to discover if the above comment about the dating of Stonehenge could possibly – in any remote configuration – be correct, I came to the startling realization that the "dating of Stonehenge" is based on little more than assumption. Excavations in 1966 and 1988 uncovered burnt bone and charcoal in several substantial pits which were dated to the Mesolithic. The results suggest that timber was used in the area for 300 to 1600 years, between 8500-7650 cal B.C. and 7500-6700 cal B.C. The early date and longevity of activity prompted researchers to question the quality of the charcoal samples (typical!). Researchers say they aren't related to the Stonehenge monument because they are simply too early, a clear assumption. Material suitable for radiocarbon dating is scarce, and yet evidence of early activity as always rejected as "residual". (See: http://www.eng-h.gov.uk/stoneh/start.htm#methods and http://www.cassiopaea.org/cass/prince.htm)

A: Why have you not brought up Stonehenge?

Q: (L) Was Stonehenge put there because of the location, or did Stonehenge create ...

A: Location attracted those spirit types on the proper frequency, who in turn, placed stones in proper location to receive the coded communications in code telepathically, in order not to have to chase around the countryside reading encoded pictographs.

Q: (L) What was the technique used within the circle to receive the information telepathically? [Planchette spiraled in, and spiraled out.]

A: Transcendent focused thought wave separation. *The spiral serves to translate message by slowing down the wave and focusing thought wave transference energy. Utilizes/transduces electromagnetic waves, the conduit, by breaking down signal from universal language of intent into language of phonetic profile.* This is for multiple user necessity who must hear and feel and understand precisely the same thing. The molecular structure of the rock, when properly sculpted sing to you. *Stonehenge is a vector of energy derived from Solar and Cosmic rays.* Pyramids focus electromagnetic energy from the atmosphere ambiently.

Q: (L) If it was built in 8000 B.C., and the Pyramids were built 8649 B.C., which is 10,643 years ago, more or less, that means that they were built at almost the same time, or at least within 600 years of each other. If they were built at almost the same time, were they built by the same, or similar groups of people?

A: Atlantean descendants.

Q: (L) Obviously the Great Pyramid is a marvel of engineering – and Stonehenge is as well – yet the two structures are so dissimilar. The Pyramid presents such a finished and sharp and elegant appearance, and Stonehenge might give a person – of course that is based on how it appears today – a more primitive presentation.

A: Was not originally.

Q: (L) Did they work in conjunction with one another and did the two groups that built them communicate with one another?

A: No and yes. Offshoots of same group.

Q: (L) If the flood of Noah, as you have said before, occurred 10,662 B.C., that means that the Pyramid and Stonehenge were built more than 2,000 years after this event.

A: Yes.

Q: (L) Did it take 2,000 years for them to develop or create the technology?

A: No.

Q: (L) What were they doing in those 2,000 years?

A: *Reassembling.*

Q: (L) In that 2,000 years of reassembling do you mean reassembling as a group through reincarnative processes ...

A: All. Built using sound wave technology.

Q: (L) When you say that it was built using sound wave technology, were these sound waves produced by human voices or by instruments or mechanical devices of some sort?

A: Mostly latter.

Q: (L) What kind of a device would this be? What would you call it?

A: Something like tuning fork.

Q: (L) It would be something that could be struck and would produce a sound that could then be directed in some way?

A: A sound enhancing collector/focuser.

Q: (L) Can we build such a thing?

A: Must be like a two-way antenna, solidly brass or bronze.

Q: (L) Other than a solid piece of metal, were there any other internal parts such as a mechanism of some sort?

A: Silicon arterial wand.

*

Q: (L) John Keel's book *Our Haunted Planet* says: "The parahuman Serpent People of the past are still among us. They were probably worshipped by the builders of Stonehenge and the forgotten ridge-making cultures of South America." Were the Serpent People worshipped by the builders of Stonehenge?

A: No.

Q: (L) Who was worshipped by the people who built Stonehenge?

A: Complicated, but the terms Spirit, stars, energy, will get you there.

*

Q: (L) Okay, in this book it says: Diodorus Siculus, writing in the 1st century B.C., said that "certain sacred offerings wrapped in wheat straw come from the Hyperboreans into Scythia, whence they are taken over by the neighboring peoples in succession until they get as far west as the Adriatic. From there they are sent south, and the first Greeks to receive them are the Dodonaeans. Then, continuing southward, they reach the Malian gulf, cross to Euboea, and are passed on from town to town as far as Carystus. Then they skip Andros, the Carystians take them to Tenos, and the Tenians to Delos. That is how these things are said to reach Delos at the present time."

So, from very ancient times, there was this practice of the Hyperboreans sending sacred offerings to the Island of Delos. Now, the Island of Delos is supposedly the birthplace of Phoebus Apollo, whose mother was Leto. Supposedly he was born on Mt. Cynthus. This is a very curious thing. This is contrary to the old view that the cultural flow was from the Mediterranean to the North, that civilization began in the Near East. It implies a cultural flow from the North to the South. What were these ancient Hyperboreans sending to the Island of Delos?

A: Leaves bearing cryptic codes.

Q: (L) What was the connection between the Hyperboreans, including the Celts of Britain, I believe, and the people of Delos?

A: Northern peoples were responsible for civilizing the Mediterranean/Adriatic peoples with the encoded secrets contained within their superior extra-terrestrially based genetic arrangement. Practice of which you speak was multi-trans-generational habit.

*

Q: (L) Is it the case that some of them communicated with higher-density beings via Stonehenge, and that these communications they received ...

A: *Stonehenge used to resonate with tonal rill, teaching the otherwise unteachable with wisdoms entered psychically through crown chakra transceiving system.* [Note: the word "rill" is new to me. Webster defines it as a small stream or a little brook; to flow in or like a rill.]

Q: (L) Was Stonehenge ever complete, with all the stones there? This author suggests that it was never completed because there are missing stones ...

A: Of course.

Q: (L) What happened to the stones that are missing? The books suggest that it was never finished because the architect must have died.

A: Nonsense. Multiple shocks registered through the ages.

Q: (L) Was Stonehenge built in stages as this author suggests? Did it start out as a circular ditch, at the time of the so-called Aubrey holes?

A: No.

Q: (L) Was it built all at once, complete?

A: Yes.

Q: (L) What about these multiple shocks. What, in particular?

A: Some were earthquakes, mini-cataclysmic in nature. Some were EM generated smashes, when terran forces clashed with outside "forces".

Q: (L) Are you suggesting that some of these rocks were vaporized, as it were, by some sort of particle beam weaponry?

A: EM activity.

Q: (L) Was Stonehenge once known as the Cloister of Ambrius?

A: Yes.

Q: (L) Who was Ambrius?

A: Druid tradition/cloak.

Q: (L) What was Ambrius?

A: They would label as a god. You might say otherwise.

Q: (L) In ancient literature, something called a Merkabah is talked about, but the definition of this extremely mysterious thing has been lost down through the centuries. There have been many "explanations" from such sources as the Midrash – Jewish commentaries –

but there is even argument there. It seems that, even then, nobody knew what it was. But now, all of a sudden, we have all these New Age folks coming along who have decided that they know what it is, and it is variously described as rotating double tetrahedrons ...

A: If no one knows what it is, that is as good as any other explanation.

Q: (L) Yes, but I want to know what the ancients who wrote about it meant? What is the definition of the word as the ancient writers used it?

A: The original definition predates this.

Q: (L) What is the original definition that predated the ancient writings that we have access to?

A: What do you think?

Q: (L) What? Well, it's a curious word because it is composed of two words or even three: mer kaba or mer ka ba. If we think of it as three part word, we have first of all, Mer, which is the Cosmic Sea of Infinite Potential. The great celestial mother. Then, we have the Egyptian Ka, which is like the astral body, and the Ba, which is similar to the Ka. I guess you could think of them as the astral body and the genetic body. Then there is the Ab, which is the sort of principle element of the life in man, like the part that is of God or the soul. The Ab was represented as a red stone. It was the part of the man that expressed desire, lust, courage, wisdom, feeling, sense and intelligence. So, all of them together sort of expresses an abstract "wholeness of being" principle. Then, Kaaba is Arabic for cube, and it is the square stone building in which the Black Stone is housed in Mecca. It was supposed to have been built by Ishmael and Abraham. So with Mer, Ka, Ab, and Ba, we have a cube made up of the principle parts of the physical, mental and spiritual self, and housing a stone. Soul stone? Mother stone?

A: By god, she's got it!

Q: (L) Okay, we've got the soul or mother stone, or the mother of all stones. Now that we have a definition, what was it?

A: *The Matriarch Stone*. Symbolism reigns supreme here. "Stone" to those you perceive as ancients symbolized communication from "a higher source".

Q: (L) What is it about a stone that made the ancients associate it with communication?

A: Radio waves. Transmission.

Q: (L) So Stonehenge was a giant transmitter and receiver. The original purpose of Stonehenge was to receive communication and to send communication. It wasn't all that Druid Hoodoo blood sacrifice or wandering-around-in-white-robes-scaring-people stuff that people do nowadays. It was a machine, so to speak. When we are talking about this Mother Stone, are we talking about something similar to the Atlantean crystals that gathered, dispersed and/or transduced energy?

THE BACCHANTES MEET APOLLO AT STONEHENGE

A: *It is more symbolic*. But you are on the right track.

Q: (L) So, in talking about Merkabah, we are not talking about spinning tetrahedrons that enable you to ascend or generate some kind of "astral vehicle". Many people are saying that visualizing yourself inside of one of these enables you to ascend, or something.

A: If you do that, it may help, though. We are going around in circles here. You should use your own abilities to complete the answers to some of these. But, then again, it is one form of "spinning", is it not?

Q: (T) Everything we have been doing here is all about gaining knowledge and increasing frequency in order to transit from third to fourth density. In ancient times, they would have had to do the same things. But, there may not have been as many experiences available. In order to get experiences, they may have had to travel. So, by going to the stones, they might have increased their frequencies to transit from third to fourth density.

(L) Or they used them as a direct machine or device to do it. Archaeologists say that the people who erected the megaliths were barbarians. They are defined as barbarians because they didn't build cities, they didn't have the wheel, they didn't have organized agriculture, and they left no written records. Those are the defined elements of civilization.

Yet, this group of people, whoever they were, did things that we cannot duplicate today, and they did it all over the globe. The groups who came along after them who *did* have all the hallmarks of what we call civilization also could not erect these gargantuan stones. I thought about this for a long time.

Archaeologists say they must have erected them as monuments to their gods, or heroes or whatever. Some of them think they were calendars to tell them when to plant the corn. Well, I think that is stretching it a bit. If you can't cross off the days on the wall and look outside and see that it is time to plant the corn, you're in pretty sad shape. You hardly need to haul stones as big as buildings across hills and valleys to set them up in special places to tell you to do that!

The psychology of the human being cannot have changed all that much over the many thousands of years from then to now, and it is true that people do not do anything without a powerful motivation; what I call the "payoff". What could be the payoff to haul these things around on greased logs as they are depicted? To create a monument or to bury their kings? To get naked and dance in the moonlight?

(A) Like they had a lot of time to do this while struggling to live the barbarian existence, too!

(L) Yeah. They are supposed to be howling savages who must constantly hunt to get food, yet they are spending all their time, occupying all their strongest men, to push rocks around! Meanwhile, according to the archaeologists and paleontologists, these folks only live to about forty years at max!

(T) They got a lot of mileage out of those forty years!

(L) Exactly! But, we are supposed to be thinking about the things they didn't have: cities, wheels, agriculture, and writing.

(F) Maybe they didn't need it.

(L) And why would that be? Because the stones did it all!

(T) Maybe they were fourth-density STO beings who planted all those stones all over the place.

(L) Well, if you think about a group of people who are setting up these massive stones like they were pieces of Styrofoam. The stones collect energy and information. They then transduce the energy or amplify it. These people know things about movement, dances or spinning or something, that enables them to behave in concert with the stones so that they all become part of a grand machine that does things!

All of the legends talk about stylized dances and the oldest things about Stonehenge say that it was the Temple of Apollo and that Apollo danced there all night at certain periods of time. Every 19 years, I believe.

When you think about that, and the other places Apollo appeared, the inversions and redactions of the legends, and we come to these magical stones that produce things. Then we come to the head of Bran the Blessed, which supposedly produced endless supplies of bread and fish or whatever else was desired. Bran's head was the giver of all good things. But more than that, it was an oracle. It could speak.

And here we have the idea of a similar function for Stonehenge: both an oracle as well as a giver of blessings and bounty. Anything you wanted or needed it provided for you. If you wanted to go somewhere, it transported you as in the legends of the flying carpets. It was magic transportation. All of these things are associated, when you track them back far enough, with a stone. The stones did everything.

This is what I have always thought about these megaliths. They *did* things. All of the things we think are the "signs" of civilization were done by the stones. Maybe Terry is right; these people were at some level of density where they could make this work. At some point, something happened, the ability was lost, and then people had to build cities, engage in agriculture, invent the wheel, and develop writing – because they could no longer do it the "easy" way.

A: *Stones were once utilized to provide for all needs, as the energies transmitted connected directly with the pituitary gland to connect spiritual realities with the material realms of 3rd and 4th densities. So you see, the "stone" was viewed as Matriarchal indeed!*

Q: (L) Were the beings involved in this type of activity third-density, fourth-density or bi-density?

A: Originally 4th when home was in other locators.

Q: (L) Could it be said that the pituitary gland itself is the body's own "mother stone"?

A: If you prefer.

Q: (J) What exactly is the function of the pituitary gland in your references to Stonehenge?

A: This gland is your uplink.

Q: (L) Is it possible that the pituitary can be stimulated by external sources such as radio waves, waves from a supernova, or other frequencies in the environment?

A: Yes and experiments have ensued.

Q: (L) Would it be beneficial for us to experiment with such things?

A: Not wise. You could fry yourself in your zeal. You can experiment, but not technologically.

We later asked the Cs some questions that further clarified the issue:

July 4, 2009

Q: (A**) I was gonna ask about Chaco Canyon. What was it built for?

A: Gathering place for those of unusual abilities.

Q: (A***) Did anybody actually live there?

A: More like a "conference center."

Q: (A**) So what happened to the people that used it?

A: Change of cosmic environment followed by earthly difficulties such as famine, climate etc.

Q: (J) What kind of things did those people with unusual abilities do when they gathered together?

A: Well, levitate, for one; direct manifestation for another; and "travel".

Q: (A***) So, could they travel from one spot on the planet to another?

A: Yes.

Q: (A***) Could they teleport?

A: Yes.

Q: (J) Teleport... these weren't your average human beings then. (laughter)

A: No not exactly, but it wasn't the same environment you currently enjoy either.

Q: (A**) Where did these people come from?

A: Remnant Atlanteans. Descendants for the word sticklers.

Q: (L) I think that's because once, somebody made a big deal out of them saying "remnants of Atlantis" and they meant descendants.

(A***) Do they mean that if our environment wasn't so polluted that we could have super powers? (L) They said "cosmic environment".

A: Gravity is different now.

Q: (A***) What happened to gravity? How'd it change?

A: Travels of the solar system through space. You are heading for another such changes soon.

Q: (A***) Are we going to become super again?

A: Some will.

August 5, 2009

Q: (L) Okay, next question: Who built the Hypogeum in Malta?

A: Ancient "circle people".

Q: (L) And for what purpose?

A: Rebirth, healing, manifestation. See answers previously given about Chaco Canyon.

In addition to the elevated states of consciousness achieved in the spiral dances accompanied by music and singing (*not* drunkenness with wine), it is thought that preparation or charging for these ceremonies was accomplished via "mystical sexual union". The redactors have corrupted this to wild orgies, naturally.

Many modern historians have ignorantly interpreted the accoutrements and later accounts of these rites as fertility rituals. They were supposed to have been performed with the intent of eliciting magical reproductive favoritism from nature. The ideas of gaining personal advantages, success, protection or anything else by practicing rites or rituals, spells, prayers, sacrifices and so forth are characteristic of left-brain function, *not* mystical union. (Yes, many meditators and "stupid saints" as well as practitioners of the Black Arts have in fact managed to access the gateway by "raping the maiden of the well", but the price is high and very few who do it that way survive long in this world.)

In short, the Bacchanalian celebration was to directly experience an altered state of consciousness, which brought about unification with the Cosmos and Nature, and even had the potential for transcending time and space in a direct, material and experiential manner. In the sensual, physical unification with the Cosmos, we see the *profound activation of the right hemisphere of the brain in direct experience of the world via the sensory perceptions* as distinct from *imagining* the world according to supposedly authoritative measurement and description.

In a Bacchic culture, the mutual need and inseparability of the sexes was exemplified by the principles of androgyny and the hermaphrodite, or Apollo and Artemis, the twins. The Androgyne represented the idea that every woman and man have both a male and female aspect and the hermaphrodite represented the idea that each man or woman was merely *half of a functioning unit in terms of polarity, or circuitry* that could somehow be unified to accomplish creative functions. The hermaphrodite was a macrocosmic symbol of the male/female unified Cosmos, and the androgyne is a microcosmic symbol of the male/female unity that can occur within each individual.

The goal of Bacchic culture and the secret teachings of the mystical traditions were harmony, balance, and unity between men and women and between the male and female aspects within each person.

The mystical literature tells us that the feminine principle corresponds to the intuitive, creative, intimate, immediate, unitive, nourishing, sensuous, spontaneous aspects of our consciousness. The masculine principle reflects logic, labeling, theoretical, legal, boundary consciousness, rule-following, mission-oriented, competitive characteristics. In this categorization, we can easily see that we are not referring to biophysical maleness or femaleness, but rather to the left and right modes of consciousness within all peoples.

So, when it was said that the female energy consorted with the wrong side and lost knowledge and power thereby, we can now see that it was a rewiring of the thinking, by giving dominance to the part of the brain that literally inhibits creativity and access to universal energies that can be accessed by anyone. It was by taking the direct knowledge of the Cosmos via empirical observation, i.e., knowledge and replacing it with the wishful thinking, conceptual, imaginary mode of a Creator God outside of the Cosmos, and thus only accessible via intercession, that we lost our connection. But, we can't be throwing the baby out with the bathwater here. We have to remember that science is a child of the right hemisphere, but is reared by the left hemisphere. In fact, without both aspects in proper balance, very little can be achieved. The King rules the material realm by virtue of his union with the Queen.

The direct, sensual experience of the world, unclouded by preconceptions or anticipation, is precisely what constitutes scientific empiricism and objectivity. It is at the root of the Cassiopaean motto: "knowledge protects". But knowledge only protects if it is utilized.

> Q: (L) Acquiring knowledge is akin to acquiring energy? Or light? Light energy?
> A: Not exactly. That would be like saying that "filling up" at the gas station is akin to acquiring speed.

Q: (L) So, knowledge and light are like the gas for the car, but speed comes from utilization?

A: Yes.

Q: (L) And utilization means ...

A: Knowledge application, which generates energy, which, in turn, generates light.

We know without a shadow of a doubt that the megalith builders utilized advanced mathematics, geometry and astronomy. Numbers appear to be the language by which we can translate right-brain perception into useful left-brain action. This is why the mystical traditions are written in mathematical codes.

The original splitting of the unity into two is described mathematically as the cosmos contracting infinitely, leaving a void, and everything else. This contraction or split made Divine apperception possible. Using this divine principle of creation, Gottfried Leibniz developed binary arithmetic in the 1700s, and this is the basis of all of our computer communications today. Two figures, 0 and 1 can express everything in the cosmos.

Science is not a fixed body of knowledge, even if many scientists of today wish it to be so. It is a constant observation, experiential interaction, and ever-renewing process of discovery, growth and evolution. By its very nature, it is elusive of definition, never static, and impermanent.

That is also the philosophy of the Cassiopaeans. How many times have they said: "Learn! Discover! Open! Up to you!" And because I didn't understand, it drove me crazy. I wanted the answers! I wanted the truth! I wanted the bottom line of all existence right there in my lap with ribbons and bells! But it cannot be given in a concept. It must be experienced via knowledge.

Another aspect of science that engages our right hemisphere is art and music. The numerical structure of music is thought to be the direct link between art and science, and is thus a conductor for expression of direct experience into the active left hemisphere. One can experience music directly, without any thinking or imagining or conceptualizing. And, at the same time, one is "experiencing" mathematics! No words can accurately and completely convey what something sounds like. It is an act of direct perception.

Now, what does all this have to do with sex? Well, actually, nothing, but it has everything to do with making love. You see, sex as *sex*, is left-brain. It is desire and goal oriented. It is loaded with anticipation. When one thinks about having sex, one has an image in the mind's eye of the end result. Even if it is not a visual image, it is an abstract image or concept of orgasmic repletion. It is a focusing on a physical act without due consideration of the spiritual connections and implications.

Nowadays sex comes in a variety of plans which relate back to specific conceptual purposes. There is the plan of technical performance and variety with the purpose of being a good lover. There is neurotic celibacy or abstinence to avoid guilt. There is masturbation that occurs either alone or with a partner with the purpose of relieving tension. There is submission to a partner for duty. There is just doing it because it has always been done to maintain the status quo or habit. There is keeping up with the modern trends, to avoid shame. One can have brief, promiscuous affairs out of fears of intimacy. One can have sex for reproduction. You can even make love just to enjoy sex, for intimacy and pleasure for the idea of love and affection. In all of these, there is an abstract audience and idea behind the act.

And that is where the full power of the right-brain is short circuited and caused to release its creative potential to a momentary contraction to a void that is uncontrolled, undirected, and unusable. After such an act, one is indeed in a condition where frequency resonances can be used to chemically or physically alter the DNA, or "put out the eyes". Going after sex in any of the above ways is a raping of the right-brain function. But, we will come back to this further on.

Now, let's go back for just a bit to our book *The Solarion Legacy*. Mr. Von Ward makes another interesting observation:

> Another constraint on the power of mind appears to be the innate mortality of ordinary matter. ... *The power of any level of consciousness less than that which created the universe must operate within inherent constraints. Discovery of the constraints operative in this stellar neighborhood would make it possible to infer the degree of power its beings have for conscious co-creation.* ... Another constraint is the reverse flow of influence of matter on consciousness. ... The conscious being has to continually deal with such material influences on its mind and energy ... (Von Ward, 2001; emphasis added)

Here is where the Cassiopaeans have given an even more suggestive clue to getting out of the soup, so to speak:

> Q: (L) Well, the situation we find ourselves in is the only way of getting out of this time loop, so to speak, to move into another density, or is there a loop in the other density as well?
> A: No. Yogis can do it. How they control their own physicality.

Controlling physicality. Right-brain and left-brain unity. How does one learn these things without having to resort to activation of the left-brain imagining which we pretty much have figured out only makes it harder? Well, this brings us back to the remarks made by don Juan to Carlos Castaneda in *The Active Side of Infinity*:

> Don Juan had said that by means of discipline it is possible for anyone to bring the energy body closer to the physical body. Normally, the distance between the two is enormous. Once the energy body is within a certain range, which varies for each of us individually, anyone, through discipline, can forge it into the exact replica of their physical body – that is to say, a three-dimensional, solid being. Hence the sorcerers' idea of the other or the double. By the same token, through the same process of discipline, anyone can forge their three-dimensional, solid, physical body to be a perfect replica of their energy body – that is to say, an ethereal charge of energy invisible to the human eye, as all energy is …

This sounds almost as though don Juan was describing energy bodies that relate to the separated hemispheres of the brain. The unification of the two sounds like the activation of the Divine androgyne.

> Don Juan explained that sorcerers see infant human beings as strange, luminous balls of energy, covered from the top to the bottom with a glowing coat, something like a plastic cover that is adjusted tightly over their cocoon of energy. He said that *that glowing coat of awareness was what the predators consumed, and that when a human being reached adulthood, all that was left of that glowing coat of awareness was a narrow fringe that went from the ground to the top of the toes. That fringe permitted mankind to continue living, but only barely.* … To his knowledge, man was the only species that had the glowing coat of awareness outside that luminous cocoon. Therefore, *man becomes easy prey for an awareness of a different order, such as the heavy awareness of the predator.*

Is the "heavy awareness of the predator" the "imaginary beliefs of mankind" that are thrust upon us by our state of reduced knowledge?

> … this narrow fringe of awareness was *the epicenter of self-reflection, where man is irremediably caught.* By playing on our self-reflection, which is the only point of awareness left to us, the predators create flares of awareness that they proceed to consume in a ruthless, predatory fashion. They give us inane problems that force those flares of awareness to rise, and in this manner they keep us alive in order for them to be fed with the energetic flare of our pseudoconcerns. … what we have against us is not a simple predator. It is very smart, and organized. It follows a methodical system to ren-

der us useless. Man, the magical being that he is destined to be, is no longer magical. ... There are no more dreams for man but the dreams of an animal who is being raised *to become a piece of meat: trite, conventional, and imbecilic.* ...

All we can do is discipline ourselves to the point where they will not touch us. How can you ask your fellow men to go through those rigors of discipline? They'll laugh and make fun of you, and the more aggressive ones will beat the shit out of you. And not so much because they don't believe it. *Down in the depths of every human being, there's an ancestral, visceral knowledge about the predators' existence.* ... Discipline is the only deterrent. But by discipline I don't mean harsh routines. I don't mean waking up every morning at five-thirty and throwing cold water on yourself until you're blue. Sorcerers understand discipline as the capacity to face with serenity odds that are not included in our expectations. For them, discipline is an art: the art of facing infinity without flinching, not because they are strong and tough but because they are filled with awe.

Sorcerers say that *discipline makes the glowing coat of awareness unpalatable to the flyer [predator].* The result is that the predators become bewildered. An inedible glowing coat of awareness is not part of their cognition, I suppose. After being bewildered, they don't have any recourse other than refraining from continuing their nefarious task.

If the predators don't eat our glowing coat of awareness for a while, it'll keep on growing. ... The sorcerers of ancient Mexico used to say that the glowing coat of awareness is like a tree. If it is not pruned, it grows to its natural size and volume. *As awareness reaches levels higher than the toes, tremendous maneuvers of perception become a matter of course.*

The grand trick of those sorcerers of ancient times was to burden the flyers' mind with discipline. They found out that if they taxed the flyers' mind with inner silence, the foreign installation would flee; giving to any one of the practitioners involved in this maneuver the total certainty of the mind's foreign origin. *The foreign installation comes back, I assure you, but not as strong, and a process begins in which the fleeing of the flyers' mind becomes routine, until one day if flees permanently. A sad day indeed! That's the day when you have to rely on your own devices, which are nearly zero. There's no one to tell you what to do. There's no mind of foreign origin to dictate the imbecilities you're accustomed to. This is the toughest day in a sorcerer's life, for the real mind that belongs to us, the sum total of our experience, after a lifetime of domination has been rendered shy, insecure, and shifty. Personally, I would say that the real battle of sorcerers begins at that moment. The rest is merely preparation.* ...

When one is torn by internal struggle, it is because down in the depths *one knows that one is incapable of refusing the agreement that an indispensable part of the self, the glowing coat of awareness, is going to serve as an incomprehensible source of nourishment to incomprehensible entities. And, another part of one will stand against this situation with all its might.*

The sorcerers' revolution is that they refuse to honor agreements in which they did not participate. Nobody ever asked me if I would consent to be eaten by beings of a different kind of awareness. My parents just brought me into this world to be food, like themselves, and that's the end of the story." (Castaneda 1998; emphasis added)

The Cassiopaeans say that it is *awareness* that protects, but awareness is only possible with knowledge of the truth of our reality. I am not talking about your reality as opposed to my reality, or your illusion as opposed to my illusion or any such thing. It is that sort of nonsense that is referred to by don Juan as "the epicenter of self-reflection, where man is irremediably caught". Most of the propagation of the you-create-your-own-reality ideas amount to the Predator "playing on our self-reflection, which is the only point of awareness left to us". If your reality is significantly different from mine, then one or both of us is not seeing the objective reality. The truth.

What is the objective reality?

Well, we cannot know without a full field of awareness; we cannot have a full field of awareness without bringing to a halt the process of our awareness being devoured; we cannot bring this to an end without knowledge; and we cannot have knowledge without discipline. With discipline, knowledge and awareness, we become unpalatable to the Predator. The Cassiopaeans have said it this way:

Q: (A) There are those who are happy in the STS mode; and there are those who are trying to get out of the STS mode ...
A: STO candidate.
Q: (A) These STO candidates cannot just simply BE, even theoretically, because then, STS would eat them.
A: No.
Q: (L) Why not?
A: STS does not eat according to protocol. STS "eats" whatever it wants to, if it is able.
Q: (L) That's what we said. If you are STO in an STS world, you are basically defenseless and they eat you.
A: No.
Q: (L) Why? What makes STO unavailable or "inedible"?
A: Frequency resonance not in sync.

Don Juan said that *discipline makes the glowing coat of awareness unpalatable to the flyer.* The result is that the predators become bewildered. An inedible glowing coat of awareness is not part of their cognition. That is precisely what the Cassiopaeans have said when they termed it not being in sync. They echoed don Juan's remark about "grabbing onto the vibrating force that holds us together," i.e., frequency resonance. The end result is: via knowledge we can learn to use discipline, which then enables us to grow back the awareness. Don Juan said: "*As awareness reaches levels higher than the toes, tremendous maneuvers of perception become a matter of course.*"

It seems that it is here, at this higher level of awareness, that one is able to have some ability to create their own reality. Naturally, everyone who has been hypnotized to believe they are a magician will think, "That's me, Baby! I'm there already!" And that may be true. But we do have a clue as to what is entailed when one has achieved higher awareness: *"Facing odds that are not included in our expectations"* and, *"facing infinity without flinching ... filled with awe."* That suggests some stupendous realizations that might cause a weak-willed person to want very desperately to take the Blue Pill as it was allegorized in the movie, *The Matrix*.

A concrete example of the many contexts in which the Predator plays on our epicenter of self-reflection is exemplified in the Nexus Seven "Top Secret/Demon" document, which says at the end:

> Mommy Goddess and Daddy God are coming into direct contact with us in a new radical fashion – not as physical ETs like the government or evil ETs would have us believe, but as personalized loving, forgiving and powerful spiritual energies and entities from beyond this physical universe. They are returning, big time, in non-physical terms, to reconnect and co-create with their original soul substance in this universe, located in (guess what?) human hearts.
>
> This Human-Spiritual heart reconnection is feared by the 'fallen' Luciferians mindsets – their game is up. Because once the true reconnection happens, it makes individual human beings hundreds of times more powerful than our high yield hydrogen bombs, in terms of potential spiritual influence. Remember the power of our historical Messiahs? They did not show what they were really capable of, despite the wonders they did demonstrate. And remember how all Messiahs claimed that any human was capable of the same as they?
>
> It was all only ever about growing love in the human heart. It was about growing the capacity for caring and intimacy, the incorruptible means for humanity not falling this time for well-laid traps. The alien-human alliance engineered fail-safe awareness traps on the human evolutionary experiment. And they work.
>
> The ETs just hope we humans as a whole species learn our lessons before we get so much power. Since most of us wouldn't trust

anyone we know with too much power, and treat other species on our planet like chattel without feelings, that ought to help explain to you why ETs have us under a form of embargo and quarantine.

The idea presented above makes it seem that love or emotions are the answer rather than direct knowledge of the Cosmos. We are told repeatedly, "You are God!" and "Mommy Goddess and Daddy God are coming ... to reconnect and co-create with their original soul substance ... located in ... human hearts" and on and on. Do we not see a similar pattern here? "You could have this! You could do this!" And the focus is placed on emotion that is stimulated by an idea or a concept, not direct knowledge via observation and experience. By propagating these twisted lie sandwiches, which do include partial truths, and getting people worked up to do things they have no understanding about, "the predators create flares of awareness that they proceed to consume in a ruthless, predatory fashion."

You see, the thing that they so cleverly leave out of the equation is that, if one would become like God, one must *know* like God. Or, to put it the other way: "If one would know God, one must become like God." That means that one must connect the hemispheres of the brain, not the emotions. Yes, it is true that emotions are observed by the right-brain, but they are created by the left-brain through thought–imagination. The *Corpus Hermeticum* (XI) says:

> If then you do not make yourself equal to God, you cannot apprehend God; for like is known by like. To realize this state of being requires a radical transformation of consciousness and perception, *a change in the way in which we know and perceive*, "for all things which the eye can see are mere phantoms and unsubstantial outlines; but the things which the eye cannot see are the realities ..."

Now, of course, there are those who claim that to know God, and to become Godlike, one must access the blissful states of Godlike Love. So they work all their lives to achieve this emotional ecstasy of God using an image or a concept. They have missed the key that becoming Godlike consists of observing and experiencing the Cosmos directly, which results in knowledge. Knowledge leads to awareness of what is out there. Awareness of what is out there gives one the ability to think with the left-brain in concord with what the right-brain observes. This merging of the two halves of the brain – observation and thinking/formulating – is the thing that can discipline emotions so that there is no negative expression that can feed the Predator.

Q: (T) Who talks to me when I am having conversations with myself in my head?
A: You.
Q: (L) Am I talking to other beings?
A: Have.
Q: (T) Can you tell me who they are?
A: Lizards.
Q: (T) Why are they talking to me?
A: Trying to convert you. Remember, T, your chronic depression represents a "battle" zone.
Q: (T) I no longer am depressed and they are talking to me more.
A: Watch out!
Q: (T) Can I turn them off?
A: Yes.
Q: (T) Who is "Sing"?
A: Leader of forces assigned to influence you.
Q: (T) Forces, as in many are assigned to me personally?
A: Yes.
Q: (T) How many are in this force?
A: Seven.
Q: (T) Do they do this because of the implants that are in me?
A: All part of process.
Q: (T) These implants are what they use to control my emotions and amplify them so that they can feed off of them?
A: Not control, influence.
Q: (T) No, not to control, influence. But when, say, I get angry, then I'm angry for a short time but then I'm angry for a long time because they have used this technology to amplify and extend this; is this what they do?
A: Yes. Knowledge protects, ignorance endangers.
Q: (T) Can I feed back through their equipment what I choose?
A: Not necessary.
Q: (T) In other words, if I get angry and realize that I am being more angry than I should be, and I change that to something positive, and feed that back to them while they have their amplifiers wide open, will that affect them? Sour their milk, so to speak?
A: Now you are "fighting fire with fire."
Q: (T) Well, is that something that we are supposed to be doing?
A: Open. But what does phrase imply?
Q: (L) What they are saying is, I think, when you feel yourself getting angry, the only way to stop the whole thing is to stop being angry and be happy or at peace. When you are happy and at peace there is not in you the desire to send anything back.
A: Bingo.

Q: (T) What I am getting at is, is it possible to do that, to change the emotional state to something more positive than what they are expecting and feed that back to them? Is that a possibility?

A: Why? How effective is a light socket without a plug in it? How effective is a motor that is never turned on? Implants are ineffective if not used.

Q: (J) The power source has to be on for the implant to work for them to get the juice and the power is negative thoughts and emotions. (T) But I am still a third-density being. I have all the emotions of a third-density being, the whole gamut, and that is part of what makes me a third-density being. Therefore I can't turn one emotion off without upsetting the balance of the other emotions, emotions are almost an analogy to the light and the dark.

A: No. If you *choose*, you may have only positive emotions.

Q: (T) Now, if I have only positive emotions, which is a nice thing to have and I'd like to have that, what does that do to the sensor equipment of the Lizzies?

A: Cancels them.

Q: (T) So they are tuned to negative frequencies?

A: Yes.

Q: (T) Having positive feelings cuts off the implants. If I cut off the sensors by having positive feelings, what will the Lizards do?

A: Go elsewhere.

Q: (L) Be aware, though, that when you first start turning this off that they may increase their efforts for a period and then finally they realize that you are really in charge here and then they go away.

A: Exactly.

Q: (L) So, when you first get a clue and you start getting a grip on your emotions and dealing with everything that happens to you with acceptance and knowledge that all is a manifestation of your own creation and for your ultimate good, for a period of time they may try ten times harder to get you back as a food source, but then once they realize they can't, then they do finally let loose?

A: You and Frank are experiencing this right now.

Q: (L) This is true. (F) We have both been under massive attack. Just doing this work has been a struggle to keep at it with everything coming from every direction. (L) The hardest has been to stay in a frame of mind to do it.

Q: (T) Is the attack I have been under the past few months the first assault?

A: Yes. Only first assault.

Q: (T) So, the more positive I become, the more they are going to continue trying, and I am assuming that because you said I have seven beings of some kind assigned to me, that they find something interesting in me that they want to keep?

A: Close.

Q: (T) Should it make me happy that they think I am important enough to have seven beings assigned to me personally? Should I take that as a compliment?

A: No.

Q: (J) Is T's level of negativity what makes him attractive to them? His capability for strong negativity?

A: Vice versa.

Q: (J) Please explain. What makes him attractive to them?

A: Not attractive, a threat.

Q: (L) I think there are a lot of people they start working on very early in life because they do like a scan and determine that a person has potential for great light so they start working on them when they are young and defenseless to try and take them out of the game, so to speak. (F) Not only great good, but also potential for knowledge. (L) Is this the case here?

A: Yes.

Q: (L) It isn't your potential for negativity; it is your potential for good. (F) Right. If you look around you then you will see the mainstream of society, and they just seem to move through life and enjoy wallowing in materiality, these people don't seem to suffer as much. (L) There seems to be two classes of people the Lizzies like to go after, extremely weak ones and those they haul off and eat or experiment on; and those who have potential strength and positivity. (F) The people they don't attack are those who they already have and they don't have to work on them. If you have the potential to rise above the Service-to-Self orientation, then you are a threat. (T) Okay. Where were we? Just by being positive will shut off the Lizzies desire to mess with me?

A: Yes.

Q: (T) That's all there is to it? But the implants will still be there?

A: So what?

Q: (T) Do the implants do anything besides transmit the frequency?

A: No.

Q: (T) And, as long as I am being negative it is transmitting and they can track me that way?

A: Close.

Q: (T) If I shut them off by being positive, they can't track me any longer?

A: Can track but not influence.

Q: (T) I am not buying into the victim line. (L) The major point here is that knowledge breeds awareness which gives you the ability to detect it when they try to influence you in very subtle ways so that you can begin to control your mind and resist early on and that is the key.

A: Close enough.

Q: (L) And you have to be disciplined and persist with positive thoughts and feelings sometimes in the face of incredible adversity. No one said it was going to be easy, but it is worth it.

The Cassiopaeans have said that what we are here to do, what we must "be about" in terms of preparation to graduate to the next level, the level of true self-creation is to learn the lessons of this density. This is related to the idea of being able to correctly discern what is in the reality and how it is working and if it is part of the control process. Awareness can help a person avoid situations that will lead to pain and suffering and negative feelings. Awareness of the reality behind events that would ordinarily be perceived as either frightening or painful can greatly facilitate the maintenance of positivity.

A: You see, my dear, when you arrive at 4th density, then you will see.

Q: (L) Well, how in the heck am I supposed to get there if I can't "get it"?

A: Who says you have to "get it" before you get there?

Q: (L) Well, that leads back to: what is the Wave going to do to expand this awareness? Because, if the Wave is what "gets you there", what makes this so?

A: No. It is like this: After you have completed all your lessons in "third grade", where do you go?

Q: (L) So, it is a question of ...

A: Answer, please.

Q: (L) You go to fourth grade.

A: Okay, now, do you have to already be in 4th grade in order to be allowed to go there? Answer.

Q: (L) No. But you have to know all the third-density things ...

A: Yes. More apropos: you have to have learned all of the lessons.

Q: (L) What kind of lessons are we talking about here?

A: Karmic and simple understandings.

Q: (L) What are the key elements of these understandings, and are they fairly universal?

A: They are universal.

Q: (L) What are they?

A: We cannot tell you that.

Q: (L) Do they have to do with discovering the *meanings* of the symbology of third-density existence, seeing behind the veil ... and reacting to things according to choice? Giving each thing or person or event its due?

A: Okay. But you cannot force the issue. When you have learned, you have learned!

> Q: (L) I just want to make sure that I am doing the most I can do. I don't want to have to come back to third density. If I can accelerate things a little ...
> A: You cannot, so just enjoy the ride. Learning is fun!

Notice that I specifically stated the possible answer: "Discovering the meanings of the symbology of third-density existence and reacting to things according to choice; giving each thing its due" and the Cassiopaeans responded: "But you cannot force the issue. When you have learned, you have learned!" So, I am not going to force the issue on anyone! Everyone who reads this book is free to accept or reject any or all of what is said here.

Our Nexus Seven guys complain:

> We need a language of hyper-dimensional symbols that codify human relationship with nature. Symbols and ritual that codify the elements and forces of nature codify the life processes of nature, from the little insects all the way up to the supposedly angelic and demonic ETs. Without this language there is no means for intelligent contact to have a basis for occurring. And it could be that some symbols from history have their basis in being received alien communications.

I would like to point out that we *do* have such a language. It is called Nature. Nature is going to teach us quite a bit. The more one contemplates Nature, the more awe one must feel regarding the creation. The problem is, for some people, the more they learn, and the more miserable they are. The person who learns, for the first time, that the cat toys and tortures the mouse before killing and eating it, is stunned that such cruelty exists in Nature. It is seen as evil. Such people then seek to construct imaginary worlds of spirit where no cat ever tortures the mouse before eating it. They quote the scripture where it says, "The lion lies down with the lamb", assuming that they will all eat grass, I suppose. Well, what about the grass? Isn't it alive also? So, in creating such fantasies, they cheat themselves of the truth about the natural world, which is the organ of the Prime Creator's expression.

This distortion grows and extends to all that they learn and consider. When they discover something that is not nice, or of the darkness, or negative, they recoil in fear and horror. What's more, they immediately begin to plan how to fix it, because obviously in their minds such a reality is broken.

The plain fact is the evil which we read into the world and all the imperfections which we believe we have discovered are simply a result of the limits of our understanding. The narrower the point of view from which we look upon, view or observe things, the more evil and the more imperfections we see.

There are many who have written to me about the "fear based" information in my books and online writings. They assume, automatically, that because we talk about reality in pretty plain terms, including all aspects of it, that I must be sitting here at my desk, quaking and quivering in terror with every word I type. Nothing could be further from the truth. I have to state right here and now that I have *never* been in a state of fear once I have learned the true nature of what energies are behind the manifestations of our world.

For all the many years that I have studied evil and darkness in an attempt to reconcile its existence to the idea of a perfect, loving God, it was the perception of the darkness as an error or mistake or flaw that made me afraid. What is more terrifying than to think that your soul and life can be subject to either an accident or a trick of temptation? What is more terrifying than to think that an accident or error can exist ontologically in the universe that is supposed to be God's creation? The only conclusions I could ever come to with that thinking was that humankind was either a sick joke or a plaything of God – and neither of those ideas are conducive to love and faith.

As I gained more and more knowledge about the world, my point of view broadened. And, as my perspective expanded, the more the evils disappeared. Now, don't get me wrong. When I say they disappeared, that does not mean they went away or were transformed. Not at all. I just stopped seeing them as evil. Not only that, I began to see the incredible humor in the situation. When I became aware of a Control System maneuver in my life, I almost laughed with glee at the challenge of a worthy opponent.

No indeed. I still can see demons in the world and at work; I still see the creeping darkness shadowing the souls of humankind, blotting out their access to their creative potential. I still see war and genocide and famine and plague as part of our reality. Not only that, I see these things as part of the reality that are not going to change into something that we call good by the powers of concentrated love and light. It is not a good idea to send love and light to the negative forces because they don't want it. But that doesn't mean that I don't love them! Semantics? No. Subtle but important distinction? Yes.

And even though for convention, I use terms such as dark and light, and good and evil and positive and negative in order to talk about things in a practical way, I no longer see these things as an essential error or that which must be done away with or transformed in order for humankind to grow and ascend from this vale of tears.

The fact is, most of humankind is not done with the lessons in this school and to try to change it for those who aren't finished with the lessons would be to violate their free will, not to mention their whole cosmic plan and purpose.

What I see now is that all of these things exist, the light and the dark, the good and the evil, the positive and the negative, the STS and STO beings, as part of the superb framework of the infinite Creator or Prime Source.

What is more, I see the reason for it to be this way, above and beyond just the simple choice of humankind to experience learning at a faster rate. That issue is not relative to our particular Group Soul only; there are a potentially infinite amount of other souls and Group Souls and beings in the Cosmos who partake of the same conditions as we do, at different levels. There is far more to this state than that.

In one sense, you could say that it is a vast and glorious self-regulating organism that is One; but it is One in Manyness. It is only when we perceive this actual Unity as already existing, and not as something that one has to imagine or pretend will come into being, (which means excluding all that one finds unpleasant or not of love and light), will the literal fact of this state manifest in one's life.

But, I am getting ahead of myself here. Let's look at nature in some interesting contexts and discover our spiritual beloved in all the many moods and faces that will be shown to us.

CHAPTER 25
A WALK IN NATURE AMONG THE NAMES OF GOD WHERE WE HAVE AN INTERVIEW WITH THE VAMPIRE AND DISCOVER A COSMIC EGG

At this point, I want to share with you the fact that, like many of you who write to me, coming to understand the whys and wherefores has been a process that has had its moments of extreme frustration and rebellion against what *is*. Even if our observations of reality are constantly telling us things that are true, we all tend to want to stay asleep and dreaming in the *Matrix*-like illusion. In the following excerpt, I only wish I could reproduce in writing the frustration and puzzlement in my voice. The words that are capitalized were practically shouted:

> Q: (L) I *am* in a little bit of a quandary here because, here we are talking to you guys who are supposed to be "us" in the future; here we are in this period of time on this planet, where things are in a very strange state; there is some kind of huge transition going on, and I am just wondering what is the whole point? Why are we talking to you? What's the point?
> A: It is the lesson. Do you not understand still? The lesson, the lessons, that is all there is. They are all immeasurably valuable.
> Q: (L) Okay, we are having these lessons. You have told us what is going on. We see it going on around us. I am convinced that what you have said is so from a LOT of other evidence as well as the research of others who have come to the same conclusion and, DAMN IT, IT'S UGLY! DO YOU UNDERSTAND ME?! IT'S UGLY!
> A: That is your perspective.
> Q: (L) Well, as C** said on the phone the other day, what are we supposed to awaken to? Are we supposed to just awaken to the fact that we can SEE all this stuff going on?
> A: Yes.

Q: (L) Okay, once we wake up and SEE it, why can't we just check out at that point? If you know what the script is, you don't have to watch the movie!

A: But then you miss out on the experience.

Q: (L) So, we are all here to experience being munched and crunched ...

A: No.

Q: (L) Imprisoned, controlled, being treated like rats in a cage in a laboratory ...

A: Ecstasy, remember?

Q: (L) Ecstasy?! WELL SWELL! We can just ALL be BURNED AT THE STAKE! I understand that is QUITE an ECSTATIC experience! I'm sure William Wallace felt perfectly ecstatic when they castrated him and removed his bowels and burned them in a brazier in front of his face!

A: Not so long ago, your face smashed upon the pavement ... [18]

Q: (L) Was that an ecstatic experience?

A: Yes.

Q: (L) So, when you say "ecstatic" you could just be talking about jumping out a window and croaking? You gotta understand here! The perspective here on third density! You don't have faces to smash on pavements!

A: Neither will/do you/us.

Q: (A) You say knowledge protects. It protects against *what*?

A: Many things. One example: *post transformational trauma and confusion.*

Q: (L) So, knowledge is going to protect us against post transformational trauma and confusion. You are implying that this transition to fourth density is going to be traumatic and confusing. Do you mean transformation from third to fourth density, or third to fifth density, i.e., death?

A: Both.

Q: (L) So, if one does not have the shock and trauma and the confusion and so forth, one is then able to function better?

A: Yes.

Q: (L) Well, you said "both". That implies that persons can transition directly from third to fourth density without dying. Is that correct?

A: Yes.

Q: (L) How does that feel? How is that experience ...

A: Alice through the looking glass.

---

[18] This is an allusion to my "immediate past life" in Germany where I jumped to my death after the Nazis took my Jewish husband and children away to a camp. See my autobiography, *Amazing Grace*, for details.

> Q: (A) Okay, you say that knowledge is supposed to protect from trauma and confusion. On the other hand, all is lessons, so trauma is a lesson. Why are we supposed to work to avoid a lesson?
> A: You are correct, it is a lesson, but if you have foreknowledge, you are learning that lesson early, and in a different way.
> Q: (L) So, if you learn the lesson in a different way, does that mitigate the need or the way or the process of the way of learning at the time of transition?
> A: Yes. Smoother.

My beloved grandmother always said to me, "A wise man learns from his mistakes; a genius learns from the mistakes of others." (I wonder if there is a special school that grandmothers attend to learn all these clever sayings?) But her point is exactly what we are dealing with here. We need to learn not only from the mistakes of others, but from our own mistakes, and from applying our greatest assets, our minds, to the matter. If "all there is is lessons", then it seems only logical to think that we can infer some principles from the world around us, from our studies, and from *direct observation*.

Many occult teachings state that one can learn all of the secrets of creation by studying nature. The alchemists say that the truth is hidden in plain sight. As I quoted in the last section, the Nexus Seven guys think that we need "a language of hyper-dimensional symbols that codify human relationships with nature. Symbols and ritual that codify the elements and forces of nature codify the life processes of nature, from the little insects all the way up to the supposedly angelic and demonic ETs." And I respond that we already have it. It is nature itself.

The only problem is, you cannot obtain knowledge and understanding of nature by simply reading about it or wandering around in the garden. You have to *think*.

> A: You see when you speed too quickly in the process of learning and gathering knowledge; it is like skipping down the road without pausing to reflect on the ground beneath you. One misses the gold coins and the gemstones contained within the cracks in the road.

We cannot rush the process. Nature's greatest secrets are always close to us. In nature, God manifests in all his many faces. Nature is the organ which proclaims the creator. It is important to learn everything you can about the physical world before you begin to investigate the spirit world because, as Chittick writes, "there are innumerable realms in the unseen world, some of them far more dangerous than the worst jungles of the visible world."

Once you have learned about the physical world many things about the spiritual world, which have previously been inexplicable to you, will then be understood.

> A: All there is is lessons. This is one infinite school. There is no other reason for anything to exist. Even inanimate matter learns it is all an "illusion". Each individual possesses all of creation within their minds. Now, contemplate for a moment. Each soul is all-powerful and can create or destroy all existence if [they] know how. You and us and all others are interconnected by our mutual possession of all there is. You may create alternative universes if you wish and dwell within. You are all a duplicate of the universe within which you dwell. Your mind represents all that exists. It is "fun" to see how much you can access.
> Q: (L) It's fun for whom to see how much we can access?
> A: All. Challenges are fun. Where do you think the limit of your mind is?
> Q: (L) Where?
> A: We asked you.
> Q: (L) Well, I guess there is no limit.
> A: If there is no limit, then what is the difference between your own mind and everything else?
> Q: (L) Well, I guess there is no difference if all is ultimately one.
> A: Right. And when two things each have absolutely no limits, they are precisely the same thing.

Now, notice that the Cassiopaeans have said, "It is *fun* to see how much you can access". What we are supposed to be accessing is universal creative powers that exist within our own minds – the zero point energy as suggested by David Bohm. But that coy little remark about fun also tells us something very important. It tells us that there are constraints in place to make the game more interesting.

The very idea that the whole of creation is a game or a challenge that God has set up for him/herself is totally repugnant to some people, and, admittedly, when any one of us is in the midst of many of the various challenges, it is hard to see the humor. Does the mouse see the humor of God when the cat toys with it before eating it? Is it a monstrous blasphemy to reduce the sufferings of humankind throughout millennia to a cosmic round of hide and seek? The following will certainly illustrate my point:

> Q: (L) What is the meaning of the number 666 in the book of Revelation?
> A: Visa.
> Q: (L) You mean as in credit card?

A: Yes. Isn't just credit, also debit.
Q: (L) Are credit cards the work of what 666 represents?
A: Yes.
Q: (L) Should we get rid of all credit cards?
A: Up to you. How are you going to do this? World will soon have nothing but credit and debit. Have you not heard of this new visa debit cards this is the future of money as controlled by the world banking system, i.e., the Brotherhood, i.e., Lizards, i.e., antichrist.
Q: (L) If I don't have a credit card then I don't have to belong to this system?
A: No. You will have no choices: belong or starve.
Q: (L) What happened to free will?
A: Brotherhood AKA Lizards AKA antichrist has interfered with free will for 309000 years. They are getting desperate as we near the change.
Q: (V) It has always been my nature to rebel against that which I did not feel was good for me. Is rebellion against this system possible?
A: If you are willing to leave the body.
Q: (L) Leave the body as in death, croak, kick the bucket?
A: Yes. Changes will follow turmoil; be patient.
Q: (L) We would like to move into the country. Will it be possible to get along without this credit/debit card leading that kind of life?
A: No.
Q: (L) Are they going to have the kind of capability of controlling everything and everybody no matter where they are?
A: Yes.
Q: (L) Even if we moved to Guyana and built a log hut in the rain forest and didn't bother anybody, we'd still get sucked into this thing?
A: Laura you will feel the effect of the Lizard beings desperate push for total control no matter where you go.
Q: (L) That is inexpressibly depressing. Do you understand?
A: Why? *Change will follow.* Refer to literature *Bringers of the Dawn*. Challenge will be ecstasy if viewed with proper perspective, which is not, we repeat: not of third level reality, understand?
Q: (L) In the reference cited, Joan of Arc is described as feeling ecstatic while burning at the stake. Is that what you mean?
A: Sort of, but you need not burn at the stake.
Q: (L) That's small comfort. There are other ways to die.
A: We are not speaking of death, Laura. If you listen to those who are firmly rooted in 3rd level this is when you run the risk of slipping in your knowledge learned no matter how good the intentions.
Q: (L) What do you mean, "Challenge will be ecstasy"? What sort of challenge?
A: Living through the turmoil ahead.

Q: (L) Several books I have read have advised moving to rural areas and forming groups and storing food, etc.

A: Disinformation. Get rid of this once and for all. That is 3rd level garbage.

Q: (L) We feel pretty helpless at the mercy of beings who can come in and feed off of us at will. Do we have someone on our side, pulling for our team, throwing us energy or something?

A: Whom do you think you have been communicating with?

Q: (L) Are you going to be able to assist us through this turmoil?

A: Yes. All you have to do is ask.

Q: (L) Will we go through any periods when we may be cut off from help?

A: You are never ever cut off.

Q: (L) Oh, I don't want to suffer!

A: You need not suffer. Stop thinking 3rd level.

Q: (L) I don't want anybody I love to suffer either. I don't want any pain. I've suffered enough!

A: You are stuck at 3rd level tonight.

I guess you can tell that I was feeling pretty desperate and sorry for myself with all of this. So desperate, in fact, that I didn't really pay attention to the important things. Notice a couple of keys above: "*Change will follow*", and the challenge of living through the turmoil will be "ecstasy".[19]

As human beings, it seems that an essential part of our nature is to feel that there is more to life than the immediately apparent material world. We don't like to think that our lives are a game of chance played by the gods. Yet, we can observe that the heartless randomness of the world is at odds with the religious views of a loving, caring God.

It seems, upon observation, that the only constant factor of the physical universe is change. As the Sufis say, "Every day God is upon some different task". However, we can also observe that change operates in a sequential and progressive manner manifested as patterns recognizable to human consciousness. These patterns take shape as the forms inherent in the nature of the instant of time when they are observed. They are manifestations of the present state of cosmic being and have much to tell us of the nature and potential development of that state. Even those things that seem to be random, according to chaos theory, conform to certain mathematical principles of randomness. We also have synchronicity, which tells us that all things are in some way linked to each other.

---

[19] This passage is a lot more meaningful after 9-11, eh?

The eighteenth century Icelandic mystic, Jon Jonsson said, "God plays at *Forkjaering* with man in this world". *Forkjaering* is a dice game. Later, Albert Einstein said, "God does not play dice" with the universe. I think the truth is somewhere in between. We are pawns in a game, only the players are, in some sense, ourselves. And we are pawns as long as we don't know the rules of the game. Once we have served our apprenticeship as playing pieces, we are then able to take our place with the players.

The important thing is that we have to gain a perspective on our existence that is not third density in order to fully enter into third density with the "proper perspective". This is reflected in the saying of Jesus that we are to be "in the world, but not of it". The Cassiopaeans have reiterated this point by saying:

> A: You would not exist if someone didn't "dream you up".
> Q: (L) Who dreamed me up?
> A: You literally are the "figments" of someone's imagination, and nothing more!!! Remember, "God" is really all existence in creation, in other words, all consciousness. This is because all existence in creation is consciousness, and vice versa.
> Q: (L) Then what is the explanation for the "manyness" that we perceive?
> A: Perception of 3rd density.
> Q: (L) The problem is accessing it, stripping away the veils.
> A: That is the fun part.

Well, ha ha ha! Aren't we having fun? It reminds me of a passage from the book of Romans that used to just make me foam at the mouth!

> What shall we conclude then? Is there injustice upon God's part? Certainly not! ... It is not a question of human will and human effort, but of God's mercy. ... So then he has mercy on whomever He wills (chooses) and He hardens – makes stubborn and unyielding the heart of – whomever He wills. You will say to me, Why then does He still find fault and blame us? For who can resist and withstand His will? But who are you, a mere man, to criticize and contradict and answer back to God? Will what is formed say to him that formed it, Why have you made me thus? Has the potter not right over the clay, to make out of the same mass one vessel for beauty and distinction and honorable use, and another for menial or ignoble and dishonorable use? (Romans 9:14-21)[20]

---

[20] All Biblical quotations are taken from Zondervan's Amplified Bible.

Of course, at this point, Paul diverts off into his wrathful theology and starts ranting about divine judgment and doom. But, what he was saying above is actually quite similar to the mystery teachings that were prevalent at the time, and which were preserved and expanded in the Gnostic and Sufi paths. It is in these teachings that we will find the rest of the story.

But, getting back to the Bible for just a moment: in my reading of years past, I came across several passages that really struck me as curious, considering their origins. The first is, of course, one that I quote frequently from the Book of Romans in the New Testament. It is generally attributed to Paul, and actually has been computer analyzed and the result of this analysis was that whoever wrote the book of Romans, also wrote the two epistles to the Corinthians as well as the epistle to the Galatians. Internal evidence from these documents indicates that they were written before 70 CE, probably close to 60 or even 40 CE. That is to say, they were written *before* the Gospels.

These epistles make no allusions to Jesus as a historical figure as depicted in the Gospels. They say absolutely nothing about the parents of Jesus, the virgin birth, a time or place of earthly existence, a trial before the Romans, an execution in Jerusalem, or any of the main characters of the Jesus story, with the exception of Peter who is referred to as a hypocrite by Paul.

If there had been a real incident such as the denial of Jesus by Peter, it is fairly certain that Paul would have brought it up and used it in his flame war against the Rock of the Church. When Paul does refer to Jesus' death, he says repeatedly that he was crucified or delivered up but never that he was killed. And we know from many ancient sources that to be crucified meant an initiatory event rather than being nailed to a wooden cross and dying in a physical sense.

When Christianity originated, Jewish writings included a considerable body of wisdom literature that had been, to a great extent, "borrowed" from more ancient sources with which the Jews had come in contact throughout their period of formation as a national entity. A lot of this literature derived from Egyptian and Babylonian sources. Very often, this material was modified or interpreted to suit the Hebrew perspective, and was often ascribed to their god, Jehovah or Yahweh in terms of source, even though more contemporary research clearly shows it to have been more or less plagiarized. Thus, within the pages of the Bible there are many passages in which this ancient wisdom literature makes itself known.

The interesting thing is that, even though much of the wisdom literature was borrowed and redacted, it often appears to have been included with very little modification. Apparently, those who were engaged in assembling the Bible either did not understand the material fully, or they were unable to change it completely because it was so generally well known. So it happens that in some passages wisdom is not merely abstract, but personified as a supernatural being created by God before he created heaven or earth. Very often, wisdom or knowledge figured as "a breath of the power of God". It is written that "*she* is the sustainer and governor of the universe who sits by the throne of God", (Wisdom of Solomon, 8:1; 9:4) and "*she* comes to dwell among men and bestow her gifts on them", but most of them reject her. Hmm. The "Mother Stone" that is rejected as the corner of the foundation?

Paul, as an educated Jew, was strongly influenced by the wisdom traditions. Paul's Jesus, like wisdom, "assists God in the creation of all things." (I Cor. 8:6) If we do not begin with the assumption that Jesus was a historical person as depicted in the Gospels, there is little in the writings of Paul to suggest that he was, while there is a great deal to suggest that a different explanation for the expression "Christ Crucified" must be considered. That said, our purpose here is simply to point out that in Paul's day, the Wisdom literature did exist, and he seemed to be in the habit of musing on it and extracting meanings from it to serve his own ends. With this in mind, let's have a look at something else Paul said:

> For that which is known about God is evident to them and made plain in their inner consciousness, because God has shown it to them. For ever since the creation of the world His invisible nature and attributes, that is *His eternal power and divinity have been made intelligible and clearly discernible in and through the things that have been made – His handiworks ...*" (Romans 1:19-20)

This remark is so similar to the following, from ibn-'Arabi that one cannot help but think that they are obtained from the same ancient source.

> Each creature is a word (*kalima*) of God. 'Though all the trees in the earth were pens, and the sea – seven seas after it to replenish it – were ink, yet would the words of God not be spent.' [*Koran*, 31:27]
> There is nothing in existence save God, His names, and His acts.

As noted, there is much of the wisdom literature preserved in the Old Testament even if it is interspersed with plagiarized myths, mythicized histories, and entirely fabricated genealogies. Many of the Psalms have been identified as preexistent Egyptian songs and writings:

> The heavens declare the glory of God, and the firmament shows and proclaims His handiwork. *Day after day pours forth speech, and night after night shows forth knowledge.* There is no speech nor spoken word; their voice is not heard yet their voice goes out through all the earth, their sayings to the end of the world. (Psalm 19:1-4)
>
> To every thing there is a season, and a time for every matter or purpose under heaven: A time to be born, and a time to die, a time to plant, and a time to pluck up what is planted. A time to kill, and a time to heal; a time to break down, and a time to build up; a time to weep, and a time to laugh; a time to mourn, and a time to dance; a time to cast away stones, and a time to gather stones together; a time to embrace, and a time to refrain from embracing; a time to get, and a time to lose; a time to keep, and a time to cast away; a time to rend, and a time to sew; a time to keep silence, and a time to speak; a time to love, and a time to hate; a time of war, and a time of peace. ... He has made everything beautiful in its time; he also has planted eternity in men's heart and mind so that man cannot find out what God has done from the beginning to the end. ... That which is now, already has been; and that which is to be, already has been; and God seeks out that which has passed by. (Ecclesiastes, 3)

These passages, which reflect very ancient sources, reveal to us a very great truth: nature and the cycles of nature reveal to us the Faces and Names of God. God has many faces, not all of them pleasant to behold.

All around us in the natural world there are wonders and horrors. Mountains are not only being built but also simultaneously worn down by glaciers and rivers. Rivers clog and change their courses. Lakes fill with sediment and turn into swamps and eventually grasslands. Some creatures adapt and survive these changes, and some do not. On almost every corner of the planet, from the highest mountains to the lowest valleys, from the hottest to the coldest climates, above the oceans and within them, there are populations of interdependent plants and animals. Most of the time this term interdependence really means that they eat one another.

At the bottoms of the deepest oceans, there are enormous tube worms that feast on bacteria that consume the chemicals that result from volcanic energy of the planet. On the summits of high mountains, where nothing else can survive the most ferocious winds and lethal cold on earth, there are lichens composed of symbiotic algae and fungi. The fungus produces an acid, which etches the surface of the rock, enabling the colony to attach to the smooth surface, and the acid also dissolves the minerals into a chemical form that the alga can absorb. The fungus provides a spongy framework for the colony, which absorbs moisture from the air. The alga, with the help of sunshine, synthesizes the rock minerals, the water and carbon dioxide from the air into food substances on which both it and the fungus feed. Both plants reproduce separately and the next generations have to reestablish the liaison afresh. The partnership is not equal, however. Sometimes the fungal threads inside the lichen wrap themselves around the algal cells and consume them. And the alga, if separated from the fungus, can lead an independent life; the fungus cannot survive without the alga. The fungus seems to be using the alga as a slave to enable it to colonize these bleak areas otherwise closed to it.

> In the Himalayas and the Andes, in the Alps and the mountains of the Antarctic, some stretches are as pink as a slice of watermelon. ... Only with a microscope can you discover, among the frozen particles, the cause of the color – a great number of tiny single-celled organisms. These, too, are algae. Each contains green particles with which it photosynthesizes, but this color is masked by a pervasive red pigment which may well serve the alga in the same way as your snow goggles serve you – by filtering the harmful ultraviolet rays in the sunshine.
>
> At one stage in its life, each of these algal cells has a tiny beating thread, a flagellum which enables it to move through the snow to reach a level, just below the surface where there is exactly the amount of light that best suits it. There, sheltered from the wind by the snow itself, temperatures are not as cripplingly low as they are in the open air.
>
> These tiny plants take nothing from the world except sunlight and a minute quantity of nutrients that are dissolved in the snow. They feed on no other living thing and nothing feeds on them. They scarcely modify their surroundings except to bring a blush to the snow. They simply exist, testifying to the moving fact that life even at the simplest level occurs, apparently, just for its own sake.[21]

These examples of life existing in some of the most extreme conditions on our planet serve not only to frame the picture of our reality, they manifest great truths about our own state of being. Creatures of all sorts live under all kinds of conditions, from icy tundra to seething swamps, from incandescent deserts to sweltering jungles. And all of them express fundamental essences of the Names of God just as humans do, individually and collectively.

On the great Serengeti plains of Africa there are herds of many different kinds of animals. Anybody who has seen the circle of life presented in the animated movie, *The Lion King*, can see a colorful

---

[21] Attenborough, *The Living Planet*, 1984; emphasis added.

depiction of the play of forces that exist in our natural world. There are elephants, antelope, giraffes and zebras moving across the landscape in great herds, eating the plant life and moving on. There are lions and cheetahs on the plains, and crocodiles in the rivers, lying in wait for a young, weak, or feeble member of the antelope, zebra or giraffe herds to become available so that they can have dinner. Then there are the hyenas and vultures that eat the remains of the predators' feasts. In the jungles, there are great serpents among the amazing varieties of predators and prey. There is also a great assortment of plant life, much of which serves as food for some of the creatures.

In the simple garden behind my house, there are birds and lizards, insects and plants of all sorts. The lizards eat many insects and the birds in turn, eat them. There are roses – beautiful but deadly – which grow in soil composed partly of plant detritus converted by earthworms into usable nutrients. There are also grubs and mole crickets that seem to do nothing but destroy what I work so hard to produce and maintain. In the evenings, the bats and mosquitoes both come out in force, the former preying on the latter (thankfully) and the night blooming jasmine opens to feed a particular species of night moth that delights in its nectar.

The earth spins around its axis bringing night to cool the planet and to provide rest for the sunlight seekers of our world. Night also provides an environment for the night creatures to come forth in their shy or sinister forays for food.

The earth, spinning on its axis, circles ponderously around the Sun, which drags all its planets in a mad dash around the outer reaches of the galaxy. The companion planets seem to have significant influence on the life forms on earth, most particularly our own satellite, the Moon. Not only that, but they mark seasons. And, according to the wisdom literature, the celestial bodies "pour forth knowledge".

There is Spring, when I spend eight hours a day getting the garden in shape; there is Summer, when I relax and watch my efforts grow and blossom; there is Fall, when I pull up the dead annuals and prune the overgrowth; and there is Winter when everything rests and builds strength to burst forth the following Spring, to initiate a new cycle. Cycles within cycles; birth, growth, maturity, reproduction, decline, and death. To everything there is a season.

Now, imagine that you are observing the Earth with a high-powered telescope out in space. This telescope gives you detailed close-ups of any point on the planet, but you cannot hear anything. You can only see. Forget everything you think you know about the principles of biological life. Forget that you think you know anything about what living things are or how they are supposed to behave. Now, what do you see?

The first thing you notice is that the surface of the planet is teeming with activity. This includes areas under the soil and deep within the ocean. The activity on the surface of the planet consists of an immense number of different shapes and sizes of living things going about in circles *eating* each other.

Further, you notice that there is a whole class of these living things that are, essentially, immobile; incapable of escaping being eaten. In fact, they don't seem to object being eaten at all. Maybe if they could run away, they would, but they can't, so it may only seem that they don't object. But, the fact of the matter is that these immobile beings, (call them plants) use this fact of being eaten to their advantage. By being eaten, they are often able to propagate themselves in far distant places that they would otherwise be unable to populate on their own.

However, all the other living things clearly resent being eaten. They very often make strenuous efforts to not be eaten.

By now, you have probably decided that this planet is a monstrous environment, and hideously dangerous to boot! We are already learning from nature.

Nevertheless, if you begin to examine the situation in another way, you begin to notice that many of the living things have fundamental similarities in shape and behavior and this leads you to think that maybe they all have something in common. After a bit of reflection, you come to the idea that this thing they all have in common is the faculty of assimilating a food and transmuting it. This process of transmutation of food seems to be directed at reproduction. When the living being achieves this aim, the organism begins to deteriorate and die. But this death is not an extinguishing of life in all the component parts of the being, because they are assimilated by other forms and recycled into new life whether animal or vegetable.

But, in considering the matter even more deeply, we discover that even those things that are not considered to be capable of assimilating and transmuting food are part of the cycle. Such things as minerals become part of the cycle and therefore partake of the process through various chemical reactions.

So, perhaps we are looking for an even deeper principle: that of the faculty of reaction. The vital phenomenon is that of reacting.

But, to have reaction, or life, there must be action and resistance to action.

Action + Resistance = Reaction/Life. We have learned something else from nature. There are two fundamental forces that result in a third.

So, we begin to think that all of these many living beings we are observing have a common, structurally very simple origin. We begin to think they are all not only manifestations of a single source, but that they have all been changing their shapes over an immense period of time. And we now come to the critical questions as to how and why this endless process of change has been occurring.

Of course, we can easily comprehend the question how in a general sense: all the changes occur via reproduction. These creatures we are observing, not having eternal life, begin to reproduce themselves as early in their life cycle as possible.

Now, in a static and stable environment, it might be expected that all the creatures would be exactly alike. They would reproduce copies of themselves that would be the same from the beginning to the end. But there is something else to consider. The planet is constantly bombarded by cosmic rays of various sorts that affect the "blueprints" or genetic codes, which determine the offspring's likeness to the parent. Sometimes, these blueprints get changed in one way or another. Many of these altered copies do not survive – in fact, most of them don't. But every once in a while, one of them does and reproduces. And sometimes the altered copies have some features which actually makes them better than the original. These individuals not only reproduce, they thrive.

So, we see a certain pattern emerging here: the variations of biological systems have to do with whether or not one variety of creature can survive the competition in the terrifying planetary game of life and death. It is clear that danger is omnipresent and only the most vigorous and adaptable survive. This is another important rule that Nature teaches us.

Many of the creatures often considered prey are equipped with elaborate sensing organs that help them to stay out of harm's way. Many of the predators have horrifyingly efficient organs of destruction such as teeth and claws.

This terrible vista is what we see when we look at nature. So, what are we to think? Is it mindless cruelty, or purposeful activity from another level of being?

Are we to think that this is the sinful natural world that has nothing at all to do with our spirituality? Is this what we are to "change" or "lift up" or "spiritualize" so that all of this monstrous eating and being eaten is done away with or transformed into a blissful garden where the Lion lies down with the Lamb and everybody munches on, well, something?

Is this dreadful condition of nature an error? Is it the result of the sin of Adam and Eve?

Or, is there a great truth there for those who will open their eyes and look?

The secrets of nature are there for all to see. Nature is its own teacher. She initiates and shows her inner sanctum to those who search and labor in the vineyard. Even the most wholesome herb can turn into a dangerous poison, if we lack knowledge of its power. It is the nature of the moth to fly into the flame because it lacks the knowledge of what effect the flame has. It is the nature of a spider to spin a web. It is the nature of the cat to torture the mouse before eating it. It is the nature of some creatures to eat their own young. It is the nature of the black widow spider and the praying mantis to eat their mates during the act of mating.

In *Hostage to the* Devil, Jesuit and exorcist Malachi Martin wrote: "A bird doesn't fly because it has wings; it has wings because it flies." That is to say: a bird is the incarnation of "Bird-ness", which includes flight and, in many species, song.

Taking this idea a little further, we could think of a black widow spider that kills and eats her mate right after mating as the embodiment of a certain combination of Names at that moment. Destroyer, Slayer, Devourer, and Terrible come to mind. The same would be true for a cat torturing a mouse before eating it. But, when not torturing the mouse, the cat is embodying other Names or Ideas. A cat is a Dreamer, Sensitive, Proud, and many other things. The same is true for many creatures, but it might be thought that each class of them has some essential spiritual idea that is exclusively theirs. But, in their physical nature, they are basically devourers and slayers.

Human beings, individually and collectively, are the incarnation of specific ideas as well. In fact, it could be said that they are the embodiment of all the things we see in the natural world.

> Q: (L) I would like to know what is the source and nature of these nearly universal visions that occur in shamanistic practices; the various creatures including serpents and bird-headed dudes, and so forth? What is the source of these hallucinations? In these chemically induced trances, why is there the common experience of seeing these bird-headed or serpent-like creatures?
>
> A: While you have physicality, some part of you will maintain the connection to its roots.

Q: (L) Are you saying that all these people who say that human beings have reptilian genetics, are telling the truth? Do we have reptilian genetics?
A: Yes.
Q: (L) Do we also have bird genetics?
A: Yes.
Q: (L) And that is our physical connection or basis?
A: Yes, as third density bioengineered beings, you lead the smorgasbord parade of that which surrounds you in the physical realm.

We have a clue then that we can learn a great deal about ourselves, our reality, our destiny, and the proper response to our environment by studying that which surrounds us in the physical realm. But, it is not just observation of the outer structure that we are after; it is the discovery of the inner nature, or the idea of a thing. The Platonic Idea of a thing is referred to in some philosophical systems as noumena. In Kantian philosophy, this is an "object reached by intellectual intuition without the aid of the senses". It is the essence of the thing, independent of the mind, the *thing-in-itself.*

We have already mentioned the fact that the Sufis, using Islam as their operational platform, refer to something that amounts to an inclusive principle. The Sufis refer to the qualities or essences as the Names of God. A Name is thus a principle or function. These Names include Alive, Knowing, Life Giver, Slayer, Powerful, Weak, Forgiving, Vengeful, Mercy, Compassion, and so on.

Now, an important thing to consider about this is that these Names are ordered according to a sort of essential preeminence. This means that the highest Name designates the widest specific reality, or relative relationship. It does not mean that any one of them is better than any other in terms of value. A man who is a genius is as valuable as an idiot in the scheme of the cosmos, just as a maggot is as valuable as a peacock. All are made of the stuff of God, and therefore, all are equal in those terms.

But, what we are talking about here is something akin to the Cassiopaean concept of density, or relative relationship. For example: the Names of fatherhood and sonhood are based on the relationship that the son comes into being through the father. In this sense, neither the father nor the son are more important, it is just that the son archetype is relationally an offshoot of the father archetype.

The relationships of the Names distinguish between God and the Cosmos and, according to the Sufis; the Names manifest the realities of the Divine. That is to say, the Names or faces are like templates through which the Divine creative force extrudes into being-ness, and this process of extrusion is followed by mixing and mingling the principles and functions to result in a great variety of engendered or created beings. Some of these Names have more inclusive connections than others and some make use of others; some of them are opposites, and it seems that they all occur in balance.

For example: the Name Alive designates the precondition for the existence of all the Names, and is thus at the top of the scale. It is all inclusive. The Sufis then go on to postulate that knowledge is born from Alive and that it includes awareness of all the other Names as intrinsic to its own existence. Knowledge, as an all-inclusive principle, necessitates knowledge of all.

We also know that the knowledge of the Name of Knowing is more inclusive in connections and more tremendous in compass than the Name of Powerful or Desiring, since these Names have less inclusive connections than Knowing. They are like gatekeepers for Knowing. There is a similar situation to be seen in the fact that the Name of Hearing, Seeing, Thankful, Clemency, Compassion, and other similar Names, are less inclusive in connection. All of them stand lower than Knowing.

In thinking about the Sufi concept of the Names of God, and hypothesizing that each and everything that exists is a manifestation of one or more of these Names in its essential nature, we begin to get the idea of what it is we must understand in terms of our reality. The Sufis say that we are to learn to put each thing in its proper place. That means we are supposed to learn from it so that we can name it.

Umberto Eco writes in *The Search for The Perfect Language*:

> God spoke before all things, and said, 'Let there be light'. In this way, he created both heaven and earth; for with the utterance of the divine word, 'there was light.' Thus Creation itself arose through an act of speech; it is only by giving things their names that he created them and gave them an ontological status: 'And God called the light Day and the darkness He called Night ... And God called the firmament Heaven.'
>
> In Genesis 2: 16-17, the Lord speaks to man for the first time, putting at his disposal all the goods in the earthly paradise, commanding him, however, not to eat of the fruit of the tree of the knowledge of good and evil. We are not told in what language God spoke to Adam. Tradition has pictured it as a sort of language of interior illumination, in which God, as in other episodes of the Bible, expresses himself by thunderclaps and lightning.
>
> ... It is at this point, and only at this point (Genesis 2:19), that 'out of the ground the Lord God formed every beast of the field, and every fowl of the air; and brought them unto Adam to see what he

would call them.' The interpretation of this passage is an extremely delicate matter. Clearly we are here in the presence of a motif, common to other religions and mythologies – that of the nomothete, the name giver, the creator of language. Yet it is not at all clear on what basis Adam actually chose the names he gave to the animals. ... The Vulgate has Adam calling the various animals 'nominibus suis,' which we can only translate, 'by their own names'. The King James Version does not help us any more: 'Whatsoever Adam called every living creature, that was the name thereof.' But Adam might have called the animals 'by their own names' in two senses. Either he gave them the names that, by some extra-linguistic right, were already *due* to them, or he gave them those names we still use on the basis of convention initiated by Adam. In other words, the names that Adam gave the animals are either the names that each animal intrinsically ought to have been given, or simply the names that the nomothete arbitrarily and ad placitum decided to give to them.

> From this difficulty we pass to Genesis 2:23. Here Adam sees Eve for the first time; and here, for the first time, the reader hears Adam's actual words ... 'This is now bone of my bones, and flesh of my flesh: she shall be called Woman ...' In the Vulgate the name is virago (a translation from the Hebrew Ishha, the feminine of ish, 'man'. If we take Adam's use of virago together with the fact that, in Genesis 2:20, he calls his wife Eve, meaning 'life', because 'she was the mother of all living', it is evident that we are faced with names that are not arbitrary, but rather – at least etymologically – 'right'. (Eco 1995)

Aside from the fact that in pre-biblical myths Adam was a creature formed by the Goddess of Earth from her own clay, and given life by her blood, the issue of the Nomothete, as Dr. Eco points out, is a theme common to other religions and mythologies. Nevertheless, when we consider the later Tower of Babel issue, in which the theme was the confusing of languages, we find that Names or words as a significant motif keep coming up to remind us of something crucial.

The theme of names or words as something that gave one power is brought forward again in the Bible when we are told that, after the Flood of Noah, "the whole earth was of one language, and of one speech". (Genesis 11:1) At this point, humankind decided to build a tower. The passage reads:

> "Come, let us build us a city, and a tower whose top reaches into the sky; and let us make a *name* for ourselves, lest we be scattered over the whole earth." (Genesis 11:4)

Now, it is very curious that the very idea we are discussing is specifically identified here. "Let us make a *name* for ourselves." What happens next is most interesting.

> The Lord came down to see the city and the tower, which the sons of men had built. And the Lord said, Behold, they are one people, and they have all one language; and this is only the beginning of what they will do; and now nothing they have imagined they can do will be impossible to them. Come, let Us go down and there confound (mix-up, confuse) their language, that they may not understand one another's speech. (Genesis 11:5-7)

Now, just what the heck happened here? We can easily figure out that it had nothing to do with language in the sense of variations in spoken speech because in Genesis 10:5, 10:20 and 10:31 we find references to the diffusion of the descendants of Noah after the flood: "... In their lands, each with his own language ... their families, their languages, their lands, and their nations ..." and so forth.

So again we find ourselves in the presence of a very subtle idea that needs our attention. Why is it that the tradition focuses on a story in which the confusing of speech was understood as a tragedy, as a divine malediction? If the languages of man were already numerous after Noah, why does this story of the confusion of tongues exist as an allegory of a curse upon humankind?

> Ba-Bel, 'God's Gate', was the Babylonian heaven-mountain of ziggurat where the god descended from the sky to the Holy of Holies, the genital locus of his mating with Mother Earth. ... Babylon's famous Hanging Gardens occupied the seven stages of the ziggurat, to create a Paradise like that of Hindu gods: 'Seven divisions of the world ... in seven circles placed one above another ...' The ziggurat was a 'temple' of the seven spheres of the world. ... The Babel myth is found all over the world, including India and Mexico. It was familiar in the Greek story of the giants who piled up mountains to reach heaven. *Hindus said it was not a tower but a great tree that grew up to heaven ...* (Walker 1983; emphasis added)

We already have disclosed a little clue from the Cassiopaeans on this matter, but let's look at it one more time and see if we can discover something more that will help us to understand:

> Q: (L) What was the event a hundred or so years after the flood of Noah that was described as the confusing of languages, or the tower of Babel?
> A: Spiritual confluence.
> Q: (L) What purpose did the individuals who came together to build the tower intend for said tower?
> A: Electromagnetic concentration of all gravity waves.
> Q: (L) And what did they intend to do with these concentrated waves?
> A: Mind alteration of masses.
> Q: (L) What intention did they have in altering the mind of the masses?

A: Spiritual unification of the masses.

Q: (L) Who were the "gods" that looked down on the tower of Babel, at those who were building it with the intention of unification, and decided to destroy their works?

A: Lizards.

Having already talked about humankind being a "Fragmented Soul Unit", we now have the idea that making a *name* as it was described in the Biblical text, had something to do with spiritual unification of the masses – possibly reassembling members of that soul unit.

We also have a clue that this action was not acceptable to the Control System because the Bible clearly says:

> "And the Lord said, Behold, they are one people, and they have 'all one language'; and this is only the beginning of what they will do; and now nothing they have imagined they can do will be impossible to them." (Genesis 11:6)

Aside from the fact that this passage pretty much confirms the Cassiopaeans' interpretation of the event, it suggests other possibilities that we need to consider, namely the idea that with spiritual unification "nothing they have imagined they can do will be impossible to them".

What a concept!

But we need to note another thing about this Tower of Babel business: The Cassiopaeans also said that it was designed to function via "electromagnetic concentration of all gravity waves" and that this would accomplish the "mind alteration of masses".

Now, let's think about this for a moment. They said "all gravity waves"/ Plural.

Let's go to another series of curious remarks made by the Cassiopaeans. And, it should be noted that this series of remarks was initiated by my questions about the *Sufi* teachings:

> Q: (L) As you know, I have been studying the Sufi teachings, and I am discovering so many similarities in these Sufi "unveilings" to what we have been receiving through this source, that I am really quite amazed, to say the least. So, my question is: could what we are doing here be considered an ongoing, incremental, "unveiling", as they call it?
> A: Yes.
>
> Q: (L) Now, from what I am reading, in the process of unveiling, at certain points, when the knowledge base has been sufficiently expanded, inner unveilings then begin to occur. Is this part of the present process?
> A: Maybe.

Q: (L) My experience has been, over the past couple of years, that whenever there is a significant increase in knowledge, that it is sort of cyclical – I go through a depression before I can assimilate – and it is like an inner transformation from one level to another. Is there something we can do, and if so, is it desirable, to increase or facilitate this process in some way?

A: It is a natural process. Let it be.

Q: (L) One of the things that Al-'Arabi writes about is the ontological levels of being. Concentric circles, so to speak, of states of being. And, each state merely defines relationships. At each higher level you are closer to a direct relationship with the core of existence, and on the outer edges, you are in closer relationship with matter. This accurately explicates the seven densities you have described for us. He also talks about the "outraying" and the "inward moving" toward knowledge. My thought was certain beings, such as fourth-density STS, and other STS beings of third density, who think that they are creating a situation where they will accrue power to themselves, may, in fact, be part of the "out raying" or dispersion into matter. Is this a correct perception?

A: Close.

Q: (L) Al-'Arabi says, and this echoes what you have said, that you can stay in the illusion where you are, you can move downward or upward. Is this, in part, whichever direction you choose, a function of your position on the cycle?

A: It is more complex than that.

Q: (L) Well, I am sure of that. Al-'Arabi presents a very complex analysis. Nevertheless, it almost word-for-word reflects things that have been given directly to us through this source.

A: Now, learn, read, research all you can about unstable gravity waves. Meditate too! We mean for you, Laura, to meditate about unstable gravity waves as part of research.

Q: (L) Okay. So, we are onto something with the Sufi teachings. It is clear that there is something under the surface, and, I was convinced by seeing this underlying pattern that it was possible to penetrate the veil, and that gave me the impetus to push for a breakthrough.

A: Unstable gravity waves unlock as yet unknown secrets of quantum physics to make the picture crystal clear.

Q: (L) Gravity seems to be a property of matter. Is that correct?

A: And antimatter! Gravity binds all that is physical with all that is ethereal through unstable gravity waves!!!

Q: (L) Is antimatter ethereal existence?

A: Pathway to. Doorway to.

Q: (L) So, through unstable gravity waves, *you can access other densities*?

A: Everything.

And we have just discovered that "Ba-Bel" means "God's Gate". Hmm …

Q: (L) Can you generate them mechanically?

A: Generation is really collecting and dispersing.

Q: (L) Okay, what kind of a device would collect and disperse gravity waves? Is this what spirals do?

A: On the way to. When you wrote "Noah" where did you place gravity?

Q: (L) I thought that gravity was an indicator of the consumption of electricity; that gravity was a byproduct of a continuous flow of electrical energy …

A: Gravity is no byproduct! It is the central ingredient of all existence!

Q: (L) I was thinking that electricity was evidence of some sort of consciousness, and that gravity was evidence that a planet that had it, had life …

A: We have told you before that planets and stars are windows. And where does the gravity go?

Q: (L) Well, where does gravity go? The sun is a window. Even our planet must be a window!

A: *You have it too!!* Gravity is all there is. Gravity is "God".

Q: (L) [So we have our own inner "window".] But, I thought God was light?

A: If gravity is everything, what isn't it? Light is energy expression generated by gravity.

Q: (L) Is gravity the "light that cannot be seen", as the Sufis call it: the Source.

A: Please name something that is not gravity.

Q: (L) Well, if gravity is everything, there is nothing that is not gravity. Fine. What is absolute nothingness?

A: A mere thought.

Q: (L) Do thoughts produce gravity?

A: Yes.

Q: (L) Does sound produce gravity?

A: Yes.

Q: (L) Can sound manipulate gravity?

A: Yes.

Q: (L) Can it be done with the human voice?

A: Yes.

Q: (L) Can it be done tonally or by power through thought?

A: Both. Gravity is manipulated by sound when thought manipulated by gravity chooses to produce sound which manipulates gravity.

Q: (L) Now, did the fellow who built the Coral Castle spin in his airplane seat while thinking his manipulations into place?

A: No. He spun when gravity chose to manipulate him to spin in order to manipulate gravity.

Q: (L) Does gravity have consciousness?

A: Yes.

Q: (L) Is it ever possible for the individual to do the choosing, or is it gravity that *is* him that chose?

A: The gravity that was inside him was all the gravity in existence.

Q: (L) Well, I thought the Sufis were tough! (F) Well, it's probably because of your studies that this door opened. (L) Good grief! What have I done! All right. I am confused.

A: No you are not.

Q: (L) Then, just put it this way: I am befuddled and overloaded.

A: Befuddling is fun! How many times do we have to tell you?!?! Learning is fun! The entire sum total of all existence exists within each of you, and vice versa.

Q: (L) Then what is the explanation for the "many-ness" that we perceive?

A: Perception of 3rd density.

Q: (L) The problem is accessing it, stripping away the veils.

A: That is the fun part.

Q: (L) So, the fellow who built the Coral Castle was able to access this. Consistently or only intermittently?

A: Partially.

Q: (L) According to what I understand, at the speed of light, there is no mass, no time, and no gravity. How can this be?

A: No mass, no time, but yes, gravity. Gravity supersedes light speed.

Q: (L) What would make a gravity wave unstable?

A: Utilization.

Q: (L) I feel like I am missing a really big point here …

A: You are, but you can only find it at your own pace.

Now, let's run some of those key points by one more time:

> Gravity is no byproduct! It is the central ingredient of all existence! Gravity binds all that is physical with all that is ethereal through unstable gravity waves!!! We have told you before that planets and stars are windows. And where does the gravity go? *You have it too!!* The entire sum total of all existence exists within each of you, and vice versa. Gravity is all there is. Gravity is "God". Gravity is manipulated by sound when thought manipulated by gravity chooses to produce sound, which manipulates gravity.

Now, remember that the Cassiopaeans said that the Tower of Babel was designed to artificially concentrate all gravity waves and that this would result in unification, which the Control System immediately saw as a threat. From the above, we can conjecture that the remark about concentrating all gravity waves must refer to the aligning of individuals as being able to access God, considering that the "sum total of all existence exists within each" human being in the form of gravity. Sounds to me like they are describing what is known today as the zero-point energy state.

David Bohm computed the zero-point energy due to quantum-mechanical fluctuations in a single cubic centimeter of space, and arrived at the energy of 10^{38} ergs (a unit of energy in the centimeter-gram-second system of units). This is the energy equivalent of about ten billion tons of uranium. Joseph Chilton Pearce compares this zero-point energy proposal to the saying of Jesus that if we have the faith of a grain of mustard seed, we might move mountains. There is a little catch, however. According to David Bohm, under present conditions this energy is inaccessible in the material sense. It is merely a mathematical representation of a theoretical state. But, as we have already proposed, this zero point energy source is really the state of pure non-anticipation of the left-brain in its analysis of the observations made through the right-brain thought processes. It is the mirror of mirrors of *Grail consciousness*.

On the subject of alphabets, Nigel Pennick wrote:

> Because they contain the potential to describe and transmit all the knowledge in the universe, alphabets have a magical quality. ... Several ancient alphabets have names for each character, which are descriptive of an object or quality, and to which magical and divinatory possibilities are attached. ... The Roman alphabet in use today is not usually considered to be of any magical or divinatory significance ... (Pennick 1992)

Ancient alphabets were more than a means by which phonetic symbols were put together to make words that denoted people or things. These signs had concepts associated with them. The word rune is related to the meaning to whisper (as Wisdom is described doing above) or to give indications of the nature of something. Each sign of the ancient symbol systems was a unit encapsulating a wealth of information. They represented a formless eternal reality, which is manifested in the world we experience as objects, powers, feelings and attributes.

Going back to our right and left-brain functions, we find that it is the left side of the brain that possesses the abilities needed for reading and writing in our modern sense of the words. But the ancient symbol systems represented logographic imagery that was more efficiently recognized by the right side of the brain. The key is to unify the two halves of the brain in response to a sign.

In the Prose Edda (Snorri Sturlson), Odin makes this synthesis. In the Song of Havamal (The Utterances of the High One), stanzas 138-139, we read:

> "I know that I hung on the windswept tree,
> Through nine days and nine nights,
> I was stuck with a spear, and given to Odin,
> Myself given to myself,
> On that tree, which no man knows,
> From which roots it rises.
> They helped me neither by bread,
> Nor by drinking horn.
> I took the runes,
> Screaming, I took them,
> Then I fell back from there."

What does this have to do with "making a name" for themselves? What can it tell us about the Names of God? How does this relate to our individual access to the zero-point energy function?

A name, in esoteric terms, is considered identical with the thing itself; it is a spiritual handle by which one becomes aware of how to deal with a person, thing or issue. Ancient Britons believed that the name and the soul were the same and there are many stories about Celtic heroes refusing to give their names to strangers. In some myths, knowledge of the name could bring destruction as is noted in the fairy tale of *Rumpelstiltzkin*.

From all the things we have discussed so far, it seems reasonable to assume that the oldest civilizations had some knowledge of sound as a means of creation and destruction. The belief that pronouncing a divine name could activate such forces is only a pale remnant of that knowledge. It could even be said that there was some element of this idea behind the saying of Jesus that "In my name shall they cast out devils". It is also reflected in the idea that one could only be saved "in the name of Jesus".

However, if we track this idea back to the wisdom literature, we find that Wisdom is the sustainer and governor of the universe who sits by the throne of God, and She comes to dwell among men and bestow her gifts on them, but most of them reject her.

Nevertheless, the tradition has been passed down that the holy names were not merely symbols because words spoken in the name of Jesus or in the name of the Father, son and holy spirit were supposed to have absolute efficacy in expelling demons. The Christian church taught that no demon could be exorcised before his own name was known, following the example of Jesus who demanded to know the names of the devils that were possessing the Gadarene.

We can see that there is a key in this shadow of truth. If these ideas are twisted perversions of the idea of knowledge and wisdom as the giver of all good things and protector of humankind, then we come face to face with the realization the naming something is to know it. And, by the same token, naming it is to separate it!

In the passage quoted from Genesis about the creation of the world being accomplished by naming things, the thing that we really need to notice here is that the "let there be light" business was essentially the fact that God separated the light from the Darkness by naming them. The One became Two. The "parent" produced the "child". The un-manifest sea of potential contracted infinitely, leaving a void, or zero-point, and everything else, or One. Everything in the cosmos can be expressed by two figures, 0 and 1, on or off, STO or STS, creation or entropy.

This zero point function with its incredible energy potential is known in the Sufi teachings as the Breath of God. God was constricted and so breathed out to ease His constriction. This breath is the cloud, or the mirror in which God sees his reflection. And the reflection is seen in everything that comes into being through the constant fluctuation of God's being as he looks in the "mirror". As God looks he is activating the positive creative potential of the idea which is responded to by the zero-point energy potential of the breath, and all creation comes into being. That which is dispersed toward the periphery, the Breath of God, becomes the clay of creation. Without it, light would not shine and the cosmos would not come into existence. And, once this full outward manifestation is achieved, it is time for the unitive movement to take over, and an active and conscious participation in this movement is the prerogative of human beings.

Here, we come to another great mystery:

> The root of the Breath is the property of love. Love has a movement within the lover, while "breath" is a movement of yearning toward the object of love, and through that breathing enjoyment is experienced. And God has said, as has been reported, "I was a Treasure but was not known, so *I loved to be known*". Through this love, breathing takes place, so the Breath becomes manifest and the Cloud comes into being. (*Koran*, II 310.17)

As an aside, we deduce from the above that love serves knowledge, not the other way around.

Getting back to the matter at hand, thus breath is a vapor, relieves constriction in the breast, and is the vehicle for words. The existent things or words come into existence within the breath as the result of God's speech. This word is described as "Be!" yet this word is addressed to each thing in its state of nonexistence. And, thereby, the thing becomes existent. The place of articulation is that which determines what comes into being. In bringing the cosmos into existence, the breath of God assumes the contours defined by the Names. Just as each word that a human speaks issues from a particular point, known as the place of articulation within the vocal apparatus, in the same way, each letter/reality of the cosmos manifests Being in a specific mode different from other modes. Each, therefore, is connected to a specific Divine Name.

According to Ibn al-'Arabi, "The One" or the Divine Presence comprises Essence, Attributes and Acts. This embraces all that *is*. The Essence is God without reference to relationships. The Acts are all created things, including man. The Names are the *Barzakh*, or isthmus between Essence and Creation. In other words, the Names define the relationships between God and the Creation. The Names are not like the creatures of the universe, which can be noted as separate things; rather, they are relationships, attributes, ascriptions or correlations between God and the cosmos. The Created things are the secondary causes of the Names.

> Once God has created the cosmos, we see that it possesses diverse levels and realities. Each of these demands a specific relationship with the Real. These names allow us to understand that they denote both His Essence and an intelligible quality that has no entity in existence. Examples of these intelligible qualities include: creation, provision, gain, loss, bringing into existence, specification, strengthening, domination, severity, gentleness, descent, attraction, love, hate, nearness, distance, reverence, contempt and so on. Every attribute manifest within the cosmos has a name known to us.
>
> The Divine Names allow us to understand many realities of obvious diversity. The names are attributed only to God, for He is the object named by them, but He does not become multiple through them.
>
> God knows the names in respect of the fact that he knows every object of knowledge, while we know the names through the diversity of their effects within us. (Koran, III 397.8)

The Names are also called realities. As qualities or essences they are the genetic code of the offspring of God – and it is really uncertain how many there are. Each system has its own list. Some commentators on Judaism say there are 72 Names of God. The Islamic view is that there are 99. Some esoteric literature lists the "Twelve Pairs of Twin Characteristics". My guess is that to try to list them all would be limiting. And it should be noted that the Judeo-Christian view is that those which are not "Beautiful Names" do not apply to God, but rather are the result of sin. In this respect, they effectively judge and condemn half of creation, and seat this judgment upon half of humanity, i.e., women.

> The multiplicity of relationships that can be discerned in God results in a multiplicity of relationships in the cosmos. All things in the universe manifest the effects and properties of the divine names. Even conflict, quarrel, strife, war have roots in God. The cosmos is a great collection of things, and things go their own ways, not necessarily in harmony with other things on the level where they are being considered. True knowledge of God demands knowing Him through both kinds of names. (Chittick 1989)

Now here we come back to the same issue the Apostle Paul was working with when he was musing about why one vessel should be called to grace and the other to wrath. Paul's view is exposed as very narrow and presumptuous when compared with the Sufi view.

> The properties of the divine names, in respect of being names, are diverse. What do Avenger, Terrible in Punishment, and Overpowering have in common with Compassionate, Forgiving, and Gentle? For Avenger demands the occurrence of vengeance in its object, while Compassionate demands the removal of vengeance for the same object. So, those who look at these manifestations will think that it is Divine Conflict, or error or accident.
>
> This conflict is because, as Al-'Arabi explains, *different Names call the creatures in different directions!* If the object of the call responds, he is named 'obedient' and becomes 'felicitous'. If he does not respond, he is named 'disobedient' and becomes 'wretched'. (Chittick 1989)

The word demon comes from the Greek *daemon*, which was something like a guiding spirit or guardian angel. The medieval concept of the demon evolved from the Christian blanket condemnation of all Pagan ideas. According to St. Thomas Aquinas, all bad weather and natural catastrophes were brought about by demons. But, we can see that the archaic idea that the daemon, as a divine power, inner spirit, fate or secondary divinity is rather close to the idea of the Names of God.

Now, in this following dialogue from the writings of the Great Shaykh, Ibn al-'Arabi, note how close to the concept of the daemon, as the ancients understood it, the Names are:

The Shayhk says: You should know that the divine call includes believer and unbeliever, obedient and disobedient. ... This call derives only from the divine names. One divine name calls to someone who is governed by the property of a second divine name when it knows that the term of the second name's property within the person has come to an end. Then this name which calls to him takes over. So it continues in this world and the next. Hence everything other than God is called by a divine name to come to an engendered state to which that name seeks to attach it. If the object of the call responds, he is named 'obedient' and becomes 'felicitous'. If he does not respond, he is named 'disobedient' and becomes 'wretched'.

You may object and say: 'how can a divine name call and the [person] refuse to respond, given that [he] is weak and must accept the divine power'?

We will answer: [He] does not refuse to respond in respect of [himself and his] own reality, since [he] is constantly overpowered. But since [he] is under the overpowering sway of a divine name, that name does not let [him] respond to the name which calls to [him]. Hence there is conflict among the divine names.

However, in terms of power, the names are equals, so the ruling property belongs to the actual possessor, which is the name in whose hand the [man] is when the second name calls to it. The possessor is stronger through the situation.

You may object: 'Then why is a person taken to task for his refusal?' We answer: Because he claims the refusal for himself and does not ascribe it to the divine name which controls him.

You may object: 'The situation stays the same, since he refuses only because of the overpowering sway of a Divine name. The person who is called refused because of the name.' We answer: That is true, *but he is ignorant of that, so he is taken to task for his ignorance, for the ignorance belongs to himself!*

You may object: 'But his ignorance derives from a divine name whose property governs him.' We answer: *Ignorance is a quality pertaining to nonexistence; it is not ontological!* The divine names bestow only existence; they do not bestow nonexistence. So *the ignorance belongs to the very self of him who is called.* (*Futuhat*, II 592.32 in Chittick 1989)

Here is a huge clue to our problem. First of all, we learn that each and every human being is under the call of one or more of the Divine Names. It seems as though one particular Name must be in charge at any given time, until it has finished with the person. If another Name calls to the person, it has less influence over him than the one that possesses him at a given time.

Now, we already know that there can be a great multiplicity of Names in operation at any given time and that this is the reason for the great variety of manifestations of secondary causes or created beings and situations in the cosmos. These can be macro-beings and situations or micro-beings and situations. There are universal, galactic, solar, global, national, racial, metropolitan, social, familial and personal manifestations of or dispute among the Names.

Gurdjieff talked about this problem in a somewhat different way, though we can see his Sufi roots showing through rather plainly.

> 'I want you to understand what I am saying. Look, all those people you see,' he pointed along the street, 'are simply machines – nothing more'.
>
> 'I think I understand what you mean', I said. 'And I have often thought how little there is in the world that can stand against this form of mechanization and choose its own path.'
>
> 'This is just where you make your greatest mistake', said G. 'You think there is something that chooses its own path, something that can stand against mechanization; you think that not everything is equally mechanical.'
>
> 'Why, of course not!' I said. 'Art, poetry, thought, are phenomena of quite a different order.'
>
> 'Of exactly the same order', said G. 'These activities are just as mechanical as everything else. Men are machines and nothing but mechanical actions can be expected of machines.' ...
>
> 'Can one stop being a machine?' I asked.
>
> 'Ah! That is the question', said G. '... It is possible to stop being a machine, but for that it is necessary first of all to know the machine. A machine, a real machine, does not know itself and cannot know itself. When a machine knows itself it is then no longer a machine, at least, not such a machine as it was before. It already begins to be responsible for its actions. What to do? It is impossible to do anything. A man must first of all understand certain things. He has thousands of false ideas and false conceptions, chiefly about himself, and he must get rid of some of them before beginning to acquire anything new.
>
> '... Man's chief delusion is his conviction that he can do. All people think that they can do, all people want to do, and the first question all people ask is what they are to do. But actually nobody does anything and nobody can do anything. This is the first thing that must be understood. Everything happens. All that befalls a man, all that is done by him, all that comes from him – all this happens. And it happens in exactly the same way as rain falls as a result of a change in the temperature in the higher regions of the atmosphere or the surrounding clouds, as snow melts under the rays of the sun, as dust rises with the wind.
>
> '... Man is a machine. All his deeds, actions, words, thoughts, feelings, convictions, opinion, and habits are the results of external

influences, external impressions. ... To establish this fact for oneself, to understand it, to be convinced of its truth, means getting rid of a thousand illusions about man, about his being creative and consciously organizing his own life, and so on. There is nothing of this kind. Everything happens – popular movements, wars, revolutions, changes of government, all this happens. And it happens in exactly the same way as everything happens in the life of individual man. Man is born, lives, dies, builds houses, writes books, not as he wants to, but as it happens. Everything happens. Man does not love, hate, desire – all this happens.

'But no one will ever believe you if you tell him he can do nothing. This is the most offensive and the most unpleasant thing you can tell people. It is particularly unpleasant and offensive because it is the truth, and nobody wants to know the truth. It is one thing to understand this with the mind and another thing to feel it with one's whole mass, to be really convinced that it is so and never forget it.

'With this question of doing, yet another thing is connected. It always seems to people that others invariably do things wrongly, not in the way they should be done. Everybody always thinks he could do it better. They do not understand, and do not want to understand, that what is being done, and particularly what has already been done in one way, cannot be, and could not have been, done in another way. ... Actually everything is being done in the only way it can be done. If one thing could be different, everything could be different. ... Everything is dependent on everything else, everything is connected, nothing is separate. Therefore everything is going in the only way it can go. If people were different everything would be different. They are what they are, so everything is as it is.

'In order to Do, it is necessary to Be. And it is necessary to understand what to Be means. ... Then one must learn to speak the truth. In most cases, people think they speak the truth. And yet they lie all the time, both when they wish to lie and when they wish to speak the truth. They lie all the time, both to themselves and to others. ... But they cannot help lying. To speak the truth is the most difficult thing in the world; and one must study a great deal and for a long time in order to be able to speak the truth. The wish alone is not enough. To speak the truth one must know what the truth is and what a lie is, and first of all in oneself. And this nobody wants to know.' (Ouspensky 1949)

And then, in the same vein we have don Juan telling Carlos Castaneda in *The Active Side of Infinity*:

'I want to appeal to your analytical mind,' don Juan said. 'Think for a moment, and tell me how you would explain the contradiction between the intelligence of man the engineer and the stupidity of his systems of beliefs, or the stupidity of his contradictory behavior.

> Sorcerers believe that the predators have given us our systems of beliefs, our ideas of good and evil, our social mores. They are the ones who set up our hopes and expectations and dreams of success or failure. They have given us covetousness, greed and cowardice. It is the predators who make us complacent, routinary, and egomaniacal.'
>
> 'But how can they do this, don Juan?' I asked, somehow angered further by what he was saying. 'Do they whisper all that in our ears while we are asleep?'
>
> 'No, they don't do it that way. That's idiotic!' don Juan said, smiling. 'They are infinitely more efficient and organized than that. In order to keep us obedient and meek and weak, the predators engaged themselves in a stupendous maneuver – stupendous, of course, from the point of view of a fighting strategist. A horrendous maneuver from the point of view of those who suffer it. They gave us their mind! Do you hear me? The predators give us their mind, which becomes our mind. The predators' mind is baroque, contradictory, morose, filled with the fear of being discovered any minute now.'
>
> 'I know that even though you have never suffered hunger ... you have food anxiety, which is none other than the anxiety of the predator who fears that any moment now its maneuver is going to be uncovered and food is going to be denied. Through the mind, which, after all, is their mind, the predators inject into the lives of human beings whatever is convenient for them. And they ensure, in this manner, a degree of security to act as a buffer against their fear.'
> (Castaneda 1998, 213-220)

All of the above sounds absolutely crazy! Here we have a Sufi mystic from hundreds of years ago, a peripatetic jack of all trades, including mysticism, from Asia Minor living in the first half of the 20th century, and a semi-mythical shaman who may have been a figment of the imagination of a peyote-eating, contemporary anthropologist, all saying something that is absolutely savage to our ideas of the Love of God, self, personal sovereignty, free will and enculturated belief systems!

They are all saying there is clearly some larger force, being or influence behind our reality about which we desperately need to become aware. Are they the only ones saying such things?

Barbara Hort, Ph.D., a Jungian psychologist is saying something quite similar. In *Unholy Hungers* she writes:

> The Beast has always been with us. For as long as our hearts have pumped blood, for as long as our souls have glowed with life, for as long as we have yearned for love, the beast has always been there. Sneering and stalking, drooling and scheming, it licks its full, soft lips in anticipation of its next warm meal. For the beast is essentially a feeding thing. Oh, yes, it has many faces, all of them human, and it

> has our endearing manners as well. But those human graces are a camouflage born of necessity – they are the disguise that enables the beast to prevail. Beneath its veneer of humanity, the core of the beast is hunger, and survival is its only goal.
>
> The beast hungers for survival, but not for life as we know it. ... It has a clever mind and an insatiable hunger. To survive, the beast must appease its hunger, and it can feed only on the thing it lacks – the essence of life. So the beast must prey upon us, the living. It must suck our lifeblood and drain our force.
>
> If we are lucky, we will merely die. If we are less fortunate, we will succumb to the deepest horror of the beast's predation, which is that most of its victims will not die. Instead, we will become the thing to which we have fallen prey, and we will be compelled to feed in the same parasitic way. Thus the feeding frenzy spreads, swelling into a bestial legion whose progenitors haunted prehistory. The beast is ancient and global and growing. I have many stories, and shapes without number, and all are like shadows – elusive and dim. But the name that we call the beast itself is clear and cold and precise. We call the beast vampire.
>
> The story of the vampires is as old, as tangled, and as evil as any on earth. ... So many, many names, and among them lies a hard truth. *The vampire stalks the living in every corner of the human world.* Dracula is only a single vampire among a global horde, and what's more, he is a young member of the clan, for he was born in the mind of Bram Stoker only one hundred years ago, and he was based on a warlord who lived less than six hundred years ago – a mere breath of time, considering it was more than three thousand years ago that the Assyrians and Babylonians described the monster *ekimmu*, an undead corpse who preyed upon the blood and flesh of the living in an effort to evade its own death. So it is between us and the vampire. Wherever we have lived, whenever we have lived, the beast has always been with us.
>
> What can account for the ancient, global presence of the vampire in myth and lore? (Hort 1996)

Well, that's a good question. There are other Jungian psychiatrists and psychologists who have been working with the idea of archetypes who have suggested that our myths and folktales have a great deal to tell us about our reality, both apparent and that which is hidden. The plain fact is, the stories about vampires are so widespread and prevalent that trying to account for it by many of the modern theories of disease, sexual perversity, sadism, necrophilia, and people who have mental aberrations causing them to steal, drink, or bathe in human blood simply doesn't cut the mustard.

According to Jung, every human psyche is composed of basic elements called archetypes. We can define archetypes as the constellations of energies or traits that make up our personalities. The images used to symbolize archetypes can help us comprehend the variety of psychic energies that compose who and what we are. According to Jungian theory, when our archetypes are activated, we feel as if we are moved by internal characters who are acting out gripping stories upon the stages of our lives. Sometimes we feel that we possess these powerful psychic energies, and at other times it feels as if they have possessed us. Jungian analyst Marion Woodman, quoted by Dr. Hort, writes:

> When we contemplate the archetypal energies that move us, it seems as if each archetype has a distinct personality with positive and negative aspects. ... The energies of our archetypes can 'fill us with radiant light, or overwhelm us with destruction and despair. They are our gods, within, spiritually and instinctually. Relating to them [consciously] allows us to work at incarnating our angels.' ... I would add that relating to an archetype unconsciously leads us to incarnate our demons as well. ... Archetypes 'are like hidden magnets [that] attract and repel. Gods and vampires, goddesses and witches are alarmingly close in this domain. They make us or break us, depending on our conscious relationship to them.'" (Hort 1996, 5; emphasis added)

Jung's idea was that when an archetype was activated in a group the images of its energy would appear in the group's stories, myths, and folktales. He also believed that any story that was widespread through space and time was an important clue to a psychological experience that was common to all. If Jung was right, then the story of the vampire, the oldest and most widespread myth of all, is more than a byproduct of ignorant people in bygone times. The vampire archetype has been with us since the dawn of history, and the fact is, it is with us in ways we are only beginning to comprehend.

I would like to draw your attention to some remarks made in the previous two sections. The first is my statement that evil is a real and cogent manifestation in our world:

> I can assure you that evil insinuates itself into our lives in the guise of goodness and truth. The difficulty in talking about evil nowadays lies not in the weird or bizarre, but rather from the insistence by our culture that religious views of good and evil are outdated. ... The fact is, the selves which create evil and wish to perpetuate it are those at higher density levels and against whom we have no defense except through knowledge of who they are and how they work. We must learn about the lies in order to perceive the truth.

Later, I again referred back to this evil:

> As my perspective expanded, the more the evils disappeared! Now, don't get me wrong. When I say they 'disappeared', that does *not* mean that they went away or were transformed. Not at all. I just stopped seeing them as evil. ... No indeed. I still can see demons in the world and at work; I still see the creeping darkness shadowing the souls of mankind, blotting out their access to their creative potential. I still see war and genocide and famine and plague as part of our reality. ... And, even though, for convention, I use terms such as dark and light, and good and evil and positive and negative, in order to talk about things in a practical way, I no longer see these things as an essential error ... What I see now is that all of these things exist, the light and the dark, the good and the evil, the positive and the negative, the STS and STO beings, as part of the superb framework of the infinite Creator or Prime Source. ... What is more, I see the *reason* for it to be this way, above and beyond just the simple 'choice' of humankind to experience learning at a faster rate.

Those who have read the previous volume may recall that as soon as I fully entered into the Christian Fundamentalist mindset which posits the idea that one needs to seek salvation for one's self as well as the world at large, my reality immediately crashed around me and I did indeed need salvation!

The offshoot of this Christian Fundamentalism, the New Age idea that "you create your own reality" by excluding any thoughts about anything that is unpleasant, was also a disaster that nearly killed me. Clearly, there was some sort of relationship between my view of the world and my experiences within it, though it was not precisely that which was suggested to be true by either of these paths.

I then continued to consider the likelihood that the reason for these manifestations is that, indeed, we do create our own reality in some obscure way, but that the devil is in the details, so to speak. I then examined the idea that when one is trying to change the reality, the truly creative part of the mind understands that the reality is broken and that this is what gets created. What this really boils down to is "however you judge, you are judged".

I would like to take just a moment here to make a point: *judging*, in a general sense, is something altogether different from examination, assessing, evaluating or forming an opinion. It suggests acting for or against something "other", since a judgment generally carries with it the idea of a "sentence" or reward and punishment. This is a crucial issue since it is at the root of the you-create-your-own-reality controversy.

Joseph Chilton Pearce, in his classic, *The Crack in the Cosmic Egg*, wrote:

> There is a relationship between what we think is out there in the world and what we experience as being out there. There is a way in which the energy of thought and the energy of matter modify each other and interrelate. A kind of rough mirroring takes place between our mind and our reality.
>
> We cannot stand outside this mirroring process and examine it, though, for we are the process, to an unknowable extent. Any technique we might use to 'look objectively' at our reality becomes a part of the event in question. We are an indeterminately large part of the function that shapes the reality from which we do our looking. Our looking enters as one of the determinants in the reality event that we see.
>
> ... The procedure of mirroring must be considered the only fixed element, while the products of the procedure must be considered relative. ... We represent the world to ourselves and respond to our representations. ... A change of worldview can change the world viewed.
>
> Metanoia is the Greek word for conversion: a 'fundamental transformation of mind'. It is the process by which concepts are reorganized. ... The same procedure can be found in worldview development [and] can be traced in the question-answer process, or the proposing and eventual filling of an 'empty category' in science. The asking of an ultimately serious question, which means to be seized in turn by an ultimately serious quest, reshapes our concepts in favor of the kinds of perceptions needed to 'see' the answer. ... A question determines and brings about its answer just as the desired end shapes the nature of the kind of question asked.
>
> Exploring this reality function shows how and why we reap as we sow, individually and collectively – but no simple one-to-one correspondence is implied. The success or failure of any idea is subject to an enormous web of contingencies. (Pearce 1975)

"A change of world view can change the world viewed." What a concept!

Most importantly, "Our looking enters as one of the determinants in the reality event that we see. ... The asking of an ultimately serious question, which means to be seized in turn by an ultimately serious quest, reshapes our concepts in favor of the kinds of perceptions needed to 'see' the answer."

These remarks take us, again, to the idea of Grail Consciousness, which is the "asking of the question", and of course to ask a question with no assumption about the answer is the key to being able to more completely *see* the universe as it is. And here we arrive at another sticking point. Once you *see* something in the reality, what are you then supposed to *do*? What is the proper reaction? Or is it that you are not supposed to react at all? How can you tell?

This is where we find "the success or failure of any idea is subject to an enormous web of contingencies". It is the contingencies or reactions that we will begin to explore.

First of all, let me remind the reader what we are trying to accomplish: we are learning about our present world so that we can arrive at the "simple understandings" that are supposed to be the final exam of third-density reality. Those understandings apparently will not only determine if we do graduate, but will also determine how prepared we are to begin the lessons of the next grade. It seems that an important part of this preparation is the achieving of this Grail Consciousness.

> The God Odin, discovering the secret spring of wisdom and poetry, asked the guardian of the spring for a drink. He was told: 'The price is your right eye.' ... The 'universal pool' is as much 'in here' as anywhere. ... Anything desired can be gotten from it, if one is willing to pay the price and has an ultimate commitment around which the process can orient. ... The mirrors of reality play are brought into alignment by a non-ambiguous commitment from a conscious mind. The 'other mirror' is automatically unambiguous. (Pearce 1975)

We already know the "right eye" that must be paid to drink from the spring of wisdom and poetry is our linear, conceptual thinking which defines a certain narrow scheme of things as good and designates all others as aberrant energy that is somehow amiss or at odds with the universe. With our left-brain, we pick and choose what we like to believe. We ignore and dampen and obscure what we don't like. We invest what we like with "faith", believing that focusing on these concepts will make them part of our reality, while forgetting that our organism, our right-brain, is observing reality in a clear and unbiased way. The possibilities and realities that are excluded from conscious acknowledgment create a mind divided, confused and robbed of power. The body will reflect this by acting as a "machine out of phase, working against itself, tearing itself up".

> Robert Frost saw civilization as a small clearing in a great forest. We have hewn our space at no small cost, and the dark 'out there' seems ever ready to close in again – a collapse into chaos should our ideation fail. ... I shall consider the dark forest to be the primal stuff, the unconscious, the unknown potential. ...

> Our clearing is a worldview, a cosmic egg structured by the mind's drive for a logical ordering of its universe. The clearing is an organization imposed by us on a random possibility.
>
> Teilhard de Chardin saw human destiny spreading the light from our small clearing out into the dark beyond. In archaic times we feared lest the dark engulf our fragile construction of reason, and all actions were oriented toward keeping the cultural circle intact.
>
> ... We have been passionately involved in strengthening our ideation, cataloging and indexing our clearing in the forest. Some unanimity of opinion has begun to form. But the nature of the dark forest is the real problem. For our attitude toward the forest influences sharply the way we look upon our clearing, and affects the kind of new clearing we can make. (Pearce 1975)

These words of Pearce bring our problem into focus. It is our attitude toward what *is* that creates our reality, because it is this attitude that determines the "center" of our consciousness. The center of our consciousness is the zero-point energy access of reality. It is in this sense that we have to look at some things in order to find what is the true source of the center of consciousness and how to shift this in order to truly change our reality.

Now it is time to form a little hypothesis in order to better analyze the situation.

CHAPTER 26
THE TREE OF LIFE

> "In the beginning was the Word, and the Word was with God, and the Word was God Himself. He was present originally with God. All things were made and came into existence through Him; and without Him was not even one thing made that has come into being. In Him was Life and the Life was the Light of Men. And the Light shines on in the darkness, for the darkness has never overpowered it, and is unreceptive to it." (John 1:1-5)

The word *logos* means word in Greek. When it was used in archaic, esoteric terms it had a more specific meaning – that "Divine Essence" was concentrated in its Name. This theory of creation was passed from Tantrism to Neoplatonic philosophy, and was later absorbed into Christianity and from there, it was suggested to apply only to Jesus. The Christian enthusiasm for this idea may have been related to the fact that it provided exclusively male gods the means by which to give birth. They could just speak the word and that was that. Thus, it has become a widely known and popular theological construct.

However, the ability to create and destroy with words was originally the domain of the Goddess in all her many manifestations. She created alphabets, languages and secret words of power, or mantras. Every manifestation of life was brought into being by the supreme syllable and mother of all sounds, Ohm.

The Logos idea is actually almost identical to the Oriental concept of the Oversoul, which was supposed to be the essence of the Great Mother. Origen, one of the early fathers of the Christian church, wrote:

> As our body while consisting of human members is yet held together by one soul, so the universe is to be thought of as an immense living being which is held together by one soul, the power of the Logos.

The doctrine of the Logos was so widespread in the ancient world that it would have been impossible for Christians to ignore it. However, not only did they appropriate its use to their own ends, they also destroyed the ancient Logoi, the sacred writings of the Orphics, mentioned by Plato and other philosophers. This was a large portion of the wisdom literature which survived in part in the Bible, and was also preserved in fragments in certain Gnostic writings discovered at Nag Hammadi in 1945. The Gospel of Truth says:

> When the Word appeared, the Word which is in the hearts of those who pronounced It. ... It was not only a sound, but It had taken on a body as well. (Pagels 1978)

Christians gave the idea a very simplistic interpretation, assuming the "body" was Christ's. The more perceptive of the ancient writers intended to say that man, the nomothete, creates all his gods from his Word.

And here we find ourselves back in the domain of the Names of God.

Q: (L) Is there only one ultimate creator of the universe?

A: All is one. And one is all.

Q: (L) How does thought become matter?

A: Bilaterally.

Q: (L) What do you mean by "bilaterally"?

A: Dual emergence.

Q: (L) Emergence into what and what?

A: Not "into what and what", but rather, "from what and to what".

Q: (L) What emerges from what?

A: The beginning emerges from the end, and vice versa.

Q: (L) And what is the beginning and what is the end?

A: Union with the One.

Q: (L) What is the One?

A: 7th density, i.e., all that is, and is not.

Q: (L) In terms of major STS, this may or may not be related, could you tell us the nature of a Black Hole?

A: Grand Scale STS. Black Holes are a natural force reflection of Free Will consciousness pattern of STS. Notice that Black Holes are located at center of spiral energy forces, all else radiates outward. All in creation is just that: a radiating wave.

Q: (L) Where does the energy go that gets sucked into a black hole?

A: Inward to total nonexistence. Universe is all encompassing. Black holes are final destination of all STS energy. Total nonexistence balances total existence. Guess what is total existence? "God." Prime Creator. As long as you exist, you are of the Prime Creator.

Q: (L) Now, this stuff that goes into Black Holes, that goes into nonexistence, is that, then, not part of the Prime Creator?

A: Correct.

Q: (L) How can Prime Creator lose any part of him or itself?

A: Prime Creator does not "lose" anything.

Q: (L) Well, then, how would you describe this energy that was in existence and then is no longer in existence because it has become or gone into a Black Hole?

A: Reflection is regenerated at level 1 as primal atoms. 1st density includes all physical matter below the level of consciousness. Seventh density is union with the one ... it is timeless in every sense of the word, as its "essence" radiates through all that exists in all possible awareness realms. And, remember, there is only one "God", and that the creator includes all that is created and vice versa!

*

Q: (L) Okay, who created the Cassiopaeans?

A: Your super ancient spiritual ancestors.

Q: (L) Do these beings have a name?

A: No. They are Transient passengers.

Q: (L) What is the meaning of this term and who are these beings?

A: Transient passengers are not beings. Transient passengers are unified thought form.

Q: (L) Why are they called Transient Passengers?

A: Because they transit all forms of reality. And they spring forth from the Unified form of existence.

Q: (L) Well, are these Transient Passengers Realms?

A: Yes. So are you.

Q: (L) Are the sixth-density Orions, also known as Transient Passengers, are they the same Transient Passengers that have been referred to as the ones who genetically engineered us or put us here?

A: Close. They are Wave riders.

Q: (L) Is "riding the Wave" part of the definition of Transient Passengers?

A: Yes.

Q: (L) Do they like to ride this wave?

A: Is it "fun" for you to live on earth?

Q: (L) Well, I like living on earth a great deal, but I don't like pain and suffering, and I don't like man's inhumanity to man and I don't like to see other people suffer.

A: Do you live on earth for amusement?

Q: (L) I would like to live on Earth for amusement but I haven't had a whole heck of a lot of laughs since I have been here this time. I would like to have a life on the planet where things were pleasant ...

A: You misunderstood.

Q: (L) I see what you are saying. That's where they live because that's where they live.

A: Yes.

Q: (L) Are there Service-to-Self beings at sixth density that some call the sixth-density Orions?

A: These are only reflections of individuals, not unified entities. These reflections exist for balance. They are not whole entities, just thought forms.

Q: (L) Are these sixth-density beings what the Bible describes as a "gathering" of angels as in the story of Job where "Lucifer" came in before the Lord ...

A: Yes.

Q: (L) So, in addition to STO, there are STS at sixth density which balance? And they are just there, they exist?

A: Reflection for balance.

Q: (L) Is there any kind of hierarchy to this thing? Do these beings come before some kind of "Grand Council" and make plans and discuss things, and make decisions and implement them?

A: No.

Q: (L) Well, how do things happen? Do things just sort of happen as a natural interaction of things and energies?

A: Yes.

*

Q: (L) You say that you are unified thought forms in the realm of knowledge.

A: Yes.

Q: (L) Ibn al-'Arabi describes unified thought forms as being the "Names of God". His explication seems to be so identical to things you tell us that I wonder ...

A: We are all the names of God. Remember, this is a conduit. This means that both termination/origination points are of equal value, importance.

Q: (L) What do you mean? Does this mean that we are a part of this?

A: Yes. Don't deify us. And, be sure all others with which you communicate understand this too! Remember: 1st density includes all physical matter below the level of consciousness. 6th density is uniform in the level pattern of lightness, as there is complete balance on this density level, and the lightness is represented as knowledge. 7th density is union with the one ... it is timeless in every sense of the word, as its "essence" radiates through all that exists in all possible awareness realms. The light one sees at the termination of each conscious physical manifestation is the Union, itself. Remember, 4th density is the first that includes variable physicality!! Ponder this carefully!!! And, remember, there is only one "God", and that the creator includes all that is created and vice versa!

Now, let's form a little hypothesis here – a working model. Let's say that Unified Thought Forms at sixth density are the Names of God. This is a level of pure consciousness; the Platonic level of ideas, or essences or noumena.

The sixth density level of knowledge of all would be just "below" the One at seventh density. We would call this the Name of Knowledge; it is the logos or "word" that engenders all existence. It could be symbolized by the ancient yin-yang symbol since it includes *all* of the Names. It could also be symbolized as the universal hermaphrodite or androgyne. It is the "Two in One" where the work of generation begins. It is the first manifestation of the eternal parent and is a bisexual universal being. It combines within itself the elements and principles of both masculinity and femininity. However, we have to note the distinction between knowledge of all and the Wrathful and Beautiful Names.

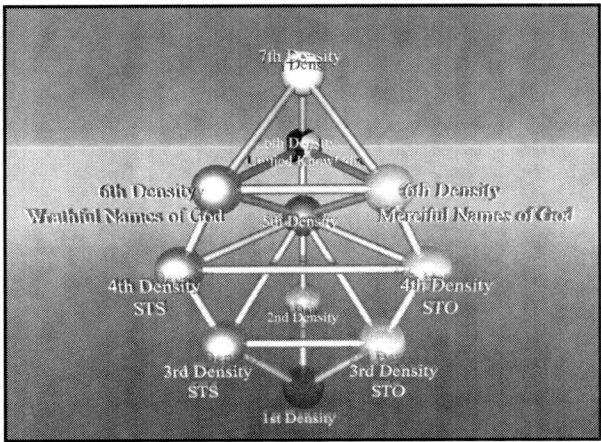

In trying to think through this idea, I wanted to have a visual image. I struggled for months to think of a way to present it with little success. Finally, it occurred to me that the Cabalistic Tree of Life might be a useful form to work with. I found an image in a book and it didn't seem quite the thing, but I thought I could play with it a bit, modify it, and get it to do what I wanted, so I scanned it onto the computer. When I did, the way the scanner was sitting forced me to place the book upside-down. When the image came up on the screen, upside-down, I immediately recognized that this was useful! So here is my little modification of the Tree of Life that represents the cosmos, or body of God.

Now, I want you to notice first of all that the vertical axis has seventh-density union with the One at the top, and first-density matter at the bottom. If I were able to present this in a hyperdimensional manner, the position at the top would include Being and Non-being that serves as a sort of Möbius connection between first density and seventh. In other words, they are not really separate – they connect in an endless cycle. "The beginning emerges from the end and vice versa." It might be useful to think of a tesseract so as to realize this is a three-dimensional representation of something that is not three-dimensional![22]

Now, the next thing we want to consider about this vertical axis is the placement of the sixth-density level of Knowledge on the vertical axis *as a* mirror image of the placement of second density as the realm of nature, that is, flora and fauna. There is an important key here that we must realize. If sixth density is "uniform in the level pattern of lightness, as there is complete balance on this density level, and the lightness is represented as knowledge", then we must think of the realm of nature as being the physical reflection of this principle. That is to say, nature – all of creation – is a reflection of all of consciousness.

We also notice that second density is only able to recycle through fifth density in order to graduate to any of the other densities, and this is reflected in our observations of nature. We do not ever see any creatures from the animal kingdom suddenly developing self-consciousness in the sense of the nature of human consciousness.

Actually, we don't necessarily have any hard evidence that it is possible for humans to graduate to the higher densities which might be indicated by the lateral axes in the figure that show direct channels between third, fourth and sixth densities. Yet we have been told that this is possible; there is circumstantial evidence in esoteric literature that this has occurred.

We do have some idea that certain divine beings who have appeared throughout history have a more or less human form. So we might assume that, generally speaking, there is not so great a barrier between our third-density state and the higher densities as there is between second density and the densities that are reflected in human self-consciousness and awareness.

So, second density is shown without a direct conduit to the higher densities except through fifth, the "recycling zone".

One thing that occurs to me as I look at this little modification of the Tree of Life is that it sure seems to model and define in pretty simple and precise terms the relationships we are coming to understand about our reality, as well as the potentials for moving from one point on the Tree to another. But, don't think that I have even begun

---

[22] Tesseracts are 4D analogs of cubes and are discussed in volume one, *Riding the Wave*.

to analyze and think of all the possibilities. I am hoping that the reader will see things that have not even occurred to me.

It should be understood, again, that the conduits of connection are actually hyperdimensional in nature and not really separated as they appear on the model. Not only that, but the two lateral axes identified as STS and STO represent literally infinite dimensions in number. These dimensions can represent different Names of God and their extensions down through the densities either as single individuals or as groups of individuals. However, there is always balance, so for every STO axis there is an equal and corresponding STS axis.

Another thing that occurs to me as I examine the relationships is that from any of the lateral axes, by accessing nature/knowledge one is also aligning with the vertical axis of Being which could be defined as the axis of gravity within each of us. Perhaps by aligning with this axis, one could theoretically open a doorway into this axis. Once one was in this axis, one could then open a doorway into any of the other positions of either the lateral or vertical axes. Of course, talking about it and doing it are two different things! Apparently this is one of the aspects of the great Work of alchemy. And in studying alchemy we find some warnings that would do us well to heed.

The alchemists wrote that the study and contemplation of the metaphorical philosopher's stone along with the chemical work was a necessary component to elevate the mind and prepare the soul for transmutation.

> By invigorating the Organs the Soul uses for communicating with exterior objects, the Soul must acquire greater powers not only for conception but also for retention, and therefore if we wish to obtain still more knowledge, the organs and secret springs of physical life must be wonderfully strengthened and invigorated. The Soul must acquire new powers for conceiving and retaining. ... That this has not been the case with all possessors was their own fault. ... Those who study only the material elements can at best discover only half the mystery ... alchemy is a mystery in three worlds – the divine, the human and the elemental ... alchemy in the hands of the profane becomes perverted ...
>
> Man's quest for gold is often his undoing, for he mistakes the alchemical processes, believing them to be purely material. He does not realize that the Philosopher's Gold, the Philosopher's Stone, and the Philosopher's Medicine exist in each of the four worlds and that the consummation of the experiment cannot be realized until it is successfully carried on in four worlds simultaneously according to one formula.
>
> Furthermore, one of the constituents of the alchemical formula exists only within the nature of man himself, without which his

chemicals will not combine, and though he spend his life and fortune in chemical experimentation, he will not produce the desired end [which is] the subtle element which comes out of the nature of the illuminated and regenerated alchemist. He must have the magnetic power to attract and coagulate invisible astral elements. (Eugenius Philalethes, quoted in Hall 1988; emphasis added)

The alchemical literature includes stories of alchemists who blew themselves up, who suffered horrible diseases, who came under the power of demonic influences because their technical abilities surpassed their spiritual development, or who shot to stardom like a meteor, and then crashed and burned in ignominy.

But, we are gathering more clues here. We have a remark that "alchemy is a mystery in *three* worlds", and that the work takes place in *four* worlds simultaneously. The three worlds are defined as "divine, human and elemental". The Cassiopaeans have also talked about these three worlds:

October 5, 1996
A: Each soul has its own patterning, which is held in place by the three bodies of existence "thought center, spirit center and physical center". There are specific methodologies for adjusting these, and traveling into or out of other planes of existence. When one does not properly utilize these, one tears the fabric of their trilateral continuum when they seek to travel. This can be very problematic, and may lead to the soul being unable to reconnect with the body, thus causing the physical center to perish!!!

They have also spoken of the "four worlds".

October 10, 1998
A: And remember, your consciousness operates on four levels, not just one! [They are] Physical body, genetic body, spirit-etheric body, and consciousness. [These are] the four composites of the human manifestation in 3rd and 4th densities.

Now, as I pondered these things, it occurred to me that this modified Tree of Life could be used to represent each individual human being since, as the Cassiopaeans have pointed out, all of creation exists within each and every one of us. When we align with the central axis, we are aligned with seventh density, which is the origin of all other engendered beings, and we thereby have access to all of Creation in very literal terms.

However, since man is a mirror image of God, we now need to reverse the image as the Cabalists constructed it with, again, my little modifications.

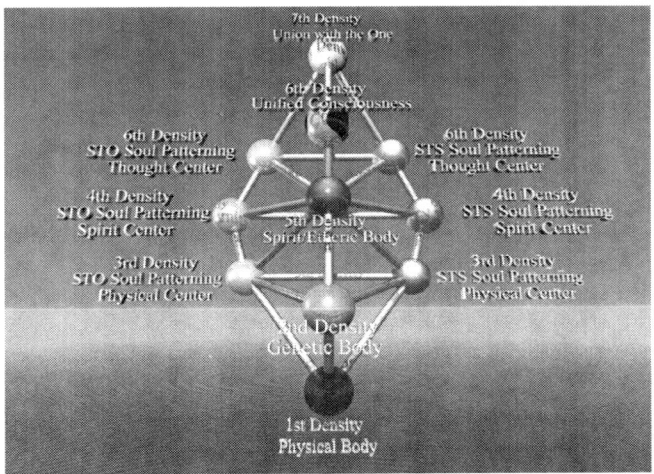

Now, look at this Tree. Note that, on the vertical axis, below the level of Union with the One, or seventh density, there are four positions. If this is the relationship we are looking for, then we see that the physical body relates to first-density matter, the genetic body relates to second density, the spirit-etheric body relates to fifth density, and consciousness relates to sixth density knowledge. At the same time, we always retain our connection to seventh density, so that must be considered the pivot or "true dimension".

> Q: (L) Physicists talk about multi-dimensional universes. The idea is that our three-dimensional space and one-dimensional time is an illusion of plane beings, while the true universe has more dimensions perpendicular to the above ones. Physicists have different guesses here: 5, 6, 7, 11, 256. How many dimensions does the true universe have?
> A: Not correct concept. Should be: How many universes does the "true" dimension have?
> Q: (L) All right, then. I think that from a previous session we were told that the number of universes was not countable. Is that correct?
> A: Infinite, maybe, but more to the point: *variable and selective.*
> Q: (L) Explain variable and selective, please?
> A: For those who know how, universes can be created at will in order to transmodify reality merge.
> Q: (L) What is a reality merge?
> A: What does it sound like?

Q: (T) Merging of realities from one universe into another? A creating of a new reality which is then merged with the old to create a new universe. (L) Maybe it means the realities of different people merge to create a sort of "mutual universe"? Like the idea "you create your own reality"?

A: T is closer; Laura is playing "left field".

Q: (T) A structure of the universe that holds the levels together ... everything is connected. The consciousness of sixth density is perfectly bonded and balanced with third density, and the quasi-physical level of fourth density, and the totally physical levels three through one, and the total One of seventh, and whatever fifth is. (L) We have four levels of physical expression, so to speak, going from the really solid, minimal consciousness level one to ...

A: Yes, but the Terran scientists have been programmed to believe that nothing can exist unless it can be measured, estimated, calculated and represented in some way in the physical material plane. Not true!!!!!!!! For example: We are in *no way* physical.

Q: (L) Well, I also want to know why you refer to a technological device that supposedly transports someone from one density to another, as a "Trans-Dimensional Atomic Remolecularizer"?

A: In order to reconstruct 3rd density into 4th density physical, other dimensions must be utilized in the process. Remember, we are talking about exact duplicates which are merged.

Q: (L) But, a little while ago you said there was a single dimension and many universes, and now you are saying utilizing another dimension, so the terminology is getting to be a little bit confusing ... (T) It is like a program loading onto a computer. Some programs just load straight in. Others need to create a space on the hard drive to put files that they need to *load* the program, but are not *part* of the program, and when it is finished loading, it erases all the "loading instructions". The hard drive is still the hard drive, but for a time, the program used a sector of the hard drive, and created a temporary dimension, let's say. (L) Is this what we are looking at here?

A: Close. And remember, we said "true" dimension!

Q: (L) So, it is like one hard drive, many programs, loading instructions for new programs that are then erased, etc. If there is one "true dimension", and infinite universes within it, does one particular universe exist, of and by itself, at any given time, until it is merged into a new one, or *is there within this one true dimension, multiple universes as real as ours is, to which we could go, and could be there alongside ours, so to speak?*

A: Yes to the latter.

Q: (L) And, can infinite numbers of "dimensions" exist within each level of density, even if temporary?

A: Yes. If you want to go back and change "history", either for individuals or for universal perception, you must first create an alternate universe to do it. Your 4th density STS "friends" have been doing this a lot.

Q: (L) If you, being a general term, create an alternate universe, does the former one continue to exist, or does the former one merge into the new one?

A: Both.

Q: (L) If the former one continues to exist, does it exist and evolve on its own, disassociated with the second one, or this offshoot?

A: Clarify.

Q: (T) The universe you are in: you are going along and say, "I think I will create a new Universe". You do it, and move to it, and you bring your universe with you. That is the merging of realities. But, when you move to the new universe, you are no longer in the original one, which continues along on its own. The pattern of the old universe, you bring *into* the new one, and when you become part of the new universe you have just created, you are no longer part of the old one you just left which just goes along with everybody else there, only without you. Is this possible?

A: Sort of ... remember, one can create all ranges of types of alternate possibilities.

Q: (L) So you could create a new universe with a new "past", even?

A: Yes.

Q: (L) So, in that way, both actually occur and you can change the whole thing?

A: When merged, the former never existed.

Q: (T) Not for the person creating the new universe, but the former will continue for everybody else.

A: Close.

Q: (L) So, for the person creating a new universe, the former never existed, but the other beings who are satisfied with that old universe, and "go" with it, are still continuing along as though ...

A: Your 3rd density mind restrictions limit the scope of your comprehension in this area.

Q: (L) If you decide you don't like your present universe, and you work like crazy to learn how to create a new one, and you do it, do you, essentially, forget that you did this? And why you did this? And forget the other universe?

A: If you wish.

Q: (L) So you can or you can't ... (T) Going by what you just said: "an unhappy universe" exists maybe because you're perceiving the universe you are in as being unhappy because that is the way *you* are and *where you are* at, in terms of learning, and by creating a new universe, you are simply wishing to change the way the universe is around you, and really it's not the universe that has a problem, but you ...

A: Off track. [So much for *that* version of "you create your own reality"!]

Q: (L) So, the universe you are in, is what it is, and you are in it for some reason ... (T) You're in it to learn lessons ... just to change the universe because you don't want to learn the lessons you've chosen to learn ... (L) Or, you have learned them and thereby *can* change the universe ... (T) When you learn, you just move on automatically, you don't have to change the universe. The universe will change for you.

A: Deja vu comes to you compliments of 4th density STS.

Q: (L) Is deja vu a result of some sensation of the universe having changed?

A: Or ... some sensation of reality bridging.

Q: (L) What is reality bridging?

A: What does it sound like?

Q: (T) A bridge is something you put between two things ...

A: You wish to limit, wait till 4th density, when the word will be obsolete!

Q: (L) That still doesn't help me to understand déjà vu as a "sensation of reality bridging". Is déjà vu because something comes into our reality from another?

A: One possibility.

Q: (T) Didn't we talk about this? That it is a bleed through from other dimensions ... that when we think we have been someplace before, it is because in another dimension we have ...

A: Yes.

Q: (L) If you are now in a particular universe that has been created and merged by fourth-density STS, and there is still the old universe existing, and you feel a connection, or a bridging, because some alternate self is in that alternate universe, living through some experience ... or a similar thing?

A: No limits of possibilities.

Q: (L) So it can be any and all of those things, and bridging realities of "past" and "future", as well. Is it possible to change the past within a discrete universe, or does every change imply a new or alternate universe?

A: Discrete does not get it.

Q: (L) Well, within a particular, selected one of the universes, can you go back in time, within that universe, change the past, and have it change everything forward, still within that selected universe, like a domino effect?

A: In such a case, yes.

Q: (L) But, you said that if you want to change the past, you have to create an alternate universe ... (T) No, you asked about changing the past, and they said you have to create a temporary place to work from, a position from which you can manipulate the reality ...

A: That is for specialized activities. What was described is not the same as an "alternate universe".

Q: (L) It is a temporary file that will go away when you are finished loading the program. And that is not creating an alternate universe, but rather a temporary dimension ...

A: Close.

Q: (L) In our particular universe, what is the primary mode? Are we constantly shifting and merging universe to universe, or is our past being changed and reacting like the domino effect ... at least in the past few years ... (T) But, we wouldn't know if the past has been changed because we wouldn't see it ...

A: Measurements are inadequate.

Q: (L) Is it that any and all possibilities will and do take place?

A: Closer.

Q: (L) Are the words "universe" and "dimension" synonymous?

A: Yes and no. For you, these are "gray" areas, and no matter how hard you try, until your perception shifts fundamentally, you ain't gonna get it!

Q: (L) Okay, there are four physical densities ...

A: No, three.

Q: (L) Okay, there are three physical densities, and the fourth is ...

A: One is variable. Three ethereal.

Q: (L) Okay, three that are physical, three ethereal, and one in between that is both.

A: Close.

Q: (L) Is awareness the only thing that determines what density one exists in?

A: No. Awareness is the bond that unites the reality.

Q: (L) You have said that gravity is the binder of all reality.

A: Yes.

Q: (L) And now you talk about perception bonding.

A: Yes. Now, try to picture how gravity is the binder of all reality!!!

Q: (L) If gravity is the binder, is gravity consciousness?

A: Not exactly. Did you know that there is no "right" or "left" in 4th density through 7th density? If you can picture this exactly, then you may be able to understand the responses to all the questions you are asking. If not, best "give it a rest". Because it will only be productive learning when you ponder and reflect/review "later".

Regarding the three worlds, divine, human and elemental – or, as the Cassiopaeans put it, the soul's three bodies of existence: thought center, spirit center, and physical center – we look again at the tree and note that each of the lateral axes has three positions: sixth density, fourth density, and third density. In other words, our third-density physical body is directly connected to our spirit center at fourth density, which emerges from the sixth-density thought center, which is the level of the Names of God.

However, in keeping with our mirror image of the cosmic tree, we have designated the two axes as STS (entropic) and STO (creative). On the STS axis, beings that graduate become more and more "encapsulated" until, at fifth density, they exist completely in entropic thought with no activity whatsoever. At some point, these contractile energies gain sufficient "weight" to graduate to sixth density, at which point, in contact with knowledge of all, they perceive their true function which is to regenerate at level One as primal atoms. They become matter. This occurs at the same instant that STO energies have gained weight on an opposing axis, and rise to union with the One. In short, a constant cycling.

> Q: (T) Now, another force in what we term as the past, defeated you and used the power of the light in order to alter us in different ways, is this correct?
> A: Yes. Now understand this: It is all part of natural grand cycle.
> Q: (L) You say it is a natural thing or part of a natural grand cycle. Is this natural grand cycle just part of the interaction between light and darkness, which just simply must be?
> A: Yes. We are at "front line" of universe's natural system of balance. That is where one rises to before reaching total union of "The One". 6th level.
> Q: (T) Now, the battle you had with the other side ...
> A: Are having.
> Q: (T) This battle goes on ... do you have the light power back?
> A: Never lost it, you did.
> Q: (T) Okay, I guess that for us the Lizzies are the main force even though they have others on their side ...
> A: Yes.
> Q: (T) They took our light, not yours?
> A: Not against you. Currently in union with you.
> Q: (T) So we are but one battle in the universe in an overall, ongoing struggle?
> A: Yes. Balance is natural. Remember, it's all just lessons in the grand cycle.
> Q: (T) When we put out energy as positive or negative energy, there are beings on other levels that feed on this energy. Is this true?
> A: Yes.
> Q: (T) Okay, and you said that the Lizzies feed on the negative energy?
> A: Yes.

Q: (T) Who feeds on the positive energy?
A: You do.
Q: (T) How do we feed on the positive energy?
A: Progression toward union with the one, i.e., level 7.
Q: (L) In other words, you fuel your own generator instead of fueling someone else's. (T) You are at level six, what do you feed on?
A: You have the wrong concept. We give to others and receive from others of the STO. We feed each other.
Q: (L) So, by feeding each other you move forward and grow but those of the STS path do not feed each other so must feed off of others. (T) Now, you are talking to us now. This is considered STO?
A: Yes.
Q: (T) We are providing energy for the channel also, does that provide you with energy?
A: No.
Q: (L) What do you want from us?
A: We don't want when pure STO. We came because YOU wanted. But that is STS until you share with others.
Q: (S) Why are you choosing Laura and Frank to transmit this information?
A: Because balancing fields are correct.
Q: (B) Is this channeling going to go beyond the primitive method of one letter at a time, or is it going to go into the method of writing or typing or direct channeling consciously or unconsciously?
A: Can now, less danger of corruption through this method.
Q: (B) What is the purpose of this contact?
A: To help you to learn, thus gain knowledge, thus gain protection, thus progress.
Q: (B) What do the Cassiopaeans gain from this contact?
A: By helping you, we are moving toward fulfilling of our destiny of union with you and all else, thus completing the Grand cycle.
Q: (B) Is this the only probability open to you or is this the best probability open to you?
A: Both.
Q: (B) Are you a great distance from us in light years?
A: Distance is a 3rd density idea.
Q: (B) Light years is third density?
A: Yes.
Q: (B) What do you mean by traveling on the Wave?
A: Traveling on thoughts.
Q: (L) Whose thoughts are they?
A: Thoughts unify all reality in existence and are all shared.
Q: (S) You travel on a wave of energy created by all thought forms?
A: Thought forms are all that exists!

Q: (B) Have those that are STS acknowledged that those that are STO are going to win in this race or conflict?

A: No, absolutely not! In fact, the STS cannot conceive of "losing" but instinctively feel pressure building upon them, that is the reason for the impending turmoil.

Q: (B) What happens to them when they lose, does this mean that they are degaussed, or does that mean that they have to go back and do the whole evolutionary process all over again on the other polarity?

A: Latter.

Q: (B) So, there is a nexus point coming up?

A: Close. When we said "close" we meant concept was "close" to reality. Not close in terms of time or distance.

Q: (B) At that point do they experience the pain that they have caused?

A: No, that is what happens on 5th level only.

When considering thought centers, a particular remark of the Cassiopaeans may give us another clue for our quest:

August 12, 1995
A: Remember, most all power necessary for altering reality and physicality is contained within the belief center of the mind. This is something you will understand more closely when you reach 4th density reality where physicality is no longer a prison, but is instead, your home, for you to alter as you please. In your current state, you have the misinterpretation of believing that reality is finite and therein lies your difficulty with finite physical existence. We are surprised that you are still not able to completely grasp this concept.

This suggests to us that the way to change our reality is to access something called a thought center or "belief" center. The only problem is, it seems that by aligning ourselves with the fourth-density Service-to-Self reality, we have also come under the domination of the STS thought center or control center. Let's have a look at some of the references to thought centers to determine if we can sort out the matter:

Q: (L) Who created the Lizzies?

A: Ormethion.

Q: (L) And who is this individual?

A: Thought center.

Q: (L) Located where?

A: Everywhere.

Q: (L) Can you give us a little more of a clue?

A: Another sector of reality.

Q: (L) Is this a sentient, self-aware being that created the Lizzies?
A: Yes and no.
Q: (L) And who created this Ormethion?
A: Not being. Thought center.

One thing we notice is that thought centers are slightly different from unified thought forms that are identified as transient passengers. This is another clue that our Tree of Life model is set up correctly, since the unified thought forms would exist at the sixth-density level of knowledge, which contains the thought of STS for balance, but no STS unified thought beings, so to say. But, the thought center realm is apparently a sixth-density level of being in a relative sense. The difference is easily identified by looking at the tree. The sixth-density thought center for STS does not transit all densities and realities – it is restricted to the STS realm. The same is true for the purely STO thought center level – it is restricted to the STO realm. However, the sixth-density unified consciousness level is located on the central, vertical axis as the logoic offspring of seventh density.

Q: (L) Where does gravity emanate from?
A: Thought center.
Q: (L) You have mentioned thought centers of many occasions. Is there more than one?
A: All are one and all.
Q: (L) If you have a thought center, how do thought centers relate to seventh density, the One?
A: Exactly!
Q: (L) Are thought centers seventh density?
A: All is.
Q: (L) All is thought centers?
A: No. All is 7th density. We have told you before that gravity is the foundational force of absolutely everything!!! This means at all density levels, all dimensions ... It is the "stuff" of all existence. Without it, nothing would exist. Your thoughts are based in gravity, too!!

On the occasion of the board photograph discussed in book 1 (as well as *Secret History*), thought centers were also mentioned in a way that gives us another clue to their significance:

Q: (L) What is this geometric figure?
A: Was a visual representation of the conduit, indeed!!! The reason for such clear luminescence is that *thought centers were clear and open in you at the moment of the photograph.* In other words, there was an imbalance of energy coming from 6th density transmission point.

This suggests that I was in a state of total non-anticipation at the moment of the photograph, which allowed a sort of "zero-point energy" function to activate in a psychic way. But, more importantly, it suggests the idea that we are connected via some sort of conduit to these archetypal thought centers as depicted in our Tree of Life image.

Another remark about thought centers demonstrates again that our Tree of Life figure is going to take us somewhere:

> A: First of all, confusion abounds here due to incorrect interpretations of the last subject discussed. Dimensions are not densities!!!! Dimensions are strictly the result of the universal consciousness as manifested in the imagination sector of thought. Density means level of development as measured in terms of closeness to union with the one ...

We might think, then, that the lateral axes represent dimensions resulting from various thought centers. And, again, we cannot limit them to just two, since they may be infinite even if they do fall under the general categories of STS and STO or the Wrathful and Beautiful Names of God.

In trying to understand the relationships of our given position at the third-density level to the vertical lateral axes, or the densities three, four, and six, to which we are connected in a direct way, we might look at this bit of information as a clue:

> Q: (A) Which part of a human extends into fourth density?
> A: That which is effected by pituitary gland.
> Q: (L) And what is that?
> A: Psychic.
> Q: (A) Are there some particular DNA sequences that facilitate transmission between densities?
> A: Addition of strands.
> Q: (L) How do you get added strands?
> A: You don't get; you receive.
> Q: (L) Where are they received from?
> A: Interaction with upcoming wave, if vibration is aligned.
> Q: (L) How do you know if this is happening?
> A: Psychophysiological changes manifest.
> Q: (A) When you speak of an upcoming wave, it is a wave of what?
> A: Think of it as a wave of reflection from the beginning and end point.
> Q: (A) But what vibrates? Energy? Aether?
> A: Energy and aether are directly symbiotic. "Aether" is Terran material science's attempt to address ether. The trouble is, there is simply no way to physicalize a plane of existence, which is com-

posed entirely of consciousness. It is the union of perfect balance between the two "states" or planes that is the foundation and essence of all creation/reality. You cannot have one without the other!

Q: (L) When you say the two states or planes, you are saying the physical state and the state of consciousness ...

A: Yes.

Q: (L) And you can't have one without the other. And the state of consciousness and the state of material existence are so completely connected, that both are infinite? One cannot exist without the other ...

A: Yes, connected, intertwined, bonded ... Merged.

Q: (A) When this aether-energy-matter vibrates, then in which dimension does it do this?

A: The densities three and four at transition junction.

Q: (A) If not in linear time, then in what?

A: Cyclical "time".

Q: (A) What measures the distance between one crest and another?

A: Ending/beginning of cycle.

Q: (A) Is DNA acting as a superconductor?

A: Yes!!! But variably.

Q: (A) I am trying to understand the universe in terms of a triad: matter – geometry – information. Is it the right idea?

A: If one thinks of matter as "living" rather than "dead". And now, when you merge densities, or traverse densities, what you have is the merging of physical reality and ethereal reality, which involves thought form versus physicality. When you can merge those perfectly, what you realize then, is that the reason there is no beginning and no end is merely because there is no need for you to contemplate a beginning or an end after you have completed your development. When you are at union with the One at Seventh density, that is when you have accomplished this and then there is no longer any need for difference between physical and ethereal forms.

This brings us back in a curious way to the study of nature – all of Creation – as a means of drawing closer in alignment with the central, vertical axis.

> By invigorating the Organs the Soul uses for communicating with exterior objects, the Soul must a acquire greater powers not only for conception but also for retention, and therefore if we wish to obtain still more knowledge, the organs and secret springs of physical life must be wonderfully strengthened and invigorated.

In a previous segment, the pituitary connection was mentioned, and now, it becomes more significant:

Stones were once utilized to provide for all needs, as the energies transmitted connected directly with the pituitary gland to connect spiritual realities with the material realms of 3rd and 4th densities. So you see, the 'stone' was viewed as Matriarchal indeed!

And the alchemists say:

> The study and contemplation of the metaphorical "Philosopher's Stone" along with the chemical work was a necessary component to elevate the mind and prepare the soul for transmutation.

The Cassiopaeans relate the alchemical transmutation to fourth density:

> Q: (L) Were the beings involved in this type of activity third density, fourth density or bi-density?
> A: Originally 4th when home was in other locators.
> Q: (L) Could it be said that the pituitary gland itself is the body's own "mother stone"?
> A: If you prefer.
> Q: (J) What exactly is the function of the pituitary gland in your references to Stonehenge?
> A: This gland is your uplink.
> Q: (L) Is it possible that the pituitary can be stimulated by external sources such as radio waves, waves from a supernova, or other frequencies in the environment?
> A: Yes and experiments have ensued.
> Q: (L) Would it be beneficial for us to experiment with such things?
> A: Not wise. You could fry yourself in your zeal.

Regarding the strictly physical aspects of our being, we look again at our Tree of Life and note specifically the arrangement of third, fourth and sixth densities on the lateral axes. The third-density position is directly connected with fifth-density contemplation zone, as are all the other densities. The Cassiopaeans once remarked about the chakras that:

> A: First of all, "chakras" are a little understood and nonproven phenomenon. Now, it just so happens they do exist, but in different form than reported by many in the so-called "psychic" community.
> Q: (L) What, exactly, is a chakra?
> A: An energy field that merges density one, two, three or four *with five*. You are all connected with level five when you are on a short wave cycle. *Chakras are the connection with physical imprint locator.*

Getting back to our hypothesis about archetypes, enters, and Names of God, let me propose that fourth density is a realm where the archetypes are embodied in group souls. These group souls then have extensions of themselves into the third-density reality in the same way a hand has five fingers. Only in these projections, each finger is a different lifetime of an individual soul, which lifetimes are not limited to sequential experience; and we cannot limit the number of hands or fingers. In this sense, it could be said that third density is a projection of sixth density through the "lens" of fourth density.

> Q: (D) When fourth-density beings communicate it's telepathic, right?
> A: Yes.
> Q: (D) Okay, since time doesn't exist, how do you communicate about happenings? If you're communicating telepathically on fourth density, and time doesn't exist, how do you communicate about events as one happens now, as opposed to later, and the next thing happens, and the next thing happens? (J) How is it sequential?
> A: Translate.
> Q: (D) Okay, let me explain what I mean. I mean, we talk about 1907 something happened ...
> A: That is how it is done.
> Q: (T) You translate the experience?
> A: From 4th density to 3rd density. And vice versa.
> Q: (L) So, in other words, it's almost like making movies. So, in other words, if you're a fourth-density being, everything is more or less happening, excuse the term happening, everything is simultaneous, and if you wish to discuss or communicate or have any focus upon any particular aspect of this unified dimension, then what you do is you kind of extract it out, project it into third density like a movie ...
> A: Close. But you will not understand fully until you get there.

Now, each of these archetypal qualities or Names of God manifest on fourth density in archetypal dramas. This relates us back to Mircea Eliade's concept of the archetypal gesture – *illud tempus* – from the beginning.

> Every hero repeated the archetypal gesture, every war rehearsed the struggle between good and evil, every fresh social injustice was identified with the passion of a divine messenger, each new massacre repeated the glorious end of the martyrs. ... All religious acts are held to have been founded by gods, civilizing heroes, or mythical ancestors. ... Not only do rituals have their mythical models, but any human act whatever acquires effectiveness to the extent to which it exactly repeats an act performed at the beginning of time by a god, a hero, or an ancestor. (Eliade 1954)

This expresses the idea that the world in which we live is a form, or reflection or double of another cosmic world that exists on a higher level. These were celestial archetypes.

Q: (L) Earlier Eva and I were talking on the phone about mythological figures possibly representing group souls. That is, on our level of third density, groups of individuals who are separated by flesh, might be extensions of group souls at a higher level ...

A: Whom does Zeus represent?

Q: (F) The father of the gods?

A: And the implication is ...?

Q: (L) Does Zeus represent seventh density?

A: Or does Zeus represent the grasping for 7th density?

Q: (L) Are we saying grasping in ways that are not suitable?

A: No grasping is "not suitable".

Q: (L) Okay. Are we all pieces of ... are there groups and groups and groups that are pieces of a larger whole, or larger wholes, and they can only graduate when they assemble?

A: More to the point would be that that makes the progress speed up for most of those involved in such a process.

Q: (C) Are we part of a group soul or group entity?

A: What do you think?

Q: (C) Yes.

A: And ...

Q: (C) I think that we are part of a group soul ... whatever that means, we have a purpose; I think we have a similar interest, and that is to discover the truth. And it is also to advance us.

A: And ...

Q: (C) When one group advances, then it filters down to others ...

A: How does it "filter down"?

Q: (C) Because I believe that all are connected.

A: How so?

Q: (L) I get it! The Zeus thing. The whole Zeus thing, the bearing of children, the moving out in all these various ways, manifestations or patterns as defined by the "children of the gods" through all the various levels, so that it eventually all comes back around to seventh density.

A: and what does it mean when it "comes back around"?

Q: (L) Union with the One. And it all just keeps going around and around.

A: And C*** says ...

Q: (C) If we are patterned after the myths of Zeus, and we have gone forth, and there are lots of smatterings of fragments upon the earth having many experiences, and as we grow and advance, we come to the truth and the full meaning, we merge back together again with all of the wisdom of all of these experiences.

A: Yes, but is not just the "Earth".

Q: (C) They are in the same process.

A: Yes.

Q: (C) Do they have different myths?

A: They have different everything ... But, in the final analysis, it is really just the same!

Q: (C) Then I would say that when everyone graduates from their finite, physical existence, then they occupy the same space at a different vibration, and go onto other lessons and experiences and advances that I cannot conceive of at the moment.

A: But what is "the moment"?

Q: (C) The moment? I haven't thought that far ahead yet!

A: Or have you, but you simply do not perceive it as such?

Q: (C) Probably so. How many people are in this particular group that Laura and I are in, for the purpose of this work?

A: Up to you to discover.

Q: (C) Well, I thought I'd give it a shot! Thinking is electrical. Does a person leave an electrical echo and can certain combinations produce harmony which is cumulative and exponential, thereby certain groups thinking can produce more than others, or individually?

A: Close. Now, Suggestion: Combine frequencies to witness the development of a directed wave effect; packs a potent "punch".

Q: (LC) I'm really curious. I feel like all of us here have been drawn together for a reason. We had a hell of a time getting here, every one of us, but we did, and I'm just wondering what is this all about? Why did all of us feel so drawn that we just *had* to be here?

A: You are not wondering so much as you are seeking confirmation.

Q: (LC) I don't know. I just feel something powerful.

A: Every one here thinks on more than one level. This already puts everyone into a different category than the status quo. You all have quite well developed senses, a more difficult task is learning to trust the messages. Remember, you all have received negative programming at the third density level, which is designed to derail your higher psychic awareness. You by now know that this is false programming, but we realize that *the subconscious centers are more difficult for you to overcome.* Patience will pay off for you big time!!!

Q: (P) This is my feeling about the whole thing: us coming together, the energy created by each of us being in each other's presence is a key; it's unlocking something that we agreed to come together at this time, though it may not be apparent now, it's going to be. That's the way I have felt about this whole thing. (LC) Okay, another question, and this is a kind of selfish one I am thinking about ...

A: Wait a minute, remember, your plane of existence is STS by its very nature and that is okay, because you're all where you are for a reason ... Now L***, fire away and be just as selfish as you please, dear. [Laughter]

Q: (LC) Well, if that's the case! I want to ask about past life relations between us. I'm sure there is. Are there any specific past life connections between any of the women in this room?

A: Before we answer that, we wish to hear from you what you perceive a past life circumstance to be. How do you perceive the reincarnation process to be?

Q: (LC) I perceive it as you come back with people you choose to come back with, and that you choose people that you are karmically connected to. (I) I see it a little bit differently than that ...

A: Aha! We have a variance!

Q: (I) I think that when we die and go to fifth density, that we make pacts with people in each incarnation, so when you come back, it is coming back to fulfill that pact. (LC) Yes, that is the way my line of thinking is going. But, when they asked that question, I was thinking that you have people you come back with because of closeness. Somebody may be your mother in one life, and there is a love bond, and then there are other people that you come back with because you have to resolve something to let go of that person rather than to get closer.

A: This is partially correct. But, there is more to it than this. For example, one can incarnate on various planes of existence, not just the one you perceive currently. And, one may actually reincarnate on more than one plane concurrently, if one is advanced enough to do this.

Q: (L) Are you suggesting that that we are all part of the same soul unit here?

A: Yes, we are! To an extent, but you may not yet understand what exactly a "soul unit" is in that sense. And of course, there is more than one sense for this as well. The "trick" that 3rd density STS life forms will learn, either prior to transition to 4th density, or at the exact juncture, is to think in absolutely limitless terms. The first and most solid step in this process is to not anticipate at all. This is most difficult for you. We understand this, but this is also why we keep reiterating this point. For example, imagine if one of your past lives is also a future life?

Q: (P) Now, I just want to say that I think that we have all of us here traveled back in time to change the way things are now. We inserted ourselves into this time period to wake up and see what is really happening. This is third-density thinking, I know, but it is the only way I can describe it. We looked back on the way things happened, the way the world is now, and we have come back to change things. We have come from the future, to wake up now, because we didn't wake up before. Because the world is going in this direction, and *something* had to be done. That's what I see. Not just that, things happen to keep us from waking up period! We've all been bombarded with stuff all our lives.

A: That is surprisingly close to the truth. Now just a moment ... reflect please.

Q: (L) P*** was saying that we have come back from the future and inserted ourselves into this timeline ...

A: Yes. That is close to being totally correct!

Q: (L) In terms of reincarnation, which we were talking about a few minutes before that, we are possibly incarnations of ourselves incarnated at different levels. This just happens to be one of the levels of reality that we are occupying, but there are other selves at other levels thinking and doing other level stuff, and these other levels are perceived by us as the future ...

A: Maybe for some of you, but let us not get ahead of ourselves.

Q: (P) The Cs say that they are *us* in the future. So, we, being *them* in the future, some of who they are in the future, have come back as us, to do what we are doing, to undo what is happening on Earth ...

A: Close, but more complex than that. It would be difficult for you to completely understand at this point, but let us just say that you are close. You should reflect upon all that is in the reflection!

Q: (L) What is the reason for the use of the term "reflection"?

A: "Alice through the looking glass."

Q: (L) When she went through the mirror, she was in an alternate reality. (I) Are we in an alternate reality?

A: Yup. But then again, are not all realities "alternate"?

Q: (P) I think we are creating a possibility that would not have existed if we had *not* come together here.

A: Yes, but that is generally true in most similar circumstances. The question is the degree to which there is significance.

We encounter in these myths the idea that man only repeats the acts of the gods; his calendar commemorates, in the period of a year or other longer cycles, all the cosmogonic phases which took place in the beginning or which take place repeatedly at another level of reality.

Myths are only a much later formulation of an archaic content that presuppose an absolute reality, or levels of reality that are extra-human. If we begin to think that our reality is but a sort of slide show projected from a hyperdimensional realm, we have to begin to think about the archetypal dramas themselves. If we come to the idea that we are extensions of our higher selves, fulfilling the purposes of the great cosmic dramas, we come up against a couple of important concepts.

The first of these concepts is free will. Going back to what the Shaykh Ibn al-'Arabi had to say about it:

> You should know that the divine call includes believer and unbeliever, obedient and disobedient. ... This call derives only from the divine names.
> One divine name calls to someone who is governed by the property of a second divine name when it knows that the term of the second name's property within the person has come to an end.
> Then this name which calls to him takes over. So it continues in this world and the next.
> Hence everything other than God is called by a divine name to come to an engendered state to which that name seeks to attach it.
> If the object of the call responds, he is named 'obedient' and becomes 'felicitous'. If he does not respond, he is named 'disobedient' and becomes 'wretched'." (*Futuhat*, II 592.32, Chittick 1989)

This gives us a clue as to the true extent of our so-called free will. Basically, it amounts to the fact that we can identify which archetypal drama we are living and acknowledge it, witness it in our mind, and accelerate or extend the concluding of it. We accelerate by our obedience to the call or we extend it by our rejection and disobedience. In the first case, the outcome can be felicitous if we are careful to finish the drama within the archetype, even if only symbolically, which is often the wisest choice in the event of being caught in a drama of great negative potential. In the second case, we can refuse to acknowledge the drama, continue to struggle against it like a bug striking a window over and over again, and be wretched as a result.

Of course, the problem many people have is in understanding they don't have to remember their past lives in order to learn. The soul has a memory of its own.

> Q: (L) Okay, let me ask this question. In talking about time, I would like to ask, in relation to time, what is memory? Some understanding of time refers to it as the "now", the ever-present now. Well, a lot of people remember a lot of other "nows", some people don't remember any "nows" at all, and it seems like memory is almost like a reverse function of anticipation. Anticipation being almost like a memory of the "future" and memory being like a reverse anticipation into the past. So, what I would like to know is if time is merely a "now", what is memory?
> A: Conscious and subconscious record of perceptions.
> Q: (L) Okay. If memory is subconscious or conscious recording of perceptions, when one accumulates a sufficient amount of memory, does one then become "timeless"?
> A: One is always timeless.
> Q: (L) Okay, but does one then become aware of one's timelessness?
> A: In 4th density.

Q: (L) Okay. Does an electron have a memory?

A: Electron is borrowed unit of 7th density.

Q: (L) All right, in the picture of the crop circle you designated as being "Atomic Structure", there was the concentric circles and then these three things on the outside corners of the triangle, one being zigzag, one being plain and round, and the other one kind of like a wheel, it had like little divisions. Would the zig-zaggy one be the electron?

A: Not correct concept atomic structure unifies elemental atoms.

Q: (L) What is an elemental atom, as opposed to an ordinary atom?

A: Elemental defines singular body of structure. Within, as in: "element of". Electron is element of atomic structure.

Q: (L) Is there anything about an atom that holds memory?

A: Memory is subjective, atom is not.

Q: (L) Well, some atoms seem to be somewhat subjective.

A: No, it is your interpretation.

Q: (L) If memory is conscious and subconscious record of perception, as you have stated, and there occurs a "reality merge", as you also described previously, some sort of time manipulation, does this automatically change individual perceptions?

A: Perceptions "leap" into place according to markers in the eternally present continuum.

Q: (L) What are these markers?

A: Experiential breaks in the perceptual realm of continuance.

Q: (L) Markers are experiential breaks. So, one experiences breaks and they become markers ... perceptions leap into place ... Is this saying that, when there is a perception of a break, that some part of the psyche seeks to bridge this break by leaping into some sort of ...

A: The definition of the previous responses will become clear for you only after some reflection, my dear!

Q: (L) Okay, you said that memory is subjective and an atom is not. If memory is subjective, what you have just been describing means that each and every person has a slightly different perspective, even if they are involved with the same incident or the same time sequence.

A: Of course! That is the treasury of learning.

Q: (L) Who is the treasurer?

A: The learner.

Q: (L) But still, what you said still implies that an atom has an objective existence. Is this correct?

A: Yes.

Q: (L) Would you please tell us what constitutes objectivity?

A: The effort on the part of the observer to leave prejudice "at the door".

Q: (L) How does the effort on the part of the observer to leave prejudice at the door relate to the objective existence of an atom?

A: An atom, as with absolutely everything else, cannot exist without an observer.

Q: (L) So, in the case of the objectivity of an atom, if the human observers are not objective, where is the observer who makes the atom objective, or *does the atom not exist if there is no observer?*

A: Yes to the latter comment.

Q: (L) So there must be an observer. Must the observer be human?

A: The observer must be a consciousness.

Q: (L) If you say that an atom has an objective existence, yet it only exists if it is perceived by a consciousness, then an atom does not have an objective existence, correct?

A: No.

Q: (L) Okay, what is the distinction? You say that objectivity is the *attempt* on the part of the observer to leave prejudice at the door.

A: Without consciousness, there is neither objective nor subjective!!

Q: (L) So the crux is the attempt to leave prejudice at the door in the same manner as one would be non-anticipatory in order to create?

A: Yes.

Q: (L) Well, that is a *very* tricky ... (A) Is consciousness objective?

A: Consciousness is objective, until it has the capacity to choose to be otherwise.

Q: (L) What is the stimulus for the change, for the giving of the capacity to choose?

A: The introduction of prejudice.

Q: (L) In a cosmic sense, cosmic consciousness, in the sense of The One Unified Consciousness, what is the stimulus there for the ability to choose?

A: When the journey has reached union with The One, all such lessons have been completed.

Q: (L) But, that doesn't answer the question.

A: Yes, it does!

And this is where the study of nature comes in. In our quotes about nature as a source of knowledge, there was a passage from Psalms:

> The heavens declare the glory of God, and the firmament shows and proclaims His handiwork. Day after day pours forth speech, and night after night shows forth knowledge. There is no speech nor spoken word; their voice is not heard yet their voice goes out through all the earth, their sayings to the end of the world. (Psalm 19: 1-4)

The Alchemists tell us:

> In order to respect the principle of hermetism adopted by the Tradition, we must understand that esoteric teachings are given in a sibylline form. St Isaac the Syrian points out that: The Holy Scriptures say many things by using words in a different sense from their original meaning. Sometimes bodily attributes are applied to the soul, and conversely, attributes of the soul are applied to the body. The Scriptures do not make any distinction here. However, enlightened men understand.

This is the point at which we begin to understand our reality. The Celestial myths are the archaic representations of the archetypes. In studying these stories and their characters we can have access to very deep knowledge about any human situation or drama in which we may find ourselves. We can also identify which character, or part, we are being activated to play. Once we have identified the drama of the moment (which may extend over years or even an entire lifetime, or merely be a mini-drama of a few minutes, hours or days' duration), we can fully activate our participation with some degree of control.

By recognizing the play, by acknowledging our part, we have formed a link between ourselves and the director, producer and writer of the production at higher densities. We are psychically linked to them in a real and symbiotic way. And, by being linked, we can have access to a free will that is not ordinarily accessible.

Joseph Chilton Pearce was aware that there was something deeper and more involved in our reality than many suppose, and he called it the Cosmic Egg. Well, he may have been more right about this than he ever suspected. If thought centers are cosmic eggs laid from sixth density into fourth density via fifth density, and hatched into third density, then we have only one issue to deal with at this density, and that is which egg is ours?

More than that, if we don't like the present egg, can we crack it and get out?

Well, here we come up against the ever-present problem of the "Catch 22":

> Q: (L) When we are talking about dimensional curtains we are talking about divisions at the same level of density, is that correct?
> A: Maybe.
> Q: (L) Can dimensional curtains be between dimensions at the same level of density?
> A: Yes.
> Q: (L) Are dimensional curtains also something that occurs between levels of density?

A: Yes.

Q: (L) So, a dimensional curtain is a point at which some sort of change takes place ... what causes this change?

A: Nature.

Q: (L) What defines this change?

A: Experience.

Q: (L) Is it in any way related to atomic or quantum physics or the movement of atoms?

A: Yes.

Q: (L) Okay. An atom is in third density. What distinguishes it from an atom in fourth density?

A: Reality.

Q: (L) What distinguishes one realm from another?

A: Assumptions.

Q: (L) Okay, what you assume or expect is what you perceive about that atom depending upon which reality you are in, is that correct?

A: Close.

Q: (L) What determines your assumptions?

A: Experience. Every thing that exists is merely a lesson.

Q: (L) Okay, so once we have learned certain lessons, as in experience of certain things, then our assumptions change?

A: Yes.

Q: (L) Okay, is this wave that is coming our direction going to give us an experience that is going to change our assumptions?

A: Catch 22: One half is that you have to change your assumptions in order to experience the Wave in a positive way. All is merely a lesson, and nothing, repeat nothing, more.

How do we get the experiences that will change our assumptions? Well, let's look at our Tree of Life again. We notice that in both versions, the cosmic and the human mirror, the different densities "recycle" through fifth density on the central axis. There does exist a sort of conduit between the centers, but these conduits do not have an exchange point on the central axis that would facilitate a shift of thought centers or assumptions. From this we can conjecture that it's somewhat difficult to change polarity without some sort of facilitator. This is why the way of the Monk, the Yogi and the Fakir are so difficult. They attempt to bridge the gap without a facilitator on the Central axis.

We notice that, on the cosmic tree, the position of knowledge is a facilitator for the cycling of sixth-density energies to move into union with the one which is, in effect, an instantaneous (or timeless) Being and Non-being. This then initiates a new cycle of consciousness that regenerates as dense matter and consciousness that emerges bilaterally into the Beautiful Names and Wrathful Names of God to initiate the drama all over again.

When we look at the human Tree of Life, which is the mirror image, we see that the position of knowledge is now held by the genetic body, which is on the central axis. We then realize that *this* is our facilitator.

The genetic body is the control center for the physical body since it transduces the central axis energies, so whichever thought center is dominant will control the physical experience. Not only that, but we can see another possibility – namely, that knowledge and genetics are directly interactive. At the third density level, genes are the logos.

> In the beginning was the Word, and the Word was with God, and the Word was God Himself. He was present originally with God. All things were made and came into existence through Him; and without Him was not even one thing made that has come into being. (John 1:1–3)

Sounds like cosmic chromosomes! It is through our genetics that we have the potential of aligning with the central vertical axis and changing thought centers. And, just as second-density nature is a reflection of sixth-density Knowledge in the cosmic tree, so is our genetic code the second-density reflection of all that exists as potential within us as human beings. It could even be said that all of nature exists within us.

> A: As third density bioengineered beings, you lead the smorgasbord parade of that which surrounds you in the physical realm. Each individual possesses all of creation within their minds. Each soul is all powerful and can create or destroy all existence if know how. You may create alternative universes if you wish and dwell within. You are all a duplicate of the universe within which you dwell. Your mind represents all that exists. It is "fun" to see how much you can access. Challenges are fun. Where do you think the limit of your mind is? If there is no limit, then what is the difference between your own mind and everything else? And when two things each have absolutely no limits, they are precisely the same thing.

Is that so? You see, our genes are more or less encoded copies of all the possible dramas of which we can be participants. Much of this information is like closed books, stored in a room that is never opened. We have the potential, via knowledge and exercising certain functions, to open these books and link up with the central axis and thereby make a shift in the essence or Name by which we are dominated. And in doing this we have the possibility of participating in a different drama, myth or fourth-density movie being projected into third density.

Q: (SV) I want to ask one question: If there is no time, there is no past and no future; there are no past lives and no future lives, there is no such thing as reincarnation, then how can you be us ...

A: Yes, there is reincarnation. You are getting ahead of yourself there. We never said there is no reincarnation.

Q: (SV) But, if there is no time? (L) It is all happening simultaneously. We are having all of these lifetimes at once. (SV) Is there a way that we can connect ourselves with all our other selves?

A: Picture it this way: we will access some of your memory banks and give you another reference ... you know what a slide projector looks like? To give you some feeling of what this expanded nature of reality really is, picture yourself watching a big slide presentation with a big slide wheel on the projector. At any given point along the way you are watching one particular slide. But, all the rest of the slides are present on the wheel, are they not? And, of course, this fits in with the perpendicular reality, which fits in with the circles within circles and cycles within cycles, which also fits in the Grand Cycle, which also fits in with what we have told you before: All there is is lessons. That's all there is and we ask that you enjoy them as you are watching the slide presentation ... and, if you look back at the center of the projector, you see the origin and essence of all creation itself, which, is level seven where you are in union with the One.

*

Q: (V) Do I feel this despair due to past life issues or due to this life?

A: Both. Like another "slide" in the slide projector carrousel.

Q: (V) What? (L) In the carrousel of many lifetime issues?

A: Close.

Q: (V) One of my biggest despairing things right now is my disgust with humanity and what they are doing, and how nasty it is ... but that's probably just another slide in the carrousel. I don't think I can hear anymore ...

A: Yes you can, and it would be wise if you did. You see, V***, there is nothing preventing you, or anyone else for that matter, from falling into the correct slot of their balanced contentment learning profile, but simply advancing that carrousel until the correct slot aligns, then just falling, or "sliding" into place!

Q: (L) You use this allegory; what would consist of advancing the carrousel?

A: Discover ... because learning is fun!

Q: (L) Is there a physiological relationship to this carrousel, or is it just strictly psychic, psychological, or learning related?

A: Hide and seek, locate and retrieve.

Here we have one of the major clues to how it will help us to study nature. If our genetics are the physical interface between us and the vertical axis, if they are the physical manifestation of the thought centers through which our existence is extruded, then we might very much want to examine nature and the creatures within it in order to be able to determine just exactly what potentials we may be enacting, what potentials we *can* activate that may not be activated, and how to suppress those potentials that belong to thought centers that we do not choose to be the arbiters of our destiny.

> By invigorating the Organs the Soul uses for communicating with exterior objects, the Soul must a acquire greater powers not only for conception but also for retention, and therefore if we wish to obtain still more knowledge, the organs and secret springs of physical life must be wonderfully strengthened and invigorated. The Soul must acquire new powers for conceiving and retaining ...

We can study nature and discover what archetypes are manifested in our lives and, if we don't like the script, we can discover the ways and means to change the selection, so to speak. That means that we can create our own reality in the sense of changing channels in terms of which thought center is in control of our lives. It also means that we can have a choice as to which face of God we behold!

> Like attracts like. When a candidate has developed virtue and integrity acceptable to the adepts, they will appear to him and reveal those parts of the secret processes which cannot be discovered without such help.
>
> Those who cannot progress to a certain point with their own intelligence are not qualified to be entrusted with the secrets which can subject to their will the elemental forces of Nature.

In the study of nature, we have been given a tool, a means of assessment that, if used rightly, can lead us to make felicitous decisions that activate our DNA in ways that align the three worlds of our soul centers with the four worlds of our bodies of existence.

In reference to the 353535 code (discussed further in the next volume), I asked the Cs:

> Q: (L) What does this code relate to?
> A: Infinite power.
> Q: (L) How is infinite power acquired by knowing this code? If you don't know the correspondences, how can you use a numerical code?
> A: Lord of Serpent promises its followers infinite power which they must seek infinite knowledge to gain, for which they pledge allegiance infinitely for which they possess for all eternity, so long as they find infinite wisdom, for which they search for all infinity.
> Q: (L) And that is the meaning of the number 33? Well, that is a round robin ... a circle you can't get out of!

A: And therein you have the deception! Remember, those who seek to serve self with supreme power, are doomed only to serve others who seek to serve self, and can only see that which they want to see.

Well, that particular session nearly drove me nuts trying to figure it out. We came back to the subject again and this time around it was even stranger:

Q: (L) Okay, let me jump over to this other subject of the number 33 and the number 11. Is there anything beyond what was given on 11-11-95, that you could add at this time, about any of the mathematics or the use of these numbers?

A: Prime numbers are the dwellings of the mystics.

Q: (L) What do you mean, "prime numbers are the dwellings of the mystics"?

A: Self-explanatory, if you use the tools given you.

Q: (L) How can a number be a dwelling?

A: Figure of speech. [Planchette spirals several times, vigorously] And how interesting that we have a new "cell" phone company called: "Primeco".

Q: (L) And how does a cell phone company called "Primeco" relate to prime numbers being dwellings of mystics?

A: Not for us to answer.

We stopped at this point and did a little exercise in word association. Some of the words we came up with were: encryption, cells of monks, prisons, prime number divisible by one or self.

Q: (L) Is encryption the key?

A: Oh, there is so much here. One example is: "Snake eyes" is not so good as 7, 11, eh?

Q: (T) They are all prime numbers, too; seven and eleven. (L) What kinds of documents or writings ... or what would be applicable ...

A: No, Laura you are trying to focus, or limit the concept, my dear. Think of it, what is the Judaic Christian legend for the creation of a woman?

Q: (L) That woman was taken from the rib of Adam. That Eve was created from the rib of Adam.

A: Ever heard of a "prime rib"?

Q: (L) [Groans] (T) I hate being in kindergarten and not knowing what the subject is. Okay, prime rib. We have a prime rib, so ...

A: What happens in a "Primary".

Q: (L) An election. You narrow down the candidates. What happens in a primary?

A: Who gets "picked" to run?

Q: (L) Okay, keep on ...

A: "Prime Directive"? "Prime time"?
Q: (L) The first, the best ... and ...
A: Not point.
Q: (L) I know that's not the point! Is what we're saying here, is that we can use these prime numbers to derive something out of something else?
A: We told you about the mystics.
Q: (L) So, mystics ... the mystics, the mystical secrets ... dwell in the prime numbers if used as a code.
A: Name the primary mystical organizations for key to clue system.

We named: Catholicism, Christianity, Judaism, Cabalism, Sufism, Mysticism, Jesuits, Masons, Knights Templar, Rosicrucians ...

Q: (L) All right. With our little list that we're making, are we on to something or are we completely off track?
A: Yes, now check out those crop circles photos ... any prime number combos there?
Q: (L) Do you mean in terms of dimension, or do you mean in composition?
A: Composition and dimensions ... anything you can find.

We stopped again and discussed sacred geometries and the fact that all the sects listed use prime numbers. We also noted that in Genesis 2:22 it says "rib taken from the man and made woman". We also noted that 2 is the only even prime number and that it was referred to as "snake eyes". In Genesis 3:5 (the 3/5 code in mind) it says "your eyes shall be opened and ye shall be as the gods", referring to the temptation of the serpent in Eden – a serpent that may very well represent the coiling DNA.

Q: (L) Are we thinking in any of the lines of something we ought to follow, or are we drifting?
A: All are lines you ought to follow.

Gurdjieff addressed the issues of this chapter as well, showing that the source of his information was very similar to the "Q source" of Jesus' alchemical teachings. This is evident in the answer he gave to Ouspensky when the latter asked, "Can it be said that man possesses immortality?" Gurdjieff replied:

"Immortality is one of the qualities we ascribe to people without having a sufficient understanding of their meaning. Other qualities of this kind are 'individuality', in the sense of an inner unity, a 'permanent and unchangeable I', 'consciousness', and 'will'. All these qualities can belong to man, but this certainly does not mean that they do belong to him or belong to each and every one.

> "In order to understand what man is at the present time, that is, at the present level of development, it is necessary to imagine to a certain extent what he can be, that is, what he can attain. Only by understanding the correct sequence of development possible will people cease to ascribe to themselves what, at present, they do not possess, and what, perhaps, they can only acquire after great effort and great labor.
>
> "According to an ancient teaching, traces of which may be found in many systems, old and new, a man who has attained the full development possible for man, a man in the full sense of the word, consists of four bodies. These four bodies are composed of substances which gradually become finer and finer, mutually interpenetrate one another, and form four independent organisms, standing in a definite relationship to one another but capable of independent action." (Ouspensky 1949)

Gurdjieff's idea was that it was possible for these four bodies to exist because the physical human body has such a complex organization that, under certain favorable conditions, a new and independent organism can actually can develop and grow within it. This new system of organs of perception can afford a more convenient and responsive instrument for the activity of an awakened consciousness.

> "The consciousness manifested in this new body is capable of governing it, and it has full power and full control over the physical body.
>
> "In this second body, under certain conditions, a third body can grow, again having characteristics of its own. The consciousness manifested in this third body has full power and control over the first two bodies; and the third body possesses the possibility of acquiring knowledge inaccessible either to the first or to the second body.
>
> "In the third body, under certain conditions, a fourth can grow, which differs as much from the third as the third differs from the second, and the second from the first. The consciousness manifested in the fourth body has full control over the first three bodies and itself.
>
> "These four bodies are defined in different teachings in various ways. The first is the physical body, in Christian terminology the 'carnal' body; the second, in Christian terminology, is the 'natural' body; the third is the 'spiritual' body; and the fourth, in the terminology of esoteric Christianity, is the 'divine' body. In theosophical terminology the first is the 'physical' body, the second is the 'astral', the third is the 'mental', and the fourth the 'causal'.
>
> "In the terminology of certain Eastern teachings the first body is the 'carriage' (the body), the second is the 'horse' (feelings, desires), the third the 'driver' (mind), and the fourth the 'master' (I, consciousness, will).

"Such comparisons and parallels may be found in most systems and teachings which recognize something more in man than the physical body. But almost all these teachings, while repeating in a more or less familiar form the definitions and divisions of the ancient teaching, have forgotten or omitted its most important feature, which is: that man is not born with the finer bodies. *They can only be artificially cultivated in him*, provided favorable conditions both internal and external are present.

"The 'astral body' is not an indispensable implement for man. It is a great luxury which only a few can afford. A man can live quite well without an 'astral body'. His physical body possesses all the functions necessary for life. A man without 'astral body' may even produce the impression of being a very intellectual or even spiritual man, and may deceive not only others but also himself.

"When the third body has been formed and has acquired all the properties, powers, and knowledge possible for it, there remains the problem of fixing this knowledge and these powers. Because, having been imparted to it by influences of a certain kind, they may be taken away by these same influences or by others. By means of a special kind of work for all three bodies the acquired properties may be made the permanent and inalienable possession of the third body.

"The process of fixing these acquired properties corresponds to the process of the formation of the fourth body.

"And only the man who possesses four fully developed bodies can be called a 'man' in the full sense of the word. This man possesses many properties which ordinary man does not possess. One of these properties is immortality. *All religions and all ancient teachings contain the idea that, by acquiring the fourth body, man acquires immortality; and they all contain indications of the ways to acquire the fourth body, that is, immortality*." (Ouspensky 1949; emphasis added)

CHAPTER 27
STRIPPED TO THE BONE
THE SHAMANIC INITIATION
OF THE KNIGHTED ONES:
TECHNICIANS OF ECSTASY

It may seem to you, the reader of these pages, that I have been hitting very hard on the concept that man is asleep and it is almost impossible to awaken. For some of you, this may evoke a sense of despair, or helplessness. Some of you feel confident that Love is the answer, and that everyone will be saved (which is to assume that somebody is damned) if they just have love, so we needn't worry about it anyway. Others very likely will outright reject such an idea. Some of you are definitely certain that you are not asleep.

In a general sense, to almost everyone and including yours truly, the very idea of time traveling, mind marauding, hyperdimensional beings with full power to create and maintain a reality of illusion and restriction in which we are confined like sheep, waiting daily to see which of our number will be taken for their wool, skins, or flesh, is so horrifying a concept that accepting it as a real possibility is tantamount to being stripped of all hopes, dreams and comfort.

Like many of you, I began this work full of frustration with teachings that don't work or don't make sense when compared with honest observation of reality and experience. There was such a labyrinth of contradictions everywhere I searched, and I knew it was necessary to go beyond everything hitherto known or tried. I did have the idea that this knowledge had been available in ancient times, judging by the evidence of the megaliths and other incomprehensible structures all over the globe, but whether or not it would be possible to rediscover this path was uncertain.

It was very clear that there was a serious discrepancy between the observable reality and some deeper reality from which, presumably, ours derives something of its form and structure, but I knew there was something that separated "us" from "them". Also, when searching for answers, it always ended in a maze of insupportable assumptions and irreconcilable facts. Yes, to all of you who have written to ask me if I have checked "this" source or "that" source, it is very likely I have, and more. And I repeat, when you read all of them, you find, as Blaise Pascal said:

> I reject equally the religion of Mahomet, of the Chinese, of the Romans, and of the Egyptians, for this simple reason that since one has no greater marks of truth than another, my reason cannot be disposed to receive any one in preference to the rest. (*Pensées*, Chapter XI)

You can add a hundred other sources to Pascal's list on my behalf. They all end in a maze of assumptions and irreconcilable "facts".

But when the Cassiopaeans began to communicate, to say things that did explain the problems I was finding in science, religion and philosophy, and those things they told us were not part of my expectations, I became furious and railed at such a bleak picture of our existence.

I had already gone through some of this process in earlier years while reading Gurdjieff and Ouspensky, but I found that what the Cassiopaeans were saying was far more dispiriting than I was prepared to receive.

I rejected ideas that suggested our fairy tale beliefs just might be imposed on us to keep us asleep and unaware because I didn't like them either. As time went by and evidence from other sources mounted, I raged at lessons that drove home these points in my personal life; and I have wept oceans for the loss of my innocence. So, believe me when I say to those of you who write to me struggling to grasp this, trying to reason and rationalize some way to hang on to the old, false belief systems – I *do* understand!

But, when all is said and done, I think I wept even more for all the years wasted in stupidity and blindness. After a time, I realized that we are only stupid and blind exactly as long as we need to be stupid and blind, and not one second longer. I am enormously grateful for all those experiences because they did teach me in a very deep way.

Now, a curious thing about the teachings of both Gurdjieff and Castaneda, both of which claim that man is food for something "other", is the lack of really specific information about this other. Yes, Castaneda goes further than Gurdjieff in telling us some of the history of the flyer, or the Predator, but it is still somewhat vague and amorphous.

We have often speculated as to whether Gurdjieff knew the truth the way the Cassiopaeans have explicated it and just simply could not bring himself to tell anyone; or if he did tell some of his students, was this something that only those on the inside knew, and held back?

My husband, Ark, met with Henri Tracol, one of Gurdjieff's students, in Marseilles back in July of 1986. It was a brief meeting in an airport restaurant, lasting about two hours at most. His interest was in determining if joining with such a school as the Gurdjieff Foundation in Paris would be helpful to his own awakening. He asked many questions, most particularly relating to this idea of "being eaten" by "something". His assessment (which is highly developed from many years as both a scientist and an instructor) of Mr. Tracol's reaction to this question was that the man was *afraid to answer*.

As he recalls it, Mr. Tracol glanced about nervously as though he might be overheard, though there was clearly no one to overhear, and made a somewhat vague allusion to "interdimensional beings".

Since it is over 15 years since this meeting, it is hard for Ark to remember exactly what was said, but the entries in his journal in the days the following the meeting reflect his state of mind at the time:

Marseilles, July 21, 1966

I am an energy transformer and a converter. That is the essence of my existence. That is my only possible goal. I can choose to serve this goal or not. I can serve only as an energy transformer. So it seems to not make much difference what I do. The result will be the same.

Or, I can serve as a channel. This is the choice between self-will and discipline. What "I" do, that is "I-Personality", is self-will. What acts through me is not self-will. Thus I wish to allow, "that which can act through me" that is not self-will. For this end I need to eliminate self-will. But, God forbid, not to eliminate control!

So I wish to eliminate self-will. I wish to eliminate identification. Eliminating identification is most important. I wish to self-remember. I wish to plan to account for each and every hour. I wish to get rid of my hump. To cease being a camel.

How? Through elimination of identification. I want to listen. And to consider internally.

July 23, 1996

All this world is vanity. A vanity which will pass. The sky will pass, earth will pass, trees will pass, and people will pass too. Human aspirations will pass. Science will pass. All that keeps me together – will pass. A goal – at this level – does not exist. To set a goal – at this level – is to lie to oneself.

Humanity, truth, knowledge – these are empty words. Words surrounded by suffering which is meaningless. When I say I want to "help humanity" – these are empty words. When I say "science", "knowledge", "truth", "cognizance" – these are phantom words.

I am an energy transformer, and I need to serve as such. And that is what I can do.

Where is the way out?

Nothing will remain of what I am doing. I might as well not exist at all. To think that I am "different"? That I am "exceptional"? That I can accomplish things that no one has succeeded in accomplishing – but I will because I will have the luck? Oh Lord, that it is possible to believe these vain illusions! I will die and nothing will be left. Nothing will succeed. Nothing will remain. No goal will be reached. Only one goal seems possible – that when the end is near, suffering will be so great that I will pass with relief.

Where is the way out? What purpose do humans serve? This is an experiment! What originates in me does not count. The only thing I can do is to allow something more powerful to speak through me. To allow something more knowledgeable to talk to me and through me. To allow something more powerful to act through me. To allow something more powerful to use me. I am just a shell, I am a machine. I am a device. I am a means to an end. I am a possibility for something more powerful to be in me and to act through me. I am a place that waits to be filled. I am a carriage without a driver and without a master. True, there is brain, there are body members, there are senses. But I am just a carriage. With no driver and no master. A personality that pretends to have rights. Which play the roles – sometimes of a driver, sometimes of a master – which says "I" continuously. Yet I am just a carriage, which goes nowhere, and is doomed to crash in some ditch.

My aspirations, my ambitions, my wants – all these belong to an empty carriage and horse that is left without control. All that I am doing means nothing. All that I am doing is personality. And that comes from personality is ballast. All that comes from personality is a camel's hump.

How to pass through a needle's eye while carrying a hump? Personality must be left aside. Aspirations and whims – that is not me. Blessed are those who are meek. To be meek – that is what I need. Nonattachment. Eliminating unnecessary things. And also being conscious of the fact that *every moment is a branching of the universe.*

So, this was the state of mind produced by a single two-hour talk with Henri Tracol.

But what is it that "acts through" or controls humankind or creates the conditions of this sleep as Gurdjieff taught? Ark and I have discussed this, combing through the available resources, trying to determine if this was one of the big secrets of the Gurdjieff work, but with little result.

At the same time, I have long pondered the possible true teachings of Jesus. What we know, factually, from the available ancient documents that are generally assessed to be contemporary with the time of early Christianity, is that the Romans and about everyone else in the Pagan world considered Christianity to be an "abominable superstition".

This is actually an astonishing statement. When you consider this fact alongside Christianity, as we know it today, it makes absolutely no sense. Christianity *as it is today* is simply a conglomeration of archaic religious beliefs and rites that are fundamentally no different from the cultic religions of the Pagans of the time. The crucified and resurrected savior god was pretty standard. And most of the teachings from the New Testament are just plagiarized versions of what was accepted by the Romans and their subjects as "normal".

In fact, if you think about this period of time and what was believed and practiced, including haruspicy, which was the going thing at the time, and involved killing an animal and reading the omens from its liver, you have to think that for these people to call something an abominable superstition, it must have been pretty bizarre. And yet, nothing remains of Christianity that could be considered by the ancient Romans as superstition because it is exactly what they did believe and practice in their various cults.

So, we have a real problem here in figuring out just what these ancient peoples would have considered an abominable superstition, and the only thing that fits the definition is the teaching that man is food for hyperdimensional beings. That is pretty objectionable at *any* time in history!

If the early Christians were talking this way, we can easily see why the Romans, who had inherited or subsumed the Greek ideas of the heavenly pantheon, would consider this to be utterly barbaric. And, if this *is* what Jesus understood and expounded to his disciples in private, it is no wonder that the forces came along and completely obliterated any trace of the original teaching, replacing it with the standard Pagan rites and ceremonies and beliefs. And, if I am on the right track with this, it certainly gives new meaning to the statement: "Ye shall know the truth, and the truth shall set you free!"

If it is true that humans are being bred and raised like cattle in a global stockyard and fed upon both psychically and sometimes even physically, we have a truly serious situation going on here, to put it mildly. As I have explained before, I have never seen a Lizzie except in dreamlike states or almost hypnopompic semi-sleep states. So, when the Cassiopaeans began to talk about them, it was truly *Twilight Zone* time, in my opinion!

I have also stated that, whenever the Cassiopaeans tell us anything, I work very hard to discover if there is any form of what I call vertical or lateral corroboration. Vertical data is that which is located in history at any point different from the present. Lateral data consists of collecting reports, witness information, and other data that amounts to circumstantial evidence from the present time. It is always better if the two types of data cross or intersect, but it is still not the same as having a smoking gun. When you are dealing with hyperdimensional realities, smoking guns are unlikely to be found.

In the case of the idea of man being food for hyperdimensional beings, there is an enormous amount of both vertical and lateral corroboration of all kinds. So much so that, in fact, it is almost impossible to understand why it is not generally known. Clearly, there have been deliberate efforts to hide this fact, and the fact that it is hidden may itself tell us something.

The point is, when don Juan and Gurdjieff and the Cassiopaeans and others tell us that our religions, our social structure, our values, our beliefs about our spiritual nature and condition have been deliberately created to perpetuate the illusion that we are free; that we are (or can be) "special and adored children of a loving God"; that we are or can be co-creators with God, that we can do anything at all of a positive and powerful nature, we need to carefully examine this issue.

It is work to examine it objectively, *hard work*, because it consists of long and difficult self-examination in order to be able to overcome the emotions that prevent us from discovering what illusions we are hanging onto, what illusions are preventing us from seeing and acting in such a way as to become free.

And yet, we *can* see that something is evolving here. With the maturation of the group mind, the stakes get higher and the deceptions deeper!

For many centuries, millennia even, simplistic religions and social dynamics were dominant over most of the world. This was possible because even when there was an intrusion by one of these hyperdimensional beings into our reality, when they did drop in for dinner, so to speak, it was easy to conceal because of the lack of communication between tribes and peoples.

When we sit in our comfortable homes and look at our reality, including that which is outside our windows, we see a stable front. Cars pass on the street, taking people to and from their homes in their varied daily activities; the sun shines; children pass by, talking and laughing. Everyone is involved in their life in an immediate and identified way, believing that this life they are involved in is what *is*.

But, once in a while, something bizarre happens to someone and they struggle to deal with this anomaly in the space-time continuum. Usually, it is sufficiently minor that they can dampen it and forget about it, which they must, because it is too aberrant in the normal accepted course of events. It must be shoved under the rug.

Once in awhile, bigger things happen in the reality – evidence of the hyperdimensional control system intrudes, or the screen breaks down in some way – and it becomes news and gets reported. Charles Fort spent many years collecting these types of things from the newspapers and magazines all over the world.

When this happens, the accepted belief system hurries to damp down the item so that everyone can go along in their respective and collective illusions. Since the events are localized, it is easy to cover it up. And, in the past, this was a lot easier than it is today.

When you read the collected information of Charles Fort, you see that the alien reality that is so widely reported today was just as active then as it is now. In fact, you see that it may even be somewhat cyclical. Just as we have cycles of food production, planting, growing and harvesting, so may hyperdimensional beings harvest us according to some "seasonal" rule.

In any event, before people began to become literate it was a lot easier to keep the lid on the matter. Then, books, papers and magazines were published and distributed. Travel became easier and information from around the world about these odd intrusions into our reality could be collected, giving an overall pattern that something was not right.

Before Charles Fort, there were a few people who already smelled a rat, but Mr. Fort kindly shoved it right under our noses and the reaction has been quite interesting. The cover-up machine went into full operation through the most effective vectors of mainstream science and religion.

But, the rat had been smelled and some people couldn't just shove it back under the rug. The stench kept wafting in the open window. And so, certain people began to start searching for the source of this stinky rat. They began to gather knowledge and information.

We can even note *how* the cover-up machine began to do this damage control. When you study the history of social and religious movement and change, you can see the control system morphing with every discovery or realization made by human beings. As they outgrew the old religions, the simplistic explanations, new religions were put in place. At exactly the right time – the period of scientific expansion and growing knowledge of the nature of reality that brought the old religious views into serious question – the whole spiritualist movement began, leading to channeled information that was designed to patch up the holes in the control net. Newer and more elaborate explanations of the higher realms came into our reality. With each new question, the control system had a new answer to help everybody calm down, relax, and stop asking questions.

At the present time, this is even more amazingly evident. A few years ago, when we first began sharing the Cassiopaean information, many of the issues we dealt with were not even addressed by these other sources. But, with everything we release, the other side brings some new candidate forward with new explanations to patch the holes we are tearing in the fabric of their reality. And, of course, since Ark is a physicist with degrees beyond Ph.D., some of these new sources are becoming more educated and articulate as if to counterbalance and damp down what we are presenting here.

For me, the idea of connecting the dots has always consisted of using everything available to me in terms of peeling that blasted onion right down to the center. If I have to spend weeks buried in books about genetics to verify or disprove something the Cassiopaeans have said, I will do it. Not only that, I will write to known experts in the field using my husband's cachet in the scientific world to get in the door and get the latest, most up-to-date *inside* information so that I can be sure what I am sharing is as accurate and balanced as I can make it.

Over and over again I come to the idea that all of these things were known long ago, and that we were sent a message in a bottle so to say, in the form of myths and archaic practices that were drilled into the participants who have long since forgotten the meaning.

Of course, it does seem that many of the ancient schools and mystical paths kept some of this information intact. But, for the most part, even that was faded on the page due to the long period of time since such things were known and acknowledged. Even then, there are those who have seen the contradictions in our reality and our beliefs and who have sought in these ancient teachings to discover what *might* be known. And many of them have made discoveries that, when considered with information from many other fields, assists us in this essential discovery of our true condition and purpose.

Gurdjieff was one of these.

And so, because he did it, he made it possible for others to do it.

Even though it seems that each person who makes progress in this discovery gets damped down or obfuscated by their followers, each person who blazes a trail makes it easier for the next traveler to follow in their footsteps. Of course, each trailblazer is in the position of having to cut and slash their way through the thickest and most dangerous jungle surrounding the truth, and this takes them only so far. But, having arrived at a new vantage point through this great effort, they can see more of what is ahead, in the center. Perhaps they can only get glimpses, but these glimpses at least assure them that they are on the right track. On the other hand, they may even see the whole picture and, in keeping with the maturity of the group mind in their time period, attempt to express the revelation in terms understandable to that generation.

Gurdjieff's teachings became known as the Fourth Way as opposed to the three ways that had existed within and utilized the very religious and social structures in place to keep us imprisoned. This is what Gurdjieff meant when he said that many are hypnotized into believing they are men or magicians. The problem with these three ways, as we have already discussed, is that they concentrate on only one of the three centers in man: bodily discipline, mental development or the way of the heart – love. Gurdjieff's way incorporated all of these through a form of conscious labor and intentional suffering.

What did Gurdjieff mean by these things? No two of his students have given the same answer. The only thing we can think about this fact is that the understanding of his students was based upon their effort, experience and level of being.

Conscious labor quite obviously does not refer to digging ditches or breaking rocks, though it could. It refers to efforts we are not accustomed to making in our ordinary lives. Intentional suffering obviously cannot be present if a person is asleep because it depends on conscience and, according to Gurdjieff, until an individual is awake, they are neither conscious nor do they have a real conscience. For Gurdjieff, conscience and consciousness cannot be separated.

There are now many Fourth Way methods scattered around the world, all of them partial and incomplete, it seems. But, the point is: Gurdjieff made a big step, he cut away a great deal of the obstructions in the path of finding ways to bring the technology back to the awareness of the group mind, and because he did, those who came after him were able to go even further in this effort.

Unfortunately, the Control System immediately put damage control into operation to patch the holes of revelation, and fences of secrecy and restriction were erected so that *if* anybody in the organization had the deeper knowledge, it became so hidden that it was likely the process of distortion and corruption would proceed on its normal course there as well.

Even so, we have to see each of these things as steps. We can't leave out Sufism, Alchemy, Catharism, and other persecuted systems of knowledge that were the stepping-stones before Gurdjieff. By looking at the overall picture, we can pretty safely say that when a revelation is seen to be useful, that it helps the people who are involved in it to lead fuller, more meaningful lives, the powers that be will immediately go into overdrive to destroy or conceal it. And, if they cannot do that, they will ensure that it is distorted and corrupted by putting their own agents in place on the inside to see the job done. Witness the development of Christianity via the Catholic Church.

Yes, Gurdjieff may have achieved the level of a true sage himself, leaving us a legacy of process and application, but our job at present is to go further. And, as we do, we must expect a continuous effort to counteract, to obfuscate, to corrupt and co-opt the concepts from all quarters. Gurdjieff addressed these very problems:

> "The humanity to which we belong, namely, the whole of historic and prehistoric humanity known to science and civilization, in reality constitutes only the outer circle of humanity, within which there are several other circles ...
>
> "The inner circle is called the 'esoteric'; this circle consists of people who have attained the highest development possible for man, each one of whom possesses individuality in the fullest degree, that is to say, an indivisible 'I', all forms of consciousness possible for man, full control over these states of consciousness, the whole of knowledge possible for man, and a free and independent will.
>
> "They cannot perform actions opposed to their understanding or have an understanding which is not expressed by actions.
>
> At the same time there can be no discords among them, no differences of understanding. Therefore their activity is entirely coordinated and leads to one common aim without any kind of compulsion because it is based upon a common and identical understanding.
>
> "The next circle is called the 'mesoteric', that is to say, the middle.
>
> "People who belong to this circle possess all the qualities possessed by the members of the esoteric circle with the sole difference that their knowledge is of a more theoretical character.
>
> "This refers, of course, to knowledge of a cosmic character. They know and understand many things which have not yet found expression in their actions. They know more than they do. But their understanding is precisely as exact as, and therefore precisely identical with, the understanding of the people of the esoteric circle.
>
> "Between them there can be no discord, there can be no misunderstanding. One understands in the way they all understand, and all understand in the way one understands. But as was said before, this understanding compared with the understanding of the esoteric circle is somewhat more theoretical.

"The third circle is called the 'exoteric', that is, the outer, because it is the outer circle of the inner part of humanity.

"The people who belong to this circle possess much of that which belongs to people of the esoteric and mesoteric circles but their cosmic knowledge is of a more philosophical character, that is to say, it is more abstract than the knowledge of the mesoteric circle.

"A member of the mesoteric circle calculates, a member of the exoteric circle contemplates. Their understanding may not be expressed in actions. But there cannot be differences in understanding between them. What one understands all the others understand.

"In literature which acknowledges the existence of esotericism humanity is usually divided into two circles only and the 'exoteric circle' as opposed to the 'esoteric', is called ordinary life.

"In reality, as we see, the 'exoteric circle' is something very far from us and very high. For ordinary man this is already 'esotericism'.

"'The outer circle' is the circle of mechanical humanity to which we belong and which alone we know.

"The first sign of this circle is that among people who belong to it there is not and there cannot be a common understanding. Everybody understands in his own way and all differently.

"This circle is sometimes called the circle of the 'confusion of tongues', that is, the circle in which each one speaks in his own particular language, where no one understands another and takes no trouble to be understood.

"In this circle mutual understanding between people is impossible excepting in rare exceptional moments or in matters having no great significance, and which are confined to the limits of the given being.

"If people belonging to this circle become conscious of this general lack of understanding and acquire a desire to understand and to be understood, then it means they have an unconscious tendency towards the inner circle because mutual understanding begins only in the exoteric circle and is possible only there.

"But the consciousness of the lack of understanding usually comes to people in an altogether different form.

"So that the possibility for people to understand depends on the possibility of penetrating into the exoteric circle where understanding begins.

"If we imagine humanity in the form of four concentric circles we can imagine four gates on the circumference of the third inner circle, that is, the exoteric circle, through which people of the mechanical circle can penetrate.

"These four gates correspond to the four ways described before.

"The first way is the way of the fakir, the way of people number one, of people of the physical body, instinctive-moving-sensory people without much mind and without much heart.

"The second way is the way of the monk, the religious way, the way of people number two, that is, of emotional people. The mind and the body should not be too strong.

"The third way is the way of the yogi. This is the way of the mind, the way of people number three. The heart and the body must not be particularly strong, otherwise they may be a hindrance on this way.

"Besides these three ways yet a fourth way exists by which can go those who cannot go by any of the first three ways.

"The fundamental difference between the first three ways, that is, the way of the fakir, the way of the monk, and the way of the yogi, and the fourth way consists in the fact that they are tied to permanent forms which have existed throughout long periods of history almost without change. At the basis of these institutions is religion. Where schools of yogis exist they differ little outwardly from religious schools. And in different periods of history various societies or orders of fakirs have existed in different countries and they still exist. These three traditional ways are permanent ways within the limits of our historical period.

"Two or three thousand years ago there were yet other ways which no longer exist and the ways now in existence were not so divided, they stood much closer to one another.

"The fourth way differs from the old and the new ways by the fact that it is never a permanent way. It has no definite forms and there are no institutions connected with it. It appears and disappears governed by some particular laws of its own.[23]

"The fourth way is never without some work of a definite significance, is never without some undertaking around which and in connection with which it can alone exist.

"When this work is finished, that is to say, when the aim set before it has been accomplished, the fourth way disappears, that is, it disappears from the given place, disappears in its given form, continuing perhaps in another place in another form.

"Schools of the fourth way exist for the needs of the work which is being carried out in connection with the proposed undertaking. They never exist by themselves as schools for the purpose of education and instruction.

"Mechanical help cannot be required in any work of the fourth way. Only conscious work can be useful in all the undertakings of the fourth way. Mechanical man cannot give conscious work so that the first task of the people who begin such a work is to create conscious assistants.

"The work itself of schools of the fourth way can have very many forms and many meanings. In the midst of the ordinary conditions of

---

[23] In my opinion, the ancient ways that Gurdjieff claimed no longer exist were, in fact, the "Fourth Way" as he described it, though more "permanent".

life the only chance a man has of finding a 'way' is in the possibility of meeting with the beginning of work of this kind. But the chance of meeting with such work as well as the possibility of profiting by this chance depends upon many circumstances and conditions.

"The quicker a man grasps the aim of the work which is being executed, the quicker can he become useful to it and the more will he be able to get from it for himself.

"But no matter what the fundamental aim of the work is, the schools continue to exist only while this work is going on. When the work is done the schools close. The people who began the work leave the stage. Those who have learned from them what was possible to learn and have reached the possibility of continuing on the way independently begin in one form or another their own personal work.

"But it happens sometimes that when the school closes a number of people are left who were round about the work, who saw the outward aspect of it, and saw the whole of the work in this outward aspect.

"Having no doubts whatever of themselves or in the correctness of their conclusions and understanding they decide to continue the work. To continue this work they form new schools, teach people what they have themselves learned, and give them the same promises that they themselves received. All this naturally can only be outward imitation.[24]

"But when we look back on history it is almost impossible for us to distinguish where the real ends and where the imitation begins. Strictly speaking almost everything we know about various kinds of occult, masonic, and alchemical schools refers to such imitation. We know practically nothing about real schools excepting the results of their work and even that only if we are able to distinguish the results of real work from counterfeits and imitations.

"But such pseudo-esoteric systems also play their part in the work and activities of esoteric circles. Namely, they are the intermediaries between humanity which is entirely immersed in the materialistic life and schools which are interested in the education of a certain number of people, as much for the purposes of their own existences as for the purposes of the work of a cosmic character which they may be carrying out. The very idea of esotericism, the idea of initiation, reaches people in most cases through pseudo-esoteric systems and schools; and if there were not these pseudo-esoteric schools the vast majority of humanity would have no possibility whatever of hearing and learning of the existence of anything greater than life because the truth in its pure form would be inaccessible for them.

---

[24] This is certainly what happened to Gurdjieff's work.

> "By reason of the many characteristics of man's being, particularly of the contemporary being, truth can only come to people in the form of a lie – only in this form are they able to accept it; only in this form are they able to digest and assimilate it. Truth undefiled would be, for them, indigestible food.
>
> "Besides, a grain of truth in an unaltered form is sometimes found in pseudoesoteric movements, in church religions, in occult and theosophical schools. It may be preserved in their writings, their rituals, their traditions, their conceptions of the hierarchy, their dogmas, and their rules. (Ouspensky 1949)

As I hinted in the previous chapter, circumstantial evidence points to the existence of a secret fraternity unknown in its entirety to the human race. Other so-called "secret" groups (Rosicrucians, Illuminati, Freemasons, Modern day Templars, Priory of Zion, etc.) are generally red herrings to distract and divert the seeker. Gurdjieff points out that these groups do serve a useful function because the very idea of esotericism reaches people through the pseudo-esoteric systems that such groups promote. And so it is that I say most if not all of the great religions of antiquity were symbolic representations of the alchemical work.

During the sixteenth, seventeenth, and eighteenth centuries a considerable number of alchemical adepts traveled around Europe, appearing and disappearing at will. According to tradition, these adepts were immortal and kept themselves alive by means of the Elixir of Life, which was one of the goals of alchemy. That such mysterious men did exist there can be little doubt, as their presence is attested to by scores of reliable witnesses.

This brings us to the most interesting remark that Gurdjieff made above about the inner circle:

> The inner circle ... consists of people who have attained the highest development possible for man, each one of whom possesses individuality in the fullest degree, that is to say, an indivisible 'I', all forms of consciousness possible for man, full control over these states of consciousness, the whole of knowledge possible for man, and a free and independent will. They cannot perform actions opposed to their understanding or have an understanding which is not expressed by actions. At the same time there can be no discords among them, no differences of understanding. Therefore their activity is entirely coordinated and leads to one common aim without any kind of compulsion because it is based upon a common and identical understanding. (Ouspensky 1949)

And we are reminded again of the alchemical maxim, "Like attracts like".

> When a candidate has developed virtue and integrity acceptable to the adepts, they will appear to him and reveal those parts of the secret processes which cannot be discovered without such help. Those who cannot progress to a certain point with their own intelligence are not qualified to be entrusted with the secrets which can subject to their will the elemental forces of Nature.

So, certainly some process must be followed to achieve the requisite level for attracting help.

When we dig as deeply into all of these matters as possible, over and over again we come upon the idea that self-knowledge is the key. It is not the end, but it is the means; the first stage in self-development and the beginning of awakening from sleep is to be able to know the self in an objective way so that the Predator's mind can be controlled. Note very clearly that I say controlled and not merged.

Gurdjieff said that we have many "I's" and at the same time, we have an animal and a spiritual nature. Self-observation and other disciplined efforts were taught as the means of crystallization of a single I. William Baldwin thought that the real source of these many "I's" was the spirit attachment problem. In working with this, he found that his techniques could assist the person in eliminating this barrier manifesting the true self, in the effort to grow the will.

The downside of it is the failure to encourage the assimilation of other knowledge as a means of having a context in which to place the discoveries that the self makes in the processes.

But what good is this knowledge when it seems that all the Cassiopaeans have to say is that we are helpless in the face of so great a deception? The fact is, they have said or suggested a lot more than that. More importantly, if we understand the Cassiopaean communication properly, we see that it is truly a Fourth Way work, and that the Cassiopaeans are the teachers who appeared to reveal the parts of the secret processes that could not be discovered without help.

What is that big secret?

Gurdjieff refers to the evil magicians. The alchemists said the same thing. Eugene Canseliet, in his preface to the second edition of Fulcanelli's *Dwellings of the Philosophers*, writes:

> Philippe de Mallery engraved with a delicate touch: 'Image of the World, in which Calamities and Perils are emblematically presented along with the opposition in feeling between the Love of God and that of man.'
>
> The first emblem straightforwardly points to the original, if not unique, source of all ills of our Humanity. It is also underlined by

the Latin inscription which, in the parenthesis, is another pun of phonetic cabala: 'Totus mundus in maligno positus est'; the whole world is established inside of the devil. (Fulcanelli 1999)

What is this world inside the devil? It is the world of lies and confusion:

> "'The outer circle' is the circle of mechanical humanity to which we belong and which alone we know.
> "The first sign of this circle is that among people who belong to it there is not and there cannot be a common understanding. Everybody understands in his own way and all differently.
> "This circle is sometimes called the circle of the 'confusion of tongues', that is, the circle in which each one speaks in his own particular language, where no one understands another and takes no trouble to be understood.
> "In this circle mutual understanding between people is impossible excepting in rare exceptional moments or in matters having no great significance, and which are confined to the limits of the given being. (Ouspensky 1949)

To many of you, it may seem that the Cassiopaeans offer nothing but repeated statements that we are "damned no matter what we do", as one correspondent suggested. But, that is not entirely the case. Yes, it is true that up to this point I have presented mostly the information that relates to these matters, attempting to penetrate and tear the veils of illusion under which humankind has been hidden from his higher nature or potential. But this has only been done with the intention of having a relatively clear view of what possibilities of doing we may actually have. Actually, I have been trying to accomplish something else, something deep and essential. For those who are asking, I have been trying to help you find your free will.

The point is, I am trying to shock you. I am trying to make you think about things in new ways. I am trying to get you to look at yourself, study yourself, discover your illusions and then apply yourself to becoming free of them. If humankind has any hope of surviving, it will have to have a major change of mind, or *metanoia*, which is incorrectly translated in the New Testament as repentance. For a change of mind to even be possible, it has to *know itself.*

And this brings us to that all-important remark made by a member of our group, TR:

> What we have been told ... is that this universe was created as a Free Will Universe. It was created specifically to allow all souls to do whatever they wish to do; they have complete choice about what they wish to do. The Grays, the Lizards, whoever they are who ab-

duct and put implants in people, have the right to do that because it's their free will to come here and do that to us. And, they have the right to tell us whatever they want to tell us to rationalize their behavior. Our right is to *not* believe what abducting entities tell us. We have free will to believe or not believe them. If they tell us in one lifetime that they have the right to do this to us, and we choose to believe them then, and then, in this lifetime, they try the same tricks and we choose *not* to believe them, in each case, we are exercising our free will and so are they. This is a Free Will universe. We can change our mind. They are trying to convince us that we have no choice in that, whether we believe them or not is *our* choice.

In the view of the monotheistic religions, as expounded by Aquinas and Descartes, free will involves the power of the will to choose or not to choose. That is, we are free insofar as we can choose among alternatives as being either good or evil.

In other words, you can choose good, or not. And if you do not choose what is presented to you as good, you have by default chosen evil. There is only one good option. You can take it or leave it. That is what constitutes your free will. It is, in the words of a Mafia Don or Nazi Officer, "an offer you cannot refuse" because the other option is clearly unpalatable and will subject you to unpleasant consequences. This view makes a mockery of the essential idea of free will.

Clearly, in our reality, we are in the face of this very teaching from one religion, philosophy, New Age channeled source or another. Once we understand that the reality itself, the illusions of what is or is not good or evil, are masks, or symbols of something deeper, we begin to realize that the two alternatives presented to us are clearly not equal. "The thirsty person chooses water, not oil; the hungry person, bread not tree bark; the poor person, the dry patch under the bridge, not the bench in the rain."

Some choice. By this definition, free will becomes little more than a joke, a logical inconsistency. It is also the chief mode of the Service-to-Self pathway – to induce choice by "weighting" it.

This view of free-will-that-is-not-free becomes the chief mask of those seeking to deny free will.

Any religion, philosophy or teaching that sets itself up as the only way a man can be saved has immediately aligned itself with the Mafia/Nazi/STS school of free will. You can easily see that a person who chooses to love or send love and light because it might gain salvation for them, or even because it feels good, is really in the position of the thirsty person choosing water and not oil to drink. And further, if they think this is the only thing they can do because the entire social and philosophical structure has been designed to make it seem this is the only viable choice in line with God's will, they are still in the same position. But, the chief thing about it is that they *believe* the illusion, the lie, that this choice is to drink water and that choice is to drink oil. In fear, they don't even consider that they don't have to choose *either*.

There are other definitions of free will that are interesting to speculate about. I am not going to engage in a lengthy monologue on the views of the philosophers because, even though some of them are quite fascinating and really make you think, that would be counterproductive to the issue at hand here.

The short version is that Hobbes and Tolstoy suggest we are free insofar as we may do as we wish without hindrance or constraint. Locke and Hume extended Hobbes's freedom-to-do-without-restriction to the power to do or not as one wills. Spinoza's view was that we are free insofar as we alone determine our behavior. We are not free when others dictate or hamper our decisions, or for reasons of illness or incapacity we cannot determine our actions.

When we consider being able to do what we choose without hindrance or restraint, and defining free will in this way, we have to then consider not only whether our free will conflicts with the free will of others, but also whether our free will itself may be less free because of unconscious psychological or physiological forces. And, if the issues of government mind-control programs and hyperdimensional beings enter the equation, whether we may be under the absolute control of external forces must also be taken into account. In the first case we may choose to rob and steal because of extreme poverty, a broken home, and an ineffective educational system. In the latter case, we may choose to "go postal" because some fiendish government programmer's toast got burned that morning or because some lurking Lizard being thought Suzy Smart was getting too close to the truth, and she needed to be eliminated on her morning trip to buy stamps.

So we begin to think that we are not so free after all. In very real terms, all of us are under the influence of external forces or programming of one sort or another.

If we are free in this way, the issue of free will, in third-density terms, becomes meaningless. This is a very shallow interpretation because it means that freedom is defined as whether a person can do what he chooses, not to the choosing itself. It refers to the freedom of the action, not to the choice of action, because all of your choices are programmed. Yet, whatever the individual decides to do, even if programmed to do it, it is considered that he has free will if he *can* do it.

What a cheap shot!

These concerns highlight the issue of the many forces that may restrain or compel behavior against one's will, which, if one was aware of them, one might or might not choose otherwise. The point is: we are not free if our potential or actual choices are restricted. Locke makes an example of a man locked into a room in which he prefers to stay. The man desires to stay in the room, is able to do so, and is thus free by Hobbes's definition, but the man does not have the power to leave the room and is thus not free according to Locke.

It is in exactly this sense that most people are deceived by the Control System to believe that they have free will. The room in which they are locked is the illusion that their beliefs and objectives are the full reality of creation, and their choice to remain in the room is acquiescence to beliefs imposed on them from the outside.

Most of humanity spend endless lifetimes locked in this room. But the fact is, after a period of time, the confinement of the room and the sameness of the experiences become objectionable because, all the while the prisoner is lulled into inactivity, something may be growing inside him, some urge to see what is outside the room. But, until this inclination is fully developed, he may make no effort to even check the door. And, once he does check the door and discovers that it is locked, he may not yet have sufficient drive to do anything more than return to his position and continue to wait for something to happen. After a bit longer, the drive grows, and this, with the realization that he *is* locked in may drive him to discover how to get out. But this process can take many lifetimes. And to attempt to open the door of the prison in which another is held when they are not ready to come out because they are not strong enough, will only frighten them, will only deprive them of the building force that is inside them that could, given time to develop, sustain the effort to emerge from the room on their own.

In such terms, whether or not a person has the power to do as he wills remains a fundamentally empirical question. He may think he has complete freedom to do or not as he wills, yet, his will, his choices which are based on his awareness, may be determined subconsciously or physically by things of which he is not aware. In this sense, any choice or act that is based upon lack of awareness, must lead us to discover the source of the lack of awareness as the causative factor, not the choice of the chooser.

In other words, if a person is programmed, whether via government experiments, alien abductors, religions created and imposed by hyperdimensional beings, then who is ultimately responsible?

Is it the programmers, or is it the person who has effectively chosen to be unaware?

Yes, the individual may be unaware due to fear of reprisals by God, demons, or his alien or government handlers. He may be afraid for his body or his soul or the body and soul of someone he loves. But these fears are beliefs that constitute the locked room in which he has chosen to remain not realizing that his own choice is the lock!

If the person is unaware, not because of fear, but simply because he is asleep is he then responsible for his lack of awareness?

According to the Cassiopaeans, yes. It is his choice. He has chosen it for a reason at some level, and he is entitled to it. He has chosen his environment; he has chosen his grade and his lessons. Perhaps chosen in the conscious sense is an inappropriate term. It is more like he is there because that is where he "fits". He is a consciousness unit, and he is learning. Only when he reaches a certain level will he begin to wake up. Only when something has grown in him. Will.

Gurdjieff seemed to have the idea that a will could be nurtured in a man and accelerated, so to say. He made the following remarks with this in mind:

> "To awaken for a man means to be dehypnotized. In this lies the chief difficulty and in this also lies the guarantee of its possibility, for there is no organic reason for sleep and man *can* awaken. Theoretically he can, but practically it is almost impossible because as soon as a man awakens for a moment and opens his eyes, all the forces that caused him to fall asleep begin to act upon him with tenfold energy and he immediately falls asleep again, very often dreaming that he is awake or is awakening.
>
> "… Only a man who fully realizes the difficulty of awakening can understand the necessity of long and hard work in order to awake.
>
> Speaking in general, what is necessary to awake a sleeping man? A good shock is necessary. But when a man is fast asleep one shock is not enough. A long period of continual shocks is needed. Consequently there must be somebody to administer these shocks. There is also the possibility of being awakened by mechanical means. A man may be awakened by an alarm clock. But the trouble is that a man gets accustomed to the alarm clock far too quickly, he ceases to hear it. Many alarm clocks are necessary and always new ones. … Alarm clocks must be wound up; in order to wind them up one must remember about them; in order to remember one must wake up often.
>
> "… But there is very little chance of a man doing all the work of winding up, inventing, and changing clocks all by himself, without outside help. It is much more likely that he will begin this work and that it will afterwards pass into sleep, and in sleep he will dream of

inventing alarm clocks, of winding them up and changing them, and simply sleep all the sounder for it.

"Therefore, in order to awaken, a combination of efforts is needed. It is necessary that somebody should wake the man up; it is necessary that somebody should look after the man who wakes him; it is necessary to have alarm clocks and it is also necessary continually to invent new alarm clocks.

"But in order to achieve all this and to obtain results a certain number of people must work together. One man can do nothing. If several people decide to struggle together against sleep, they will wake each other. It may often happen that twenty of them will sleep but the twenty- first will be awake and he will wake up the rest. It is exactly the same thing with alarm clocks. One man will invent one alarm clock, another man will invent another, afterwards they can make an exchange. Altogether they can be of very great help one to another, and without this help no one can attain anything. Therefore, a man who wants to awake must look for other people who also want to awake and work together with them." (Ouspensky 1949)

Clearly Gurdjieff was aware of the damage control factor of the Control System and how quickly it moves in to damp down any rips in the fabric of the illusion. His idea that we must continually invent new alarm clocks is a clear indication that he knew that his method would have to be reworked, revised, added to and expanded. His hope to accelerate the awakening of man seems to have been the driving force behind everything he did, and he was aware of what might happen to his work. It wasn't just the idea of distortion; he knew that it had to be constantly reinvented to keep pace with the evolving Control System.

Can we accelerate the awakening?

The Cassiopaeans have indicated that, yes it is possible:

> Q: (L) Is there a tool that enhances free will?
> A: No tool is needed because all there is is lessons. The learning cycle is variable, and progress along it is determined by events and circumstances as they unfold.
>
> Q: (L) So, when a person is being hypnotized and controlled from outside, because that is the matter of concern we were discussing earlier, they are hypnotized and controlled until they learn to stop it?
> A: Yes.
>
> Q: (L) So, using the analogy of the pigsty, they just have to wallow in it and suffer until they have had enough?
> A: Using your analogy of the bicycle: Is there a tool, which makes it unnecessary for the child to learn how to ride the bicycle, in order to know how to ride it?!?
>
> Q: (MM) Don't you get more free will by assimilating knowledge?

A: Yes!! Yes!!

Q: (L) So, in other words, knowledge and awareness makes you aware that you have free will, and also makes you aware of what actions actually *are* acts of free will, and therefore, when you know or suspect the difference between the lies and deception and truth, then you are in a position to be in control of your life?

A: Yes. Remember, you learn on an exponential curve, once you have become "tuned in". This means that you become increasingly able to access the universal consciousness. Please learn to trust your increasing awareness. All who are present here are at one point or another on that cycle of progression, some further along than others. If you properly network without prejudice, you may all wind up at the same point on this cycle.

What does it mean to be "tuned in"? We return again to the issue of "Like attracts like".

"When a candidate has developed virtue and integrity acceptable to the adepts, they will appear to him and reveal those parts of the secret processes which cannot be discovered without such help.

"Those who cannot progress to a certain point with their own intelligence are not qualified to be entrusted with the secrets which can subject to their will the elemental forces of Nature."

The Cassiopaean transmissions are just such an "appearance". The process is best described by Eugene Canseliet in his preface to the second edition of Fulcanelli's alchemical masterpiece, *The Dwellings of the Philosophers:*

"According to the meaning of the Latin word adeptus, the alchemist has then received the Gift of God, or even better, the Present, a cabalistic pun on the double meaning of the word, underlining that he thus enjoys the infinite duration of the Now. ...

"In the Kingdom of Sulphur there exists a Mirror in which the entire World can be seen. Whosoever looks into this Mirror can see and learn the three parts of Wisdom of the entire World."

After thirty years of study and two years of dedicated experimentation, detailed in my autobiography, *Amazing Grace*, the Cassiopaean communications began.

"We are you in the future", they said. "We transmit "through" the opening that is presented in the locator that you represent as Cassiopaea, due to the strong radio pulses aligned from Cassiopaea, which are due to a pulsar from a neutron star 300 light years behind it, as seen from your locator. This facilitates a clear channel transmission from sixth density to third density."

Through this "gift of God" I have been enabled to look into the "mirror in which the entire world can be seen" from my own omnipresent self, in a state of full awareness. In short, based on all the details, the Cassiopaean transmissions are a true Fourth Way work, and exactly as Gurdjieff described, the first order of business of such a work is to network, to teach and train others.

> "Schools of the fourth way exist for the needs of the work which is being carried out in connection with the proposed undertaking. They never exist by themselves as schools for the purpose of education and instruction.
>
> "Mechanical help cannot be required in any work of the fourth way. Only conscious work can be useful in all the undertakings of the fourth way. Mechanical man cannot give conscious work so that the first task of the people who begin such a work is to create conscious assistants." (Ouspensky 1949)

So, learning, networking with others who are further along on the cycle of progression, and doing this without prejudice can make a difference, it seems.

What is the specific purpose of the Cassiopaean work? Let's stop and consider that. At the beginning of World War I, Ouspensky speculated to Gurdjieff that the war was a consequence of life in the industrial age, wherein humans were becoming more mechanized and had stopped thinking for themselves because they had things too easy. Gurdjieff replied:

> "There is another kind of mechanization which is much more dangerous: being a machine oneself. Have you ever thought about the fact that all people themselves are machines? ... Look, all those people you see are simply machines – nothing more. ... You think there is something that chooses its own path, something that can stand against mechanization; you think that not everything is equally mechanical."

At this point, Ouspensky raised what would seem to be a most logical objection: "Why of course not! ... art, poetry, thought, are phenomena of quite a different order."

Gurdjieff replied: "Of exactly the same order. These activities are just as mechanical as everything else. Men are machines and nothing but mechanical actions can be expected of machines." He then continued:

> "[Western civilization] armed with 'exact knowledge' and all the latest methods of investigation, has no chance whatever and is moving in a circle from which there is no escape.

> "That is because people believe in progress and culture. There is no progress whatever. Everything is just the same as it was thousands, and tens of thousands, of years ago. The outward form changes. The essence does not change. Man remains just the same. 'Civilized' and 'cultured' people live with exactly the same interests as the most ignorant savages. Modern civilization is based on violence and slavery and fine words.
>
> "... What do you expect? People are machines. Machines have to be blind and unconscious, they cannot be otherwise, and all their actions have to correspond to their nature. Everything happens. No one does anything. 'Progress' and 'civilization', in the real meaning of these words, can appear only as the result of conscious efforts. They cannot appear as the result of unconscious mechanical actions. And what conscious effort can there be in machines? And if one machine is unconscious, then a hundred machines are unconscious, and so are a thousand machines, or a hundred thousand, or a million. And the unconscious activity of a million machines must necessarily result in destruction and extermination.
>
> "It is precisely in unconscious involuntary manifestations that all evil lies. You do not yet understand and cannot imagine all the results of this evil. But the time will come when you will understand."

Again we note: Gurdjieff was speaking at the beginning of the First World War, in the opening rounds of a century of unprecedented warfare. And now, almost a hundred years later, humanity is on the edge of a precipice and no one knows what feather will plunge us into the abyss.

Wilhelm Reich wrote about the same problems that concerned Gurdjieff and Ouspensky:

> "Why did man, through thousands of years, wherever he built scientific, philosophic, or religious systems, go astray with such persistence and with such catastrophic consequences? ...
>
> "Is human erring necessary? Is it rational? Is all error rationally explainable and necessary? If we examine the sources of human error, we find that they fall into several groups:
>
> "Gaps in the knowledge of nature form a wide sector of human erring. Medical errors prior to the knowledge of anatomy and infectious diseases were necessary errors. But we must ask if the mortal threat to the first investigators of animal anatomy was a necessary error too.
>
> "The belief that the earth was fixed in space was a necessary error, rooted in the ignorance of natural laws. But was it an equally necessary error to burn Giordano Bruno at the stake and to incarcerate Galileo? ...
>
> "We understand that human thinking can penetrate only to a given limit at a given time. What we fail to understand is why the

human intellect does not stop at this point and say: 'this is the present limit of my understanding. Let us wait until new vistas open up.' This would be rational, comprehensible, purposeful thinking. ...

"What amazes us is the sudden turn from the rational beginning to the irrational illusion. Irrationality and illusion are revealed by the intolerance and cruelty with which they are expressed. We observe that human thought systems show tolerance as long as they adhere to reality. The more the thought process is removed from reality, the more intolerance and cruelty are needed to guarantee its continued existence." (Reich 1949)

Who or what is responsible for this state of humankind is a major issue, most particularly if we assume a benevolent God and a hierarchy of benevolent beings guiding the destiny of humankind. Gurdjieff commented on this in the following way (edited for clarity):

"We must remember that the ray of creation ... is like a branch of a tree ... growth depends on organic life on earth. ... if organic life is arrested in its development, in its evolution, and fails to respond to the demands made upon it, the branch may wither. This must be remembered.

"To this ray of creation, exactly the same possibility of development and growth has been given as is given to each separate branch of a big tree. But the accomplishment of this growth is not at all guaranteed. It depends upon the harmonious and right action of its own tissues.

"Organic life on earth is a complex phenomenon in which the separate parts depend upon one another. General growth is possible only on the condition that the 'end of the branch' grows. Or, speaking more precisely, there are organic life tissues which are evolving, and there are tissues which serve as food and medium for those which are evolving. Then there are evolving cells within the evolving tissues, and cells which serve as food and medium for those which are evolving. In each separate evolving cell there are evolving parts and there are parts which serve as food for those which are evolving. But always and in everything it must be remembered that evolution is never guaranteed, it is possible only and it can stop at any moment and in any place.

"The evolving part of organic life on earth is humanity. If humanity does not evolve it means that the evolution of organic life will stop and this, in its turn will cause the growth of our ray of creation to stop.

"At the same time if humanity ceases to evolve it becomes useless from the point of view of the aims for which it was created and as such it may be destroyed. In this way the cessation of evolution may mean the destruction of humanity.

"We have no clues from which we are able to tell in what period of planetary evolution we exist. We cannot know this but we should bear in mind that the number of possibilities is never infinite.

"At the same time in examining the life of humanity as we know it historically we are bound to acknowledge that humanity is moving in a circle. It one century it destroys everything it creates in another and the progress in mechanical things of the past hundred years has proceeded at the cost of losing many other things which perhaps were much more important for it.

"Speaking in general there is every reason to think and to assert that humanity is at a standstill, and from a standstill there is a straight path to downfall and degeneration.

"A standstill means that a process has become balanced. The appearance of any one quality immediately evokes the appearance of another quality opposed to it. The growth of knowledge in one domain evokes the growth of ignorance in another; refinement on the one hand evokes vulgarity on the other; freedom in one connection evokes slavery in another; the disappearance of some superstitions evokes the appearance and growth of others; and so on.

"A balanced process proceeding in a certain way cannot be changed at any moment it is desired. It can be changed and set on a new path only at certain 'crossroads'. In between the crossroads nothing can be done.

"At the same time if a process passes by a crossroad and nothing happens, nothing is done, then nothing can be done afterwards and the process will continue and develop according to mechanical laws; and even if the people taking part in this process foresee the inevitable destruction of everything, they will be unable to do anything.

"I repeat that something can be done only at certain moments which I have just called 'crossroads' and which in octaves, we have called the 'intervals'.

"The process of evolution, of that evolution which is possible for humanity as a whole, is completely analogous to the process of evolution possible for the individual man. And it begins with the same thing, namely, a certain group of cells gradually becomes conscious; then it attracts to itself other cells, subordinates others, and gradually makes the whole organism serve its aims and not merely eat, drink and sleep.

"In humanity as in individual man everything begins with the formation of a conscious nucleus. All the mechanical forces of life fight against the formation of this conscious nucleus in humanity, in just the same way as all mechanical habits, tastes, and weaknesses fight against conscious awareness in man.

"Can it be said that there is a conscious force which fights against the evolution of humanity?" Ouspensky asked.

"From a certain point of view it can be said," said G.

"Where can this force come from?" Ouspensky asked.

"There are two processes which are sometimes called 'involutionary' and 'evolutionary'. The difference between them is the following: An involutionary process begins consciously in the absolute but at the next step it already becomes mechanical – and it becomes more and more mechanical as it develops; an evolutionary process begins half-consciously but it becomes more and more conscious as it develops.

"But consciousness and conscious opposition to the evolutionary process can also appear at certain moments in the involutionary process.

"From where does this consciousness come?

"From the evolutionary process of course. The evolutionary process must proceed without interruption. Any stop causes a separation from the fundamental process. Such separate fragments of consciousnesses which have been stopped in their development can also unite and at any rate for a certain time can live by struggling against the evolutionary process. After all it merely makes the evolutionary process more interesting.

"Instead of struggling against mechanical forces there may, at certain moments, be a struggle against the intentional opposition of fairly powerful forces though they are not of course comparable with those which direct the evolutionary process.

"These opposing forces may sometimes even conquer.

"The reason for this consists in the fact that the forces guiding evolution have a more limited choice of means; in other words, they can only make use of certain means and certain methods. The opposing forces are not limited in their choice of means and they are able to make use of every means, even those which only give rise to a temporary success, and in the final result they destroy both evolution and involution at the point in question.

"Are we able to say for instance that life is governed by a group of conscious people? Where are they? Who are they?

"We see exactly the opposite: that life is governed by those who are the least conscious, by those who are most asleep.

"Are we able to say that we observe in life a preponderance of the best, the strongest, and the most courageous elements?

"Nothing of the sort. On the contrary we see a preponderance of vulgarity and stupidity of all kinds.

"Are we able to say that aspirations towards unity, towards unification, can be observed in life?

"Nothing of the kind of course. We only see new divisions, new hostility, new misunderstandings.

"So that in the actual situation of humanity there is nothing that points to evolution proceeding.

"On the contrary when we compare humanity with a man we quite clearly see a growth of personality at the cost of essence, that is, a growth of the artificial, the unreal, and what is foreign, at the cost of the natural, the real, and what is one's own.

"Together with this we see a growth of automatism.

"Contemporary culture requires automatons. And people are undoubtedly losing their acquired habits of independence and turning into automatons, into parts of machines.

"It is impossible to say where is the end of all this and where the way out – or whether there is an end and a way out. One thing alone is certain, that man's slavery grows and increases. Man is becoming a willing slave. He no longer needs chains. He begins to grow fond of his slavery, to be proud of it. And this is the most terrible thing that can happen to a man. (Ouspensky 1949)

Carlos Castaneda puts the problem another way:

"You have arrived, by your effort alone, to what the shamans of ancient Mexico called the topic of topics. I have been beating around the bush all this time, insinuating to you that something is holding us prisoner. Indeed we are held prisoner! This was an energetic fact for the sorcerers of ancient Mexico. ... They took over because we are food for them, and they squeeze us mercilessly because we are their sustenance. Just as we rear chickens in chicken coops, the predators rear us in human coops. Therefore, their food is always available to them ...

"I want to appeal to your analytical mind', don Juan said. 'Think for a moment, and tell me how you would explain the contradiction between the intelligence of man the engineer and the stupidity of his systems of beliefs, or the stupidity of his contradictory behavior. Sorcerers believe that the predators have given us our systems of beliefs, our ideas of good and evil, our social mores. They are the ones who set up our hopes and expectations and dreams of success or failure. They have given us covetousness, greed and cowardice. It is the predators who make us complacent, routinary, and egomaniacal ...

"In order to keep us obedient and meek and weak, the predators engaged themselves in a stupendous maneuver – stupendous, of course, from the point of view of a fighting strategist. A horrendous maneuver from the point of view of those who suffer it. They gave us their mind! Do you hear me? The predators give us their mind, which becomes our mind. The predators' mind is baroque, contradictory, morose, filled with the fear of being discovered any minute now ...

"Through the mind, which, after all, is their mind, the predators inject into the lives of human beings whatever is convenient for them." (Castaneda 1998, 213-220)

This, of course, takes us to Gurdjieff's story of the evil magician, which we have already discussed. We should pay particular attention to this remark made by Gurdjieff:

> "The evolving part of organic life on earth is humanity. If humanity does not evolve it means that the evolution of organic life will stop and this, in its turn will cause the growth of our ray of creation to stop.
>
> "At the same time if humanity ceases to evolve it becomes useless from the point of view of the aims for which it was created and as such it may be destroyed. In this way the cessation of evolution may mean the destruction of humanity."

In short, based on an objective assessment of the world around us, we are in deep trouble. In another place, Gurdjieff makes a rather spooky remark:

> "There is a definite period", he said, "for a certain thing to be done. If, by a certain time, what ought to be done has not been done, the earth may perish without having attained what it could have attained."
>
> "Is this period known?" I asked.
>
> "It is known", said G. "But it would be no advantage whatever for people to know it. It would even be worse. Some would believe it, others would not believe it, yet others would demand proofs. Afterwards they would begin to break one another's heads. Everything ends this way with people."

Gurdjieff gave other hints about this, though I expect he didn't fully know the details since his own work was that of one who prepares the ground and plants the seeds that are crucial to us now when considering the Cassiopaean mission. In this passage, Gurdjieff returns again to the subject of evolution, which, as he pointed out, has stopped in humanity.

> "Everything I have said till now I have said about the whole of humanity. But as I pointed out before, the evolution of humanity can proceed only through the evolution of a certain group, which, in its turn, will influence and lead the rest of humanity.
>
> "Are we able to say that such a group exists? Perhaps we can on the basis of certain signs, but in any event we have to acknowledge that it is a very small group, quite insufficient, at any rate, to subjugate the rest of humanity. Or, looking at it from another point of view, we can say that humanity is in such a state that it is unable to accept the guidance of a conscious group."
>
> "How many people could there be in this conscious group?" someone asked.
>
> "Only they themselves know this", said G.
>
> "Does it mean that they all know each other?" asked the same person again.
>
> "How could it be otherwise?" asked G.

"Imagine that there are two or three people who are awake in the midst of a multitude of sleeping people. They will certainly know each other. But those who are asleep cannot know them. How many are they? We do not know and we cannot know until we become like them.

"It has been clearly said before that each man can only see on the level of his own being. But two hundred conscious people, if they existed and if they found it necessary and legitimate, could change the whole of life on the earth. But either there are not enough of them, or they do not want to, or perhaps the time has not yet come, or perhaps other people are sleeping too soundly." (Ouspensky 1949)

Gurdjieff was right that it was not the right time then. Based on observation and research, it is apparent that humanity has now reached a great historical crossroads. We have come to the end of a two thousand year history of intolerance, cruelty and stupidity, which has created our present state of global, collective madness. Humanity, as a collective whole, is arriving at a state of collective spiritual bankruptcy, or "death". And yet, we cannot assume that this is meaningless.

Those who understand the principles of electricity will comprehend when I say that this present global estate is the way nature works and is the establishing of sufficient contact potential difference for the inflow of energy of cosmic light. But just as it is in the case of the individual, when that point is reached – that dark night of the soul – there is a choice that becomes apparent: the soul is offered the way "up" or the way "down". In order for this coming inflow of energy to act in positive ways, to create a new reality of free will and balance, there must be a point of contact that can conduct the energy. There must be human "micro-chips" or "circuits" sufficient to sustain this energy or all of humanity will perish. This means that only the development of human beings of a certain sort – with a certain wiring, so to say – will result in the global capacity to confront the energies of the crossroads.

The only other turning point in history that can be compared with the present one is that of the Great Flood. Thus, we come to the idea that the search for the Holy Grail and the alchemical work of distillation of the Philosopher's stone is *also* the building of an Ark in order to pass over into the New World.

That is the Fourth Way work of the Cassiopaeans.

With all of this in mind, we want to now return to Kant's definition of free will.

Kant defined free will as the ability to initiate a new causal series. For Kant, freedom is independence of the influence of motivations, character, and external causes. It is more than just the power to choose. Freedom is the power to exercise will as reason directs, to be a first cause of events, regardless of physical constraints.

This means the ability to choose freely between at least two alternatives. It means that these (at least two) alternatives *must not be weighted* to one side or another in intrinsic terms. That is, there must be nothing that compels the chooser to choose one over the other. In fact, it seems to be that the choice is more potent if it is made in an act of deep and pure faith, in opposition to all that is evident in material terms.

Freedom, thus defined, captures the essence of the choice between STS and STO. To be thus free means we can see with our reason all or most of the influences that are imposed on us by the many forces acting in our environment, and we can then *choose* based on knowledge of those forces, irrespective of them.

Our physical bodies are phenomena subject to natural third-density causality because we are part of the third-density world and subject to its laws. Our actions, based on third-density interpretations alone, are then subject to the same empirical third-density causality, and because causal series are continuous in time (each event has a prior cause which is an effect of another prior cause), we have no freedom at this level of phenomena.

The totality of the fourth-density field of possibilities is veiled from us and leaves us with no more freedom than the causally simple stimulus-response theories of the behaviorists. Our actions are a result of causal processes, controlled and devised at the fourth-density or noumenal level of reality, and freedom at this third density level is impossible unless we access the fourth-density causal level by seeing via the clues apparent in third density. If we can see the true field of options, we can choose our alignment. But, alignment choices seem to have far-reaching effects in terms of third-density empirical experience.

What this means is that, as long as we do not engage in disciplined efforts to widen our perception, we appear to have little freedom within the field to behave other than we do. The more aware of the noumenal or causal realm we are, the more free will we can have. And this is because we are overcoming the damping effect of matter and the Predator's mind. By doing this, we are increasing our polarization.

What can be, what might have been, or what should be are ideas that can be dealt with via reason even if there are no apparent manifestations of them in the reality. And this is where the mind – consciousness, awareness – comes into the picture in disciplined effort to envision what has not (apparently) existed and does not (apparently) exist, but which must exist by virtue of the fact we can conceive it.

In the deepest terms, reason is more than the domain of possibilities; it is also the realm of possible empirical worlds, of analytic constructions, of alternate conceptions, and of potential frameworks for the very conditions of experience. Because we can think about things that we have never experienced with any of our senses, and understand that reason, making use of knowledge and awareness, can be independent of the "real world".

Therefore, it is also possible that reason, supported by knowledge and awareness and followed by choice, stands in causal relation to phenomena.

In other words, if your knowledge and awareness of the reality lead you to the conclusion, via reason, that the reality is controlled, and you are not free within it, yet you can develop or comprehend the idea of a world that is *not* controlled, that is *not* limited. You can *choose* to align yourself with such a *possible world* in a deep and conscious way. This choice of alignment then becomes your connection to a thought center. And the stronger your connection to the thought center, which is in the causal realm, the more it will manifest in your reality.

Kant is concerned only with whether an action can be both causally necessary and free at the same time. His answer is yes, *if we are aware.* Kant also argues that this is possible because we can have two different perspectives simultaneously on the same action.

To be free in Kant's sense gives us the power to create a new world, to redo the old, to change ourselves and correct our deficiencies with awareness, which then puts our choices into an entirely different category. We can see it as an ordinary action, a choice brought into focus because of the forces around us, or other choices in our past; and at the same time we can be aware of all of those factors and choose from that position of awareness in a completely different "platonic reality" than the ordinary world.

We can argue that whether or not we have freedom is unprovable (Kant argues that the "how and why" of our possible freedom is unknowable), but given its possibility through reason we can presume freedom to exist. And once we presume it to exist, we can then make choices based on this presumption and observe the results empirically.

Reason is the crucial concept in Kant's approach, and it is here that he makes the critical point. Reason is distinct from what we can know through our five senses, because it deals with the possibility and not actuality of experience.

What do I mean by that? Well, let me try to explain it this way. A correspondent recently wrote of his despair when he realized that what the Cassiopaeans were saying truly did do a better job of explaining the order of the universe and the meanings behind the experiences and symbols of reality.

> [Tonight] we had a ... big annual fireworks presentation that is synchronised with a radio broadcast ... the whole thing is massive and hyped up. There's lots of flashing lights (people even joined in and flashed their house lights), lots of aerial traffic and lots of flashing fireworks. All this backed by a radio broadcast that is impossible to escape since *everyone* is playing it. As beautiful as it is, I got immensely depressed. All that I know so far, all the knowledge in me just caused me to [be unable to] escape the awful feeling of alienation and despair.
>
> All these people, the kids, the elderly, the mothers and grandparents – they are all screwed – most likely including me. We're like sheep – we'll be happy with a bunch of flashing lights and then we'll go off to earn more money. To run the program. I think the most disturbing moment was when I saw this really gorgeous boy – five maybe seven. He had an incredibly smooth face; he was watching the fireworks and clapping his hand in happiness. Pity that Lizzies might eat him tomorrow. ... It's just too much to handle on your own!
>
> We will be taken over with no problems at all. This is our destiny and only a small percentage of us worldwide will have any clue as to what is happening when the sky turns red. The rest will get burned in the packed-out churches. And what can I do?
>
> Well, not much ... it's like one of those prophetic dreams – they happen and you can't change anything. Yeah, I tried but my acts led to the dream FULFILLING it. So either way – whether you do something or not, little difference will be made. It makes no difference how many people I help. It makes no difference how many old ladies' days I make. It makes no difference how many books I read and how many riddles I solve. It is all predestined anyway. I'm tired of giving already!
>
> And so the night goes on. I am alone, with no one to truly see what I mean in a face-to-face conversation. All the people I've ever met had something wrong with them (and there's literally thousands of them). No amount of unconditional love could turn them normal. I'm running out of possibilities here (maybe there's something wrong with ME then). I'm tired of fighting, asking, probing, observing and not being able to share properly. It's a doomed existence and I'm here to watch. Whatever happened to love, compassion and understanding? Where on Earth (HELL) has the internal beauty gone? Is all this bickering ever going to end? Enough already! [Name of correspondent withheld for privacy]

Indeed! And how passionately eloquent. Having been there, more than once, my heart bled for him. And, which is worse: to see what he is seeing as a young man with his whole life before him? Or to see what there is to see in middle age, with five children for whom you have given most of your life; seeing not only that you have been lying to yourself by believing lies and deception, but that you have conveyed those same lies to the people you love the most? What do you do when you realize that most of your life you have given away your free will and, at the same time, have taken away the free will of those dearest to you? More horrible still, what do you do when you realize it has all been done in the name of love?

Is there light at the end of this tunnel? Is there "Balm in Gilead"?

Yes, many times I experienced what my correspondent described so well. And it is only in the past few years that I am able to see it for what it was: a series of initiations. Step by step I was led through one level after another, stripping away all my beliefs and expectations until I had no more illusions in which to hide. And what I was being taught by the universe was the deepest and most essential thing to know – about myself.

When the last illusion was stripped away and I was left with nothing but the skeleton of my being, I reached what Kafka describes as "Von einem gewissen Punkt gibt es keine Rückkehr mehr. Dieser Punkt ist zu erreichen." There is a point of no return. This point has to be reached.

When you have been stripped of all your illusions, when you have nothing left to believe in, there is no one there at all but yourself. It felt rather like falling endlessly in icy, black, meaningless space. No rhyme nor reason, no truth nor beauty, no anything that I had ever believed in could be seen anywhere. I had peeled away the layers of all the warm, fuzzy, comforting beliefs and found that it was all a lie, a deception, a mask for feeding and manipulation. And by believing the lies, I had participated in the feeding and manipulating to so great a degree that my grief and regret became an ocean in which I was drowning. No wonder we resist giving up our beliefs. Without them, we have to face the truth about ourselves. And, as much as we think we are loving, caring, giving beings, when we see the truth, when we see that most of our ideas about loving and caring and being have been manipulated to deprive us of our free will and to pass the infection on to those we love the most, it is like looking into the pit of Hell.

And when you look into the pit of Hell and realize that you have been feeding that black and bloody, sucking and gaping gore-filled maw waiting to swallow you, and that you have taught those you love to feed it as well, the horror of the realization is enough to drive you mad with grief and despair. And you search for a meaning, some little point of illumination, and there is no light anywhere, not even a single candle to dispel the darkness.

But, while falling in this dark, empty space, something begins to form inside you. In the beginning it is very small, but it catches your attention and, since it is the only thing that is different in the sucking, feeding darkness, you become riveted on it. You cannot be sure exactly what it is at first, but your attention gives it energy and it begins to grow inside you.

What you have found is your will.

And once you have found your will you see "the choice". Choice is a function of will. Where will exists, choice comes into being. You can choose.

What you see is that you can choose the orientation of your soul.

The thought came to me as: "Well, okay, I don't see any light or love or truth or beauty anywhere; and the universe may just blink out one day without it ever having really existed. But that would be a tragedy." Desolation overwhelmed me and I felt so great a pity and love for what might have been – for what radiant and sublime dreams may be in the mind of God that might never be fulfilled; because the deceptions are so deep, and the reality is so monstrous – who can really see it and survive? And I became aware of the feather-like weight of my inclination, my true will to be. It was not more than an inclination, a propensity, a preference. But as I noted it and focused on it, it became firmer and more purposeful.

And I realized, "I am just one single, solitary, lone being in the darkness and there really and truly might never ever be anyone or anything in existence of real love, truth and beauty". The sadness and despair vaulted from my soul into darkness that enveloped me. But nothing answered. And my attention was drawn back again to this small thing that was growing inside me, which had now begun to glow and give off warmth in that soul-chilling blackness. Somehow my thoughts were making it grow. My thoughts were aligning me with it. Resolution and steadfastness began to blossom. And then I realized it was connected to some greater source of light and by my penitential love for the dream of love and Truth, the light was growing.

And I understood that this darkness was also God; creation; Existence.

Disasters, misfortunes, tragedies, ruin, destruction, adversity, suffering, pain, anguish in all the varied manifestations we find them in our world are expressions of the idea of nonexistence. I understood that the idea of nonexistence exists only as an idea, and only because in a realm of infinite possibilities, even the potential of nonexistence exists as Non-being. In the two fundamental ideas of Being and Non-being, all creation is manifested. In the act of creation, the out rush of creative energy; half of the consciousness of God formed itself into a reflection of this idea of Non-being as part of the grand experience. And this reflection of Non-being is matter – it is only the half of the consciousness of God gone to sleep to offer itself as the clay from which the cosmos is formed.

I also understood that, in that eternal instant of falling asleep there was a sensation of loss in this half of God that "volunteered" for the role of matter, and that this sensation is expressed as a recoil, a contraction upon itself. It is this contraction in flux interaction with outraying creative consciousness. This establishes the tension of polarization, which is the dynamic by which the cosmos is manifested. And, in third-density terms, this recoil or contraction is the essence of STS; those who choose this mode recycle into sleeping matter.

The creative consciousness half of God uses the matter that is formed by the recoil of the other half of God to take on form, to engage in exploration of all the ideas in the mind of God. This results in an increase of its relative energy. This using of matter to increase energy is felt by the sleeping consciousness or matter as fear of loss of self. To assuage the fear, the matter-oriented consciousness must circumscribe, limit, and restrain. It must believe that the grand constructions of illusion are not only real, but also *all that exists*. Physicality becomes the standard, the measure, and the object of veneration. The physical universe is, in effect, God. This is the essential dynamic of all physical or partly physical realities, including the hyperdimensional fourth-density STS.

And I finally understood the reason for the masks and mazes of our world: it is "The Parable of the Sower".

> A man went out to sow, and as he sowed, some seeds fell by the roadside, and the birds came and ate them up. Other seeds fell on rocky ground, where they had not much soil, and at once they sprang up, because they had no depth of soil; but when the sun rose they were scorched, and because they had no root they dried up and withered away. Other seeds fell among thorns, and the thorns grew up and choked them out. Other seeds fell on good soil and yielded grain, some a hundred times as much as was sown, some sixty times as much, and some thirty. He who has ear, let him be listening and consider and perceive and comprehend by hearing.
>
> … To you it has been given to know the secrets and mysteries of the kingdom of heaven, but to them it has not been given. For whoever has to him will more be given and he will be furnished richly, so that he will have abundance; but from him who has not, even what he has will be taken away.

> While any one is hearing the Word of the kingdom and does not grasp and comprehend it, the evil one comes and snatches away what is sown in his heart. This is what was sown along the roadside. As for what was sown on thin, rocky soil, this is he who hears the Word and at once welcomes and accepts it with joy; Yet it has no real root in himself, but is temporary – inconstant, lasts but a little while and when afflictions or trouble or persecution comes on account of the Word, at once he is caused to stumble ... and he falls away. As for what was sown among thorns, this is he who hears the Word but the cares of the world and the pleasure and delight and glamour and deceitfulness of riches choke and suffocate the Word, and it yields no fruit.
>
> As for what was sown on good soil, this is he who hears the Word and grasps and comprehends it; he indeed bears fruit, and yields in one case a hundred times as much as was sown, in another sixty times as much, and in another thirty. (Matthew 13:3–23)

Our reality is masked as a medium for growth. And what we are growing is our will which, when aligned with a given thought center, allows that thought center to manifest its will in our reality to the extent we are in alignment and can be amplified. To be in alignment with the STO thought centers results in an increase of spiritual consciousness and a diminishment of the sleeping consciousness of matter. To align with the STS thought centers, as we currently are by circumstance, results in an increase of the sleeping consciousness, or wishful thinking of matter, and a diminishment of spiritual consciousness.

Karl von Eckartshausen tells the tale of the *Path to the Temple of Secrets:*

> The Temple of Secrets is located on a high mountain, and everywhere thorns are covering the path leading to the Temple. The inconceivable, mysterious height of the mountain is the reason why many people doubt the existence of the Temple of Secrets. Some think of it as a Fairy Tale, some consider it an old Myth and others believe it to be the Truth.
>
> "At the entrance of the narrow path stands Ignorance, with her sisters Stupidity and Laziness, and they tell awful tales to the travelers and of horrible adventures the travelers will encounter if they set foot on this path. That is how lazy Human Beings and fearful Human Beings can easily be persuaded to turn back.
>
> "There are a few Human Beings on which ignorance attempts her deceptions in vain. They climb up the first part of the thorny steep path, and when they are about half way up the mountain, they reach a plateau on which they find the Temple of Self-Love. Next to this Temple stands Self-Conceit, Pride and Know it-All and they offer

the traveler a cup, out of which he drinks his own Self in great gulps and thereby becomes intoxicated with himself, with his own "I".

"These travelers then become so intoxicated with themselves that they imagine that their Temple, the Temple of Self-Love is the Temple of Secrets and there is nothing, but nothing, above them. The inscription on this temple, the Temple of Self-Love, reads as follows: The Sanctuary of the Wisdom of the World.

"Desires, passions and wantonness are the servants of these priests. However, those whose heart searches for the truth will not find any satisfaction with this and they will keep on searching.

"A few thousand steps from this Temple you will find a very secluded little hut, inhabited by a hermit, with the following inscription above the door: The Residence of Humility.

"The man who lives here guides the strangers to the residence of humility, which in turn leads them to Self-Recognition. This Divine Beauty becomes the traveler's companion, and with her, he conquers the inaccessible mountain. Whosoever tries to reach the Temple of Secrets without this Divine Beauty can very easily be misled by his Self-Love, and as a result, will follow the wrong path. His greed for knowledge will lead him to the Temple of Curiosity. The inhabitants of this Temple are: fraud, seduction and deception, the founders of most of the secret societies, and those Human Beings who, in search for the Truth and for the Temple of Secrets will, if they join these Secret Societies, be robbed of the ability to see with their Soul. They are then led to the top of the mountain, where they fall into the abyss or into the labyrinth or maze, in which they will walk in circles for eternity without finding the Truth.

"Humility alone is the best guide. This alone will lead the seeker to the Master of Teachers of all secrets. This Master Teacher is the *pure will*.

"This pure will becomes the friend of the highest of knowledge and they enter into a bond of eternal union.

"The knowledge of the effects of the Eternal Light of godliness in all created beings is True Magic in Theory.

"The conception of this Light, or the transition from the intellect to the will, is True Magic in Practice." (von Eckartshausen, 1788/1989)

Now, note the sequence above; those who align with the thought centers of STS manifest *ignorance*, *stupidity* and *laziness* in the sense that they believe awful tales and horrible adventures of travelers, and they are easily persuaded to turn back. That is to say that they are persuaded that knowledge will bring them to grief, or that asking questions is a "lack of faith" that will earn them condemnation at best, and a quick ticket to Hell at worst. The comparison between this analogy and the Parable of the Talents in which the servant who buried his talent because he was afraid and was cast into outer darkness are interesting, especially when we consider the end result of the STS alignment, which is to recycle into primal matter. I would suggest that people such as these are eaten rather quickly just as the seeds that fell by the wayside were immediately consumed by the birds in "The Parable of the Sower".

Then, we have another class of STS alignment. They aren't easily put off by terror tactics, so special deceptions are set up for them. They *do* reach the "plateau on which they find the temple of self-love. Next to this temple stands Self-Conceit, Pride and Know it-All and they offer the traveler a cup, out of which he drinks his own self in great gulps and thereby becomes intoxicated with himself, with his own 'I'." We can see that these are the ones that achieve the higher levels of STS orientation. The key in the analogy is that they become so intoxicated with themselves that they imagine that their Temple, the Temple of Self-Love is the Temple of Secrets and there is nothing, but nothing, above them. This is what the Cassiopaeans have described as "ultimate in wishful thinking". And, of course, these are the purveyors of most of the deceptions in our world today because one of the things that these individuals most wishfully think is that they are the purveyors of the wisdom of the world!

Von Eckartshausen tell us that "desires, passions and wantonness are the servants of these priests". We know from this that these individuals may be very high in the STS hierarchy of the Control System themselves. And they use the nature of hunger within humanity, the Predator's mind, to do their will.

> Q: (L) It says here: In 1979, Project Phoenix, with the assistance of the Grays, was successful in producing a mind amplifier. This was used in conjunction with putting people with exceptional psychic or mental capabilities under drug influence, hooking them up to this machine and keeping them in a state of pre-orgasmic sexual excitation wherein they were able to create some type of physical form. They say: "The fire within man that is characterized as passion is the secret that can be utilized. The secret to all things is passion. With passion all things are possible. The amplification experiments of the Phoenix Project have been explained as having amplified brain waves. In fact, it amplified the passion of the subject. It was that 'inner will' of the subject that was amplified, that inner spirit within all of us is that driving force is manifested as electrical energy. Master that force and you cannot be controlled, the universe is yours. Master the inner spirit and you shall master the physical." Comments please.
>
> A: "Passion" does not set one "free", quite the opposite!

Q: (L) But what if your passion is for knowledge? What is it that gives some people this drive, this steamroller compulsion that they are determined to get to the absolute bottom of everything and strip away every lie until there is nothing left but the naked truth? What is the source of this desire?

A: That is not passion, it is soul questing. It is simply that one is at that point on the learning cycle. At that point, no drive is needed.

Q: (L) So, you more or less are there because some critical mass has been reached that "jumps" you to the point where seeking truth is simply who you are? It defines the parameters of your being?

A: Yes.

However, there is a kind of person who has some sort of inner inclination for truth. They are simply unable to accept anything else. They cannot be satisfied until they have peeled the onion to the very core. And these keep their eyes on the goal of truth.

The seeker of truth continues to gather knowledge in the same way the servants in the "Parable of the Talents" continued to invest their money. Gathering knowledge without prejudice inevitably leads to humility. Humility combined with knowledge inevitably leads to self-recognition. And self-recognition becomes the companion that enables us to navigate the emotions and illusions that seek to distract us and blind us! Finally, self-recognition, which is the ultimate state of humility, leads us to *pure* will.

Now, notice, I didn't say *strong* will, just pure. A person's will to be is his natural frequency. And when you marry will to knowledge you have the hope of using your will in a particular way. This will is the mustard seed of the Biblical parable. Again: will to be, or orientation, is *frequency*.

Application of will via knowledge to choices produces *frequency resonance vibration* in the consciousness, which can then manifest in the individual's experience in very particular ways, as I will try to explain.

Any given system has a natural frequency. A human being has several frequencies. They relate to the atomic signature of the cellular structure, etheric body frequency, and the frequency of the consciousness, which is a function of will or orientation.

If you record a pure tone, you can connect the output line that would normally connect to a speaker to an oscilloscope instead. In this way, you can see the sound rather than hear it. As you observe it, you will note that it oscillates. You are seeing a wave. Frequency is the number of crests of a wave in a designated unit of time. That is what determines frequency. More units in time mean higher frequency. Frequency is in inverse ratio to the length of the wave. The higher the frequency, the shorter the wave. (It is important to note here that a unit of time is an arbitrary measurement, so assigning a number to a frequency is merely a matter of convention.)

Frequency resonance vibration is directly related to what is called forced oscillation. Any wave system may be driven by a force from the "outside". Whenever a system is made to vibrate by a periodic force, the resulting motion is called forced oscillation. An example would be the glass that shatters when an opera singer hits the right note.

Forced oscillations take place with the frequency of the driving force rather than with the natural frequency of the system. The amplitude of the response depends on how the driving frequency is related to the natural frequency. If these frequencies are nearly the same, even a very weak driving force can, in time, feed enough energy into the system to give it a large amplitude of motion. This condition is called resonance.

Everybody has probably pushed a child on a swing. What you notice is, after a series of very strong pushes to get the swing going, you can stand there and just give an occasional push or tap to keep the same swinging motion going. But, as every parent knows, it has to be given at exactly the right instant. The tap must be applied in the same direction, and at the very instant of the swinging away motion for it to work. If you give a push at intervals instead of at every return, you will find that an increase of force is necessary depending on how many times you let the swing come and go before applying another tap. If you set up a series of every other return before pushing, you will have to apply the exact same force at each of these arbitrarily determined intervals, which will be a multiple of the force you would have to apply if you pushed with every single return.

These intervals of pushing at arbitrarily designated returns are submultiples of the natural frequency. And, as you see from this example, they can also produce the same resonance. The frequency resonance vibration is the swinging that results from being pushed.

If the pushes continued and if the swing had long enough ropes and a brave enough child, a regular series of pushes could eventually launch the child into outer space!

But, you will notice that if the pushes are not given at the right moment, if they are not constantly delivered either with every swing or in a submultiple, if no periodicity is maintained, the swing will slow down and stop. You will also notice that if you do not apply the pushes in a fixed period, the motion of the swing is erratic. And you will definitely notice that if you push at the wrong moment, or against the swing direction, you will cause it to slow down. In such a case, you are taking energy away from the system.

The very same principles apply to forced oscillation of any wave, whether it is a sound wave, radio wave, light wave or whatever. In fact, it could be said that light produced is forced oscillations of atoms. All things in nature, which are a response to a stimulus, are forced oscillations.

A human being could be considered a series of forced oscillations. And here we come to the problem:

> "Besides depending on how close the driving frequency is to the natural frequency, the amplitude of response of the forced vibrations of a system also depends on the strength of the damping. The less damping there is, the greater the response of resonance. *The resonance frequency is always lower than the natural frequency but gets very close as the damping is reduced."* (Freeman 1973)

Now, as we have said, a human being is a combination of frequencies of the cellular structure, the etheric or genetic body, and the consciousness orientation. If these different frequencies operate in harmonious submultiples of a certain fundamental frequency, we say that the system is in harmony. That is to say, there is harmonious frequency resonance.

We can also say that by changing one of the frequencies and amplifying it, the others may be brought into harmony by the process of forced oscillation *if* the natural frequency of each is a harmonic of, or is close to, the driving frequency.

At the same time, the act of changing any of the frequencies can be accomplished by forced oscillation from the "outside", whether in harmony or not. That is to say, if the forced oscillation is not close to the natural frequency there will be less amplitude.

Now, a human being, in general, is under the powerful influence of the matter of which his body is constructed. Matter is the result of the STS. The thought of Non-being or sleeping consciousness of God. Therefore, by being in third density, to a great extent, man is asleep. He is under the influence of the frequency of the STS polarity. His frequency resonance vibration is STS, or that of matter. The Predator's mind.

But, man has a possibility of changing frequency, aligning with STO polarity, *if* he can find that part of him that is truly of Service-to-Others and amplify it through the process of frequency resonance vibration, resulting from the forced oscillation of alignment with the STO thought center. It is only his will that can do this, and it is only when it is married to knowledge so that he can truly know what his choice is and how to implement it. These choices are the pushes of the swing. If sufficient amplitude is achieved, all of his other frequencies will also gradually be forced into frequency resonance vibration.

Of course, this process is not only dependent upon the natural frequency of the individual, but also upon the dampers that may be in place that can restrict the amplitude. The fewer dampers, the greater the amplitude that can be achieved with the least application of energy.

We have to discover and remove the dampers to our systems.

Again, it is in the gaining of knowledge through which we can remove the dampers, little by little. It is hard work and it is painful. But as we do this, we come, step by step; to the position of humility and self-knowledge that enables the alignment of the will. If the natural frequency of STO is present in the moment of choice, this pure will becomes the "friend of the highest of knowledge" and they "enter into a bond of eternal union". One is then able to connect with the eternal creative light within, which then becomes the forced oscillator that changes the frequency resonance vibration in dramatic and life changing ways. This amounts to giving up self-will to allow the greater will of the thought center to manifest. The manifestation of this in one's daily life via choices become pushes of the swing of the etheric body and the atomic signature of the cellular structure, which then changes the entire reality.

When we finally achieve self-recognition and humility, we understand that it is implementation of our choices at *this* third density level that increases the amplitude of our frequency resonance vibration, which is, in actuality, our polarization. Amplitude constitutes our ripeness" fo advancement to the next density. What we are choosing is, in effect, which part we will play in the next cycle of creation. What we do now determines our course into either consciousness that creates or the intensely contractile thought of Non-being that goes to sleep as primal matter. Neither of them are higher frequencies, they are simply different.

Mass and "spring constant" are the determinants of frequency in material terms. Using the principle of "As above, so below", we must assume that similar constructs apply to spiritual frequencies. The Spring Constant is the measure of the force needed to extend the spring by an arbitrary measure. Mass, since it relates to matter, in spiritual terms is analogous to sleeping consciousness or ignorance. This means that the fundamental ignorant or sleeping nature of the STS orientation equates to greater mass *and* spring constant. Greater mass and spring constant require greater strength of forced oscillation to produce frequency resonance vibration even if the natural frequency is very close to the frequency of the forced oscillator. Thus, since the natural frequency of the human being is that of matter to the greatest extent, it is more inclined to be influenced by the STS polarity's forced oscillation.

Less mass and spring constant are the result of knowledge. Knowledge is a function of consciousness and all knowledge that *is* knowledge and not assumption, prejudice or illusion, increases consciousness.

> Q: (L) We have been discussing memories and how memories of, say, past lives are stored, and that leads to the question of what is the structure and composition of the soul? How does the soul remember? How does it carry its memories from lifetime to lifetime, from body to body, whether simultaneous or sequential? How does the soul "store" them?
>
> A: Has to do with atomic principles. These with gravity present the borderland for the material and the nonmaterial. Which theoretical atomic particulates would you think form the basis here?
>
> Q: (L) How about tachyons?
>
> A: Maybe neutrons? Neutrinos.
>
> Q: (A) Neutrinos are funny particles because they are massless. But, some people don't believe that neutrinos exist. Do they exist?
>
> A: Okay, we are going to throw caution to the "winds", and say yes. [Laughter.]
>
> Q: (L) In terms of these neutrinos and soul composition, how are memories formed or held or patterned with these neutrinos?
>
> A: Contained within for release when and if suitable.
>
> Q: (L) Memories are contained within the neutrinos?
>
> A: Sort of.
>
> Q: (L) Are they contained within patterns formed by the neutrinos?
>
> A: Closer.
>
> Q: (L) So, that means that if one "consciousness unit", or soul has more memories or experiences than another consciousness unit, it would have more neutrinos?
>
> A: No.
>
> Q: (L) What's the difference?
>
> A: More data per unit, sort of.
>
> Q: (L) Does that mean that an individual neutrino can be, in and of itself, more "dense" in data, so to speak?
>
> A: So to speak.
>
> Q: (L) Does this increased density of data change the nature or function of the individual neutrino?
>
> A: Maybe it changes the function of the awareness, thus the environs.

Q: (L) Is there a specific number of neutrinos that constitutes a consciousness unit, or soul?

A: Number is not quite the right concept. Orientation is closer.

Q: (L) What are the orientational options?

A: Vibrational frequencies.

Q: (L) Do the vibrational frequencies increase or decrease with density of data?

A: Change; better not to quantify.

Note that the nature of the soul is fundamentally altered not only by a change in the orientation of the basic units, which has to do with changing frequencies. This process is also dependent on increasing the data within the basic units; vibrational frequencies change with increase of the density of data.

The increase of data changes the frequency in a natural way from the orientation of STS to that which is closer to STO. This results in a reduction in mass and spring constant, which means less energy must be input from the forced oscillator in order to produce frequency resonance vibration.

This is why it is easier to increase amplitude via the STO alignment. This is why it is easier to graduate to fourth density via the STO alignment. This is also why all the dampers and controls are held so tightly in place. The Control System does not want humans to graduate to fourth density and that is why they create beliefs and illusions and controls designed to induce us to make STS choices no matter what we do. As long as we believe lies, we are aligned with STS. As long as we are aligned with STS, our mass and spring constant make it impossible for us to increase our amplitude for graduation.

And this brings up another fact. In order to graduate to fourth density via the STS pathway, several conditions must be met. First, nearly *all* of the dampers to STS for the individual must be removed and all of the STO inclinations of the individual must be removed to increase the potential for amplification.

Second, the natural frequency of the individual, which we already know is a function of choice, must be so close to the pure STS frequency as to be almost identical for the forced oscillation from the higher-density thought center to have any effect at all. This means that the degree and depth of depravity, malignity, malevolence, degeneration and contraction must be extremely pure in the individual.

> A: We wish to review some things ... The concept of a "master race" put forward by the Nazis was merely a 4th density STS effort to create a physical vehicle with the correct frequency resonance vi-

bration for 4th density STS souls to occupy in 3rd density. It was also a "trial run" for planned events in what you perceive to be your future.

Q: (L) You mean with a strong STS frequency so they can have a "vehicle" in third density, so to speak?

A: Correct. Frequency resonance vibration! Very important.

Q: (L) So, that is why they are programming and experimenting? And all these folks running around who some think are "programmed", could be individuals who are raising their nastiness levels high enough to accommodate the truly negative STS fourth density – sort of like walk-ins or something, only not nice ones?

A: You do not have very many of those present yet, but that was, and still is, the plan of some of the 4th density STS types.

When you "grok" the level of STS that has to be present in an individual in order to graduate to fourth-density STS, the purity of the evil – the consciousness of it – well, it is a pretty horrifying thought. It's like Ted Bundy, Albert Fish, Ed Gein, and Jeffrey Dahmer all rolled into one and amplified exponentially! Not only that, smarter!

Such beings would not have the damping effect of any STO frequencies on the STS frequency. Efforts would be made to reduce, or eliminate entirely, any residual STO inclinations that might act to expose them in their moments of STO "weakness". That is truly scary and is something we need to keep in mind.

Such a being would be able to act in any way they chose, without glitches that give them away, and be able to disarm and deceive to get their prey exactly where they want them.

Unfortunately, a mixture of STS and STO choices do not add up to graduation to fourth-density STS. All they do is damp each other, thus making it less likely for any amplification will occur. The person who wishes to pursue the STS pathway with the intent of graduating has to give up any and all thoughts of experiencing love or kindness that is freely given. Yes, they can be in love relationships and can act kind. But, at this level, it is all pure manipulation for the purpose of owning or subsuming to the self the energies of others. Yet, there are those to whom this path is attractive.

However, this is not clearly seen at the lower densities until the masks are stripped away. The deepest implications of this are hidden by many veils. And even the fourth and fifth-density STS participants do not necessarily comprehend the ultimate dissolution at the end of their philosophies. This is why there are so many higher-density sources that are convinced they are teaching love and light and truth and beauty, and why so many on third density are deceived by these teachings. Those who are deceived believe in these teachings because they "feel" good, or because they "want" to. This belief that is sustained in the face of all empirical evidence to the contrary amounts to wishful thinking. It is seeing what one wants to see, rather than what is: ultimate wishful thinking.

The deepest implication of wishful thinking means that those who adopt this view of reality cannot see that they do not become God by what amounts to assimilation and control of other selves; but that the real result is a gradual compaction and implosion and dissolution into primal matter and Non-being. The negative hierarchy is a pyramidal food chain; the apex of the pyramid is comprised of the most persistent of the negative graduates, the one who has stuck it out against every evidence of diminishment, and is the ultimate example of wishful thinking.

And this is the most important point of all. It is a way home because, at the eternal moment when those that return to the light do return, those that hold the idea of Non-being, or darkness *also* return. In an eternally instantaneous unification and disbursement act that was, is and always will be, the energies of darkness and lightness fall into their respective roles eternally. When you realize that it is never going to end, that neither path will take you to "heaven" and "eternal bliss", or oblivion or any of the illusions perpetrated upon humankind, it then becomes simply a matter of preference. And that preference is only an inclination. It literally has the weight of a feather.

And that, my friend, is the choice that I faced. The possibility of Service-to-Others in a realm composed of matter, which is by its nature Service-to-Self, under the control of higher-density beings who are oriented by Service-to-Self. That's where we are. That is what *is* in this realm.

And, by understanding that either choice ultimately leads back to God, since there really is no back to God because in real terms there is no separation from God to begin with, we find that we have an unweighted choice.

That's it. The whole banana. That's the choice. Either way, nothing is going to come to an end with union with God because the instant there is union with the one, it all starts over again. That's what is. Our choice is to actualize what is *in* us; To choose our orientation and begin to discover how to amplify it.

Of course, that means we have some details to hammer out here. Like the fact that every single day we make choices and every one of these choices either amplifies our frequency resonance vibration, or damps it. The Control System wants to damp all our choices so that we will neither be able to polarize nor increase amplitude. They have a nice little thing going here and they will do anything to keep it going.

So, we need to get down to the nitty gritty of what is really Service-to-Others and Service-to-Self.

In the simplest of terms, Service-to-Others is a creative impulse. It is to find delight and satisfaction in variety and change. It is to serve God in others, which means to give all others the right to be what they choose, to give them the right to their own free will. It does not mean to give them your energy, your love, or any part of your creative force unless there is willing exchange. In an STO exchange, all parties give freely to all others and therefore all are sustained and grow.

Service-to-Self is, at the deepest level, just the thought of Non-being that manifests as fear of losing self in the act of creation. Thus, difference, variety, change, spontaneity, and all creative functions are feared and must be carefully controlled.

Service-to-Self naturally forms itself into a controlling hierarchy where each level is narrower and more exclusive and contractile than the level below it. It is a process of consuming conscious awareness and stuffing it into the black hole of the hought of Non-being in an effort to fill up that hole, thereby assuaging the fear evoked by the thought of Non-being. The thing that happens, though, is that a consciousness which has been subsumed into this thought is then defined by it and contracts and contracts until it becomes, eventually, primal matter.

One of the problems we face is the fact that, very often, the desire of human beings at this third level of density to experience light and love and truth and beauty; to be One in a harmony of similar goals and objectives of peace and tranquility, kindness, devotion, respect and concord, is manipulated by those beings who live in fear of losing self, twisted and distorted to mean a contraction into sameness rather than harmonious variety.

In human terms, this fear of losing self and need to become One is not always expressed by overt domination or subjugation. It is often expressed by the dynamic of absorption of other consciousnesses into a single ideal, narrowly defined by human terms of love and light. Very often the ideals of love and light are twisted to mean denying the free will of others to make their own choices.

In fact, the idea that evil is a rebellion, a fault, a thing to be done away with, is the twist in all the teachings of history that have laid the groundwork for domination and absorption by the forces of Service-to-Self. In terms of monotheism, this idea of saving the world has manifested the fruits of the many slaughters that have been instituted in the name of unity, and love. Because of this perceived need to fix or change or transform other people or situations, those whose inner inclination is actually STO are induced to damp their own STO frequency. If, in the act of giving or sending love, or any act whatsoever you deny the free will of another, you are damping your STO frequency resonance vibration.

And remember, we are not talking about free will in the simplistic terms of being able to do as one chooses without restriction. So we aren't talking about not putting criminals in jail for breaking the law. In fact, putting a criminal in jail so that he can fully enter into his freely chosen lesson can be pure STO. It's the old don't do the crime if you can't do the time cliché. By doing the crime, the individual has chosen the consequences at some level.

Each and every time we participate in wishful thinking, we are polarizing to Service-to-Self because wishful thinking is the essence of the constructed defense against the fear of Non-being. Thus, when we live in illusions we are, by default, electing to be part of the STS food chain.

The illusions in which we participate are generally projections of higher-density STS beings, and are set up to produce the negative polarization energy of those on third density, which supports and maintains the fourth-density STS beings so that they can continue to project the illusion. This results in the inability of human beings to see what is truly of STO, which prevents their making STO choices, which damps their frequency resonance vibration and keeps them in the cycle.

The work of developing free will is to stop believing lies. At the same time, the only way to really learn this is to try on the lies until the external evidence mounts so high that one is forced to the ultimate choice of choosing to continue with the lie in the face of the evidence that it is a lie, or to choose to see only the truth.

Such a choice is a causal act of polarization. It is an alignment of choice.

Making the choice only comes to those who are ready, those who have reached that point on the learning cycle. None of us can skip this step, and none of us can make it for others. In fact, the greatest gift we can give to save another is to release them fully into their chosen lessons.

And so, the choice comes, you are face to face with what you truly are, in the blackness of the abyss, and you choose. I realised that in terms of any action I might take in this reality, I had *no* free will except in terms of my response. I could choose how I responded. I could choose my frequency. That was it. In my case the thought came:

> I will offer myself as one who has chosen to be this light, love, truth and beauty. By being it, I am giving it to God. I will strive for as long as I am present on this Godforsaken planet, as long as I am separated from my source, drifting in the darkness, to be as much of love and truth and beauty as I can manage to manifest.

I no longer cared whether that made me a prime piece of meat for the Control System; I didn't care if they were going to eat me tomorrow or even if they ate everybody I loved and the whole universe ended in a bang and I was blotted out of existence for eternity.

I figured that for whatever it was worth, which may have been absolutely nothing, when it was all over and the stars all blinked out, there was going to be that one little memory in the physical universe's brain; the memory that one person responded with love to the right of the universe to be exactly as it is, even if what it *is* is nothing but a dark, devouring mouth that consumes its creatures as soon as they are created, including me. My response to seeing was to sound the tone of love, beauty and truth so that it would have existence in me.

I chose to end the illusion of wishful thinking about life in the flesh and all the ways we are deceived. Finally I understood the dynamics of third-density Service-to-Self. And I understood why it was that everywhere I looked there was darkness. And I understood my choice. And I made it. Yes, there is no candle to illuminate the darkness that I can see – so the only solution is to *be* my own candle.

I decided that whatever I had to do at this level in order to discover how to respond to life in order to do and be that truth and beauty implicit in the unconditional love of free will, I was going to keep searching until my last breath. If all my efforts failed, at least my response as one who held to the ideal of truth, love and beauty, from the very depths of my soul and in the face of whatever horror I faced in my search, would have existed.

I realized that this truly was the only thing that I had to give, and I was ready to give it. And the fact is it was everything in me – little though it might have been. But it was my all. And I chose to give this response as a pure, clear tone, to God with the full awareness that there was nothing I could expect to change it There was no anticipation that it would make any difference at all, and the greatest likelihood was that I would be drowned out or devoured rather quickly.

So, like a battered and bloody soldier on a battlefield with all the odds against him, like a Berserker who had lost all care for, or consciousness of, the weakness of the flesh, I picked myself up and set my eyes firmly on the center of the action, and started to walk in that direction. And I never looked back.

And for me, the universe changed in that instant.

In my own moment of choice, I was dealing with a possibility that was not an actuality. It is impossible to be a true STO being in an STS world. For me, it was such a pity, such a sadness that once I penetrated the illusion I found nothing but darkness.

I could see that real truth and beauty just simply could not be found in our reality once one began to peel away the layers of lies and deception and illusion. To realize that love given to someone or something in order to change it was clearly a judgment, and that nearly all love practiced in our world was clearly done because it was a manipulation designed to gain, whether it was salvation or to be loved in return or to feel good, all of which feed Non-being. This produced in me such a sensation of sadness and love for creation that, in that moment, the choice to manifest love and truth within, despite the fact I could know nothing of it through my five senses and third-density experience, was a choice to make a possibility real.

I was able to see with my intellect the influences that are imposed on us by the many forces acting in our environment, but I then *chose* irrespective of them. I could see, after all the years of stripping away veils like flesh from my very bones, that the whole grand scheme of things in third density merely amounted to choosing the lesser of many evils. It was a system of dampers.

For me to have to choose that way was not a choice, it was a compromise. I was no longer willing to compromise. You could even say that I chose rebellion over compromise with the forces that control our environment. The reason and intent for the choice was above this control and was made with full awareness that it may be impossible to ever do anything to effectively implement the choice.

In other words, there was no weight to the choice. I was seeing that over and over again I had been told I must drink the water and not the oil because it was the only rational choice, and I was rejecting that control. I was essentially choosing to drink neither, preferring to seek further for the ideal "living water". And it was only in myself that I found it. It was in my power to choose to continue to create rather than seek return and oblivion.

> Jesus answered [the Samaritan woman at Jacob's well], If you had only known and had recognized God's gift ... you would have asked Him and He would have given you living water. ... Whoever takes a drink of the water that I will give him shall never, no never, be

thirsty anymore. But the water that I will give him shall become *a spring of water welling up continually within him unto eternal life.* ... A time will come when the true worshippers will worship the Father in spirit and in true reality; for the Father is seeking just such people as these ... God is a Spirit and those who worship Him must worship Him in spirit and truth. (John 4:10–24)

The deepest realization of this choice hits home when you understand that the greatest illusions that are chosen by us are those of our closest relationships. Jesus said:

Do not think that I have come to bring peace upon the earth; I have not come to bring peace but a sword. For I have come to part asunder a man from his father, and a daughter from her mother, and a newly married wife from her mother-in-law; and a man's foes will be they of his own household. He who loves and takes more pleasure in father or mother than in Me is not worthy of Me; and he who loves and takes more pleasure in son or daughter than in Me is not worthy of me; And he who does not take up his cross and follow Me is not worthy of Me. Whoever finds his [lower] life will lose the [higher] life and whoever loses his [lower] life on My account will find [the higher life]. (Matthew 10: 35–39)

Every situation or dynamic in which we find ourselves demands a response. To not respond is, of course, a choice to accede to the dynamic as it is. This means that the only true response we can give is to be more fully and strongly what we have chosen. Consciously. And only by doing this do we progress to the next level.

We come then to the problem of how to do this. I realized that it was a matter of growing stronger in terms of polarity. At the level of third density, the animal man is far stronger than the spiritual man. Third density is the point at which the process of division takes place. Some will follow the unification into Oneness that leads to the "new" descent into primal matter, and some will become the consciousness that loses itself in the clay of creation for the joy of learning and experience. There are those that find the door to the inner circle of creation, and those that descend to become matter.

And on that note, I will close this volume of the Wave with the words of Gurdjieff:

"The inner circle is called the 'esoteric'; this circle consists of people who have attained the highest development possible for man, each one of whom possesses individuality in the fullest degree, that is to say, an indivisible 'I', all forms of consciousness possible for man, full control over these states of consciousness, the whole of knowledge possible for man, and a free and independent will.

"They cannot perform actions opposed to their understanding or have an understanding which is not expressed by actions.

"At the same time there can be no discords among them, no differences of understanding. Therefore their activity is entirely coordinated and leads to one common aim without any kind of compulsion because it is based upon a common and identical understanding." ...

"Everything I have said till now I have said about the whole of humanity. But as I pointed out before, the evolution of humanity can proceed only through the evolution of a certain group, which, in its turn, will influence and lead the rest of humanity.

"Are we able to say that such a group exists? Perhaps we can on the basis of certain signs, but in any event we have to acknowledge that it is a very small group, quite insufficient, at any rate, to subjugate the rest of humanity. Or, looking at it from another point of view, we can say that humanity is in such a state that it is unable to accept the guidance of a conscious group."

"How many people could there be in this conscious group?" someone asked.

"Only they themselves know this," said G.

"Does it mean that they all know each other?" asked the same person again.

"How could it be otherwise?" asked G.

"Imagine that there are two or three people who are awake in the midst of a multitude of sleeping people. They will certainly know each other. But those who are asleep cannot know them. How many are they? We do not know and we cannot know until we become like them.

"It has been clearly said before that each man can only see on the level of his own being. But two hundred conscious people, if they existed and if they found it necessary and legitimate, could change the whole of life on the earth. But either there are not enough of them, or they do not want to, or perhaps the time has not yet come, or perhaps other people are sleeping too soundly." (Ouspensky 1949)

(The Wave continues in volume four, *Through a Glass Darkly* ...)

APPENDIX
CULT-IVATING TERROR

A BRIEF ANALYSIS OF THE ORIGINS AND EFFECTS OF THE CULT PHENOMENA IN MODERN SOCIETY BY JOE QUINN[25]

The Oxford English dictionary entry for "cult" states:
1. A system of religious worship, esp. as expressed in ritual.
2. A devotion or homage to a person or thing.
2b. A popular fashion, esp. followed by a specific section of society.
3. Denoting a person or thing popularized in this way.

It is clear that the above description could easily apply to any of the organized religions prevalent today. Christianity, Judaism, Islam, Buddhism and others are replete and indeed founded on ritual and "devotion to a person or thing". However, they are not generally referred to as cults. It seems that the term cult, in its modern and widely understood form, is reserved for any group formed under a hierarchical structure, where some form *of coercion or manipulation* of the group members exists. Generally there is also some focus of worship, be it the group leader(s) or some other outside personage or thing. The justification for worship or allegiance is usually tied to the perceived or stated benefits or potential benefits to be derived from the worship or allegiance. (I know, sounds rather like accepted mainstream religions. Go figure.)

It seems at a practical level, however, that the key element in distinguishing a cult from a mainstream religion is the existence of overt identifiable coercion (physical or mental) or manipulation of members.

---

[25] http://www.cassiopaea.org/cass/cult-ivating_terror.htm

Having said that, physical coercion or attacks on the physical integrity of members in such groups, while not without precedent, is less common, (physical coercion being a more obvious violation of free will and therefore more easily identified). A much more subtle, and for this reason more effective form of coercion is intellectual, or more commonly, emotional manipulation. This is generally achieved through the aforementioned worship principle where members are encouraged to give of their time, energy, financial resources, etc. in the hope of or with the promise of achieving the stated goal and/or benefits for the individual or group.

Very often the allegation that mind control is used on cult members is made. Proving such a claim is problematic however, since the definition of mind control is broad to say the least. There can be many forms of "mind control" varying in subtlety, although they are not called by that name (see the mass media coverage of the Gulf War for one example).

In relation to alleged cults it is usually via the observation of the results of mind control that assertions are most often made as to whether it is in use or not in any given group. These results include a widely known list of supposed indicators. For example: members joining "communes", giving up possessions, extreme devotion and allegiance to a leader, and in a few cases giving up their lives by way of apparent suicide.

In line with this more practical understanding, *Wikipedia.com* gives the following definition of cult:

> Since the 1960s, in English-speaking countries, especially in North America, most English speakers have adopted the term in a pejorative sense to denote groups, many of them with religious themes, that exploit their members psychologically and financially using group-based persuasion techniques (sometimes called 'mind control'). Unlike legitimate religious movements, *cults are characterized by high levels of dependency, exploitation, and compliance with demands of leadership that are unrelated to religion.* 90% or more of cult members ultimately leave the group.

Using the above definition then, we can deduce that cults are groups characterized by "high levels of dependency, exploitation, and compliance with demands of leadership that are unrelated to religion", while legitimate religious movements can supposedly use the same "high levels of dependency, exploitation, and compliance with demands of leadership", as long as they are related to religion.

The problem then is, what defines religion? One commentator suggests the following:

> ... religion always begins in an experience that some individual has or that some small group of people shares. The response that this person or group makes to the original experience is what begins the process of interaction between the religion and the community. In extreme cases we can imagine a religion which lived and died unknown to all but the original participants, because their response turned inward and never created an interaction with others in the community; or a religion in which the response to the original experience so quickly and completely assimilated it to the traditions of the community that the germinal religion never acquired an independent identity. Most recognizable religions fall somewhere between these extremes, and thus acquire the identity by which we can recognize them.
>
> Religion originates in an attempt to represent and order beliefs, feelings, imaginings and actions that arise in response to direct experience of the sacred and the spiritual. As this attempt expands in its formulation and elaboration, it becomes a process that creates meaning for itself on a sustaining basis, in terms of both its originating experiences and its own continuing responses.[26]

If the true definition of religion is based on "belief that is a direct experience of the sacred and spiritual", then most of today's mainstream religions that are founded on the experience or hearsay of another cannot constitute a valid religion and therefore are in fact not religions at all. They continue nevertheless to retain "high levels of dependency, exploitation, and compliance with demands of leadership", essentially (under the above definition) making them cults.

In spite of this, many groups today define themselves as religious in one way or another and the term certainly has many different meanings for many different people. For example the *Watchman Fellowship* who claim they are "an independent Christian research and apologetics ministry focusing on new religious movements, cults, the occult and the New Age" state that:

> There are many groups operating which engage in the use of deception, fraud, manipulation, coercion, control, and exploitation. The constitutionally protected right of free speech serves as a check and balance against these abuses. When deception, control, and fraud are present, a person's freedom of choice is undermined. It is always right to publicly and privately expose these practices. The one exposing error or abuse has the responsibility to be accurate.[27]

---

[26] Paul Connelly, "What is Religion?", 1996,
(http://www.darc.org/connelly/religion1.html).
[27] Watchman Fellowship, A Christian Response to Cults and New Religious Movements, Copyright 2000, (http://www.watchman.org/about.htm).

Yet they see no deception, control, and fraud when *they* unilaterally decide to "witness" to unwitting members of the public, presenting a subjective interpretation of a religious text as fact. It is not however our intention here to weigh up the pros and cons of various competing religious organizations.

Essentially there would seem to be two approaches that can be taken when attempting to assess the cult status of a group: one can approach it from a theological point of view or from a sociological point of view.

One religious professor in 1994 well summarized the popular perspectives concerning the identification of cults in an online posting, shortly after the tragedy at Waco that deserves some consideration:

> As a professor of religious studies who specializes in research, writing, and teaching about America's alternative religions, I can tell all of you that the word 'cult' has become an essentially contested concept. That is, like many other words, there is no universally agreed-upon meaning.
>
> Before one can know what the term means one must know the user and his or her context religiously and socially. I tell my students there are four major approaches to using the term: journalistic (tends to be sensational), theological (defines 'cult' by some standard of orthodox truth), sociological (uses 'cult' to describe groups that self-consciously oppose the mainstream of culture), and psychological (uses a standard of psychological manipulation and coercion).
>
> What counts as a cult differs by these varying definitions. All three may agree on a certain group being a 'cult' such as Jim Jones' 'Peoples' Temple'. But a theologian might label the LDS church [Latter-day Saints (Mormons)] a 'cult' simply because it diverges considerably from standard orthodox Christianity, while a sociologist would say it isn't a cult due to its size and influence.

The theological argument seems to hinge upon interpretation of religious texts, with various groups attempting to define the boundaries of what it means to be truly Christian. The argument is unlikely to be resolved any time soon given that none of the warring factors actually possess any conclusive proof.

For example, the theological approach is taken by the Christian counter-cult movement. It considers the Church of Jesus Christ of Latter-day Saints (Mormon) a cult because the church rejects the traditional doctrine of the Trinity, has scriptures in addition to the Bible, and has various other unorthodox beliefs and practices.

In the end, size and influence seem to play a major part in deciding which religious group gets awarded cult status. The Catholic Church, for example, has approximately a 2,000 year history, 600 million followers around the world, and vast financial resources at its disposal. It seems that this provides all the protection needed from the threat of "cult headquarters" ever replacing the term Vatican, or "cult leader" the title of Pope.

Rightly or wrongly then, smaller and newly formed religious groups are much more likely to find themselves the object of scrutiny than larger established mainstream religions, regardless of the evidence or lack thereof for provable cultic behavior (if such a thing even exists from the theological point of view). Of course, given the monotheistic nature and monopoly on belief held by the major organized religions, it is certainly plausible that this situation is most acceptable to them, and that they may even contribute to its perpetuation.

In a recent article for the long established Egypt weekly paper *Al-Ahram*, Jonathan Cook, a British writer living in Nazareth, makes an interesting point about the similarity of the mind programming effects attributed to cults and the effects of mainstream religion (in this case, Judaism). He suggests that the reason the persecution of the Palestinians at the hands of the Israeli military continues unquestioned by the Jewish people is not due to ignorance of the situation but is instead dependent upon various factors, not least of which are the dictates of Judaism, he comments:

> It depends upon [Jews] passing through an education system that transmits historical and moral values of exclusiveness to the religious and the secular alike: premised for the former on a biblical mission to be realized by God's chosen people; and for the latter on the overriding need to provide a sanctuary for a people blighted by centuries of persecution culminating in the Holocaust.
>
> It also depends on a military rite of passage to adulthood that cements Israelis to their society, itself perceived as their only protection from a hatred, anti-Semitism, to which – if they are to believe their teachers, media and government – every gentile in the world is susceptible. This is their unique fate as Jews – and Israel is their one and only insurance policy.
>
> Israelis who believe this – and almost all do – feel that they have no choice but to submit to the collective good. Not a universal good, one of values shared by all mankind, but a collective good reserved only for Jews.
>
> Talk to Jewish anti-Zionists in Israel – a tiny number of people, barely reaching four figures out of a total Jewish population of five million – and most will tell you how hard they struggled to overcome the Zionist training they were given from birth. Many say they are still fighting to defeat their own racist assumptions to this day.

> Jeff Halper, an academic and leading Israeli activist against army abuses in the occupied territories, recently described to me the decades-long process of 'unlearning' his Zionist responses. *Deprogramming is what he called it. The kind of thing we read about in the papers when vulnerable youngsters need to be revived from the dangerous ideas implanted by a cult. But how do you loosen the grip of a cult when a whole nation is under its spell?*[28]

The other approach available to "cult assessors" is the sociological approach. This is the approach taken by most, and forms the basis of the most serious allegations, as it precludes the theological argument, which is fraught with difficulty and in the end comes down to a matter of belief rather than verifiable facts.

The sociological argument is essentially the cultural argument wherein it is alleged that certain groups self-consciously oppose the mainstream of culture with all its inherent accepted norms. Implicit in this argument is that mind control or manipulation that is alleged to form a part of the make-up of many cults does not form a part of the make-up of modern civilized society and culture. This argument, as we discuss a little later, is also subjective.

The aforementioned *Wikipedia.org* definition is interesting in that it states that the term cult in the pejorative sense was first adopted en masse in the 1960s. Indeed it seems that prior to this time the term cult did not have negative connotations at all, being generally used (if used at all) to denote any belief system. As noted above, the Oxford English dictionary gives the additional definitions of cult as: *2a. a popular fashion esp. followed by a specific section of society 3. denoting a person or thing popularized in this way.*

The definition of what is and what is not a cult is not officially defined by any government agency in the US. The term remains open to interpretation and, as is discussed further below, it perhaps better serves the essential goals of government for it to remain that way. As a result, the prosecution of cults or cult leaders has generally been carried out under more mundane infractions of the law, for example, kidnapping or extortion, or in the case of the Waco incident, gun control.

(Note: From here on the term cult is discussed from the above mentioned sociological point of view.)

Nevertheless, there exist several different conflicting definitions of what a cult is, in widespread use. But even if a definition were to

---

[28] Cook, Jonathan, *Al-Ahram Weekly*, "Eyes Wide Open," Issue No. 652, (21 – 27 August, 2003), (http://weekly.ahram.org.eg/2003/652/op42.htm).

be agreed upon, there still remains the problem of agreement as to what entities fit under that definition.

As stated, the main requirement for cult status would seem to be what can be broadly termed violation of free will. For this to be present it seems logical that at the outset there must be some level of deceit in the presentation of what the member benefits will be. No prospective cult would attract many devotees if among the benefits of membership it included: subtle mind control, physical beatings, incarceration, daily insult sessions, etc. In short, cults as they are popularly defined, are definitely not "what you see is what you get" organizations.

At present there are estimated to be somewhere between 3,000 and 5,000 purported cults in the US, *nominated by the various parties who find reason or need to do so*. For example, Amway[29] is a company that aggressively recruits people to recruit other people to sell its products (cosmetics, vitamins etc.). It has been accused of using cult-like tactics in the treatment of its employees (Butterfield 1985).

The Church of Scientology,[30] founded by L. Ron Hubbard, uses a form of psychotherapy called Dianetics that some people claim[31] is designed to hypnotize members into a more weak-minded and paranoid state. The church is said by some to persuade some members to become slaves. A sub-organization of the church – known as the Sea Organization – has paramilitary trappings, but is not armed. Critics also say the Church seems to function as a for-profit organization, as it requires fixed-price donations for many of its services, which are required to advance in orders.

On its Web site, Scientology says it is not a cult, but "a religion in the fullest sense of the word."

Sahaja Yoga[32] has also been accused.[33] This is a form of Yoga unlike any that most people (at least in the West) are familiar with. It involves mainly meditation and what they term "tying up your kundalini". This is done in order to achieve "self-realization" (connection with your self). Members are invited to "feel a cool breeze" emanating from the top of their heads as proof that their kundalini is indeed being activated. Self-realization is also available over the

---

[29] About Amway, (http://www.amway.com/en/General/About-Amway-10725.aspx?).
[30] Scientology: Church of Scientology Official Site, (http://www.scientology.org/).
[31] "Operation Clambake Present: What is Scientology?" (http://www.xenu.net/roland-intro.html).
[32] Sahaja Yoga Meditation, (http://www.sahajayoga.com/).
[33] Steven Alan Hassan's Freedom of Mind Center,
(http://www.freedomofmind.com/resourcecenter/groups/s/sahaja/).

Internet.[34] Just stare into the eyes of the picture of the leader, Shri Mataji Nirmala Devi, while listening to her instructions.

In the run up to the year 2000 the term millennium cult[35] became widely known. These were groups that believed that, as the year 2000 approached, unfortunately so too did the end of the world. As the year 2000 came and went with no end in sight, many were forced to recalculate their dates, most extending the millennium to anywhere between now and 2012.

While there are apparently few major "millennium cults" extolling the virtues of the "end of the world", there are various self-styled "experts" who organize group expeditions to various "sacred sites", often in Egypt, and who allegedly draw on "ancient sources of wisdom" to prepare us for the upcoming "shift" as they call it.

One such source of "wisdom" is that of ancient Egypt and the various "cults" that existed at that time. Many of these "experts", also known as "Enochian magicians", "archaic futurists", etc., apparently see themselves as tasked in some way with triggering the end of the world or "cosmos regeneration" as they call it. This is to be achieved through "magickal workings" using various "ancient" and "sacred" techniques. Among the more colorful are: "Calling down the cube of space", "aligning the celestial poles", "opening the portals", "celestial mechanics", "sacred science", "sacred geometry", and "the raising of the djed".

Disturbingly, however, there exist strong links between Enochian magick and Satanism, which the reader can confirm by doing an Internet search using the two terms.

On a more humorous note (depending on how you look at it), in regard to the above mentioned "raising the djed" – it seems that anyone involved in this activity immediately becomes a "djedi" and from various sources we find that the time when these "djedi" perform their "magickal working" will be the time of the "return of the djedi". Thus, we could consider the *Star Wars* movies as cultic in nature.[36]

As is common with many alleged cults the benefits on offer to believers are grandiose. However, due to the nature of these millennial cults their leaders probably do not envision having to make good on their promises, at least not in this lifetime. Djedis then can expect to reap seemingly fantastic benefits from their efforts, for example:

---

[34] Self-realization (Kundalini Awakening) through Sahaja Yoga, (http://www.sahajayoga.com/experienceitnow/default.asp).
[35] CESNUR – Center for Studies on New Religions, Watching Millennial Groups in the Year 2000, (http://www.cesnur.org/testi/Y2K_updates.htm).
[36] Moira Timms, *Egypt: Equinox 2000*, (http://www.portalmarket.com/history.html).

When we experience our own connection between the two (matter and spirit) a resounding 'Yessss!' will synaptically ricochet throughout the global brain, the morphogenetic field of the planet, (and the Internet.) Our conscious reconnection with the wisdom of our own origins, and the rediscovery of the archaic celestial/terrestrial technologies, initiates us into 'whole' consciousness.[37]

Each of us holds the keys, as they are but elements of our own true nature: basic human kindness, an open heart and mind, and the desire to build a loving world society. As you likely know, it is a special time on Earth, a time of global shift.[38]

Or better still:

Attune yourself to the blissful energetic current of the joyous goddesses as you enter their abundant world of passion, ecstasy and enchantment. Learn how to open yourself to the magical world of the senses, awaken your Kundalini energy, experience the sacred nature of your sexuality and fill yourself with the fertile, life-enhancing nectar of the Sensuous Goddess.[39]

One notable exponent of this type of "earth grid engineering"[40] as it is often called, is Dan Winter. After many years of lectures and workshops around the US, Mr. Winter was eventually convicted by several US courts, including the US Federal Court and the US Bankruptcy Court of North Carolina, for representing as his own work the work of various scholars, and in addition, for adulterating the contents of the other scholars' work. Moreover, Mr. Winter published under his own name and sold for profit the works of these scholars in the form of books, CDs and videos. He was forced to publicly admit his lies and deceit in a sworn statement[41] and urged his publishers and associates to do likewise. He then fled the country without paying any of the court fees that were assessed against him. At present Mr. Winter is a fugitive, and continues to conduct seminars and workshops in Europe and Australia.

There seems to be a distinct susceptibility and therefore vulnerability in many people to unquestioningly accept the word of others, particularly when these "others" present themselves as an authority on a subject. The vulnerability is further pronounced when the sub-

---

[37] Ibid.
[38] http://www.timeofglobalshift.com/.
[39] http://www.sacredmysteries.com/sacredmysteries/index.html#sharron2
[40] Implosion Group: Dan Winter – *Sacred Geometry & Coherent Emotion* – Heart Turner, (http://soulinvitation.com/indexdw.html).
[41] Corrective Notice by Daniel E. Winter, (http://www.danwinter.com/cornote.html).

ject being presented is tied to the emotional needs of the listener. It seems that this weakness is understood and used to ensure devotion, be it to an organization, a concept, another person, or a law.

In the words of the plaintiff in the case against Mr. Winter:

> Dishonest people, and people who enjoy hurting others – like Mr. Winter – count on the fact that the vast majority of healthy, caring, well-intended people are not suspicious by nature, and accept what they are told at face value. This is good. Decent, caring people should not have to be suspicious, and should not need to double-check every claim that is made. But unfortunately, this means that decent, caring people, young and old, students and professionals, are easily deceived by people like Mr. Winter, who go to so much trouble to deceive them.[42]

We can perhaps say then that the potential for a group or organization to actually be a cult is related to the extent to which the group or organization presents itself as having the answer(s) to people's problems, promising a better life, happiness, financial success, spiritual enlightenment or essentially anything that plays upon *the passive emotional needs* that are common to many, but, it seems, not to all of us.

As Mr. Tenen says in the above quote, it is unfortunate that people are forced to be suspicious and double-check everything they are told. However, based on the nature of the world we live in, to *not* do so is to place oneself at the mercy of those who make deception a way of life; and their number is legion.

What can be observed in our society at present is that in the mind of the average citizen the concept of a "cult" is understood as more of a vague threat than anything clearly defined and understood. From the generally ill-informed position of the man in the street it can perhaps be likened to the now ever present threat of "terrorists" and "terrorism"; he understands it as something bad, or threatening but would be hard pressed to give any clear examples of where it is and exactly what level of threat it poses to him, personally. This limited and distorted perception of the common person may be indicative of a certain way in which information is disseminated in our society and about the possible agenda of those that disseminate it.

What seems to be true is that the cult label is so powerful, carries so much stigma, and can be used in a directed way to damage and destroy groups and individuals exactly because of the very things that it labels as cultic manipulation, i.e., the susceptibility of the hu-

---

[42] Stanley Tenen, Meru Foundation, Nov. 2004, (http://www.danwinter.com/).

man psyche to programming and subtle suggestive techniques of one sort or another. Governments must employ the force of public opinion in order to take public action. In our modern society in which people of a predatory nature seem to thrive, any accusation can and often is made to stick when stated and stated often enough by those in apparent positions of power and influence.

Dozens if not hundreds of incidents in our recent history can be cited where the public was (and continues to be) led to believe something as truth when in fact it was not. The recent WMD debacle involving various Western governments is but one large-scale example. Human history is indeed replete with urban myths – many of them forming some of our most accepted and sacred foundational cows.[43] From science to history to religion to politics, no field of study is exempt.

Information is, and probably always has been, a highly valued commodity. Knowledge is power, as the saying goes. While originally the stated role of governments was to carry out the will of the people, it is clear today that is no longer the case. The job of governments now, it seems, is purely the control of resources, with the most important "resource" being the citizenry.

The information that society is "allowed" to receive shapes the perception of the members of that society. Therefore, control of information is key to control of perception, and control of perception is key to the control of the population. Read any of Noam Chomsky's articles or interviews on the media and control of information[44] for a more in-depth analysis of the control of information and how it is used to manipulate and coerce the masses of people to serve the elite in governments.

Today we have terms like Total Information Awareness (closely tied to and since 9/11 synonymous with the US government project Terrorism Information Awareness[45]), which is within itself a cult of information[46] (Roszak 1986), or cult of awareness. This philosophy and its importance is promoted and implemented from the top level in our society. At the time of writing, we have people like John Ashcroft, at on a whirlwind tour of the US, attempting to promote or perhaps

---

[43] Knight-Jadczyk, Laura, The Ark of the Covenant and the Temple of Solomon, excerpted from *The Secret History of the World*, (Red Pill Press, 2005), (http://www.cassiopaea.org/cass/biblewho1.htm).
[44] Talks, Interviews, & Debates (http://www.zmag.org/chomsky/talks.cfm).
[45] http://www.darpa.mil/darpatech2002/presentations/iao_pdf/slides/poindexteriao.pdf
[46] Roszak, Theodore. The Cult of Information, A Neo-Luddite Treatise on High-Tech, Artificial Intelligence, and the True Art of Thinking. University of California Press, 1986.

instill this concept into the minds of the populace, the goal being to create an environment or atmosphere wherein the masses of people will be convinced that it is in the interest of their own protection or that of the country (and thus their "patriotic duty") to funnel information about their fellow citizens upwards to their "leaders". Neighbors are encouraged to keep a watch on each other and report "suspicious behavior", with the list of just what defines "suspicious behavior" being supplied by the office of Mr. Ashcroft. We are told that mere disgruntled citizens[47] may well constitute the "enemy in our midst".

The masses are told that the benefits of compliance with the requirements of the cult of information lie in the fact that we will be safer; more secure in our beds at night. In short, the cult of information is essentially a cult of fear. Fear must first be instilled in the minds of the masses to inspire them to feed this upward flowing stream of information to their leaders – designed to facilitate the extirpation of any contrary source of information. And fear is a principle that humans seem somehow pre-designed and preprogrammed to wholeheartedly embrace.

What this boils down to is: if you control the knowledge that people have, you control the people. As such, it is not hard to see that if governments understand knowledge as power, and they seek to retain power, they must seek to control the flow of information, the aim of which must be to limit knowledge.

If you control the spread of information, you control what people think. If you control what people think, you are effectively controlling their minds. And we come around in a circle to what is truly cultic.

From this point of view, logically, any group that threatens the government monopoly on information and power, and therefore their control of the people, is a threat and must be dealt with. As Richard Dolan has written in his first volume of *UFOs and the National Security State*:

> Anyone who has lived in a repressive society knows that official manipulation of the truth occurs daily. But societies have their many and their few. In all times and all places, it is the few who rule, and the few who exert dominant influence over what we may call official culture. – All elites take care to manipulate public information to maintain existing structures of power. It's an old game. (Dolan, 2002)

As noted above, the allegation that mind control is used on cult members is often made when labeling any group as a cult. However,

---

[47] Burkeman, Oliver, Guardian Unlimited, Special Reports, "US Moves on to High Terror Alert," March 19, 2003, (http://www.guardian.co.uk/usa/story/0,12271,917247,00.html).

there can be many forms of mind control – including the mass media – although they are not called by that name. And if we are to rely on the criteria on which assertions of cult are based, i.e., observation of the results of mind control (members joining communes, giving up possessions, extreme devotion and allegiance to a leader, and in a few cases giving up their lives by way of apparent suicide), we certainly find reasonable justification for labeling the current US administration as a cult for persuading hundreds of thousands of Americans to give up their possessions and join the commune of the US military out of extreme devotion to a proven liar, George W. Bush, resulting in what could be termed apparent suicide in Iraq.

As discussed above, it seems that there exists a certain type of mentality that is predisposed to wholeheartedly and unquestioningly accept this type of establishment fear-based programming. Such individuals are easily controlled within the contexts of standard religions which, as can be noted, are also generally fear-based. However, in the 1960s, there was a popular upsurge in the awareness of the masses at large due to outrage at the Vietnam War. The US government set out to eradicate radical protests against government policies, and what is now popularly known as COINTELPRO – Counter Intelligence Program – was created.

Of course, COINTELPRO in one form or another has always existed, and was described in some detail by Machiavelli. Now, keeping in mind that the elite controllers of the masses seek most definitely to control perception via the control of information, we can deduce that this must require that any sources of information which lead to knowledge – knowledge being power – must be marginalized or even eliminated entirely in order for control to be maintained. This leads to the next logical step which is to realize that COINTELPRO must also be used to vector ideological trends.

COINTELPRO methods included sending anonymous or fictitious letters designed to cast those individuals or groups they wished to contain or destroy in a bad light; publishing false, defamatory, or threatening information; forging signatures on fake documents to make their targets look bad in some way; introducing disruptive and subversive members into organizations to destroy them from within; and so on. Blackmailing insiders in any group to force them to spread false rumors, or to foment factionalism was also common. COINTELPRO also concentrated on creating bogus organizations.

These bogus groups could serve many functions that might include attacking and/or disrupting bona fide groups, or even just simply creating a diversion with clever propaganda to attract members away in order to involve them with time-wasting activity so as to prevent them from doing anything useful. COINTELPRO was also famous for instigation of hostile actions through third parties. It is in this sense that we can best understand many of the groups that have willingly and enthusiastically taken on the role of self-appointed "cult busters",[48] going about their work in a frenzy of slandering and finger-pointing, evoking the image of the Spanish Inquisition with its motto of, "kill them all, God will know his own." Apparently irony is wasted on them and the adage, "people in glass houses should not throw stones", means nothing to them.

It is in the context of COINTELPRO that we can better understand many curious things about this issue of cults. For many years the Cult Awareness Network (CAN)[49] worked closely with US government officials to tackle the threat of purported cults. It actively urged the press, Congress, and law enforcement to act against any *non-mainstream* religious, psychological, or even political movement, which it described as a cult. After interviewing CAN's executive director, Cynthia Kisser, at the time, a reporter wrote:

> No one knows how many destructive cults and sects exist in the United States. Kisser's binder holds 1,500 names gleaned from newspaper clippings, court documents and thousands of calls to the network's hotline. Some of the groups have legitimate purposes, Kisser says. But her group's efforts show that most, despite wildly diverse beliefs, share stunningly similar patterns of mind control, group domination, exploitation and physical and mental abuse.[50]

CAN critics pointed out that so-called mind control techniques are not much different than the techniques used in education and socialization efforts used by all schools, churches, ideologies and philosophies. CAN's other successful approach was to refer relatives of group members to deprogrammers who charge thousands of dollars for their services and, according to a former national director of CAN's predecessor, the Citizens Freedom Foundation, kicked back some of the money to CAN.

Deprogramming often includes kidnapping individuals, subjecting them to sleep and food deprivation, ridicule and humiliation, and even physical abuse and restraint until they promise to leave the al-

---

[48] Knight-Jadczyk, Laura, "Rick Ross – Ross Institute: Agent of COINTELPRO or Agent of Mossad? Part II," (http://www.cassiopaea.org/cass/rickross2.htm).

[49] The group is defunct, having been forced into liquidation on June 20, 1996, after unsuccessfully seeking refuge in bankruptcy in the face of a $4.8 million damages verdict handed down in September 1995 by a U.S. District Court in Seattle.

[50] Associated Press wire story, April 23, 1993, 10:25 EDT.

leged cult – doing the very things they accuse the cult of doing! Because deprogrammers usually involve family members in these kidnappings and deprogrammings, victims rarely press charges. However, in the last few years, five deprogrammers have been prosecuted for kidnapping or unlawful imprisonment. One such deprogrammer is Rick Ross,[51] a convicted jewel thief who has boasted of more than 200 "deprogrammings". Cynthia Kisser praised him as being "among the half dozen best deprogrammers in the country." In the summer of 1993 Rick Ross was indicted in Washington state for unlawful imprisonment.[52]

The fear principle is perhaps the most prized weapon in the government's armory of population management and control tools. The apparent human predisposition for fear of the unknown, strange or the weird is undoubtedly exploited by government agencies in garnering public support for its condemnation of groups that it perceives as threatening to its monopoly on control. It understands that it can find fertile ground in the mass mind for the dissemination of negative fear based propaganda about "cults" or "terrorists", etc. This in turn feeds the growth of "cult busters" and "cult busting" mentality and essentially allows for any group it chooses to be tarred with the "cult" or the "terrorist" brush.[53]

It is indeed fortunate for the government that the existence and availability of the term "cult" with its by now well-established and immediate negative connotations can be so easily used as a weapon with which to attack and defame. Any group that the government may deem a threat to its monopoly on truth can be quickly and easily dealt with simply by assigning it the cult label. It is a remarkably effective means with which to control and, if needed, effectively neutralize any such group. For such a group the evidence, or lack thereof, of any cultic behavior becomes irrelevant.

Without doubt, real cults practicing some form of mind programming have existed and continue to exist, yet due to the aforementioned human nature and nature of governments and those that govern, it is almost inevitable that many have been and will be wrongly accused, and deliberately so.

---

[51] Knight-Jadczyk, Laura, "Rick Ross – Ross Institute: Agent of COINTELPRO or Agent of Mossad? Part II," (http://www.cassiopaea.org/cass/rickross.htm).

[52] Walker, Jessie, *Reason* magazine, "No Angels," Published by the *Seattle Scroll*, April 21, 1997, (http://reason.com/opeds/walker042197.shtml).

[53] Watson, Paul Joseph, *Propaganda Matrix*, "Endless Fake Terror Alerts: Fear Based Mind Control," (http://www.propagandamatrix.com/endless_fake_terror_alerts.html).

One such contemporary case is that of *"The Sniff Art Collective"*[54] *("dedicated to freedom of expression in the great outdoors")* recently accused of being a satanic cult (and murder), essentially for simply displaying their paintings in public. The case is ongoing.[55]

It appears that, as a result of the high profile, sensationalist news coverage on the various cults over the past half-century, the term has become widely known and at the same time assumed its negative connotations. It was through these few, well-publicized events involving alleged mind control that the popular understanding of the word cult has been firmly imprinted in the minds of the populace. The most shocking cases were those where alleged physical and mental coercion took place, resulting in deaths of a number of members.

The "Jonestown massacre" in the forests of Guyana in 1978 was one such case. At the time, there were suggestions that the CIA and even Israeli intelligence agencies were in some way involved, that the leader Jim Jones was a CIA asset, and that the members of the US embassy in Guyana who were closely involved with the members of Jonestown were CIA agents.[56]

The allegations included suggestions that the CIA's mind-control program, code-named MK-ULTRA,[57] was not stopped in 1973, as the CIA had told Congress. Instead, it is suggested MK-ULTRA had merely been transferred out of public hospitals and prisons into the more secure confines of religious cults, Jonestown being one of those MK-ULTRA experimental cults.

The implication here is that the fact that mind programming nowadays goes hand in hand with the term cult, may be due more to outside influences than due to any intrinsic or automatic part of an alleged group's makeup or function. There were also conflicting reports as to whether the 913 people who died actually committed suicide, with the Guyanese coroner at the time saying that as many as 700 members showed signs of having been murdered.[58]

What is verifiably true about the Jonestown massacre is that US congressman Leo J. Ryan had been to Jonestown with various reporters and a delegation of concerned relatives of Jonestown members on

---

[54] http://www.elsob.net/el_sob_sniff.html
[55] Johnson, Chip, San Francisco Chronicle, "Bulb Art is Devilish, Not Satanic, Artists in Turmoil after Peterson Theory," September 1, 2003,
(http://www.sfgate.com/cgi-bin/article.cgi?f=/c/a/2003/09/01/BA217393.DTL).
[56] Steel, Fiona, "Jonestown Massacre: A "Reason" to Die,"
(http://www.crimelibrary.com/notorious_murders/mass/jonestown/connections_5.html?sect=8).
[57] Cosmic Cointelpro Timeline, (http://www.cassiopaea.org/cass/timeline.htm).
[58] Steel, Fiona, ibid.

the day of the "suicides" and was he himself killed in the events that followed. This was, of course, blamed on the Jonestown cult – that they wanted to suppress Congressman Ryan's report. But the possibility exists that Congressman Ryan's report needed to be suppressed for exactly the opposite reasons, that it would be unfavorable to those labeling the Jonestown group as a cult. In the end, the question can be asked about this event: who benefits? And the answer is that it put a powerful sociological tool into the hands of the government – the idea that a cult was, indeed, a very dangerous thing. The fear of cults was literally created with this event.

Another example of a much publicized cult confrontation, where the destruction of the group and the deaths of its members in a horrific fire was the ultimate outcome, occurred at Waco, Texas in 1993.

In April 1993, eighty-nine Branch Davidians led by David Koresh died when BAFT (Bureau of Alcohol, Firearms, and Tobacco) agents stormed their compound at Mount Carmel in Waco, Texas. While the general impression among the public was – and still is – that the deaths were the result of "cultic activities", at the time there were well founded allegations that government agents acted in a disproportionate way to the threat and that the deaths were unnecessary.

Nancy Ammerman, a Visiting Scholar at Princeton University's Center for the Study of American Religion, was one of the outside experts assigned by the Justice Department to evaluate BATF and FBI's handling of the Branch Davidians. She was particularly critical of Rick Ross and the Cult Awareness Network.

> Although these people often call themselves 'cult experts', they are certainly not recognized as such by the academic community. The activities of the CAN are seen by the National Council of Churches (among others) as a danger to religious liberty, and deprogramming tactics have been increasingly found to be outside the law ... Mr. Rick Ross, who often works in conjunction with the Cult Awareness Network (CAN), has been quoted as saying he was 'consulted' by the BATF. ... The Network and Mr. Ross have a direct ideological (and financial) interest in arousing suspicion and antagonism against what they call 'cults'. ... *It seems clear that people within the 'anti-cult' community had targeted the Branch Davidians for attention.* (Justice Department Report: Ammerman: 1; emphasis added)

We note with chagrin that this "arousing of suspicion and antagonism" led to the deaths of undoubtedly innocent people – including many small children – in a particularly gruesome manner.

It would seem that financial gain is a significant motivating factor in the activities of so called cult busters such as Ross. In *Inside the*

Cult (Breault and King 1993) there appears the January 16, 1993 diary entry of a former branch Davidian, Marc Breault (also the co-author of the book) where he describes a conversation he had with Branch Davidian Steve Schneider's sister:

> Rick (Ross) told Sue that something was about to happen real soon. He urged her to hire him to deprogram Steve. Rick has Sue all scared now. The Schneider family doesn't know what to do. Rick didn't tell them what was about to happen, but he said they should get Steve out as soon as possible. I know that Rick has talked to the ATF. (Breault and King 1993, 317)

We should note carefully that Rick Ross was primarily interested in being "hired to deprogram," and that whatever he knew, he withheld for financial gain.

After the April 19th fire, Methodist Minister Joseph Bettis wrote Attorney General Reno:

> ... from the beginning, members of the Cult Awareness Network have been involved in this tragedy. This organization is widely known for its use of fear to foster religious bigotry. The reliance of federal agents on information supplied by these people, as well as the whole record of federal activity deserves your careful investigation and public disclosure. ... Cult bashing must end, and you must take the lead.

Representative Harold Volkmer charged that the initial attack on the Branch Davidians was part of a pattern of Gestapo-like tactics at the bureau.

> I fail to see the crimes committed by those in the Davidian compound that called for the extreme action of BATF on Feb. 28 and the tragic final assault.[59]

Representative John Conyers branded the April 19th gas and tank attack a "military operation" and called it a "profound disgrace to law enforcement in the United States." He told Janet Reno, "You did the right thing by offering to resign. I'd like you to know that there is at least one member of Congress who is not going to rationalize the innocent deaths of two dozen children." Reno, however, apparently recovered quickly from her attack of conscience.

Los Angeles journalist Cletus Nelson writes:

> From the very outset, the public was falsely led to believe a multiracial spiritual community was largely comprised of gunrunning 'rednecks' steeped in violent apocalypse theology and martial rhetoric.

---

[59] Isikoff, Michael, "Reno Strongly Defends Raid on Cult," *Washington Post*, April 29, 1993.

As if to further darken the picture, thinly veiled allegations of child abuse and cultic phenomenon were widely circulated on television and in the mainstream press. This egregious use of what media analysts refer to as "negative framing" would seal the fate of the controversial 7th Day Adventist sect when it was deemed politically expendable by Washington officials.[60]

Whatever the truth behind the events at Waco and Jonestown (and it is undoubtedly not as black and white as the media would have us believe), the result was to imprint on the mind of the global population the idea that small groups with alternative views were synonymous with cults, and cults were the equivalent of dangerous, fanatical religious beliefs, manipulative mind control and a host of other antisocial activities. The reader can make the logical connections between Rick Ross and his ilk and the government COINTELPRO idea on their own. Birds of a feather …

As stated, there is no definitive definition or established criteria for what constitutes a cult in the USA. However, in France there has been considerable research done by government agencies into the subject. The French National Assembly has produced a general outline of what may constitute a "cult" in modern parlance:

Report of the French Assembly Inquiry Commission on Cults
Dec. 20 1995

Section I: 2:(d) The concept retained by the Commission.

Any movement *presenting itself as religious* with the following criteria:

Mental destabilization

Exorbitant demands of a financial nature

A breaking off of contact with one's original environment

Attacks on the physical integrity of members

The recruitment of children

Having a discourse more or less antisocial

Involved in troubles of a public order nature

Involved in serious judicial problems

Misappropriation of traditional economic circuits

Attempts to infiltrate the public powers.

The Commission insists on the fact that as the definition of cults is in many ways difficult.

In conducting its work, it attempted to ensure that it did not simply accept the definition of cults proposed by those who are engaged, in one way or another, in the promotion of new religions or those

---

[60] Nelson, Cletus, "The Watchdogs of Waco: Defenders of State Terror," August 25, 2001, (http://www.lewrockwell.com/orig/nelson2.html)

engaged in the struggle against the real or supposed excesses of purported cults.

In its work, the Commission was conscious that neither newness nor the small number of members, nor even eccentricity could be retained as criteria permitting to label as a cult a so-called religious movement: *the largest contemporary religions were often at their start little more than cults with small numbers of members; many established and socially recognized rites today, in their beginning gave rise to reservations and oppositions.*[61] (emphasis added)

The very fact that that the French government has publicly sought to investigate the cult phenomena and outline criteria defining one suggests that they take the issue seriously. At the same time however, from the above definition, we see also that they approach the subject in a reasoned and logical way. First of all, rejecting what we might call the COINTELPRO standard of tarring and feathering. As the French Assembly pointed out rather succinctly, the largest contemporary religions today started as little more than cults.

---

[61] Cults in France, National Assembly Constitution of October 4, 1958, Recorded with the Presidency of the National Assembly on December 22, 1995, Full English translation, (http://cftf.com/french/Les_Sectes_en_France/cults.html)

BIBLIOGRAPHY

Bramley, William. *The Gods of Eden*. New York: Avon Books, 1990.

Breault, Marc, and King, Martin. *Inside the Cult: A Member's Chilling, Exclusive Account of Madness and Depravity in David Koresh's Compound*. New York: Signet, 1993.

Butterfield, Stephen. *Amway, the Cult of Free Enterprise*. South End Press, 1985.

Castaneda, Carlos. *The Active Side of Infinity*. HarperCollins, 1998.

Chittick, William C. *The Sufi Path of Knowledge*. Albany: State University of New York Press, 1989.

Conway, Flo, and Siegelman, Jim. *Snapping: America's Epidemic of Sudden Personality Change*. Lippincott, Williams and Wilkins, 1978.

Daniélou, Alain. *Gods of love and ecstasy : the traditions of Shiva and Dionysus*. Rochester, Vt.: Inner Traditions International, 1992.

Diodorus of Sicily, tr. C. H. Oldfather, Loeb Classical Library, Volumes II and III. London: William Heinemann, and Cambridge, Mass.: Harvard University Press, 1935 and 1939.

Dolan, Richard. *UFOs and the National Security State: Chronology of a Cover-Up*. Hampton Roads, second edition, 2002.

_____. *UFOs and the National Security State: The Cover-Up Exposed*. Keyhole Publishing, 2009.

Eco, Umberto. *The Search for the Perfect Language*. Oxford: Blackwell, 1995.

Eliade, Mircea. *The Myth of the Eternal Return*. Princeton: Princeton University Press, 1954.

_____. *Mephistopheles and the Androgyne: Studies in Religious Myth and Symbol*. NY: Sheed and Ward, 1965.

_____. *The Forge and the Crucible: The Origins and Structures of Alchemy*. 2nd ed. Translated by Stephen Corrin. Chicago, Ill.: University of Chicago Press, 1978.

Elkins, Don; Rueckert, Carla and McCarty, Jim. *The Ra Material*. Norfolk, VA: The Donning Co., 1984.

Friedman, Richard Elliot. *Who Wrote the Bible*. New York: Summit Books, 1987.

Freeman, Ira M. *Physics Principles and Insights*. New York: McGraw-Hill, 1973.

Fulcanelli. *The Mystery of the Cathedrals*. Las Vegas: Brotherhood of Life, 1984.

_____. *The Dwellings of the Philosophers*. Boulder: Archive Press, 1999.

BIBLIOGRAPHY

Godwin, Joscelyn. *Arktos: The Polar Myth in Science, Symbolism, and Nazi Survival*. Kempton: Adventures Unlimited Press, 1996.

Godwin, Malcolm. *The Holy Grail: Its Origins, Secrets & Meaning Revealed*. Viking Studio Books, 1994.

Hall, Manly P. *The Secret Teachings of All Ages*. Diamond jubilee ed. Los Angeles: Philosophical Research Society, 1988.

Hamilton, Edith. *Mythology*. Grand Central Publishing, 1999.

Hort, Barbara E. *Unholy Hungers*. Boston & London: Shambhala, 1996.

Isserlin, B.S.J. *The Israelites*. London: Thames and Hudson, 1998.

Jessup, Morris K. *The Case for the UFO*. New York: Citadel Press, 1955.

Joseph, Frank. *Lost Pyramids Of Rock Lake: Wisconsin's Sunken Civilization*. Galde Press, 1997.

Korff, Kal K. *The UFO Crash at Roswell, What They Don't Want You to Know*. Prometheus, 1997.

Marciniak, Barbara. *Bringers of the Dawn, Teachings from the Pleiadians*. Bear & Company Publishing, 1992.

O'Brien, Cathy, and Phillips, Mark. *Trance Formation of America The True Life Story of a CIA Slave*. Global Trance Formation Info, Ltd., 1995.

Osborn, Nancy. *The Demon Syndrome*. New York: Bantam Books, 1983.

Ouspensky, P. D. *In Search of the Miraculous*. New York: Harcourt, Brace, Jovanovich, 1949.

Pagels, Elaine. *The Gnostic Gospels*. New York: Random House, 1978.

Pearce, Joseph Chilton. *The Crack in the Cosmic Egg*. Pocket Book, 1975.

Pennick, Nigel. *Secret Games of the Gods*. Maine: Samuel Weiser, Inc., 1992.

Reich, Wilhelm. *Ether, God, and Devil*. New York: Orgone Institute Press, 1949.

Russell, Bertrand. *Education and the Good Life*. New York: Boni and Liveright, 1926.

Schumaker, John F. *The Corruption of Reality: A Unified Theory of Religion, Hypnosis, and Psychopathology*. Amherst, NY: Prometheus Books, 1995.

Schwartz, Regina M. *The Curse of Cain*. University of Chicago Press, 1997.

Von Eckartshausen, Karl. *Magic: the principles of higher knowledge*. Tr. and ed. Gerhard Hanswille & Deborah Brumlich. Scarborough: Merkur Pub. Co., 1989.

Von Ward, Paul. *Our Solarian Legacy: Multidimensional Humans in a Self-Learning Universe*. Hampton Roads, 2001.

Walden, James. *The Ultimate Alien Agenda*. Llewellyn Publications, 1998.

Walker, Barbara G. *The Woman's Encyclopedia of Myths and Secrets*. San Francisco: Harper and Row, 1983.